Under the General Editorship of

GORDON N. RAY

The University of Illinois

THE CHARACTER

Part Four of

OF PROSE ✒

WALLACE DOUGLAS
Northwestern University

AN INTRODUCTION TO LITERATURE

by Herbert Barrows, Hubert Heffner,
John Ciardi, and Wallace Douglas

HOUGHTON MIFFLIN COMPANY
Boston · The Riverside Press Cambridge

PREFATORY NOTE
(To the Complete Edition)

There are many volumes designed to introduce college students to literature. What novelty can be claimed for this book comes from its plan. The four skilled and experienced teachers who have served as editors were not limited in their work by any imposed uniformity of treatment. They were asked instead to organize their approaches to fiction and drama, to poetry and prose, exactly as they would their own courses in these kinds of writing.

The result is four highly idiosyncratic presentations, ranging from Mr. Barrows's catholic and persuasive survey of the short story to Mr. Douglas's lively polemic for modern prose, from Mr. Heffner's detached and orderly analysis of drama to an examination of poetry marked by all the brilliance and conviction readers have come to expect from that poet and defender of poetry, Mr. Ciardi. The customary teaching materials are here. The characteristics, the conventions, and the special effects of each kind of writing are set forth, and the necessary critical terms are introduced. But each editor has done this in his own way.

Yet the book does have a deeper unity, which derives from certain assumptions shared by the editors. I recall some twenty years ago being a member of a group of graduate students in English to whom Robert Frost offered this advice: "Don't work. Worry!" This was his counsel to poets, he said, and he thought it might apply to us as well. One or two of our professors regarded his words as subversive of discipline, but we took them, I am sure correctly, as a clue to the kind of understanding of literature that makes its study really valuable. In like manner the editors of this book see literature as an unending source of delight, not merely as a "subject" to be pursued systematically like any other. They propose formal analysis to the student, not as an end in itself, but as a means of widening his range of comprehension and deepening his enjoyment of the thing comprehended. The beginning student, eager and curious, but largely unread and uninformed, will find them reliable guides to the "extension of life" which literature uniquely offers.

GORDON N. RAY

51774

CONTENTS

THE

CHARACTER

OF PROSE

A book has its special form because of the way its author views his audience and tries to reach them; in selecting these essays, I have proceeded as if my audience consisted of readers as well as students. I think the essays are all good objects for study, because they reflect the world in important ways, and show how some good writers have explained, exhorted, argued, condemned, ridiculed, or preached. I hope they are also readable for their own sakes.

I have included several essays that are pretty light and casual, and maybe not altogether reverent. In one of them, Max Beerbohm, a carefully cultivated Ariel among England's minor geniuses, pokes some rather solemn fun at Swinburne, one of England's numerous nineteenth century poets, who had an especially whimsical life. Broader and sharper than this is the fun that P. G. Wodehouse and Robert Benchley have with Shakespeare and that notoriously major artist, Eugene O'Neill. Then there is Stanley Walker's string of notes—material for the enrichment of the American Way of Life, he calls them—about such things as a Texan with a midget butler, a Philadelphia lady who complained because social life in her town was complicated by the habit Biddles have of thinking they're Cadwaladers when they're drunk, and two New York writers who argued over whether the finest sentence in the English language is "We can sleep all day tomorrow" or "No date has been set for the wedding."

James Thurber once said that humorists or "writers of light pieces running from a thousand to two thousand words" "sit on the edge of the chair of Literature," and I hope I have plenty of essays by people who sit more firmly and comfortably. My ears are not "shut to the ominous rumblings of the dynasties of the world moving toward a cloudier chaos than ever before."[1] When I use the other kind of essay, the one by the writer who "talks largely about small matters, and smally about great affairs," I am only following the practice of successful authors that Horace described as mingling in a work material that will seem applicable to life to those who seek instruction when they read, and other material that will amuse those who only want amusement. The light essays were chosen to fill the amusement part of that ancient formula, and by their very oddity or quirkishness, I thought they might also lighten the really rather formidable job of being introduced to literature, showing perhaps that neither reading nor talking about reading need be solemn.

Besides amusement and interest, I have had to think about instruction. And first of all I have tried to sample the forms that writers use these days when they want to express their opinions or convey some information or describe something. Here at one extreme are Shaw's letters, which are personal and private expressions; at least they are in form, though the subjects of those I have chosen and Shaw's own sense of theater often make them pretty public. Perhaps the autobiographical selections, especially Gertrude Stein's arch reflections, are closest to a truly familiar kind of writing. At the other extreme are the general, rather abstract discussions by Whitehead and Barraclough, which in their deliberate movements and restrained tones, together with the suggestion that their material is very much the product of investigation and reflection, seem like the solid and somewhat conclusive dissertations that enlivened the pages of the nineteenth century magazines.

Between these extremes are a number of journalistic forms. The decorous elegance of its style may at first conceal the nature of Addison's essay, but it is, of course, an early example of the editorial essay or short-piece which is today used in newspapers that reach toward responsible journalism, as the saying goes. Alistair Cooke's "Farewell on P Street," Alfred Noyes' "Dinner at The Pines," and Dickens' "Night Walks" are all varieties of reporting, being distinguished from each other chiefly by the varying distances that the authors stand from their subjects: Cooke is on the spot, Noyes far removed in time and space, Dickens somewhat closer. Morton Hunt's "A Giant In Her Field" uses a rather unexpected subject, but it is just an example of a typically modern form of reporting: the feature story that presents information about, and the tone of, an interesting personality or event. This one is a *New Yorker* Profile, which means that the subject is out-of-the-way or at least un-

---

[1] That's part of another sentence from Thurber's "Preface to a Life." I worked it in because I wanted a sample of the sound of modern prose at its most artful.

expected, so that besides an enormous number of just plain facts, the author is able to present a good many amusing or slightly (never too much) bizarre details about which he can be, and the reader must be, urbanely detached. The selections on the present generation are examples of informational and opinion articles—the sort that report on a current situation or problem in an effort to form opinion. Finally there are a number of reviews and columns.

Considering the selections from Addison, Swift, Cobbett, Hazlitt, Smith, and Dickens, it can hardly be said that there is anything especially modern (or indeed especially "unliterary") about articles, short statements of fact or opinion, written for the moment, under a deadline and for a particular journal. Addison's essays were read in a periodical before they were studied in high schools. So far as that goes, I am not convinced that contemporary forms of exposition differ in kind from the older ones: Macaulay's "essays" and some of Matthew Arnold's were longer and more thought out than the book reviews we read, but still they were introductions to and criticisms of new books. It is a commonplace that the personal or familiar essay is no more, alas; but what are those small reflective paragraphs that appear in most issues of *The New Yorker's* "Talk of the Town," and many metropolitan dailies have staff columnists who write smally about large issues or point wryly to everyday oddities. What does seem to have happened, however, is that in the last fifty years or so, the magazines have more and more discussed *current* situations, as if trying to meet the newspapers; and they have also (for the same reason?) used more and more purely factual articles, ones which presented information without much effort at developing its significance, especially its significance in the large general terms which, apparently, nineteenth century editors could assume their readers were anxious for. But even this change in the content of articles is, perhaps, less important than the stylistic change described by Bonamy Dobrée in "The New Way of Writing," the essay that follows this introduction.

As a second purpose I have had in mind to suggest the stylistic range of modern writing: the ornate sentimentality of Strachey, and Alistair Cooke's plainer kind, Gertrude Stein's assertively commonsensical reflections, Liebling's nervy colloquialism, Forster's enervated small talk, Shaw's eloquent and Hutchins' diaconal wit, and with these quite personal styles, some examples of good journeyman prose. I have included some older writers (Dickens, Swift, Hazlitt, and a few more) for comparison. I have not bothered with the questions of what is an essay or what is "prose," as distinguished from whatever it may be distinguished from; but since this section is part of an "introduction to literature," I have included a good many articles that illustrate how people talk about books and authors.

At the beginning I have put several pieces about prose. This was not so that readers would be able to talk about prose in the abstract, without the "prejudice of particular examples," as Herbert Read once said. Instead I wanted them to get a feeling for the kind of writing that appeals to modern tastes. I have also taken some time in the introduction to analyze such writing, and to suggest what has happened to it in the twenty years since Dobrée called it "the new way of writing."

I

By now our ears have become so shaped for modern style (let us call it a conversational prose) that even the best or most academic of us can hardly believe that people could once have read with pleasure the writings of the later or minor Victorians. Of course when we think about it, we confess to philistinism, and we admit that ordinary Victorian prose differs more in degree than in kind from what habit has accustomed us to applaud. Yet who now could really be pleased by this paragraph from a Victorian schoolman and journalist?

> It is to be observed that power of style, in the sense in which I am here speaking of style, is something quite different from the power of idiomatic simple, nervous, racy expression, such as the expression of healthy, robust natures so often is, such as Luther's was in a striking degree. Style, in my sense of the word, is a peculiar recasting and heightening, under a certain condition of spiritual excitement, of what a man has to say, in such a manner as to add dignity and distinction to it . . . . So Luther's sincere idiomatic German . . . no more proves a power of style in German literature, than Cobbett's sinewy idiomatic English proves it in English literature. Power of style, properly so-called, as manifested in masters of style like Dante or Milton in poetry, Cicero, Bossuet or Bolingbroke in prose, is something quite different, and has, as I have said, for its characteristic effect, this: to add dignity and distinction.

That is Matthew Arnold, writing in the middle of the nineteenth century, and how uneasily, even suspiciously, we listen to him. He tries very hard to seem open and plain, but we end by feeling that he has only been tricky and inflated. He begins all wrong with that forensic or at least pedagogical "it is to be observed," and then he puts us off even more by "power of style," which is certainly showy and probably inaccurate, considering that he really means only one quality of a style. He makes a good play when he drops "as I have said" into his last sentence, but it doesn't in the least convince us that he had defined anything in his second sentence. He jars us with "masters of style," because it now seems pretentious; even in Arnold's day "in a striking degree" must have seemed careless. When Arnold tells us that dignity and distinction can be added to a piece of writing, we are likely to give him up for talking nonsense, since to us it is almost certain that manner and matter cannot be separated.

Basically what bothers us is Arnold's taste. If "idiomatic simple, nervous, racy expression" cannot be called style, then so much the worse for style. Today we have no feeling for a man who would want to heighten what he has to say, especially, of all things, "under a certain condition of spiritual excitement." For more than a generation most teachers and nearly all writers have been bringing us to distrust anything like "fine writing," until now almost anyone can find insincerity or falsity, or at least the impersonal artfulness of bad taste, in a passage like this:

> There are poets of the cloister and the quiet corner, of green fields and the earth serene in its changes. There are poets of streets and struggles, of dust and combat, of violence wanton or justified, of plain folk living close to a hard earth as in the great though neglected poem *Piers Plowman*. There have been poets whose themes wove through both the foregoing approaches.

This is what happens when a writer thinks about his manner instead of trying to say what he has to say. Here the writer only wanted to say that poets have different subjects, or that they make up poems about different things. Who then does he mean by "poets of the cloister and the quiet corner"? It is an elaborate way of saying that some poets write about rather simple things; does it also mean that they write about religion and families and homes? Whatever the case, didn't the author probably use "quiet corner" because "cloister" reminded him of "hearth" —which was obviously impossible? Surely he must have linked "streets" and "struggles" because he liked the alliteration. His reason for writing "violence wanton or justified" can only have been the rhythm, but we prefer one that is less theatrical, such as he would have got if he had written what he almost certainly would have said, "wanton or justified violence." But then what is "justified violence"? In referring to a "great though neglected poem," he allowed himself the kind of self-conscious allusion that lecturers like. Finally, to prove the emptiness of everything, there is the perfunctory, neutral, bureaucratic prose in his last sentence: "whose themes move through both the foregoing approaches."

The author is contriving his effects, not explaining his meaning. If he has an idea, he is certainly not keeping his eye on it. Instead of planning his paragraph, he decorates his sentences to make them memorable. Instead of talking quietly to ordinarily educated people, he listens to himself and his literary clevernesses. The result is only a collection of sentences that have more flourishes than points, that are overly insistent in both rhythm and diction, and that are really quite anonymous, in spite of their apparent color, so that they do not at all suggest their author's mind and self. The passage contains just the kind of writing that modern readers are not able to listen to, for they are all, I think, rather like the editors of *The Pelican Book of English Prose*: they may not have "a settled antipathy to ornate prose, but it is fair to admit that [they] are suspicious of its self-conscious varieties after the Restoration . . . ."

"A writer," Hemingway said, "who appreciates the seriousness of writing so little that he is anxious to make people see he is formally educated, cultured, or well-bred is merely a popinjay." "Prose is architecture," he added, "not interior decoration, and the Baroque is over." Today most people would accept his values, and indeed many might even try to write like him. They only want to put down what they feel or what they know or what they have to say, and to do it just as clearly and plainly and truly as they can. Surely only a few young and rather academic people would say that a critic was whimsical or intolerably sentimental if he praised the "simple, nervous, racy expression" of a child's writing such as this passage, which was written by a seven year old girl who was writing a book for her mother's birthday.

FORWARD

This book has three things that are not flowers but most of the things are flowers so the name of the book is flowers. the three things that are not flowers is and apple a boat and a Fawn with a bell around his neck so this book could be called plants anamals Flowers and boats but that would be too long a name and there are just one of each so we just called it flowers. Anyhow there werent any more Ship sentcils and anamal sentcils and fruit sentcils so its just flowers. We didnt get so far did we so the name of the book is just plain flowers.

The author
V.L.

The tradition of plain, easy writing is now so general that advertising copywriters accept it with positive thinking. One copywriter says that when he got into advertising, "rich, beautiful prose had recently gone out of favor."

Advertising had made the big discovery that everybody is stupid. Especially *people*. The 12-year-old mentality was the big thing. We wrote with our tongues in our cheeks, and we were kind of ashamed of what we were writing. We were writing down, being mediocre, on purpose. If it wasn't mediocre (or worse), it wouldn't sell, because the boobs wouldn't understand it.

But in the last ten years, he says, agency men like himself "learned better." What they learned, I think, is that the plain style need not be bad or cheap; indeed that it has its own dignity and strength. They must have learned that the plain style has rules like any other, for the man I am quoting goes on to give a few of the directions that composition teachers have been drumming into their freshmen for forty years or so.

We writers have learned a lot in the last ten years. We've learned how to get closer to people. Today we understand them better, like them better. The relationship is more personal. *Singular* writing. A friend writing to a friend.

We're doing less bragging and nagging. Fewer puns and rhymes and cuties. We've cut the kid stuff, the verbal showing off.

We've learned that simplicity increases interest.

We've learned to be more specific.

We've learned to be pleasanter.

We've learned that, whatever we are, we must never be dull. Dull today, gone tomorrow.

We're no longer afraid to be adult.

We're playing it simpler, straighter. And yet we're having more fun, and so are our readers. We're giving them more real news, real help, real entertainment, real interest.

The doctrine is good enough, but somehow the product doesn't quite satisfy. Wasn't that friendliness achieved too easily? And hasn't an informal style become a stylized informality? One has to wonder if this kind of writing is the necessary result of the change in value and manner that H. G. Wells discovered fifty years ago in the work of Stephen Crane:

> He began stark—I find all through this brief notice I have been repeating that in a dozen disguises, "freedom from tradition," "absolute directness," and the like—as though he came into the world of letters without ever a predecessor. In style, in method, and in all that is distinctively *not* found in his books, he is sharply defined, the expression in literary art of certain enormous repudiations. . . . Any richness of allusion, any melody or balance of phrase, the half quotation that refracts and softens and enriches the statement, the momentary digression that opens like a window upon beautiful or distant things, are not merely absent, but obviously and sedulously avoided. It is as if the racial thought and tradition had been razed from his mind and its site plowed and salted. He is more than himself in this; he is the first expression of the opening mind of a new period, or, at least, the early emphatic phase of a new initiative—beginning, as a growing mind must needs begin, with the record of impressions, a record of vigor and intensity beyond all precedent.

II

In *Modern Prose Style*, Dobrée could not quite avoid the tone of revolutionary virtue, but the book is less a manifesto than a history, and even "the new way of writing" seems to be a tradition that he observed in its high maturity. Dobrée was analyzing the results of fifty years or so of experiment that had finally (it seemed, back in 1934) made it impossible for any cultivated person ever again to write with the deadening propriety of the ordinary Victorians. All of them, teachers, editors, and writers alike, wrote as if they had been following the advice of one of the eighteenth century journalists: "Whoever wishes to attain an English style, familiar but not coarse, and elegant but not ostentatious, must give his days and nights to the volumes of Addison." When Dobrée wrote, however, most people would have said that the qualities Johnson denigrated were just the ones that prose should have. To a twentieth century ear, Johnson's prose would have been all the better if he had allowed himself some of the carelessness he found in Dryden:

> [The prefaces] have not the formality of a settled style, in which the first half of the sentence betrays the other. The clauses are never bal-

anced, nor the periods modelled: every word seems to be dropped by chance, though it falls into its proper place.

What else should a writer do, we would ask, than write the kind of clean, simple, direct writing that Johnson thought put Swift into the second class?

This easy and safe conveyance of meaning it was Swift's desire to attain, and for having attained he deserves praise, though perhaps not the highest praise. For purposes merely didactick, when something is to be told that was not known before, it is the best mode, but against that inattention by which known truths are suffered to lie neglected, it makes no known provision; it instructs but it does not persuade.

For Dobrée's audience the trouble with late Victorian prose was not (as Coleridge had said of eighteenth century prose) that it combined "triteness of thought with singularity and excess of manner of expression . . . to soothe ignorance and flatter vanity." The trouble was rather that the elegance and restraint of Addison had been flattened to a kind of characterless, anonymous politeness:

In the city of Pará, the provincial government assists to augment the splendour of the religious holidays. The processions which traverse the principal streets consist, in the first place, of the image of the saint, and those of several subordinate ones belonging to the same church; these are borne on the shoulders of respectable householders who volunteer for the purpose: sometimes you will see your neighbour the grocer or the carpenter groaning under the load.

It is a style that was useful enough in business or for writers who wanted to say their little bit quickly and easily; and inoffensively. Here is a pretty fair sample of it; I choose this passage both because it is early (1813) and because it is from a novel, where certainly any modern reader would expect to find something much less impersonal.

The housekeeper came; a respectable looking elderly woman, much less fine, and more civil, than she had any notion of finding her. They followed her into the dining-parlour. It was a larger, well-proportioned room, handsomely fitted up. Elizabeth, after slightly surveying it, went to a window to enjoy its prospect. The hill, crowned with wood, from which they had descended, receiving increased abruptness from the distance, was a beautiful object. Every disposition of the ground was good; and she looked on the whole scene, the river, the trees scattered on its banks, and the winding of the valley, as far as she could trace it, with delight. As they passed into other rooms, these objects were taking different positions; but from every window there were beauties to be seen. The rooms were lofty and handsome, and their furniture suitable to the fortune of their proprietor; but Elizabeth saw, with admiration for his taste, that it was neither gaudy nor uselessly fine; with less of splendour, and more real elegance, than the furniture of Rosings.[1]

Jane Austen, *Pride and Prejudice*, XLIII

This was a style that could be clear and readable, but never very exciting. Its conventional graces were built of clichés and tiresome metaphors, and they appealed more often to the eye and the literary memory than to the ear of the imagination. Whatever sound it had came from rotund periods that might have been lifted from orations. It was very seldom concrete, and not often economical either. On the whole its diction was pretentious, or at least imprecise and colorless. The people who used this style called it polite, we are likely to call it empty or, when an effect is reached for, bathetic.

It had one great virtue, however: almost anyone could hope to write it competently. For example, take the opening sentence of Barrett Wendell's very influential book, *English Composition* (1891).

During the past ten years I have been chiefly occupied in teaching, to undergraduates of Harvard College, the principles of English Composition. In the course of that time I have been asked a great many questions concerning the art, mostly by friends who found themselves writing for publication. Widely different as these inquiries have naturally been, they have possessed in common one trait sufficiently marked to place them, in my memory, in a single group: almost without exception, they have concerned themselves with matters of detail.

That passage has many good qualities. Perhaps the most important is that it is unassuming and utilitarian; it seems to have been written for a reading public that, because they could not believe in "known truths," would not tolerate a style that tried to make commonplaces profound instead of clear. Wendell must have thought with Coleridge and most modern writers that good writing is "the art of conveying the meaning appropriately and with perspicuity." In addition Wendell's sentences move directly; his vocabulary is a common one; considering his subject, it is rather simple. One cannot imagine that Wendell would write "their furniture was suitable to the fortune of their proprietor" instead of "their furniture was expensive." But so far as that goes, his would probably be

---

[1]The visit to Pemberley, D'Arcy's country house, that is described in Chapter XLIII of *Pride and Prejudice* is one of the events that reform Elizabeth's view of D'Arcy. As the last sentence in this passage says, the house makes Elizabeth admire his taste, and she begins to suspect that he has a different nature than the one suggested by his appearance and behavior. But notice that a modern reader, though quite aware of the dramatic function of the passage, might still find it unsatisfying, since nowhere in it would he find words that would let him visualize the details of this crucial scene. In the last clause, for example, he would most likely call "gaudy," "uselessly fine," "splendour," and "real elegance" only general counter words, finding in them none of the specific theoretical significance that they may have contained for Jane Austen's readers. Incidentally, notice how the word *elegance* has deteriorated. Nowadays it is completely a cant word of real estate people or sales-"ladies" in expensive dress stores, and not usable in any serious work.

the larger politeness anyway, and he would not allow himself such a comment at all. At any rate (to use what he calls "an apparently commercial phrase"), it seems pretty sure that Wendell would never venture any details to make us see or feel the room. But these faults, as we would call them, only keep Wendell from an individual style, not from prose that is readable and decent. His writing is just, simple, direct, and placid; it is a kind of common style of journeyman prose.

III

As Dobrée shows, modern writers re-created prose as an expressive instrument because they wrote listening to the rhythms and intonation of their own voices. They might almost have been remembering Hazlitt: "There is a method of trying periods on the ear, or weighing them with the scales of the breath, without any articulate sound." Looked at as figures in the history of literature, modern writers are seen as drawing the written dialect back to what it had been before the eighteenth century journalists made it polite. As men and women writing, though, they are perhaps better described as finding ways to express the novelty of the world they were beginning to see: its new knowledge, new values, new attitudes; new ways of doing things and of looking at them. The writers in this tradition were always free and often daring, though never in just a literary way. They seemed to be forever experimenting and exploring, not just in language but in knowledge and experience as well, so they needed new words, new metaphors, and indeed some of them even new syntactical patterns. Perhaps it is a comment on the power of their personalities as well as the ingenuity of their explorations that today nobody much feels any oddity in a statement like this: "A poet makes his discovery of poetic truth only through exploration of the meaning of words."

In other ways than their sense of freedom, these modern writers were rather like the Elizabethan journalists before them. They liked to appeal to the senses and the mind directly, and to the former perhaps more often than to the latter; and so they drew on all that they knew: no word or idea or detail was outside their taste. They were expressing themselves, and since their natures were healthy and robust, eager and inquisitive, they liked the color and vitality of common ways of saying things, like "That smoke looks pretty angry. See how it kicks about." On the whole they avoided the theatricalities of the grand style. They could recognize the effective pattern in this sentence: "And I with my own eyes have seen how brief, vain, and deceitful is the glory of this world." Yet since purple was never their favorite color, what they would have applauded and might have tried to imitate was the detail that goes before the moral: that thieves had stripped the body of Innocent III "of its precious vestments and left it almost naked and stinking in the church."

IV

Current writers, those who have started writing in the quarter century since Dobrée's book was published, still work within the tradition he described. Many use its conventions so very competently that they are almost always able to give their styles pleasantly colloquial movements and indeed even energy. It is difficult, however, not to feel that among the majority there has been a gradual collapse of personal distinctions into a kind of common conversational informality. Consider the effect of these sentences, which I have picked from several magazines more or less as my eye fell on them.

It's been some time now since there has been much excitement about "fair-trade price-fixing" laws—those state regulations, empowered by the Federal government's McGuire Act, which allow manufacturers to fix the retail prices of their branded products.

Consumer Reports

Last summer a cataract of violent, scatological eloquence suddenly burst from the boards of a London theater, scattering into the wings the well-bred platitudes to which we theater-goers here are accustomed.

The Progressive

As a "colony" Okinawa could not possibly become a "show window" of democracy, for colonialism and democracy are based on entirely different principles.

The Progressive

Throughout the five boroughs [of New York City] there are various kinds of special classes where the bright youngster can use his brain, instead of sitting bored through his classes as he might in a small-town school.

The Reporter

We are in for a golden age of satire, in my opinion, and if this is so we will be fortunate indeed.

Kingsley Amis, *The New York Times Book Review*

Outside Boston, say in Brooklyn, the author of [a book on Henry Adams] starts with two strikes on him, and it is a tribute to the excellence of the design and the skill in execution displayed by Mr. Levenson that this natural prejudice is so completely overcome.

The (London) Times Literary Supplement

The sheer number of new things requiring zippy, colorful identification is appalling to the industrialists, who live in frankly avowed dread of the day when the demand for names will, once and for all, exceed the supply.

The New York Times Magazine

These sentences, which are very workmanlike, remind us of the impersonal, professional style of the ordinary Victorians; for their differences, chiefly of rhythm and pace, are none of them so great that a reader could confidently say that the sentences were written by different people. The style (for it is *a* style; if not an official one, it is at least general and common) is the result of twenty years or so of the bureaucratization of prose. In this time editors have demanded a neutral, quickly readable prose, almost as the founders of the Royal Society in the seventeenth century insisted on "a close, naked, natural way of Speaking; positive Expressions, clear Senses; a native Easiness; bringing all Things as near the mathematical Plainness as they can; and preferring the Language of Artizans, Countrymen, and Merchants, before that of Wits or Scholars." (Did the modern writers also want to be scientifically neutral as well as commonly readable?) During these years many writers wrote too much too rapidly; often they got steady work in the Grub Street of the radio, movie, and television script factories, or on one of the news magazines. The schools helped too, with their insistence that students learn correctness and propriety by writing themes on such subjects as "Radio City—City Within A City." The result of these pressures has been a style that is as rigidly conversational and familiar as that of the eighteenth century journalists was rhetorical and formal.

Probably the most important device in this style is that of the conversational sentence. Here are three interesting or curious examples. In the first, perfectly usual sentences are completed or carried on by a loosely related absolute phrase and an unrelated appositive.

> In a six-year period came four books of poetry having a variety of faults, no other person more keenly aware of their accomplishments and shortcomings than myself. In the two books for children, in this period, are a few cornland tales that go on traveling, one about "The Two Skyscrapers Who Decided to Have A Child."

On the whole the effect there is careless more than easy; perhaps it is even garrulous.

In the second example the writer certainly needs something to lighten the effect of his first sentence which so formally carries the folk allusion. He gets what he needs by the interjection and by his short, direct, and quite emphatic last sentence. Together they are no doubt supposed to suggest a man thinking as he talks.

> A lay observer, familiar only with the fact that the next Presidential conventions will not be held for three years, might think that these five political hares are running too hard to stay the distance and that somewhere is an unnoticed tortoise who will outlast them. Maybe. But the five are running according to form.

But it would be interesting to know exactly what the last two sentences do add except an artificial finality that is rather fussy, and that contrasts oddly with the grave tone in the rest of the piece.

Here is the third example:

Magazines tell us what to buy. What to eat. How to eat it. Where to go. How to go there. How to get our children, and how to raise them. How to tell our children how to get their children. How to handle the old mumbling bumbling birds-and-the-bees job—and handle it right.

Another important device is that of the incongruous use of slang or familiar diction.

Steichen after World War I put in a year making a thousand photographs of a white cup and saucer, a quest in light and shadow. Maugham crosses up Forster on how to write a novel and both heave Walter Scott into the ash can. Shakespeare wrote a certain amount of trash— because his theater had to have a new play next Tuesday.

Another device—this one perhaps goes back to the early *New Yorker*, as do a good many others—is the skewing of stock figures of comparison. Anyone might think some man looked like just any old owl; so the owl that this man looks like is "poorly plumed but comfortable." And what is a comfortable owl?

Mr. Starkie, relaxing after a lecture tour . . . and celebrating the approaching publication of his translation . . . of *Don Quixote* . . . is learned, astute, absent-minded, gay, worldly, innocent, and who, with specs on, resembles a poorly plumed but comfortable owl.

But is Mr. Starkie like an owl and all the rest only when he is relaxing and celebrating? And notice the "and who." Where is the first who-clause?

In addition, there are such devices as the subjectless verb, the contraction, and the parenthetical question or adverb, the allusion to common experience, and the unexpected but only moderately startling detail. By now, it almost seems, writing shouldn't be any trouble at all.

In the hands of a conscientious writer, however, as for example in the following advertisement, the current common style has great vigor and grace, even some degree of personal tone.

CLIP-ON BUTTONS

By this time, most men know where they can go to get a button sewn on in an emergency. But there are times when even your nearest Wallachs is too far. A button that pops off your shirt just when you're dressing in a hurry can throw you completely off stride. And that's why we are supplementing our normal sew-on service with something new.

This something new is the clip-on shirt button. It requires no sewing and is really a variation on the old bachelor's button. Each button has two little prongs. You push the prongs through the shirt fabric and press down. The prongs won't rust, scratch or tear. And whether you later replace a clip-on with a regular button or leave it in the shirt is up to you.

[1]Adv. Copyright 1957, Wallachs.

These little white emergency buttons come three-on-a-card and we should be very happy if you would accept a card with our compliments. Ask for them in any Wallachs store.

Of course one might still object to *supplement* and *variation* as inappropriately formal; certainly "we should be" is just finicky. And *later*, besides being unnecessary, interrupts the movement of its sentence. But generally the writing has a very decent and sober swing to it.

Here is a feature story to show the good journalistic form of the current common style.

ABOUT NEW YORK

Centenarian, Resident of the Plaza 27 Years, Takes Some Brief Glimpses Into Long Past

By MEYER BERGER

In this town, probably more than in any other, women of means, when their husbands die, are likely to give up large houses or apartments to retire to the well-ordered comfort of conservative hotels. Some withdraw completely and brood over a happier past to a lonely end.

The Plaza Hotel on the south edge of Central Park, which will be fifty years old this fall, has widow guests—and some unmarried women, too—who have lived there since the place first opened. Some rarely leave their suites; they talk only with the maids and with the waiters who serve them.

Mrs. Ella Peterson Tuttle Freeman has lived in the Plaza for twenty-seven years. Before that, she had resided in the old Waldorf-Astoria before it was torn down to make way for the Empire State Building.

Mrs. Freeman will be 100 years old today. Her hair is snow-white and is laid in neat curls each day. Sight has all but faded from her blue eyes. Though her windows face across the park onto a glorious view— trees now like brown smoke, skaters on Wollman rink, wild ducks in the pond just below—she no longer sees them.

Mrs. Freeman's memory works like a rusted shutter; it sticks most of the time, then jerks open for brief glimpses into a long past. She dimly remembers childhood on Clinton Avenue, Brooklyn, when there were no paved streets, only dusty roads and open vistas; that "Father [he was William Tuttle] made radiators" and that the Pratts, of the wealthy oil family, were neighbors.

The shutter comes down again, and then: "Father just bought a whole block on Clinton Avenue and built a big house on it. He had trees planted all around it. Lanes cut across Clinton Avenue, but they had no signposts—no names." The tight shutter again. Then: "I heard Adelina Patti. When I was a little girl, I bought a vinegar pickle at the grocer's. It was wrapped in brown paper. I ate every bit. I liked it better than candy."

The blue eyes wavered. They could not see the clean-washed blue sky over the park or the white Fifth Avenue towers. Then memory broke through the cloud again: "I wore hoop skirts. I played the organ in church. I danced the Vienna waltzes. * * * I went to Adelphi and to Packer Institute. I went to private school, but my father was angry. My teacher sat on a piano and sucked chalk. I didn't know a fraction from a dog. He took me out of private school. He put me in a public school—a sheep-fold kind of place—was it on Carlton Avenue? I learned some things there."

In June, 1887, Miss Tuttle was married to Frank Stanley Freeman, a banker in Brooklyn. He lived only one month. She never remarried.

The sun gilded Mrs. Freeman's hair. She laughed in sudden recollection. It was about father. He was down South, once, wearing white spats. A native, who had never seen spats before, stared at them. He said: "Excuse me, suh, but yo' drawers is showin'." The old woman chuckled. She kept repeating: "Excuse me, suh, but yo' drawers is showin'." That was a family joke for years.

Miss Catherine Cooper, a Canadian, has been Mrs. Freeman's companion the last twelve years. She said: "Mrs. Freeman is very proud of her hats. She likes them gay. She got one downstairs the other day, and insisted on a feather for it."

Mrs. Freeman does not cross over Fifty-ninth Street to the park anymore, though she did up to some months ago. She says: "It's too chancey, now." But come summer, and she is driven out to her nieces in Syosset, L. I., for brief stays. One niece, Mrs. J. J. McDonald, was master of hounds at Meadow Brook.

There will be no formal birthday party today. Mrs. Freeman will have gifts for Bertha Meyers, the hotel maid, who likes to fill Mrs. Freeman's room with fresh flowers left behind by departing guests, and for William, her waiter. She will receive them, and her kin, in her throne-like chair by the window that faces on the park—in the chair where she sits and dreams of the great changes that have come over the city in her hundred years.

FROM *The New York Times.* Used by permission.

The story has many sharply phrased details; only a few are done with literary turns. (Compare Berger's report of Mrs. Freeman's memories with his own descriptions of Central Park.) The sentences are generally easy and direct; except for a few, especially in the last two paragraphs, they do not seem perfunctory. For the most part the diction is appropriately plain, though there are a couple of literary flourishes. Would not "She is almost blind" have done as well as "Sight has all but faded from her blue eyes"? But perhaps these criticisms too are only captious, when the greater part of the story is so pleasantly written.

In its most popular forms, the current common style is notable for slack and unaccented sentences, carelessly chosen words, sentimental or obvious details, thinly developed thought. It seems based on the attitudes and speech habits of a mass-educated, mass-entertained, mass-informed urban population. But in its more sophisticated forms, the style is not unattractive. It is brisk and unassuming and at the same time efficient. Perhaps it does not matter if it is also very often commonplace and flat. Curiously, though it is really quite impersonal, this style almost always makes us think that we are listening to somebody interesting. So in general we can be pleased by it.

And that probably is why we find it tolerable. Modern prose satisfies our taste for the natural and honest because it does almost always have the tone and sound of an individual talking; even if it often seems to be the same individual, at least we never feel we are listening to a book that has suddenly begun to make a noise.[1] Perhaps we are only naive when, reading an elaborate or un-English style, we infer pretentiousness or even falsity in thought and value; but so we do.[2] Most educated people today would agree with Professor Sutherland:

> When we wish to give high praise to a poem we say quite naturally that it is "great poetry." When we think highly of a piece of prose writing, we are more likely to say "This is good prose." Whenever I hear the expression "great prose" or "fine prose" I am apt to suspect that it is something which I should not greatly care to read: a purple passage from De Quincey, perhaps, or from Ruskin, or from Doughty's *Travels in Arabia Deserta*.

This modern prose style may be conventional and sometimes even institutional, but its convention is for the easy, the nervous, the racy, the compact way of saying things that we associate with naturalness and honesty, and with the spoken language. Probably we are not far wrong when we think that modern prose satisfies Sutherland's definition of good prose, for it is indeed a superb instrument for allowing "the writer's meaning to come through with the least possible loss of significance and nuance, as a landscape is seen through a clear window."[3]

---

[1]Because books and other printed forms of discourse are now so generally available, not very many people try to retain what they read. Whenever they need to know, they can always "look it up." Perhaps we tolerate the modern common style only because we have all become a little tone deaf.

[2]At least among educated people, the causes are H. W. Fowler's *Modern English Usage*, H. L. Mencken's *The American Language*, and H. C. Wyld's *History of Modern Colloquial English*. For more than a generation the teaching of composition in college has been influenced by Wyld's thesis: "The style of Literature is rooted in the life and conversation of the age. From these sources alone can prose renew its life from generation to generation. When Literary prose style loses touch with the spoken language it becomes lifeless and unexpressive, powerless to 'strike the ear, the heart or the fancy,' remote alike from human feeling and from the speech of man because it has never known real life or movement."

[3]James Sutherland, *On English Prose*. Toronto, University of Toronto Press, 1957, pp. 26 and 77.

ON WRITING

Three of the selections in this section are by famous stylists; I hope it can be learned from them that the modern way of writing that Dobrée describes has quite respectable historical antecedents. The plain style was not invented just the other day by Hemingway. These and the other selections will show the kind of point that can be used in criticizing or analyzing prose. And they should also give some information about the qualities of the prose style that most of the other selections in the book have been chosen to illustrate. Careful reading of the older selections should give some feeling for the kind of writing that appeals to most people today.

THE NEW WAY OF WRITING

Bonamy Dobrée

Can we say that there is, definitely, "a new way of writing"? Is there such a thing as *modern* prose, with characteristics the older prose does not possess?[1] It may seem at first sight that the question cannot reasonably be put, for if we are agreed that style is the personal voice—which pierces through even the "impersonal" manner—and that the voice is the man; and if we assume, as we plausibly can, that man does not alter except over very long periods, can we talk of a modern as opposed to an old-fashioned style?

One can make two answers to this. The first is, that though time may not change man physically, nor perhaps mentally, leaving his vocal chords and what he wants to do with them still the same, two things do change: the social being, and with him the method of speech he must use to be effective with other social beings. Man as a social animal alters in tune with what we call, since a better term is lacking, "the spirit of the age," which we gauge by the different approaches men make to the external universe, and, more important perhaps, to their own emotions. Man may be fundamentally unchanged, but in the social process of his time, different facets are polished, unfamiliar aspects emerge. To take a simple example: How would a fourteenth-century man react if he were asked to

From *Modern Prose Style* by Bonamy Dobrée. Oxford, The Clarendon Press, 1934. Reprinted by permission of the publishers.
[1] I may suggest to begin with, that had I been writing thirty years ago, I would probably have felt constrained to write "with characteristics *which* the older . . ." [Author's note]

think of "the wonders of the deep" compared with the way a twentieth-century man would react? Today we should at once let our minds turn to what we might roughly call "scientific marvels," that is to various detailed manifestations of fish life, or of corals. The fourteenth-century man would shudder deliciously at a vision of leviathans, appallingly, even incredibly shaped, of mermaids, of ghostly inhabitants. Not only, then, will men of various ages wish to *express* different things, but they will wish to *impress* men differently. What would be the good, for instance, of a member of the House of Lords rising up and saying:

> My Lords, this ruinous and ignominious situation, where we cannot act with success nor suffer with honour, calls upon us to remonstrate in the strongest and loudest language of truth, to rescue the ears of majesty from the delusions which surround it.

We can imagine a peer having similar feelings about, perhaps, the situation in India, but such language, used by Chatham in 1777, would have no result whatever now, though in its way it is splendid, and in its own age was no doubt very effective indeed. Our second answer arises out of the first: since the needs of the voice have changed, the instrument has been altered: we no longer use the same tool as our ancestors did to move other people. And there is still another consideration. If we use a different tool it is that our emotions have changed, or at any rate, if our emotions do not change, our attitude towards them differs with the age in which we live. These things, however, interact upon each other. We know, as once we did not know, that our emotions vary with the language we use in describing them: the spirit of an age may not only be reflected in its prose, it may be, indeed it is, to some extent conditioned by it. This, however, is an issue which would take us too far outside the bounds of our subject; nor am I qualified to pursue it.

Let us now take two passages, dealing with much the same range of ideas, written by men who were each in their day stylists. We have already done something of the sort in the Introduction, but we can use another example to reinforce the argument of the first. This time one writer is Sir Thomas Browne, the other William James, and I am taking Browne at his most straightforward.

> Let thy studies be free as thy thoughts and contemplations: but fly not only upon the wings of imagination; join sense unto reason, and experiment unto speculation, and so give life unto embryon truths, and verities yet in their chaos. There is nothing more acceptable unto the ingenious world, than this noble eluctation of truth; wherein, against the tenacity of prejudice and prescription, this century now prevaileth.

That is from *Christian Morals:* now let us take this from *The Will to Believe:*

> On the whole, then, we must conclude that no philosophy of ethics is possible in the old-fashioned absolute sense of the term. Everywhere

the ethical philosopher must wait on facts. The thinkers who create the ideals come he knows not whence, their sensibilities are evolved he knows not how; and the question as to which of two conflicting ideals will give the best universe then and there, can be answered by him only through the aid of the experience of other men.

I take it that anybody, even neglecting Browne's obsolete forms, would at once recognize the first passage as belonging to the seventeenth century, and the second to our own time. Can we put our finger on where exactly the difference lies?

It is pretty obvious that the difference lies in the rhythm, but that is too easy a thing to say: and as a matter of fact, if we analyse these two passages into "prose rhythms" in the way that Saintsbury did in his fascinating book, they are not, prosodically speaking at least, so different after all. Are not such cadences as

$$\bar{\text{em}}\breve{\text{bry}}\breve{\text{on}}/\text{truths, and}/\text{verities}/\text{yet in their}/\text{chaos,}$$

and

$$\text{old-fashioned}/\text{absolute}/\text{sense of the}/\text{term,}$$

of much the same order? Both are, in a sense, dactylic. What is different is the way the metres are used. In modern writing there is far less insistence on the rhythms; the unit into which the rhythms are woven, that is to say the phrase, is far more flexible, on the whole longer. The antithetical balance has gone. But what is more significant is that the written language to-day is much nearer the spoken language, with implications we shall follow up in a moment. But first I must dispose of two possible objections. The first and lesser one is that for the seventeenth-century example we have a very conscious stylist. That is true, but Jeremy Taylor or Milton will give much the same result. Why do we remember, except for its insistence on rhythm, Milton's "rousing herself like a strong man after sleep, and shaking her invincible locks"? But how do I know, it will be asked in the second place, that the older people did not speak as they wrote? The suggestion is often made, most notably by Mr. Gordon Bottomley, that in the seventeenth century, especially in Shakespeare's time, the rhythms of everyday speech were more accentuated, approached even those of blank verse, or of obviously cadenced speech. Let us look at something from a contemporary of Sir Thomas Browne's:

> Up, and by water, stopping at Michell's, and there saw Betty, but could have no discourse with her, but there drank. To White Hall, and there walked to St. James's, where I find the Court mighty full, it being the Duke of York's birthday; and he mighty fine, and all the musick, one after another, to my great content.

Pepys, you see at once, was not writing literary English: he was setting down his doings as he might have chatted about them to his wife—if, of course, he had been a brave enough man to do so.

It is fairly certain, I think, that the written language of the seventeenth century was farther from the spoken language than the written language of to-day is from our conversation, a division which probably began with Caxton. John Donne, one can be sure, never spoke at home in the way that he thundered from the pulpit. The proof is to be found in the correspondence of the time, much of which has been collected by Professor Wyld in his *History of Modern Colloquial English*, largely for this purpose; and what comes out is that the language of the Elizabethans was not essentially unlike our own. Here, for one example, is Sir Philip Sidney writing to Edward Molyneux:

> Few words are best. My letters to my father have come to the eyes of some. Neither can I condemn any but you for it. If it be so you have played the very knave with me; and so I will make you know if I have good proof of it. But that for so much as is past. For that is to come, I assure you before God, that if ever I know you do so much as read any letter I write to my father, without his commandment, or my consent, I will thrust my dagger into you. And trust to it, for I speak it in earnest. In the mean time, farewell.

The sentiments of this prose (we trust) are not ours, and the forms are not quite so, but the ring of it is. If we were to say that sort of thing, we should say it in that kind of way. Sidney's prose here, we see, is altogether different from what he wrote for the press, his "Sidneyan showers of sweet discourse." Here is another example; and making allowance for stage speech, does it sound very quaint or old-fashioned, or very heavily rhythmed?

> Thou art so fat-witted, with drinking of old sack, and unbuttoning thee after supper, and sleeping upon benches after noon, that thou hast forgotten to demand that truly which thou wouldst truly know. What a devil hast thou to do with the time of the day. . . .

Prince Hal probably spoke fairly current English; and the journalists of the time, Nashe, Greene, Dekker, wrote much in the way Prince Hal spoke, for they were not labouring after fine style, but trying to write as men talked. What appears to have happened is that in the seventeenth century a profound division developed between the spoken and the written language, a division bridged by the journalists and the comic writers. What seems to have occurred afterwards was, to cut a long story short, that the journalists, forgetting Dryden, deserted to the written side: one has only to think of Addison, and then of Dr. Johnson, who, far from trying to write as he naturally spoke, did his best to model his conversation on his writing. Everybody remembers how he let slip the remark about *The Rehearsal* not having wit enough to keep it sweet, and then, recoiling in horror from so natural an expression, hurriedly amended the phrase to "has not vitality enough to preserve it from corruption." The stylists of the eighteenth century seem to have taken their writing farther and farther away from their speech—Gibbon, Burke, Smollett. This process went on through the nineteenth century; we have only to think of Carlyle or Pater, though it is true that some people all the while kept up the spoken tradition, Defoe, Sterne, and even Lamb, for though Lamb's style is artificial as regards words, his rhythms are those of his talk, or at any rate of his possible talk. What I think is going on at the present day is a return to speech rhythms: the conscious stylists are, so to speak, ridding themselves of "style": not "style," but *a* style is what they are aiming at, a style that will faithfully reflect their mind as it utters itself naturally. What is curious is that now it is the leading authors who write naturally, style, so-called, being left to the journalists. I take the opening sentence of the first leading article of *The Times* of the day on which I happened to be taking notes for this chapter (19 August 1933): "As soon as it was announced, on the morrow of Parliament's rising. . . ." One need not go on. Who would dream of *saying* "on the morrow of Parliament's rising"? It is jargon. What we would probably say is, "the day after Parliament rose." Not that this *pompier* "style" is confined to the august heights of journalism: it runs all through, and not long ago *The Daily Worker* printed with regard to certain prisons: "No sound comes from out those walls." Does the man who wrote those words habitually say "from out"? Why does this happen? Why do people write forms which are dead, which they would never utter? In both the examples quoted one is tempted to diagnose insincerity of thought, or at least mental laziness.

Does it not seem, then, that the modern prose-writer, in returning to the rhythms of everyday speech, is trying to be more honest with himself than if he used, as is too wreckingly easy, the forms and terms already published as the expression of other people's minds? "Style . . . is not an ornament; it is not an exercise, not a caper, nor complication of any sort. It is the sense of one's self, the knowledge of what one wants to say, and the saying of it in the most fitting words."[2] And that is why it is extremely hard to achieve *a* style, for all these three things are very difficult to attain. Take only the last task, the saying of what one wants to say in the most fitting words. It seems almost impossible, for every time we speak we have virtually to re-create the instrument if we want to be faithful to our idea or feeling. Everywhere the words and phrasing of past generations interpose themselves between us and the reality. "It is . . . a true and lamentable fact that, in ultimate analysis, one cannot speak about anything without altering it to some extent."[3] It is the realization of this, a realization possibly new in our day, which impels authors to try to write as they speak in ordinary life on ordinary physical matters, for it is only in this way that one can achieve fidelity to one's self: otherwise the language and style of the literary tradition assert themselves. But the modern writer

[2]Introduction to *The London Book of English Prose*, by Herbert Read and Bonamy Dobrée, Eyre and Spottiswoode, 1931. [Author's note]
[3]*The Theory of Speech and Language*, by A. H. Gardiner, Oxford, 1932. [Author's note]

must not think of style: the man who thinks first of style is lost: the primary thing to do—this is an old observation—is to think clearly. As M. Jean Cocteau says, writing for modern authors: "Style cannot be a starting point: it happens. What is style? For a great many people it is a complicated way of saying very simple things. From our point of view it is a very simple way of saying complicated things."[4] How does a modern writer tackle this problem? Here, I think, is a good example:

> I had great ambitions. I have none now—and have not even the fear of failing. What matters to me and to many of the survivors of my generation is only that which is common to us all, our fear for our children. If it were not for that, I should know how to act in what remains of my life—that would be to withdraw as far as possible from the little world of writing and talking about books which is a microcosm of the whole, its values no finer than those accepted by the rest of the world, and only valid on the assumption that to a writer success means precisely what it means to a stockbroker or a multiple grocer. That is, material wealth, and the respect paid to it. This seems to me a denial of all the writer, the "clerk," should stand for, but I can do nothing to alter it, and therefore I ought to run away for my life.
>
> After all that turbulence of desire and ambitions it seems strange I should believe now that very little in me is real except the absolute need, intellectual and spiritual, for withdrawal, for resolving to satisfy in my life only the simple wants. It is as strange as that I am only just learning to write and don't care to.
>
> There are days when I retract all this, and think how queer I shall grow if I live alone, and think too that what is needed is some effort to create cells inside the body social, groups of angry, last-minute saints. That would be no good. I should weary in a week of the company of persons who thought and felt no differently from myself.[5]

That, as prose, is simple, easy, fluent, and flexible; what is important, however, is that it is written, apparently, in the *tones* of every day, though here and there we can detect traces of literary forms—"only that which" instead of "only what": "how to act" instead of "what to do": it is extraordinarily difficult to rid one's self of terms of that kind. But to show how new the tone is, here is a passage from another autobiography written, one always thought, in a natural, confidential manner:

> There were perhaps twenty boys in the school at most, and often fewer. I made the excursion between home and school four times a day; if I walked fast, the transit might take five minutes, and, as there were several objects of interest on the way, it might be spread over an hour. In fine weather the going to and from school was very delightful, and small as the scope was, it could be varied almost indefinitely.[6]

[4]*A Call to Order*, Allen and Unwin, trs. 1933. [Author's note]
[5]From *No Time Like the Present*, by Storm Jameson, Cassell, 1933. [Author's note]
[6]From *Father and Son*, by Edmund Gosse, Heinemann, 1907. [Author's note]

There are, we see immediately, one or two obvious "literary" turns in that passage: "I made the excursion between home and school," instead of "I went to and from school": "If I walked fast, the transit might take five minutes," instead of "I could get there or back (or do the journey) in five minutes": "objects of interest," with others of the same sort. And the general run, which is the important thing, though simple and easy, and we might perhaps admit fluent, is not flexible. Each sentence contains an idea and completes it. The mind comes to a full stop at the end of each phrase. But our minds in life do not work in that way; they are always ready to frame the next sentence, carried on by the impetus of the last. Gosse, in common with the older writers, was concerned, not to follow the movements of his mind, but to present something concrete.

To say, then, that the hall-mark of good modern prose style is an essential fidelity does not imply that writers of previous generations were charlatans and liars, only that they owed fidelity to other things. And it is here that the spirit of our age imposes itself upon our style. All the previous ages whose writers have been quoted or referred to here had something they could take for granted, and it never occurred to the older writers that they could not take themselves for granted. We can be sure of nothing; our civilization is threatened, even the simplest things we live by: we are on the verge of amazing changes. In our present confusion our only hope is to be scrupulously honest with ourselves, so honest as to doubt our own minds and the conclusions they arrive at. Most of us have ceased to believe, except provisionally, in truths, and we feel that what is important is not so much truth as the way our minds move towards truths. Therefore, to quote M. Cocteau again, "Form must be the form of the mind. Not a way of saying things, but of thinking them." Perhaps that is why we nowadays instinctively mistrust any one who pontificates: and, as a matter of experience, if we examine the writings of the pontificators, people skilled in "a way of saying things," we invariably find that their style is bad, that falsity has crept in somewhere. The writer is not being faithful to the movement of his mind; he is taking things for granted, and he fills us of to-day with uneasiness.

We have, then, to judge of the integrity of a modern writer by this sense of himself that we feel he has. If we are to respond, he must (we suppose) be aware of himself as something a little uncertain in this shifting universe: he also is part of the material which he has to treat with respect: he must listen to himself, so to speak, to hear what he has to say. He must not pre-judge, or force an issue: we must be able to imagine that he is talking to himself. In no other way can he achieve *a* style, which is the sound of his voice, which is the man himself.

It is not so simple as it sounds for a man to watch his own mind; it is as difficult as writing in the way you ordinarily talk: literary habits continually get in the way. Nor must a man write as he might lazily talk, and it is more important than ever for him to reject the dead metaphor which can never be more than an approximation, to choose the exact, the expressive word, to rid his style of fat, to make it athletic. What he must really do, as the first essential, is to keep his awareness athletic, especially his awareness of himself. And he must not watch his mind idly; he must watch it as he might a delicate piece of machinery doing its work, and he must watch it, not flickering about in every direction, as an active mind does, but only in the direction he wants it to go. Otherwise the result may be disastrous. Even the following extremely clever attempt seems to me an object-lesson:

> The problem from this time on became more definite.
> It was all so nearly alike it must be different and it is different, it is natural that if everything is used and there is a continuous present and a beginning again and again if it is all so alike it must be simply different and everything simply different was the natural way of creating it then.
> In this natural way of creating it then that it was simply different everything being alike it was simply different, this kept on leading one to lists. Lists naturally for a while and by lists I mean a series. More and more in going back over what was done at this time I find that I naturally kept simply different as an intention. Whether there was or whether there was not a continuous present did not then any longer trouble me there was or there was, and using everything no longer troubled me if everything is alike using everything could no longer trouble me and beginning again and again could no longer trouble me because if lists were inevitable if series were inevitable and the whole of it was inevitable beginning again and again could not trouble me so then with nothing to trouble me I very completely began naturally since everything is alike making it as simply different naturally as simply different as possible. I began doing natural phenomena what I call natural phenomena and natural phenomena naturally everything being alike natural phenomena are making things be naturally simply different. This found its culmination later, in the beginning it began in a center confused with lists with series with geography with returning portraits and with particularly often four and three and often with five and four. It is easy to see that in the beginning such a conception as every-thing being naturally different would be very inarticulate and very slowly it began to emerge and take the form of anything, and then naturally if anything that is simply different is simply different what follows will follow.[7]

One cannot say whether Miss Stein's mind really moves like that: pos-sibly it does, and possibly most of our minds move more like that than we are aware of, or at any rate are prepared to admit. What is clear is that the mere following of the mind, its echoes and repetitions, does not really give its shape; and this makes us realize that to write naturally as the mind would wish to utter, is just as much an art—or an artifice—as to

[7]From *Composition as Explanation*, by Gertrude Stein, Hogarth Press, 1926. [Author's note]

write in what we call an artificial style, say that of a Pater or Meredith. What has happened is that the modern writer is faced with new material, and what he has to do is to discover the new form that this material requires.

But because this new form can only be an adaptation of the old, it takes consummate art to prevent literature interposing itself between us and life. The problem, no doubt, has always existed, but if it has been realized the solution has rarely, if ever, been hit on. Yet there is Sterne, and what Mrs. Woolf has to say about him is illuminating:

> . . . With the first words—They order, said I, this matter better in France—we are in the world of *Tristram Shandy*. It is a world in which anything may happen. We hardly know what jest, what jibe, what flash of poetry is not going to glance suddenly through the gap which this astonishingly agile pen has cut in the thick-set hedge of English prose. Is Sterne himself responsible? Does he know what he is going to say next for all his resolve to be on his best behaviour this time? The jerky disconnected sentences are as rapid and it would seem as little under control as the phrases that fall from the lips of a brilliant talker. The very punctuation is that of speech, not writing, and brings the sounds and associations of the speaking voice in with it. The order of the ideas, their suddenness and irrelevancy, is more true to life than to literature. . . . Under the influence of this extraordinary style the book becomes semi-transparent. The usual ceremonies and conventions which keep reader and writer at arm's length disappear. We are as close to life as we can be.[8]

That passage is not quoted as being characteristic of Mrs. Woolf: to hear her real voice one must go to the novels: it is quoted as an aid to my argument. And it serves it in two ways, because of what it says, and because of the way it says it, for if the prose is not markedly Mrs. Woolf's, it is obviously modern: the voice that is speaking is a voice of to-day: I shall not be misunderstood, I hope, if I say that any one might have written it. Now let us compare this with the way Bagehot wrote about Sterne in the *National Review* in 1864:

> But here the great excellence of Sterne ends as well as begins. In *Tristram Shandy* especially there are several defects which, while we are reading it, tease and disgust us so much that we are scarcely willing even to admire as we ought to admire the refined pictures of human emotion. The first of these, and perhaps the worst, is the fantastic disorder of the form. It is an imperative law of the writing art, that a book should go straight on. A great writer should be able to tell a great meaning as coherently as a small writer tells a small meaning. . . .

and so it goes on. That is typical nineteenth-century prose: we get something very like it in Matthew Arnold, or Huxley, and in its way it is

[8]*The Common Reader*, ii, Hogarth Press, 1932. [Author's note]

excellent. But the rhythms and inflexions are quite different from those of to-day: it consists, not of thoughts closely followed, not of ideas suggested, but of utterances, of pronouncements. Again, as with Gosse, we have the end-stopped phrase: there is a door banged at the end of each, and we feel as though we were on parade receiving orders.

What seems to us to be lacking in the older prose is the sense of the uninterrupted flow of the mind: Bagehot, for example, appears to cut off this continuum, shall we call it, into arbitrary lengths, as we slice chunks off a cucumber. This is to force on our minds a logic that is not of their own making; and though it may be true that, as T. E. Hulme said, "All styles are only means of subduing the reader," we must not feel that our minds are being forced, and therefore distorted. Perhaps it was George Moore's principal achievement to give this sense of flow: there is hardly an instant's pause in his mental processes. His style is very distinctive; all the time one hears a voice, a personal utterance, though pursued to the lengths to which he took it, or allowed it to carry him, it becomes in the end monotonous. The mind runs on too much; it has no form but that of a stream: no solid shape emerges. But the sort of flow we are talking about can, and sometimes does, take form. Here is an extract from Henry James, whose whole being was directed to following the movement of his mind, and who gave form to this movement, not indeed in a language natural to us, but one which seems to have been natural to him, a way which he could not have escaped from even if he had wanted to:

> Momentary side-winds—things of no real authority—break in every now and then to put their inferior little questions to me; but I come back, I come back, as I say, I all throbbingly and yearningly and passionately, oh mon bon come back to this way that is clearly the only one in which I can do anything now, and that will open out to me more and more, and that has overwhelming reasons pleading all beautifully in its breast. What really happens is that the closer I get to the problem of the application of it in any particular case, the more I get *into* that application, so that the more doubts and torments fall away from me, the more I know where I am, the more everything spreads and shines and draws me on and I'm justified in my logic and my passion. . . . Causons, causons, mon bon—oh celestial, soothing, sanctifying process, with all the high sane forces of the sacred time fighting, through it, on my side! Let me fumble it gently and patiently out—with fever and fidget laid to rest—as in all the old enchanted months! It only looms, it only shines and shimmers, *too* beautiful and too interesting, it only hangs there too rich and too full and with too much to give and to pay; it only presents itself too admirably and too vividly, too straight and square and vivid, as a little organic and effective Action.[9]

We may think that artificial, but we do not feel, complicated as it is, that this is a literary language. It is the language of Henry James's speech; it

[9]*Letters*, Macmillan.

reflects his mind accurately, a mind with a very definite form. James, if you like, had a tortuous way of thinking, but he had broken down the barriers between his mind and the expression of it.

What we look for, however, is a style which shall be as free and individual as in that passage, but which smacks less of idiosyncrasy, for something we might all use, though, no doubt, not so well as our model, for something which does not give us, as some recent prose does, the uneasy effect of submitting us to a laboratory experiment. Perhaps this is what we want:

> The trouble with her ship was that it would *not* sail. It rode water-logged in the rotting port of home. All very well to have wild, reckless moods of irony and independence, if you have to pay for them by withering dustily on the shelf.
>
> Alvina fell again into humility and fear: she began to show symptoms of her mother's heart trouble. For day followed day, month followed month, season after season went by, and she grubbed away like a housemaid in Manchester House, she hurried round doing the shopping, she sang in the choir on Sundays, she attended the various chapel events, she went out to visit friends, and laughed and talked and played games. But all the time, what was there actually in her life? Not much. She was withering towards old-maiddom. Already in her twenty-eighth year, she spent her days grubbing in the house, whilst her father became an elderly, frail man still too lively in mind and spirit. Miss Pinnegar began to grow grey and elderly too, money became scarcer and scarcer, there was a black day ahead when her father would die and the home be broken up, and she would have to tackle life as a worker.
>
> There lay the only alternative: in work. She might slave her days away teaching the piano, as Miss Frost had done: she might find a subordinate post as nurse: she might sit in the cash-desk of some shop. Some work of some sort would be found for her. And she would sink into the routine of her job, as did so many women, and grow old and die, chattering and fluttering. She would have what is called her independence. But, seriously faced with that treasure, and without the option of refusing it, strange how hideous she found it.
>
> Work!—a job! More even than she rebelled against the Withams did she rebel against a job. . . .[10]

It is clear, I imagine, that that could not have been written in the last century; it speaks with the authentic voice of this. It has the ring of what we hear around us every day: it has no air of "style," yet it is extremely expressive. Certain liberties are taken, such as leaving out "It is . . ." before "all very well . . ." in the first paragraph. Here and there we feel just a touch of literary formulas, and we wish they were not there: "as did so many women" instead of "as so many women did," but these things are

[10]From *The Lost Girl*, by D. H. Lawrence, Secker, 1920. [Author's note]

very rare in Lawrence. We feel that he is nearly always completely free of "literature" and can be himself. We follow his mind working—and he speaks as it works. Or, at least, that is the impression we get. It is not true, of course: but at least he is using his material (part of which is his mind) with complete freedom, and finding a form which will make it tell.

Suppose that, before we go on to discuss experiments, we try to prophesy what direction our prose will take. We might perhaps say that it will be in that of greater flexibility and a more curious following of our mental processes, with, sometimes, violence offered to our old notions of syntax wherever we find them distorting or cumbrous. One would like to think that all of us will come to the stage of refusing to write what we would not, indeed could not, say, though that, of course, is not to limit our writing to what we actually do say. This is not to claim for a moment that by writing as we speak we shall achieve a style; before we do that we must go through at least three fundamental disciplines. First there is that of fidelity to thought, the extremely difficult task of complete honesty; we must not, as is so easy, allow language to condition our thought: then there is the labour of finding the exact words and the exact inflexion of phrase to carry the whole sense, the emotional colour, of the words; and thirdly, it is over and above these things that we have to model our prose to give it what seems to be the run and structure of our usual speaking. That is where the artifice comes in, and that is where we can achieve the art.

ON FAMILIAR STYLE

William Hazlitt

It is not easy to write a familiar style. Many people mistake a familiar for a vulgar style, and suppose that to write without affectation is to write at random. On the contrary, there is nothing that requires more precision, and, if I may so say, purity of expression, than the style I am speaking of. It utterly rejects not only all unmeaning pomp, but all low, cant phrases, and loose, unconnected, *slipshod* allusions. It is not to take the first word that offers, but the best word in common use; it is not to throw words together in any combinations we please, but to follow and avail ourselves of the true idiom of the language. To write a genuine familiar or truly English style, is to write as any one would speak in common conversation, who had a thorough command and choice of words, or who could discourse with ease, force, and perspicuity, setting aside all pedantic and oratorical flourishes. Or to give another illustration, to write naturally is the same thing in regard to common conversation, as to read naturally is in regard to common speech. It does not follow that it is an easy thing to give the true accent and inflection to the words you utter, because you do not attempt to rise above the level of ordinary life and colloquial speaking. You do not assume indeed the solemnity of the pulpit, or the tone of stage-declamation: neither are you at liberty to gabble on at a venture, without emphasis or discretion, or to resort to vulgar dialect or clownish pronunciation. You must steer a middle course. You are tied down to a given and appropriate articulation, which is determined by the habitual associations between sense and sound, and which you can only hit by entering into the author's meaning, as you must find the proper words and style to express yourself by fixing your thoughts on the subject you have to write about. Any one may mouth out a passage with a theatrical cadence, or get upon stilts to tell his thoughts: but to write or speak with propriety and simplicity is a more difficult task. Thus it is easy to affect a pompous style, to use a word twice as big as the thing you want to express: it is not so easy to pitch upon the very word that exactly fits it. Out of eight or ten words equally common, equally intelligible, with nearly equal pretensions, it is a matter of some nicety and discrimination to pick out the very one, the preferableness of which is scarcely perceptible, but decisive. The reason why I object to Dr. Johnson's style is, that there is no discrimination, no selection, no variety in it. He uses none but "tall, opaque words," taken from the "first row of the rubric":—words with the greatest number of syllables, or Latin phrases with merely English terminations. If a fine style depended on this sort of arbitrary pretension, it would be fair to judge of an author's elegance by the measurement of his words, and the substitution of foreign circumlocutions (with no precise associations) for the mother-tongue.[1] How simple it is to be dignified without ease, to be pompous without meaning! Surely, it is but a mechanical rule for avoiding what is low to be always pedantic and affected. It is clear you cannot use a vulgar English word, if you never use a common English word at all. A fine tact is shewn in adhering to those which are perfectly common, and yet never falling into any expressions which are debased by disgusting circumstances, or which owe their signification and point to technical or professional allusions. A truly natural or familiar style can never be quaint or vulgar, for this reason, that it is of universal force and applicability, and that quaintness and vulgarity arise out of the immediate connection of certain words with coarse and disagreeable, or with confined ideas. The last form what we understand by *cant* or *slang* phrases.—To give an example of what is not very clear in the general statement. I should say that the phrase *To cut with a knife*, or *To cut a piece of wood*, is perfectly free from vulgarity, because it is perfectly common: but to *cut an acquaintance* is not quite unexceptionable, because it is not perfectly common or intelligible, and has hardly yet escaped out of the limits of slang phraseology. I should hardly therefore use the word in this sense without putting it in italics as a license of expression, to be re-

---

[1] I have heard of such a thing as an author, who makes it a rule never to admit a monosyllable into his vapid verse. Yet the charm and sweetness of Marlow's lines depended often on their being made up almost entirely of monosyllables. [Author's note]

ceived *cum grano salis.* All provincial or bye-phrases come under the same mark of reprobation—all such as the writer transfers to the page from his fire-side or a particular *coterie,* or that he invents for his own sole use and convenience. I conceive that words are like money, not the worse for being common, but that it is the stamp of custom alone that gives them circulation or value. I am fastidious in this respect, and would almost as soon coin the currency of the realm as counterfeit the King's English. I never invented or gave a new and unauthorised meaning to any word but one single one (the term *impersonal* applied to feelings) and that was in an abstruse metaphysical discussion to express a very difficult distinction. I have been (I know) loudly accused of revelling in vulgarisms and broken English. I cannot speak to that point: but so far I plead guilty to the determined use of acknowledged idioms and common elliptical expressions. I am not sure that the critics in question know the one from the other, that is, can distinguish any medium between formal pedantry and the most barbarous solecism. As an author, I endeavour to employ plain words and popular modes of construction, as were I a chapman and dealer, I should common weights and measures.

The proper force of words lies not in the words themselves, but in their application. A word may be a fine-sounding word, of an unusual length, and very imposing from its learning and novelty, and yet in the connection in which it is introduced, may be quite pointless and irrelevant. It is not pomp or pretension, but the adaptation of the expression to the idea that clenches a writer's meaning:—as it is not the size or glossiness of the materials, but their being fitted each to its place, that gives strength to the arch; or as the pegs and nails are as necessary to the support of the building as the larger timbers, and more so than the mere shewy, unsubstantial ornaments. I hate any thing that occupies more space that it is worth. I hate to see a load of band-boxes go along the street, and I hate to see a parcel of big words without any thing in them. A person who does not deliberately dispose of all his thoughts alike in cumbrous draperies and flimsy disguises, may strike out twenty varieties of familiar everyday language, each coming somewhat nearer to the feeling he wants to convey, and at last not hit upon that particular and only one, which may be said to be identical with the exact impression in his mind. This would seem to shew that Mr. Cobbett is hardly right in saying that the first word that occurs is always the best. It may be a very good one; and yet a better may present itself on reflection or from time to time. It should be suggested naturally, however, and spontaneously, from a fresh and lively conception of the subject. We seldom succeed by trying at improvement, or by merely substituting one word for another that we are not satisfied with, as we cannot recollect the name of a place or person by merely plaguing ourselves about it. We wander farther from the point by persisting in a wrong scent; but it starts up accidentally in the memory when we least expected it, by touching some link in the chain of previous association.

There are those who hoard up and make a cautious display of nothing but rich and rare phraseology;—ancient medals, obscure coins, and Spanish pieces of eight. They are very curious to inspect; but I myself would neither offer nor take them in the course of exchange. A sprinkling of archaisms is not amiss; but a tissue of obsolete expressions is more fit *for keep than wear.* I do not say I would not use any phrase that had been brought into fashion before the middle or the end of the last century; but I should be shy of using any that had not been employed by any approved author during the whole of that time. Words, like clothes, get old-fashioned, or mean and ridiculous, when they have been for some time laid aside. Mr. Lamb is the only imitator of old English style I can read with pleasure; and he is so thoroughly imbued with the spirit of his authors, that the idea of imitation is almost done away. There is an inward unction, a marrowy vein both in the thought and feeling, an intuition, deep and lively, of his subject, that carries off any quaintness or awkwardness arising from an antiquated style and dress. The matter is completely his own, though the manner is assumed. Perhaps his ideas are altogether so marked and individual, as to require their point and pungency to be neutralised by the affectation of a singular but traditional form of conveyance. Tricked out in the prevailing costume, they would probably seem more startling and out of the way. The old English authors, Burton, Fuller, Coryate, Sir Thomas Brown, are a kind of mediators between us and the more eccentric and whimsical modern, reconciling us to his peculiarities. I do not however know how far this is the case or not, till he condescends to write like one of us. I must confess that what I like best of his papers under the signature of Elia (still I do not presume, amidst such excellence, to decide what is most excellent) is the account of *Mrs. Battle's Opinions on Whist,* which is also the most free from obsolete allusions and turns of expression—

> 'A well of native English undefiled.'

To those acquainted with his admired prototypes, these Essays of the ingenious and highly gifted author have the same sort of charm and relish, that Erasmus's Colloquies or a fine piece of modern Latin have to the classical scholar. Certainly, I do not know any borrowed pencil that has more power or felicity of execution than the one of which I have here been speaking.

It is as easy to write a gaudy style without ideas, as it is to spread a pallet of shewy colours, or to smear in a flaunting transparency. "What do you read?"—"Words, words, words."—"What is the matter?"—"*Nothing,*" it might be answered. The florid style is the reverse of the familiar. The last is employed as an unvarnished medium to convey ideas; the first is resorted to as a spangled veil to conceal the want of them. When there is nothing to be set down but words, it costs little to have them fine. Look through the dictionary, and cull out a *florilegium,* rival the *tulippomania. Rouge* high enough, and never mind the natural complexion. The vulgar, who are not in the secret, will admire the look of preternatural health and vigour; and the fashionable, who regard only appearances, will be delighted with the imposition. Keep to your sounding generalities, your tinkling phrases, and all will be well. Swell out an unmeaning truism to a perfect tympany of style. A thought, a distinction is the rock on which all this brittle cargo of verbiage splits at once. Such writers have merely *verbal* imaginations, that retain nothing but words. Or their puny thoughts have dragon-wings, all green and gold. They soar far above the vulgar failing of the *Sermo humi obrepens*[1]—their most ordinary speech is never short of an hyperbole, splendid, imposing, vague, incomprehensible, magniloquent, a cento of sounding common-places. If some of us, whose "ambition is more lowly," pry a little too narrowly into nooks and corners to pick up a number of "unconsidered trifles," they never once direct their eyes or lift their hands to seize on any but the most gorgeous, tarnished, thread-bare patch-work set of phrases, the left-off finery of poetic extravagance, transmitted down through successive generations of barren pretenders. If they criticise actors and actresses, a huddled phantasmagoria of feathers, spangles, floods of light, and oceans of sound float before their morbid sense, which they paint in the style of Ancient Pistol. Not a glimpse can you get of the merits or defects of the performers: they are hidden in a profusion of barbarous epithets and wilful rhodomontade. Our hypercritics are not thinking of these little fantoccini beings—

"That strut and fret their hour upon the stage"—

but of tall phantoms of words, abstractions, *genera* and *species*, sweeping clauses, periods that unite the Poles, forced alliterations, astounding antitheses—

"And on their pens *Fustian* sits plumed."

If they describe kings and queens, it is an Eastern pageant. The Coronation at either House is nothing to it. We get at four repeated images—a curtain, a throne, a sceptre, and a foot-stool. These are with them the wardrobe of a lofty imagination; and they turn their servile strains to servile uses. Do we read a description of pictures? It is not a reflection of tones and hues which "nature's own sweet and cunning hand laid on," but piles of precious stones, rubies, pearls, emeralds, Golconda's mines, and all the blazonry of art. Such persons are in fact besotted with words, and their brains are turned with the glittering, but empty and sterile phantoms of things. Personifications, capital letters, seas of sunbeams, visions of glory, shining inscriptions, the figures of a transparency, Britannia with her shield, or Hope leaning on an anchor, make up their stock in trade. They may be considered as *hieroglyphical* writers. Images stand out in their minds isolated and important merely in themselves, without any ground-work of feeling—there is no context in their imaginations. Words affect them in the same way, by the mere sound, that is, by their possible,

[1] Plain speech (creeping along the ground).

not by their actual application to the subject in hand. They are fascinated by first appearances, and have no sense of consequences. Nothing more is meant by them than meets the ear: they understand or feel nothing more than meets their eye. The web and texture of the universe, and of the heart of man, is a mystery to them: they have no faculty that strikes a chord in unison with it. They cannot get beyond the daubings of fancy, the varnish of sentiment. Objects are not linked to feelings, words to things, but images revolve in splendid mockery, words represent themselves in their strange rhapsodies. The categories of such a mind are pride and ignorance—pride in outside show, to which they sacrifice every thing, and ignorance of the true worth and hidden structure both of words and things. With a sovereign contempt for what is familiar and natural, they are the slaves of vulgar affectation—of a routine of high-flown phrases. Scorning to imitate realities, they are unable to invent any thing, to strike out one original idea. They are not copyists of nature, it is true: but they are the poorest of all plagiarists, the plagiarists of words. All is far-fetched, dear-bought, artificial, oriental in subject and allusion: all is mechanical, conventional, vapid, formal, pedantic in style and execution. They startle and confound the understanding of the reader, by the remoteness and obscurity of their illustrations: they soothe the ear by the monotony of the same everlasting round of circuitous metaphors. They are the *mock-school* in poetry and prose. They flounder about between fustian in expression, and bathos in sentiment. They tantalise the fancy, but never reach the head nor touch the heart. Their Temple of Fame is like a shadowy structure raised by Dulness to Vanity, or like Cowper's description of the Empress of Russia's palace of ice, as "worthless as in shew 'twas glittering"—

"It smiled, and it was cold!"

A LETTER
TO A YOUNG GENTLEMAN,
LATELY ENTERED INTO
HOLY ORDERS

Jonathan Swift

Dated *January* 9, 1719–20.

S I R,

Although it were against my Knowledge, or Advice, that you entered into Holy Orders, under the present Dispositions of Mankind towards the *Church;* yet, since it is now supposed too late to recede, (at least according to the general Practice and Opinion,) I cannot forbear offering my Thoughts to you upon this new Condition of Life you are engaged in.

I COULD heartily wish that the Circumstances of your Fortune had enabled you to have continued some Years longer in the University, at least, until you were ten Years standing; to have laid in a competent Stock of human Learning, and some Knowledge in Divinity, before you attempted to appear in the World: For I cannot but lament the common Course, which at least Nine in Ten of those, who enter into the Ministry, are obliged to run. When they have taken a Degree, and are consequently grown a Burden to their Friends, who now think themselves fully discharged; they get into Orders as soon as they can, (upon which I shall make no Remarks,) first sollicit a Readership, and if they be very fortunate, arrive in Time to a Curacy here in Town; or else are sent to be Assistants in the Country, where they probably continue several Years (many of them their whole Lives) with thirty or forty Pounds a Year for their Support, until some Bishop, who happens to be not over-stocked with Relations, or attached to Favourites, or is content to supply his Diocese without Colonies from *England,* bestows them some inconsiderable Benefice; when it is odds they are already encumbered with a numerous Family. I would be glad to know what Intervals of Life such Persons can possibly set apart for Improvement of their Minds; or which Way they could be furnished with Books; the Library they brought with them from their College being usually not the most numerous, or judiciously chosen. If such Gentlemen arrive to be great Scholars, it must, I think, be either by Means supernatural, or by a Method altogether out of any Road yet known to the Learned. But I conceive the Fact directly otherwise; and that many of them lose the greatest Part of the small Pittance they received at the University.

I TAKE it for granted, that you intend to pursue the beaten Track, and are already desirous to be seen in a Pulpit; only I hope you will think it proper to pass your Quarantine among some of the desolate Churches five Miles round this Town, where you may at least learn to *read* and to *speak*, before you venture to expose your Parts in a City-Congregation: Not that these are better Judges, but because if a Man must needs expose his Folly, it is more safe and discreet to do so, before few Witnesses, and in a scattered Neighbourhood. And you will do well, if you can prevail upon some intimate and judicious Friend to be your constant Hearer, and allow him with the utmost Freedom to give you Notice of whatever he shall find amiss either in your Voice or Gesture; for want of which early Warning, many Clergymen continue defective, and sometimes ridiculous, to the End of their Lives: Neither is it rare to observe among excellent and learned Divines, a certain ungracious Manner, or an unhappy Tone of Voice, which they never have been able to shake off.

I COULD likewise have been glad, if you had applied your self a little more to the Study of the *English* Language, than I fear you have done; the Neglect whereof is one of the most general Defects among the Scholars of this Kingdom, who seem to have not the least Conception of a Stile, but run on in a flat Kind of Phraseology, often mingled with barbarous Terms and Expressions, peculiar to the Nation: Neither do I perceive that any Person either finds or acknowledges his Wants upon this Head, or in the least desires to have them supplyed. Proper Words in proper Places, makes the true Definition of a Stile: But this would require too ample a Disquisition to be now dwelt on. However, I shall venture to name one or two Faults, which are easy to be remedied with a very small Portion of Abilities.

THE first, is the frequent Use of obscure Terms, which by the Women are called *hard Words*, and by the better Sort of Vulgar, *fine Language;* than which I do not know a more universal, inexcusable, and unnecessary Mistake among the Clergy of all Distinctions, but especially the younger Practitioners. I have been curious enough to take a List of several hundred Words in a Sermon of a new Beginner, which not one of his Hearers among a Hundred, could possibly understand: Neither can I easily call to Mind any Clergyman of my own Acquaintance who is wholly exempt from this Error; although many of them agree with me in the Dislike of the Thing. But I am apt to put my self in the Place of the Vulgar, and think many Words difficult or obscure, which the Preacher will not allow to be so, because those Words are obvious to Schollars. I believe the Method observed by the famous Lord *Falkland,* in some of his Writings, would not be an ill one for young Divines: I was assured by an old Person of Quality, who knew him well; that when he doubted whether a Word were perfectly intelligible or no, he used to consult one of his Lady's Chambermaids, (not the Waiting-woman, because it was possible she might be conversant in Romances,) and by her Judgment was guided, whether to receive or reject it. And if that great Person thought such a

Caution necessary in Treatises offered to the learned World; it will be sure at least as proper in Sermons, where the meanest Hearer is supposed to be concerned; and where very often a Lady's Chambermaid may be allowed to equal half the Congregation, both as to Quality and Understanding. But I know not how it comes to pass, that Professors in most Arts and Sciences are generally the worst qualified to explain their Meanings to those who are not of their Tribe: A common Farmer shall make you understand in three Words, *that his Foot is out of Joint, or his Collarbone broken;* wherein a *Surgeon,* after a hundred Terms of Art, if you are not a Scholar, shall leave you to seek. It is frequently the same Case in Law, Physick, and even many of the meaner Arts.

AND upon this Account it is, that among *hard Words,* I number likewise those which are peculiar to Divinity as it is a Science; because I have observed several Clergymen, otherwise little fond of obscure Terms, yet in their Sermons very liberal of those which they find in Ecclesiastical Writers, as if it were our Duty to understand them: Which I am sure it is not. And I defy the greatest Divine, to produce any Law either of God or Man, which obliges me to comprehend the Meaning of *Omniscience, Omnipresence, Ubiquity, Attribute, Beatifick Vision,* with a Thousand others so frequent in Pulpits; any more than that of *Excentrick, Idiosyncracy, Entity,* and the like. I believe, I may venture to insist further, that many Terms used in Holy Writ, particularly by St. *Paul,* might with more Discretion be changed into plainer Speech, except when they are introduced as part of a Quotation.

I AM the more earnest in this Matter, because it is a general Complaint, and the justest in the World. For a Divine hath nothing to say to the wisest Congregation of any Parish in this Kingdom, which he may not express in a Manner to be understood by the meanest among them. And this Assertion must be true, or else God requires from us more than we are able to perform. However, not to contend whether a Logician might possibly put a Case that would serve for an Exception; I will appeal to any Man of Letters, whether at least nineteen in twenty of those perplexing Words might not be changed into easy ones, such as naturally first occur to ordinary Men, and probably did so at first to those very Gentlemen, who are so fond of the former. . . .

THE Fear of being thought Pedants hath been of pernicious Consequence to young Divines. This hath wholly taken many of them off from their severer Studies in the University; which they have exchanged for Plays, Poems, and Pamphlets, in order to qualify them for Tea-Tables and Coffee-Houses. This they usually call *Polite Conversation, knowing the World,* and *reading Men instead of Books.* These Accomplishments, when applied in the Pulpit, appear by a quaint, terse, florid Style, rounded into Periods and Cadencies, commonly without either Propriety or Meaning. I have listened with my utmost Attention for half an Hour to an Orator of this Species, without being able to understand, much less to carry away one single Sentence out of a whole Sermon. Others, to shew that their Studies have not been confined to Sciences, or ancient Authors, will talk in the Style of a gaming Ordinary, and *White Friars*; where I suppose the Hearers can be little edified by the Terms of *Palming*, *Shuffling*, *Biting*, *Bamboozling*, and the like, if they have not been sometimes conversant among Pick-pockets and Sharpers. And truly, as they say, a Man is known by his Company; so it should seem, that a Man's Company may be known by his Manner of expressing himself, either in publick Assemblies, or private Conversation.

It would be endless to run over the several Defects of Style among us: I shall therefore say nothing of the *mean* and the *paultry*, (which are usually attended by the *fustian*,) much less of the *slovenly* or *indecent*. Two Things I will just warn you against: The first is, the Frequency of flat, unnecessary Epithets; and the other is, the Folly of using old threadbare Phrases, which will often make you go out of your Way to find and apply them; are nauseous to rational Hearers, and will seldom express your Meaning as well as your own natural Words.

Although, as I have already observed, our *English* Tongue be too little cultivated in this Kingdom; yet the Faults are nine in ten owing to Affectation, and not to the want of Understanding. When a Man's Thoughts are clear, the properest Words will generally offer themselves first; and his own Judgment will direct him in what Order to place them, so as they may be best understood. Where Men err against this Method, it is usually on Purpose, and to shew their Learning, their Oratory, their Politeness, or their Knowledge of the World. In short, that Simplicity, without which no human Performance can arrive to any great Perfection, is no where more eminently useful than in this. . . .

As I take it, the two principal Branches of Preaching, are first to tell the People what is their Duty; and then to convince them that it is so. The Topicks for both these, we know, are brought from *Scripture* and *Reason*. Upon the former, I wish it were oftner practised to instruct the Hearers in the Limits, Extent, and Compass of every Duty, which requires a good deal of Skill and Judgment: The other Branch is, I think, not so difficult. But what I would offer upon both, is this; that it seems to be in the Power of a reasonable Clergyman, if he will be at the Pains, to make the most ignorant Man comprehend what is his Duty; and to convince him by Arguments, drawn to the Level of his Understanding, that he ought to perform it.

But I must remember, that my Design in this *Paper* was not so much to instruct you in your Business, either as a Clergyman, or a Preacher, as to warn you against some Mistakes, which are obvious to the Generality of Mankind, as well as to me; and we, who are Hearers, may be allowed to have some Opportunities in the Quality of being Standers-by. Only, perhaps, I may now again transgress, by desiring you to express the Heads of your Divisions in as few and clear Words, as you possibly can; otherwise, I, and many Thousand others, will never be able to retain them, nor consequently to carry away a Syllable of the Sermon. . . .

I CANNOT forbear warning you, in the most earnest Manner, against endeavouring at Wit in your Sermons: Because, by the strictest Computation, it is very near a Million to One, that you have none; and because too many of your Calling, have consequently made themselves everlastingly ridiculous by attempting it. I remember several young Men in this Town, who could never leave the *Pulpit* under half a Dozen *Conceits*; and this Faculty adhered to those Gentlemen a longer or shorter Time, exactly in Proportion to their several Degrees of Dulness: Accordingly, I am told that some of them retain it to this Day. I heartily wish the Brood were at an End. . . .

I WOULD say something concerning Quotations; wherein I think you cannot be too sparing, except from Scripture, and the primitive Writers of the Church. As to the former, when you offer a Text as a Proof or an Illustration, we your Hearers expect to be fairly used; and sometimes think we have Reason to complain, especially of you younger Divines; which makes us fear, that some of you conceive you have no more to do than to turn over a Concordance, and there having found the principal Word, introduce as much of the Verse as will serve your Turn, although in Reality it makes nothing for you. I do not altogether disapprove the Manner of interweaving Texts of Scripture through the Style of your Sermon; wherein, however, I have sometimes observed great Instances of Indiscretion and Impropriety; against which I therefore venture to give you a Caution.

As to Quotations from antient Fathers, I think they are best brought in, to confirm some Opinion controverted by those who differ from us: In other Cases we give you full Power to adopt the Sentence for your own, rather than tell us, *as St.* Austin *excellently observes*: But to mention modern Writers by Name, or use the Phrase of *a late excellent Prelate of our Church*, and the like, is altogether intolerable; and, for what Reason I know not, makes every rational Hearer ashamed. Of no better a Stamp is your *Heathen Philosopher*, and *famous Poet*, and *Roman Historian*; at least in common Congregations, who will rather believe you on your own Word, than on that of *Plato* or *Homer*.

I HAVE lived to see *Greek* and *Latin* almost entirely driven out of the Pulpit; for which I am heartily glad. The frequent Use of the latter was certainly a Remnant of Popery, which never admitted Scripture in the vulgar Language; and I wonder that Practice was never accordingly objected to us by the Fanaticks.

THE Mention of Quotations puts me in mind of Commonplace Books, which have been long in use by industrious young Divines, and, I hear, do still continue so; I know they are very beneficial to Lawyers and Physicians, because they are Collections of Facts or Cases, whereupon a great Part of their several Faculties depend: Of these I have seen several, but never yet any written by a Clergyman; only from what I am informed, they generally are Extracts of Theological and Moral Sentences, drawn from Ecclesiastical and other Authors, reduced under proper

Heads; usually begun, and perhaps, finished, while the Collectors were young in the Church; as being intended for Materials, or Nurseries to stock future Sermons. You will observe the wise Editors of ancient Authors, when they meet a Sentence worthy of being distinguished, take special Care to have the first Word printed in Capital Letters, that you may not overlook it: Such, for Example, as the *Inconstancy of Fortune, the Goodness of Peace, the Excellency of Wisdom, the Certainty of Death; that Prosperity makes Men insolent, and Adversity humble;* and the like eternal Truths, which every Plowman knows well enough, although he never heard of *Aristotle* or *Plato.* If Theological Common-Place Books be no better filled, I think they had better be laid aside: And I could wish, that Men of tolerable Intellectuals would rather trust to their own natural Reason, improved by a general Conversation with Books, to enlarge on Points which they are supposed already to understand. If a rational Man reads an excellent Author with just Application, he shall find himself extremely improved, and perhaps insensibly led to imitate that Author's Perfections; although in a little Time he should not remember one Word in the Book, nor even the Subject it handled: For, Books give the same Turn to our Thoughts and Way of Reasoning, that good and ill Company do to our Behaviour and Conversation; without either loading our Memories, or making us even sensible of the Change. And particularly, I have observed in Preaching, that no Men succeed better than those, who trust entirely to the Stock or Fund of their own Reason; advanced, indeed, but not overlaid by Commerce with Books. Whoever only reads, in order to transcribe wise and shining Remarks, without entering into the Genius and Spirit of the Author; as it is probable he will make no very judicious Extract, so he will be apt to trust to that Collection in all his Compositions; and be misled out of the regular Way of Thinking, in order to introduce those Materials which he hath been at the Pains to gather: And the Product of all this, will be found a manifest incoherent Piece of Patchwork.

SOME Gentlemen abounding in their University Erudition, are apt to fill their Sermons with philosophical Terms, and Notions of the metaphysical or abstracted Kind; which generally have one Advantage, to be equally understood by the Wise, the Vulgar, and the Preacher himself. I have been better entertained, and more informed by a Chapter in the *Pilgrim's Progress,* than by a long Discourse upon the *Will* and the *Intellect,* and *simple* or *complex Ideas.* Others again, are fond of dilating on *Matter* and *Motion,* talk of the *fortuitous Concourse of Atoms,* of *Theories,* and *Phænomena;* directly against the Advice of St. *Paul,* who yet appears to have been conversant enough in those Kinds of Studies.

I DO not find that you are any where directed in the Canons, or Articles, to attempt explaining the Mysteries of the Christian Religion. And, indeed, since Providence intended there should be Mysteries; I do not see how it can be agreeable to *Piety, Orthodoxy,* or good *Sense,* to go about such a Work. For, to me there seems to be a manifest Dilemma in the Case: If you explain them, they are Mysteries no longer; if you fail, you have laboured to no Purpose. What I should think most reasonable and safe for you to do, upon this Occasion, is upon solemn Days to deliver the Doctrine as the Church holds it, and confirm it by Scripture. For my Part, having considered the Matter impartially, I can see no great Reason which those Gentlemen, you call the *Free-Thinkers,* can have for their Clamour against Religious Mysteries; since it is plain, they were not invented by the Clergy, to whom they bring no Profit, nor acquire any Honour. For every Clergyman is ready, either to tell us the utmost he knows, or to confess that he doth not understand them: Neither is it strange, that there should be Mysteries in Divinity, as well as in the commonest Operations of Nature. . . .

IGNORANCE may, perhaps, be the *Mother* of *Superstition; but Experience* hath not proved it to be so of *Devotion:* For *Christianity* always made the most easy and quickest Progress in civilized Countries. I mention this, because it is affirmed, that the Clergy are in most Credit where Ignorance prevails, (and surely this Kingdom would be called the *Paradise* of Clergymen, if that Opinion were true) for which they instance *England* in the Times of *Popery.* But whoever knoweth any Thing of three or four Centuries before the Reformation, will find, the little Learning then stirring, was more equally divided between the *English* Clergy and Laity, than it is at present. There were several famous Lawyers in that *Period,* whose Writings are still in the highest Repute; and some *Historians* and *Poets,* who were not of the *Church.* Whereas, now-a-days our Education is so corrupted, that you will hardly find a young Person of Quality with the least Tincture of Knowledge; at the same Time that[1] many of the Clergy were never more learned, or so scurvily treated. Here among Us, at least, a Man of Letters, out of the three Professions, is almost a Prodigy. And those few who have preserved any Rudiments of Learning, are (except, perhaps, one or two Smatterers) the Clergy's Friends to a Man: For, I dare appeal to any Clergyman in this Kingdom, whether the greatest Dunce in his Parish be not always the most proud, wicked, fraudulent, and intractable of his Flock.

I THINK the Clergy have almost given over perplexing themselves and their Hearers, with abstruse Points of Predestination, Election, and the like; at least, it is time they should; and therefore, I shall not trouble you further upon this Head.

I HAVE now said all I could think convenient with relation to your Conduct in the Pulpit. Your Behaviour in the World is another Scene, upon which, I shall readily offer you my Thoughts, if you appear to desire them from me, by your Approbation of what I have here written; if not, I have already troubled you too much.

I am, SIR,

JANUARY 9,
1719-20.

Your affectionate
Friend and Servant.

[1]*N. B. This Discourse was written Fourteen Year ago; since which Time, the Case is extremely altered by Deaths and Successions.* [Author's note]

A CORRUPT FOLLOWING

Alice Meynell

During the whole nineteenth century our language underwent a certain derogation, notorious, different in kind from the corruptions of all other ages, and as familiar as brick and slate, gas, and the architecture of stations—and apparently, of yesterday, and to-day and of a morrow seen in rather dull and discouraging prospect. But the truth is that this common speech is due to the enormous influence of a great author who was born in 1737, was for forty-seven years the contemporary of Dr. Johnson, and died well within the eighteenth century.

Whose, for instance, is the use of "I expect" for a conjecture referring to the past? It is Gibbon's: "I should expect that the eunuchs were not expelled from the palace." What is the "and which" and "who" of the slovenly? and what the "whose" applied to inanimate things by authors too fine and too modern to write "whereof"? Gear of Gibbon's style, both: "Below the citadel stood a palace of gold, decorated with precious stones, and whose value might be esteemed," etc.; and "A Menapian of the meanest origin, but who had long signalized his skill as a pilot." There is the inanimate "whose" of a more illustrious and older author, but this claims the excuse of metre.

Whence have we that peculiarly harsh vulgarism, "so much per month," instead of "so much a month," or "per mensem"? From Gibbon. And whose is the confusion of speech that cannot give the word "same" its proper completion, but saddles it with a relative pronoun? Gibbon's "The Western countries were civilized by the same hands which subdued them." "The hands which subdued them" would be correct, and certainly more majestic.

Gibbon set the example of this common lax grammar: "Instead of receiving with manly resolution the inevitable stroke, his unavailing cries and entreaties disgraced the last moments of his life"; and "The election of Carus was decided without expecting the approval of the Senate"; and "A peasant and a soldier, his nerves yielded not easily to the impressions of sympathy." And there is nothing that (Gibbon always says which) illiterate politeness is so fond of as this unconstructed and decorated phrase. Gibbon's literature was scholarly, and these errors of his alter little or nothing of the honour due to his eminent elegance of style. But it was these laxities that took the public taste mightily, and it was the "corrupt following" of this apostle that set the fashion of an animated strut of style—a strut that was animated in its day and soon grew inanimate, as the original authentic Gibbon never does. His own narrative never fails to reply to a perpetual stimulation.

FROM *Alice Meynell, Prose and Poetry*. London, Jonathan Cape, 1947. Reprinted by permission of Sir Francis Meynell.

But to deal with the rest of the grammatical ill-example, left to unlucky generations from the very middle of the century of propriety, and
made so much our own. It is very modern to have "either" or "neither"
followed by more than two things, and it is pure Gibbon; all the more
conspicuous as Gibbon dearly loves the sound of three: "The policy of the
senate, the active emulation of the consuls, and the martial enthusiasm of
the people"; "The undertaking became more difficult, the event more
doubtful, and the possession more precarious." But the three go ill with
"either": "either food, plunder, or glory"; "either salt, or oil, or wood."
"The generals were either respected by their troops, or admired for valour,
or beloved for frankness and generosity."

Finally, for a very little and silly blunder, what is more modern and
current and popular than this: "Magnus, with four thousand of his supposed accomplices, were put to death"? And even this is Gibbon.

To have done with mere grammar, there is surely no author in the
history of our literature who has so imposed a new manner of writing upon
an admiring people. He changed a hundred years of English prose. The
dregs of his style have encumbered the nation. Changes that have been
ascribed to Johnson were his doing and not Johnson's.

He belonged to the eighteenth century; but the nineteenth century belonged to him, because he possessed it. That is why he and his English
are thus modern; the times became conformed to him; and he was himself
not his own age, but that which succeeded and admired him.

It was to the broad face of astonishment and with the self-conscious face
of novelty, that Gibbon addressed his prose. That shortened sentence (for
it was he who shortened the sentence, and Macaulay did but imitate his
full stops for the pauses of historical surprise) was to strike and to demonstrate, and this with a gesture constantly renewed. "Suspicion was equivalent to proof. Trial to condemnation." "The strict economy of Vespasian
was the source of his magnificence. The works of Trajan bear the stamp
of his genius." His, too, is the full ceremony of the ushering phrase: "It
is easier to deplore the fate, than to describe the actual condition, of
Corsica." His too, the "latter and the former," which became a favourite
fashion. "Oh, do not condemn me to the latter!" exclaims a lover in one of
Mrs. Inchbald's stories, after a statement of his hopes and fears; and this
phrase of emotion was a debt to Gibbon. The reader finds that the lady
does not condemn him to the latter; she permits some prospect of the
former. "Peruse" is his verb, and "extensive" a most favourite adjective.
To him we owe "the mask of hypocrisy" and "the voice of flattery." It is
not his fault that posterity divided that property so lavishly among themselves.

And yet is there no fault in his own frigid prodigality? Take this sentence in all its splendour: "The Tyber rolled at the foot of the seven hills
of Rome, and the country of the Sabines, the Latins, and the Volsci, from
that river to the frontiers of Naples, was the theatre of her infant vic-
tories." And this: "A distant hope, the child of a flattering prophecy." This

all-inhuman image reminds us, by contrast, of Shelley, who often has this figure of a child, and never, however remote the thought, without a sense of childhood. So cold is Gibbon that when the incessant stimulation of his rhetorical intention spurs him to describe a murder thus: "A thousand swords were plunged at once into the bosom of the unfortunate Probus," we are moved to tell him trivially that he exaggerates. When Burke said "A thousand swords" he meant a thousand, and had a right to mean them, but Gibbon did not, obviously, mean a thousand.

"The unfortunate Probus" is the model of a sentence that sometimes becomes monotonous even with the carefully various Gibbon: "The prudent Atticus" begins a phrase, and "the equitable Nerva" passes it on to "the cautious Athenian," and then again to "the generous Atticus." His is a frigidity that deals broadly with massacre and the sack of cities. And from amid these generalities, as it were invisible unless viewed from afar, he suddenly plucks us this man's "smile," or that man's "blush." Whatever Gibbon's race, there never was a writer so exceedingly Latin in spirit.

"To view," by the way is one of his favourite verbs: "Viewing with a smile of pity and indulgence the various errors of the vulgar . . . and sometimes condescending to act a part on the theatre of superstition, they concealed the sentiments of an atheist under the sacerdotal robes." Readers with a sense of humour may remember under what conditions Zenobia "reiterated the experiment"; and the fatal manner in which the tradesman's circular of to-day has "diffused" (as Gibbon would say) the last ruins of his prose by post, is rather curiously illustrated thus: a little while ago some infamous face-wash was described in advertisements as a mixture of drugs brought across the desert by fleet dromedaries. And here is Gibbon's Zenobia "mounting her fleetest dromedary."

How great, nevertheless, how sombre are the nobler habits of his language: "The veteran legions of the Rhine and the Danube." What armies! what time, space! what war! "Give back my legions, Varus!" Give back our legions, Gibbon! We may count our regiments, but thou hast named, not counted, multitudes.

And when Gibbon "gratifies" these legionaries, the polite word does but make them more remote: "After suppressing a competitor who had assumed the purple at Mentz, he refused to gratify his troops with the plunder of the rebellious city." So that we do not forgive the corrupters who so scattered the word that burlesque was necessary for sweeping it out of the way. When Mr. Micawber confesses his "gratifying emotions of no common description," he rallies a lofty and a distant Gibbon.

Ruskin, student of Hooker in the further, and of Johnson in the nearer, past, was the first writer of pure prose—the first by a long tale of years—to reject the whole encumbrance of the vain spoils of Gibbon; yet even he has one little patch of them: "A steep bank of earth that has been at all exposed to the weather contains in it . . . features capable of giving high gratification to a careful observer." It is solitary in *Modern Painters*; it is the nether Gibbon, a waste product of Gibbon.

But now I spoke of burlesque; and Dickens's burlesque of style is admirable; there is also a burlesque of another and more innocent kind: When the author of a recent English work on the *Divine Comedy,* says that Paolo and Francesca were to receive from Dante "such alleviation as circumstances would allow," that also is a distant, a shattered Gibbon, a drift of Gibbon.

THE SPECTATOR *

No. 512. Friday, October 17, 1712

Joseph Addison

Lectorem delectando pariterque monendo. Hor.

There is nothing which we receive with so much reluctance as advice. We look upon the man who gives it us as offering an affront to our understanding, and treating us like children or idiots. We consider the instruction as an implicit censure, and the zeal which any one shows for our good on such an occasion, as a piece of presumption or impertinence. The truth of it is, the person who pretends to advise, does, in that particular, exercise a superiority over us, and can have no other reason for it but that, in comparing us with himself, he thinks us defective either in our conduct or our understanding. For these reasons there is nothing so difficult as the art of making advice agreeable; and, indeed, all the writers, both ancient and modern, have distinguished themselves among one another, according to the perfection at which they have arrived in this art. How many devices have been made use of to render this bitter potion palatable! some convey their instructions to us in the best chosen words, others in the most harmonious numbers; some in points of wit, and others in short proverbs.

But among all the different ways of giving counsel, I think the finest, and that which pleases the most universally, is fable, in whatsoever shape it appears. If we consider this way of instructing or giving advice, it excels all others, because it is the least shocking, and the least subject to those exceptions which I have before mentioned.

*The footnotes are by Richard Hurd, Bishop of Worcester, an early editor of Addison. They are clearly of the schoolroom and not the writer's desk. Hurd says, "Mr. Addison is generally allowed to be the most correct and elegant of all our writers; yet some inaccuracies have escaped him, which it is the chief design of the following notes to point out. A work of this sort, well executed, would be of use to foreigners who study our language, and even to such of our countrymen as wish to write it in perfect purity."

The Latin motto may be translated, "by delighting and instructing [the readers] in equal measure." It is from Horace, *The Art of Poetry,* line 349.

This will appear to us, if we reflect, in the first place, that upon reading of a fable we are made to believe we advise ourselves.[1] We peruse the author for the sake of the story, and consider the precepts rather as our own conclusions, than his instructions. The moral insinuates itself imperceptibly, we are taught by surprise, and become wiser and better unawares. In short, by this method a man is so far over-reached as to think he is directing himself, whilst he is following the dictates of another, and consequently is not sensible of that which is the most unpleasing circumstance in advice.

In the next place, if we look into human nature, we shall find that the mind is never so much pleased, as when she exerts herself in any action that gives her an idea of her own perfections and abilities. This natural pride and ambition of the soul is very much gratified in the reading of a fable: for in writings of this kind, the reader comes in for half of the performance; everything appears to him like a discovery of his own; he is busied all the while in applying characters and circumstances, and is in this respect both a reader and a composer. It is no wonder, therefore, that on such occasions, when the mind is thus pleased with itself, and amused with its own discoveries, it is highly delighted with the writing which is the occasion of it. For this reason the Absalon and Achitophel was one of the most popular poems that ever appeared in English. The poetry is indeed very fine, but had it been much finer it would not have so much pleased, without a plan which gave the reader an opportunity of exerting his own talents.

This oblique manner of giving advice is so inoffensive, that if we look into ancient histories, we find the wise men of old very often chose[2] to give counsel to their kings in fables. To omit many which will occur to every one's memory, there is a pretty instance of this nature in a Turkish tale, which I do[3] not like the worse for that little Oriental extravagance which is mixed with it.

We are told that the Sultan Mahmoud, by his perpetual wars abroad, and his tyranny at home, had filled his dominions with ruin and desolation, and half unpeopled the Persian empire. The vizier to this great sultan (whether an humourist or an enthusiast we are not informed) pretended to have learned of a certain dervise to understand the language of birds, so that there was not a bird that could open his mouth but the vizier knew what it was he said. As he was one evening with the emperor, on their return from hunting, they saw a couple of owls upon a tree that grew near an old wall, out of an heap of rubbish. "I would fain know," says the

[1]*Ourselves.* Two small inaccuracies in this sentence. 1. Instead of "*upon reading of a fable,*" it should have been, "*upon the reading of,*" or, "*upon reading a fable.*" 2. The sentence is involved and complicated—"We reflect *that*—we are made to believe *that* we advise ourselves."—To conceal or palliate the last defect, the second *that* is left out, but must be supplied by the reader.

[2]*Chose.* To avoid the fault just now taken notice of, we might say, "*choosing* to give," &c.

[3]*Which I do—which is.* The same fault again.

sultan, "what those two owls are saying to one another; listen to their discourse, and give me an account of it." The vizier approached the tree, pretending to be very attentive to the two owls. Upon his return to the sultan, "Sir," says he, "I have heard part of their conversation, but dare not tell you what it is." The sultan would not be satisfied with such an answer, but forced him to repeat word for word everything that the owls had said. "You must know then," said the vizier, "that one of these owls has a son, and the other a daughter, between whom they are now upon a treaty of marriage. The father of the son said to the father of the daughter, in my hearing, "Brother, I consent to this marriage, provided you will settle upon your daughter fifty ruined villages for her portion." To which the father of the daughter replied, "Instead of fifty, I will give her five hundred, if you please. God grant a long life to Sultan Mahmoud; whilst he reigns over us, we shall never want ruined villages."

The story says, the sultan was so touched with the fable, that he rebuilt the towns and villages which had been destroyed, and from that time forward consulted the good of his people.

To fill up my paper I shall add a most ridiculous piece of natural magic, which was taught by no less a philosopher than Democritus, namely, that[4] if the blood of certain birds, which he mentioned, were mixed together, it would produce a serpent of such wonderful virtue, that whoever did eat it should be skilled in the language of birds, and understand everything they said to one another. Whether the dervise above-mentioned might not have eaten such a serpent, I shall leave to the determinations of the learned.

QUESTIONS

1. What notions about style are shared by the authors of these articles?

2. Does the Oxford Dictionary show that Hazlitt was right in thinking that *"to cut an acquaintance* is . . . hardly yet escaped out of the limits of slang phraseology"? What examples of slang or near slang can you find in the other essays?

3. Check your handbook and dictionary (the Oxford Dictionary too) for the usages or constructions that Bishop Hurd and Alice Meynell objected to in Addison and Gibbon. Look up *colloquial* in Johnson's dictionary, the Oxford Dictionary, the unabridged Webster's, and as many desk dictionaries as you can. See what your handbook says.

4. Using Dobrée's stylistic and moral criteria, analyze the style in one of Arthur Krock's columns (in *The New York Times*). Compare Walter Lippmann's style in one of his columns and in one of his early books, say the *Preface to Morals.*

5. You have probably read some essays by Lamb. Would you agree with Hazlitt's comments on his style? Note Dobrée's too.

---

[4]"*That*—it would produce—of such virtue *that*—." Still the same fault of a too complicated construction; whence we may conclude that this paper was written carelessly, and in haste.

6. Discuss Swift's "Letter" as the product of a society in which there is a sharp separation between the metropolis and the provinces, between the Court and the "ordinary Sort."

7. How many of the words Swift lists on p. 1058 strike you as too technical or hard for ordinary purposes?

8. What is the meaning of *conceit* in "half a Dozen *Conceits*" (p. 1060)? Comment on the spelling "Excentrick" (p. 1058). Comment on the form *Intellectuals* in "Men of tolerable Intellectuals" (p. 1061).

9. How many of Swift's excellences and faults of writing can you find mentioned in your handbook? Apply his criteria to two or three paragraphs in one of your textbooks.

REMINISCENCE: SOME WRITERS AND THEIR WAYS

The first three selections in this group are examples of personal reminiscence; the last is a feature story, one based on a good deal of research and observation. All four authors have a sharp eye for the significant detail; perhaps it would be fair to say that the articles make their effect with the details rather than with reflection, comment, or analysis. Notice that Hunt keeps himself out of his article; there is a tone, but it is an institutional one, the New Yorker attitude, it might be called, and probably a good deal of re-writing was done to the article. In all the selections notice the easy, associational organization.

MR. D. H. LAWRENCE

Norman Douglas

I knew him before his marriage, in *White Peacock* days, and still hope that a certain photograph of him taken at that time may be reproduced somewhere. It was a charming likeness, with an ethereal expression in those youthful features. Then he came to see me with his newly-married wife; I cooked, in her honour, a German luncheon.

FROM *Looking Back, An Autobiographical Excursion*, by Norman Douglas. London, Chatto & Windus. Reprinted by permission of Chatto & Windus and of The Society of Authors as the literary representative of the Estate of the late Norman Douglas.

He sometimes turned up at the *English Review* office with stories like the *Prussian Officer* written in that impeccable handwriting of his. They had to be cut down for magazine purposes; they were too redundant; and I was charged with the odious task of performing the operation. Would Lawrence never learn to be more succinct, and to hold himself in hand a little? No; he never would and he never did; diffuseness is a fault of much of his work. In *Women in Love,* for example, we find pages and pages of drivel. Those endless and pointless conversations! That dreary waste of words! To give your reader a sample of the chatter of third-rate people is justifiable; ten consecutive pages of such stuff is realism gone crazy.

Lawrence never divined that conversations and dialogues are precious contrivances, to be built up *con amore;* that they should suggest a clue to character and carry forward the movement instead of retarding it; that they should be sparkling oases, not deserts of tiresome small-talk. Reading these flatulent passages, one wonders by what process his brain came to conceive them; one wonders, next, how he could bring himself to write them down, and next, how, having written them, he could bear to see them in print. He must have known they were rubbish. His state of health, maybe, engendered an imperious need of unburdening himself of every idle thought which flitted through his head.

I suppose he was not much concerned with the form of his novels. They were explorations into himself. That is why, for us, they are explorations into Lawrence. There is *Kangaroo:* well, that intrusion of a Cornish element is an artistic outrage. Yet he could not help infecting Australian surroundings with this exotic taint; *c' était plus fort que lui;*[1] and if it injures the story it certainly reveals some secrets of Lawrence's own psychology. The same applies to *The Trespasser*—the tale, a well-motivated one, of a husband entangled with another woman, who is harassed to such a point by his legitimate wife and family that, instead of pounding them all into a jelly, he hangs himself. Self-exploration! There was in Lawrence a masochistic strain, a strain of Christ, prophet and sufferer. Both of them were in disharmony with their environment; both took every opportunity of saying so, although in Jesus—if he ever existed—we find less hysteria than in Lawrence, whose Messianic utterances are delivered in shrill tones, and often in so paradoxical a language that he becomes a mere screamer, peevish and frothy. And even as Jesus performed the menial task of washing his disciples' feet, so Lawrence was never happier than when scrubbing floors or peeling potatoes: how frequently in his books are the men portrayed as doing the work of women or of servants!

Aaron's Rod lays bare another aspect of his character, namely, his love of scoring off people to whom he is under an obligation. The book teems with examples of this trait; I alone could give five of them, although not a quarter of the persons described are known to me. Here is one. The distinguished old gentleman introduced in the twelfth chapter as "Sir William" had never met Lawrence; he had been induced by some third

[1] It was stronger than he.

party to offer him hospitality. He is now dead, and those who are dispassionately interested in such problems will do well to compare Lawrence's fictitious account of "Sir William" and his household with the following extract of a letter dated 27 February 1925, giving me "Sir William's" own comments on this proceeding:

". . . Some years ago, during the War, a friend wrote me that Lawrence was on his way to Turin, where at that time it was difficult to get accommodation; would I put him up? In due time one evening when, with a party of guests, I had just sat down to dinner, a visitor was announced. I went to the door—it was a cold wet evening—and there was a homespun-clad figure, carrying some sort of travelling bag. I received him hospitably, sent him upstairs to a bedroom to wash; he joined us at the dinner table and remained until the following day. I had a good deal of conversation with him but, as the sequel showed, without creating a favourable impression, although at the time we appeared to be on terms of friendship and sympathy. He sent me a couple of his books, *Twilight in Italy,* which is a very good book, although I do not see why he named it thus, and *Sons and Lovers,* which has some remarkably effective chapters, but on the whole, left as it were a bad taste in my mouth. So when I noticed a new book by Lawrence in one of the magazines, *Aaron's Rod,* I decided to try another sample of his art and had it sent to me. To my astonishment I found in it, though with disguised names of places and persons, a description of his visit to my house. The scene was laid in Novara, but the particulars tallied perfectly with the circumstances of his arrival, the features of my entrance gate, lodge and grounds being faithfully reproduced.

"He also described the conversations at the dinner table and afterwards, all of which, according to him, were on a despicably low intellectual level. He also portrays myself and my wife, and I grieve to say that we did not impress him at all favourably, as I appear in his pages as a kind of physically decrepit and vulgarly ostentatious plutocrat. My wife he thought proper to compare to Queen Victoria, which, however gratifying to my loyal British sentiments, was unflattering in the sense that he was evidently not alluding to the admirable qualities which Queen Victoria possessed in such abundant measure, but rather to her physical shortcomings. He also referred to the staircase, to the blue silk hangings of his bedroom (and to the unpardonable circumstance that his breakfast was served with the refinement of a decent household) in disparaging terms. He had felt like throwing these indications of an effete civilization out of the window!

"Now, I have no objection to make to his chronicling his impressions with sincerity, but I can never pardon him for the fact that the considerable number of pages which he devoted to us, as well as the whole of the book, were so insufferably dull. If he had at least made me out an amusing jackanapes I would not have minded it, but, that I should have been the source of inspiration of such shockingly wearisome tirades, somewhat humiliates me. It is true that in one passage he acknowledges that I had been exceedingly hospitable to an utter stranger, but that is his only concession to what the Italians call 'creanza.'[1] . . ."

A student of Lawrence's psychology will not gloss over this trait of character—it is too persistive and too pronounced; he will not condemn, but endeavour to understand. It has given me food for thought, and my reading of the matter is this: everybody, in his heart of hearts, dislikes being under the necessity of accepting help, financial or otherwise, however willingly bestowed. It is a form of patronage. We object to being patronized; it makes us resentful. Now most of us have learnt to dominate or mask this feeling of resentment; we accept help when it is required, and then utter due expressions of gratitude. This gratefulness is an indirect reaction, a social conventionality and a modern one (the Homeric Greeks never thanked the giver of a gift; they thanked the gods, whose instrument he was, or their luck). Secondary reactions were irksome to Lawrence. In accepting aid he had placed himself in a position of inferiority and subjection; the account must be evened. This is the primary reaction; resentfulness. In this particular, and not only in this, Lawrence might be compared to a sensitive plate. He recorded instantaneously. He could not control the impulse to be longwinded in *Women in Love,* nor to be spiteful towards "Sir William" and those other protectors whom he chastises for their kindness to him. I know that state of mind. Like Lawrence, I have often felt inclined to curse people for being in a position to help me. Unlike him, I never let the cat out of the bag. Yet many of those who knew him best will prefer a simpler and less charitable explanation. They will say that his caricature of "Sir William's" household was inspired by sheer envy and cattishness. Lawrence was certainly one of the most envy-bitten mortals I have known. He was envious of other men's social rank, of their reputations and natural gifts, their health, and chiefly of their bank-balances; even the relative affluence of his own family was a grievance to him. "Sir William" was rich beyond the dreams of avarice.

For the rest, the prevalent conception of Lawrence as a misanthrope is wrong. He was a man of naturally blithe disposition, full of childlike curiosity. The core of his mind was unsophisticated. He touched upon the common things of earth with tenderness and grace, like some butterfly poised over a flower—poised lightly, I mean, with fickle *insouciance* (for his books contain strange errors of observation). This, once more, was the direct reaction, the poet's reaction; the instantaneous record. No intervening medium, no mirage, hovered between Lawrence and what his eyes beheld. These things lay before him clear-cut, in their primordial candour, devoid of any veil of suggestion or association. It was his charm. There was something elemental in him, something of the *Erdgeist.*[2]

His genius was pictorial and contemplative, impatient of causes save

[1]Politeness, or here most likely, good breeding.

[2]Perhaps in the Goethean sense of spirit of the (whole) earth, though anyone who doesn't like Lawrence could translate it as earth spirit or gnome.

where the issue was plain to an infant's understanding, as in the matter of that pamphlet on Pornography and Obscenity—a noble pronouncement. Lawrence was no Bohemian; he was a provincial, an inspired provincial with marked puritan leanings. He had a shuddering horror of Casanova's Memoirs; he was furious with a friend for keeping two mistresses instead of one, and even with Florentine boys for showing an inch or so of bare flesh above the knee—"I don't like it! I don't like it! Why can't they wear trousers?"; my own improprieties of speech he ascribed to some perverse kink of nature, whereas they were merely an indication of good health. Had he been concerned for his own peace of mind he should have left the department of exact thinking to take care of itself and devoted his energies to that of feeling, for he insisted on discovering ever fresh riddles in the Universe, and these riddles annoyed him. He could flounder in philosophy as few have yet floundered; in his descriptive writings are phrases which none save Lawrence could have struck out. His life was restless, ever moving from place to place. His work moves restlessly from subject to subject, and sometimes, as in certain of his tales, with an enviable flair, an enviable freshness, an enviable mastery.

It is true that, being inwardly consumed and tormented, he never clarified his outlook. Lawrence had neither poise nor reserve. Nor had he a trace of humour. He had courage. He knew what would be the consequence if a notorious book of his should ever be published: a howl of execration. He went ahead. I think the writings of Lawrence have done good; his influence was needed by a large class of our fellow-creatures. He has done good negatively, as a warning to thinkers and on occasion to writers; positively, because his work is in the nature of a beneficent, tabu-shattering bomb. An American friend tells me that Lawrence's romances have been of incalculable service to genteel society out there. The same applies to genteel society in England. Scholars and men of the world will not find much inspiration in these novels. Lawrence opened a little window for the bourgeoisie. That is his life-work.

I once asked him whom he was aiming at with *Lady Chatterley,* which was just then appearing. He said:

"The young writers. I want them to come out of their shells and be more frank. I want to encourage them—give them some 'kick.' As for the old ones—I don't care a pin whether they read Lady C. or not. There's nothing to be done with them; they are past human aid. Let them stew in their grease."

At that meeting I induced Lawrence to pay several whiskies-and-sodas for Orioli and myself; the surest way to win his regard was to make him suffer small losses of this kind. There must have been something wrong, however, with my masochistic theory, for not long afterwards he played a much better trick on us.

He was leaving for Germany with his wife and had invited Orioli[3] for

[3]Italian publisher and friend of Douglas. Lawrence's wife is the Frieda mentioned below.

a farewell luncheon, his train being due to start early in the afternoon. Then it occurred to him that he would like to have me too, and he sent round word to that effect. I had another engagement but threw it over: "Lorenzo" was no ordinary person and, besides that, so ill that who could say whether I was ever going to see the poor devil alive again? We sat down at midday in a certain restaurant, Orioli and myself ordering the simplest dishes in view of Lorenzo's relative impecuniosity. He himself could not make up his mind what to eat. He was not feeling particularly hungry that day, and Frieda waited for him to decide. At last he thought he could manage some fish. They brought for his inspection the usual platter of raw fish, red mullets and the rest of them. He waved it aside; these small sea-beasts with their ten thousand bones were troublesome to deal with. Then the manager himself appeared, bearing an enormous tray in his arms. On it lay a sole, a single sole, a monster, one of the largest I ever saw in Italy; it would have done credit to Bond Street. He set it down ceremoniously and observed:

"This, gentlemen, is no fish. It is a museum-piece. It is a wonder. Lucky the client who gets it."

Lorenzo fell in love with the museum-piece. Frieda and he would have that wonder for luncheon, or nothing at all. I thought: that's going to cost him fifty or sixty francs. Well, it was no affair of mine; this was Lorenzo's luncheon; let him do as he pleases! The sole was long in cooking. Frieda had patience, but Lorenzo fumed and grew more and more concerned about the possibility of missing his train. He continually looked at his watch: was that wretched fish never coming? At last it arrived, and the two of them devoured what they could with irreverential haste. Lorenzo glanced at his watch—

"Good God! We're just in the nick of time. Hurry up! I can't pay now, because I've got only a few coppers and a five-hundred franc note which they'll never be able to change; we must settle up later. Now let's rush! You, Douglas, take Frieda to the station in a taxi. I'll go with Orioli in another, because I must fetch my bags at his place."

Arrived at the station Frieda, of course, had no money for the fare, because Lorenzo always kept the cash; I paid it. Orioli paid for the other taxi and the porters, because Lorenzo had only a few coppers and a five-hundred franc note which they'll never be able to change. On our way home we also settled up the combined luncheon-bill; it amounted to a little less than a hundred francs, for which we have not yet been reimbursed. Meanwhile Lorenzo made himself comfortable in a corner seat, with his tweed overcoat thrown about him. No reference was made to the museum-piece either then or thereafter, and as the train moved out I thought to detect—it may have been imagination on my part—the phantom of a smile creeping over his wan face.

The last time I saw Lawrence was at Bandol on the 4 January 1930. They were living in one of those dreadful little bungalows built of gaudy cardboard—there may have been one or two bricks in it as well—which grow up overnight, like a disfiguring eruption, along that coast. Lawrence was a sick man; sick to death. His voice was weak, and he moved about with difficulty. He produced a bottle of French cognac: wouldn't I have a glass? He spoke of the flowers in their garden, of the clamour of the waves on stormy days. Not much later, in the beginning of March, I strewed a few red carnations on his grave at Vence—an inoffensive gesture.

PS.—Here is a characteristic passage in a letter from Lawrence to a mutual friend, now also dead (how people die off!); it is dated Fontana Vecchia, Taormina, 31 March 1920:

"Here one feels as if one had lived for a hundred thousand years. What it is that is so familiar I don't know. You remember Stopford said Sicily had been waiting for me for about 2,000 years: must be the sense of that long wait. Not that Sicily waited for me alone—

"She waits for each and other
She waits for all men born.

"—What for? To rook them, to overcharge them, to diddle them and do them down. Capri is an unhatched egg compared to this serpent of Trinacria.

"The money-changers, thieves incomparable, have shut up shop, and if you want to buy anything the natives say 'il cambio'[4] and take you metaphorically by the nose.

"I have done 50,000 words of a novel which amuses me but perhaps won't amuse anybody else. I am going to give it to Mary to criticize. I feel that as she sits in her room at Timeo she will represent the public as near as I want it. So like an 'aristo' before Robespierre I shake in my superior shoes.

"Here is very beautiful. Yes, we are north of the village, outside. We don't see Etna. Beautiful flowers are out. There is a tiny blue iris as high as your finger which blooms in the grass and lasts a day. It is one of the most morgen-schön[5] flowers I have ever seen. The world's morning—that and the wild cyclamen thrill me with this sense. Then there are the pink gladioli, and pink snapdragons, and orchids—old man and bee and bird's nest. Sicily seems so fascinating in the interior. If I can only get some money and finish this novel I shall walk into the middle of it. Perhaps away from the coast the exchange won't be stuck so tight in the native throat. Anyhow the exchange doesn't make *me* any less a human being, and it ought not to make them. But it does.

"I look up at Monte Venere and think I will set off. Why don't I? But the dawn is so lovely from this house. I open my eye at 5.0, and say Coming; at 5.30, and say yellow; at 6.0, and say pink and smoke blue; at 6.15, and see a lovely orange flare and then the liquid sunlight winking straight in my eye. Then I know it's time to get up. So I dodge the sunlight with a corner of the blanket, and consider the problem of

[4] The exchange; i.e. the rate for exchanging money.
[5] Fresh and lovely (as the morning).

the universe: this I count my sweetest luxury, to consider the problem of the universe while I dodge the dawned sun behind a corner of the sheet; so warm, so first-kiss warm. . . ."

And here is a poetic wraith, enclosed in another letter to the same mutual friend:

GREEN

The dawn was apple-green
The sky was green wine held up in the sun
The moon was a golden petal between.

She opened her eyes, and green
Her eyes shone, clear like flowers undone
For the first time, now for the first time seen.

NO. 2. THE PINES

Max Beerbohm

Early in the year 1914 Mr. Edmund Gosse told me he was asking certain of his friends to write for him a few words apiece in description of Swinburne as they had known or seen him at one time or another; and he was so good as to wish to include in this gathering a few words by myself. I found it hard to be brief without seeming irreverent. I failed in the attempt to make of my subject a snapshot that was not a grotesque. So I took refuge in an ampler scope. I wrote a reminiscential essay. From that essay I made an extract, which I gave to Mr. Gosse. From that extract he made a quotation in his enchanting biography. The words quoted by him reappear here in the midst of the whole essay as I wrote it. I dare not hope they are unashamed of their humble surroundings.—M. B.

In my youth the suburbs were rather looked down on—I never quite knew why. It was held anomalous, and a matter for merriment, that Swinburne lived in one of them. For my part, had I known as a fact that Catullus was still alive, I should have been as ready to imagine him living in Putney as elsewhere. The marvel would have been merely that he lived. And Swinburne's survival struck as surely as could his have struck in me the chord of wonder.

Not, of course, that he had achieved a feat of longevity. He was far from the Psalmist's limit. Nor was he one of those men whom one asso-

ciates with the era in which they happened to be young. Indeed, if there
was one man belonging less than any other to Mid-Victorian days, Swinburne was that man. But by the calendar it was in those days that he had
blazed—blazed forth with so unexampled a suddenness of splendour; and
in the light of that conflagration all that he had since done, much and
magnificent though this was, paled. The essential Swinburne was still the
earliest. He was and would always be the flammiferous boy of the dim
past—a legendary creature, sole kin to the phœnix. It had been impossible
that he should ever surpass himself in the artistry that was from the outset
his; impossible that he should bring forth rhythms lovelier and greater
than those early rhythms, or exercise over them a mastery more than—
absolute. Also, it had been impossible that the first wild ardour of spirit
should abide unsinkingly in him. Youth goes. And there was not in Swinburne that basis on which a man may in his maturity so build as to make
good, in some degree, the loss of what is gone. He was not a thinker: his
mind rose ever away from reason to rhapsody; neither was he human. He
was a king crowned but not throned. He was a singing bird that could
build no nest. He was a youth who could not afford to age. Had he died
young, literature would have lost many glories; but none so great as the
glories he had already given, nor any such as we should fondly imagine
ourselves bereft of by his early death. A great part of Keats' fame rests
on our assumption of what he *would* have done. But—even granting that
Keats may have had in him more than had Swinburne of stuff for development—I believe that had he lived on we should think of him as author of
the poems that in fact we know. Not philosophy, after all, not humanity,
just sheer joyous power of song, is the primal thing in poetry. Ideas, and
flesh and blood, are but reserves to be brought up when the poet's youth
is going. When the bird can no longer sing in flight, let the nest be ready.
After the king has dazzled us with his crown, let him have something to
sit down on. But the session on throne or in nest is not the divine period.
Had Swinburne's genius been of the kind that solidifies, he would yet at
the close of the nineteenth century have been for us young men virtually
—though not so definitely as in fact he was—the writer of "Atalanta in
Calydon" and of "Poems and Ballads."

Tennyson's death in '98 had not taken us at all by surprise. We had
been fully aware that he was alive. He had always been careful to keep
himself abreast of the times. Anything that came along—the Nebular
Hypothesis at one moment, the Imperial Institute at another—won mention from his Muse. He had husbanded for his old age that which he had
long ago inherited: middle age. If in our mourning for him there really
was any tincture of surprise, this was due to merely the vague sense that
he had in the fullness of time died rather prematurely: his middle-age
might have been expected to go on flourishing for ever. But assuredly
Tennyson dead laid no such strain on our fancy as Swinburne living.

It is true that Swinburne did, from time to time, take public notice of
current affairs; but what notice he took did but seem to mark his remote-

ness from them, from us. The Boers, I remember, were the theme of a
sonnet which embarrassed even their angriest enemies in our midst. He
likened them, if I remember rightly, to "hell-hounds foaming at the jaws."
This was by some people taken as a sign that he had fallen away from
that high generosity of spirit which had once been his. To me it meant
merely that he thought of poor little England writhing under the heel of
an alien despotism, just as, in the days when he really was interested in
such matters, poor little Italy had writhen. I suspect, too, that the first
impulse to write about the Boers came not from the Muse within, but from
Theodore Watts-Dunton without. . . . "Now, Algernon, we're at war,
you know—at war with the Boers. I don't want to bother you at all, but
I do think, my dear old friend, you oughtn't to let slip this opportunity
of," etc., etc.

Some such hortation is easily imaginable by any one who saw the two
old friends together. The first time I had this honour, this sight for lasting
and affectionate memory, must have been in the Spring of '99. In those
days Theodore Watts (he had but recently taken on the -Dunton) was
still something of a gad-about. I had met him here and there, he had said
in his stentorian tones pleasant things to me about my writing, I sent him
a new little book of mine, and in acknowledging this he asked me to come
down to Putney and "have luncheon and meet Swinburne." Meet Catullus!

On the day appointed "I came as one whose feet half linger." It is but
a few steps from the railway-station in Putney High Street to No. 2. The
Pines. I had expected a greater distance to the sanctuary—a walk in which
to compose my mind and prepare myself for initiation. I laid my hand
irresolutely against the gate of the bleak trim front-garden, I withdrew
my hand, I went away. Out here were all the aspects of common modern
life. In there was Swinburne. A butcher-boy went by, whistling. He was
not going to see Swinburne. He could afford to whistle. I pursued my
dilatory course up the slope of Putney, but at length it occurred to me
that unpunctuality would after all be an imperfect expression of reverence,
and I retraced my footsteps.

No. 2—prosaic inscription! But as that front-door closed behind me I
had the instant sense of having slipped away from the harsh light of the
ordinary and contemporary into the dimness of an odd, august past. Here,
in this dark hall, the past was the present. Here loomed vivid and vital on
the walls those women of Rossetti whom I had known but as shades.
Familiar to me in small reproductions by photogravure, here they *themselves* were, life-sized, "with curled-up lips and amorous hair" done in the
original warm crayon, all of them intently looking down on me while I
took off my overcoat—all wondering who was this intruder from posterity.
That they hung in the hall, evidently no more than an overflow, was an
earnest of packed plenitude within. The room I was ushered into was a
back-room, a dining-room, looking on to a good garden. It was, in form
and "fixtures," an inalienably Mid-Victorian room, and held its stolid own
in the riot of Rossettis. Its proportions, its window-sash bisecting the view

of garden, its folding-doors (through which I heard the voice of Watts-Dunton booming mysteriously in the front room), its mantel-piece, its gas-brackets, all proclaimed that nothing ever would seduce them from their allegiance to Martin Tupper.[1] "Nor me from mine," said the sturdy cruet-stand on the long expanse of table-cloth. The voice of Watts-Dunton ceased suddenly, and a few moments later its owner appeared. He had been dictating, he explained. "A great deal of work on hand just now—a great deal of work." . . . I remember that on my subsequent visits he was always, at the moment of my arrival, dictating, and always greeted me with that phrase, "A great deal of work on hand just now." I used to wonder what work it was, for he published little enough. But I never ventured to inquire, and indeed rather cherished the mystery: it was a part of the dear little old man; it went with the something gnome-like about his swarthiness and chubbiness—went with the shaggy hair that fell over the collar of his eternally crumpled frock-coat, the shaggy eye-brows that overhung his bright little brown eyes, the shaggy moustache that hid his small round chin. It was a mystery inherent in the richly-laden atmosphere of The Pines. . . .

While I stood talking to Watts-Dunton—talking as loudly as he, for he was very deaf—I enjoyed the thrill of suspense in watching the door through which would appear—Swinburne. I asked after Mr. Swinburne's health. Watts-Dunton said it was very good: "He always goes out for his long walk in the morning—wonderfully active. Active in mind, too. But I'm afraid you won't be able to get into touch with him. He's almost stone-deaf, poor fellow—almost stone-deaf now." He changed the subject, and I felt I must be careful not to seem interested in Swinburne exclu-sively. I spoke of "Aylwin."[2] The parlourmaid brought in the hot dishes. The great moment was at hand.

Nor was I disappointed. Swinburne's entry was for me a great moment. Here, suddenly visible in the flesh, was the legendary being and divine singer. Here he was, shutting the door behind him as might anybody else, and advancing—a strange small figure in grey, having an air at once noble and roguish, proud and skittish. My name was roared to him. In shaking his hand, I bowed low, of course—a bow de cœur[3]; and he, in the old aristocratic manner, bowed equally low, but with such swiftness that we narrowly escaped concussion. You do not usually associate a man of genius, when you see one, with any social class; and, Swinburne being of an aspect so unrelated as it was to any species of human kind, I wondered the more that almost the first impression he made on me, or would make on any one, was that of a very great gentleman indeed. Not of an *old* gentleman, either. Sparse and straggling though the grey hair was that fringed the immense pale dome of his head, and venerably haloed though

[1]An early Victorian popular philosopher; Beerbohm is using him as a symbol of bour-geois vulgarity.

[2]A prose romance by Watts-Dunton.

[3]With all my heart, wholehearted.

he was for me by his greatness, there was yet about him something—
boyish? girlish? childish, rather; something of a beautifully well-bred
child. But he had the eyes of a god, and the smile of an elf. In figure, at
first glance, he seemed almost fat; but this was merely because of the way
he carried himself, with his long neck strained so tightly back that he all
receded from the waist upwards. I noticed afterwards that this deport-
ment made the back of his jacket hang quite far away from his legs; and
so small and sloping were his shoulders that the jacket seemed ever so
likely to slip right off. I became aware, too, that when he bowed he did
not unbend his back, but only his neck—the length of the neck account-
ing for the depth of the bow. His hands were tiny, even for his size, and
they fluttered helplessly, touchingly, unceasingly.

Directly after my introduction, we sat down to the meal. Of course I
had never hoped to "get into touch with him" reciprocally. Quite apart
from his deafness, I was too modest to suppose he could be interested in
anything I might say. But—for I knew he had once been as high and
copious a singer in talk as in verse—I had hoped to hear utterances from
him. And it did not seem that my hope was to be fulfilled. Watts-Dunton
sat at the head of the table, with a huge and very Tupperesque joint of
roast mutton in front of him, Swinburne and myself close up to him on
either side. He talked only to me. This was the more tantalising because
Swinburne seemed as though he were bubbling over with all sorts of
notions. Not that he looked at either of us. He smiled only to himself, and
to his plateful of meat, and to the small bottle of Bass's pale ale that stood
before him—ultimate allowance of one who had erst clashed cymbals in
Naxos.[4] This small bottle he eyed often and with enthusiasm, seeming to
waver between the rapture of broaching it now and the grandeur of having it to look forward to. It made me unhappy to see what trouble he had
in managing his knife and fork. Watts-Dunton told me on another occasion that this infirmity of the hands had been lifelong—had begun before
Eton days. The Swinburne family had been alarmed by it and had consulted a specialist, who said that it resulted from "an excess of electric
vitality," and that any attempt to stop it would be harmful. So they had
let it be. I have known no man of genius who had not to pay, in some
affliction or defect either physical or spiritual, for what the gods had given
him. Here, in this fluttering of his tiny hands, was a part of the price that
Swinburne had to pay. No doubt he had grown accustomed to it many
lustres before I met him, and I need not have felt at all unhappy at what
I tried not to see. He, evidently, was quite gay, in his silence—and in the
world that was for him silent. I had, however, the maddening suspicion
that he would have liked to talk. Why wouldn't Watts-Dunton roar him
an opportunity? I felt I had been right perhaps in feeling that the lesser
man was—no, not jealous of the greater whom he had guarded so long
and with such love, but anxious that he himself should be as fully impressive to visitors as his fine gifts warranted. Not, indeed, that he

[4]That is, who had been a heavy drinker; Naxos is an Aegean island famous for its wine.

monopolised the talk. He seemed to regard me as a source of information about all the latest "movements," and I had to shout banalities while he munched his mutton—banalities whose one saving grace for me was that they were inaudible to Swinburne. Had I met Swinburne's gaze, I should have faltered. Now and again his shining light-grey eyes roved from the table, darting this way and that—across the room, up at the ceiling, out of the window; only never at us. Somehow this aloofness gave no hint of indifference. It seemed to be, rather, a point in good manners—the good manners of a child "sitting up to table," not "staring," not "asking questions," and reflecting great credit on its invaluable old nurse. The child sat happy in the wealth of its inner life; the child was content not to speak until it were spoken to; but, but, I felt it did want to be spoken to. And, at length, it *was*.

So soon as the mutton had been replaced by the apple-pie, Watts-Dunton leaned forward and "Well, Algernon," he roared, "how was it on the Heath to-day?" Swinburne, who had meekly inclined his ear to the question, now threw back his head, uttering a sound that was like the cooing of a dove, and forthwith, rapidly, ever so musically, he spoke to us of his walk, spoke not in the strain of a man who had been taking his daily exercise on Putney Heath, but rather in that of a Peri who had at long last been suffered to pass through Paradise. And rather than that he spoke would I say that he cooingly and flutingly *sang* of his experience. The wonders of this morning's wind and sun and clouds were expressed in a flow of words so right and sentences so perfectly balanced that they would have seemed pedantic had they not been clearly as spontaneous as the wordless notes of a bird in song. The frail, sweet voice rose and fell, lingered, quickened, in all manner of trills and roulades. That he himself could not hear it, seemed to me the greatest loss his deafness inflicted on him. One would have expected this disability to mar the music; but it didn't; save that now and again a note would come out metallic and over-shrill, the tones were under good control. The whole manner and method had certainly a strong element of oddness; but no one incapable of condemning as unmanly the song of a lark would have called it affected. I had met young men of whose enunciation Swinburne's now reminded me. In them the thing had always irritated me very much; and I now became sure that it had been derived from people who had derived it in old Balliol days from Swinburne himself. One of the points familiar to me in such enunciation was the habit of stressing extremely, and lackadaisically dwelling on, some particular syllable. In Swinburne this trick was delightful—because it wasn't a trick, but a need of his heart. Well do I remember his ecstasy of emphasis and immensity of pause when he described how he had seen in a perambulator on the Heath to-day "the most BEAUT——iful babbie ever beheld by mortal eyes." For babies, as some of his later volumes testify, he had a sort of idolatry. After Mazzini had followed Landor to Elysium, and Victor Hugo had followed Mazzini, babies were what among live creatures most evoked Swinburne's genius for self-abasement. His rapture about this especial "babbie" was such as to shake within me my hitherto firm conviction that, whereas the young of the brute creation are already beautiful at the age of five minutes, the human young never begin to be so before the age of three years. I suspect Watts-Dunton of having shared my lack of innate enthusiasm. But it was one of Swinburne's charms, as I was to find, that he took for granted every one's delight in what he himself so fervidly delighted in. He could as soon have imagined a man not loving the very sea as not doting on the aspect of babies and not reading at least one play by an Elizabethan or Jacobean dramatist every day.

I forget whether it was at this my first meal or at another that he described a storm in which, one night years ago, with Watts-Dunton, he had crossed the Channel. The rhythm of his great phrases was as the rhythm of those waves, and his head swayed in accordance to it like the wave-rocked boat itself. He hymned in memory the surge and darkness, the thunder and foam and phosphorescence—"You remember, Theodore? You remember the PHOS——phorescence?"—all so beautifully and vividly that I almost felt storm-bound and in peril of my life. To disentangle one from another of the several occasions on which I heard him talk is difficult because the procedure was so invariable: Watts-Dunton always dictating when I arrived, Swinburne always appearing at the moment of the meal, always the same simple and substantial fare, Swinburne never allowed to talk before the meal was half over. As to this last point, I soon realised that I had been quite unjust in suspecting Watts-Dunton of selfishness. It was simply a sign of the care with which he watched over his friend's welfare. Had Swinburne been admitted earlier to the talk, he would not have taken his proper quantity of roast mutton. So soon, always, as he had taken that, the embargo was removed, the chance was given him. And, swiftly though he embraced the chance, and much though he made of it in the courses of apple-pie and of cheese, he seemed touchingly ashamed of "holding forth." Often, before he had said his really full say on the theme suggested by Watts-Dunton's loud interrogation, he would curb his speech and try to eliminate himself, bowing his head over his plate; and then, when he had promptly been brought in again, he would always try to atone for his inhibiting deafness by much reference and deference to all that we might otherwise have to say. "I hope," he would coo to me, "my friend Watts-Dunton, who"—and here he would turn and make a little bow to Watts-Dunton—"is himself a scholar, will bear me out when I say"—or "I hardly know," he would flute to his old friend, "whether Mr. Beerbohm"—here a bow to me—"will agree with me in my opinion of" some delicate point in Greek prosody or some incident in an old French romance I had never heard of.

On one occasion, just before the removal of the mutton, Watts-Dunton had been asking me about an English translation that had been made of M. Rostand's "Cyrano de Bergerac." He then took my information as the match to ignite the Swinburnian tinder. "Well, Algernon, it seems that

'Cyrano de Bergerac' "—but this first spark was enough: instantly Swinburne was praising the works of Cyrano de Bergerac. Of M. Rostand he may have heard, but him he forgot. Indeed I never heard Swinburne mention a single contemporary writer. His mind ranged and revelled always in the illustrious or obscure past. To him the writings of Cyrano de Bergerac were as fresh as paint—as fresh as to me, alas, was the news of their survival. "Of course, of course, you have read 'L'Histoire Comique des États et des Empires de la Lune'[5]?" I admitted, by gesture and facial expression, that I had not. Whereupon he reeled out curious extracts from that allegory—"almost as good as 'Gulliver' "—with a memorable instance of the way in which the traveller to the moon was shocked by the conversation of the natives, and the natives' sense of propriety was outraged by the conversation of the traveller.

In life, as in (that for him more truly actual thing) literature, it was always the preterit that enthralled him. Of any passing events, of anything the newspapers were full of, never a word from him; and I should have been sorry if there had been. But I did, through the medium of Watts-Dunton, sometimes start him on topics that might have led him to talk of Rossetti and other old comrades. For me the names of those men breathed the magic of the past, just as it was breathed for me by Swinburne's presence. For him, I suppose, they were but a bit of the present, and the mere fact that they had dropped out of it was not enough to hallow them. He never mentioned them. But I was glad to see that he revelled as wistfully in the days just before his own as I in the days just before mine. He recounted to us things he had been told in his boyhood by an aged aunt, or great-aunt—"one of the Ashburnhams"; how, for example, she had been taken by her mother to a county ball, a distance of many miles, and, on the way home through the frosty and snowy night, the family-coach had suddenly stopped: there was a crowd of dark figures in the way . . . at which point Swinburne stopped too, before saying, with an ineffable smile and in a voice faint with appreciation, "They were burying a suicide at the crossroads."

Vivid as this Hogarthian[6] night-scene was to me, I saw beside it another scene: a grim panelled room, a grim old woman in a high-backed chair, and, restless on a stool at her feet an extraordinary little nephew with masses of auburn hair and with tiny hands clasped in supplication—"Tell me more, Aunt Ashburnham, tell me more!"

And now, clearlier still, as I write in these after-years, do I see that dining-room of The Pines; the long white stretch of table-cloth, with Swinburne and Watts-Dunton and another at the extreme end of it; Watts-Dunton between us, very low down over his plate, very cosy and hirsute,

[5] *The Comic History of the Countries and Empires of the Moon,* by de Bergerac; it is one of several probable sources for *Gulliver.*

[6] In the manner of William Hogarth, the eighteenth century British artist. It is hard to feel Hogarth's vivid, reportorial line through Swinburne's "ineffable smile" and voice that was "faint with appreciation." Presumably Beerbohm connected the suicide at night with some of Hogarth's forceful pictures of London low-life, or low high-life.

and rather like the dormouse at that long tea-table which Alice found in Wonderland. I see myself sitting there wide-eyed, as Alice sat. And, had the hare been a great poet, and the hatter a great gentleman, and neither of them mad but each only very odd and vivacious, I might see Swinburne as a glorified blend of those two.

When the meal ended—for, alas! it was not, like that meal in Wonderland, unending—Swinburne would dart round the table, proffer his hand to me, bow deeply, bow to Watts-Dunton also, and disappear. "He always walks in the morning, writes in the afternoon, and reads in the evening," Watts-Dunton would say with a touch of tutorial pride in this regimen.

That parting bow of Swinburne to his old friend was characteristic of his whole relation to him. Cronies though they were, these two, knit together with bonds innumerable, the greater man was always *aux petits soins*[7] for the lesser, treating him as a newly-arrived young guest might treat an elderly host. Some twenty years had passed since that night when, ailing and broken—thought to be nearly dying, Watts-Dunton told me—Swinburne was brought in a four-wheeler to The Pines. Regular private nursing-homes either did not exist in those days or were less in vogue than they are now. The Pines was to be a sort of private nursing-home for Swinburne. It was a good one. He recovered. He was most grateful to his friend and saviour. He made as though to depart, was persuaded to stay a little longer, and then a little longer than that. But I rather fancy that, to the last, he never did, in the fullness of his modesty and good manners, consent to regard his presence as a matter of course, or as anything but a terminable intrusion and obligation. His bow seemed always to convey that.

Swinburne having gone from the room, in would come the parlourmaid. The table was cleared, the fire was stirred, two leather arm-chairs were pushed up to the hearth. Watts-Dunton wanted gossip of the present. I wanted gossip of the great past. We settled down for a long, comfortable afternoon together.

Only once was the ritual varied. Swinburne (I was told before luncheon) had expressed a wish to show me his library. So after the meal he did not bid us his usual adieu, but with much courtesy invited us and led the way. Up the staircase he then literally bounded—three, literally three, stairs at a time. I began to follow at the same rate, but immediately slackened speed for fear that Watts-Dunton behind us might be embittered at sight of so much youth and legerity. Swinburne waited on the threshold to receive us, as it were, and pass us in. Watts-Dunton went and ensconced himself snugly in a corner. The sun had appeared after a grey morning, and it pleasantly flooded this big living-room whose walls were entirely lined with the mellow backs of books. Here, as host, among his treasures, Swinburne was more than ever attractive. He was as happy as was any mote in the sunshine about him; and the fluttering of his little hands, and feet too, was but as a token of so much felicity. He looked

[7]Full of (small) attentions.

older, it is true, in the strong light. But these added years made only more notable his youngness of heart. An illustrious bibliophile among his books? A birthday child, rather, among his toys.

Proudly he explained to me the general system under which the volumes were ranged in this or that division of shelves. Then he conducted me to a chair near the window, left me there, flew away, flew up the rungs of a mahogany ladder, plucked a small volume, and in a twinkling was at my side: "This, I *think,* will please you!" It did. It had a beautifully engraved title-page and a pleasing scent of old, old leather. It was *editio princeps* of a play by some lesser Elizabethan or Jacobean. "Of course you know it?" my host fluted.

How I wished I could say that I knew it and loved it well! I revealed to him (for by speaking very loudly towards his inclined head I was able to make him hear) that I had not read it. He envied any one who had such pleasure in store. He darted to the ladder, and came back thrusting gently into my hands another volume of like date: "Of course you know *this?*"

Again I had to confess that I did not, and to shout my appreciation of the fount of type, the margins, the binding. He beamed agreement, and fetched another volume. Archly he indicated the title, cooing, "You are a lover of *this,* I hope?" And again I was shamed by my inexperience.

I did not pretend to know this particular play, but my tone implied that I had always been *meaning* to read it and had always by some mischance been prevented. For his sake as well as my own I did want to acquit myself passably. I wanted for him the pleasure of seeing his joys shared by a representative, however humble, of the common world. I turned the leaves caressingly, looking from them to him, while he dilated on the beauty of this and that scene in the play. Anon he fetched another volume, and another, always with the same faith that *this* was a favourite of mine. I quibbled, I evaded, I was very enthusiastic and uncomfortable. It was with intense relief that I beheld the title-page of yet another volume which (silently, this time) he laid before me—THE COUNTRY WENCH. "*This* of *course* I have read," I heartily shouted.

Swinburne stepped back. "You have? You have read it? Where?" he cried, in evident dismay.

Something was wrong. Had I *not,* I quickly wondered, read this play? "Oh yes," I shouted, "I have read it."

"But when? Where?" entreated Swinburne, adding that he had supposed it to be the sole copy extant.

I floundered. I wildly said I thought I must have read it years ago in the Bodleian.

"Theodore! Do you hear this? It seems that they have now a copy of 'The Country Wench' in the Bodleian! Mr. Beerbohm found one there— oh when? in what year?" he appealed to me.

I said it might have been six, seven, eight years ago. Swinburne knew for certain that no copy had been there *twelve* years ago, and was surprised that he had not heard of the acquisition. "They might have told me," he wailed.

I sacrificed myself on the altar of sympathy. I admitted that I might have been mistaken—must have been—must have confused this play with some other. I dipped into the pages and "No," I shouted, "this I have *never* read."

His equanimity was restored. He was up the ladder and down again, showing me further treasures with all pride and ardour. At length, Watts-Dunton, afraid that his old friend would tire himself, arose from his corner, and presently he and I went downstairs to the dining-room. It was in the course of our session together that there suddenly flashed across my mind the existence of a play called "The Country Wife," by—wasn't it Wycherley? I had once read it—or read something about it. . . . But this matter I kept to myself. I thought I had appeared fool enough already.

I loved those sessions in that Tupperossettine dining-room, lair of solid old comfort and fervid old romanticism. Its odd duality befitted well its owner. The distinguished critic and poet, Rossetti's closest friend and Swinburne's, had been, for a while, in the dark ages, a solicitor; and one felt he had been a good one. His frock-coat, though the Muses had crumpled it, inspired confidence in his judgment of other things than verse. But let there be no mistake. He was no mere *bourgeois parnassien*,[8] as his enemies insinuated. No doubt he had been very useful to men of genius, in virtue of qualities they lacked, but the secret of his hold on them was in his own rich nature. He was not only a born man of letters, he was a deeply emotional human being whose appeal was as much to the heart as to the head. The romantic Celtic mysticism of "Aylwin," with its lack of fashionable Celtic nebulosity, lends itself, if you will, to laughter, though personally I saw nothing funny in it: it seemed to me, before I was in touch with the author, a work of genuine expression from within; and that it truly was so I presently knew. The mysticism of Watts-Dunton (who, once comfortably settled at the fireside, knew no reserve) was in contrast with the frock-coat and the practical abilities; but it was essential, and they were of the surface. For humorous Rossetti, I daresay, the very contrast made Theodore's company the more precious. He himself had assuredly been, and the memory of him still was, the master-fact in Watts-Dunton's life. "Algernon" was as an adopted child, "Gabriel" as a long-lost only brother. As he was to the outer world of his own day, so too to posterity Rossetti, the man, is conjectural and mysterious. We know that he was in his prime the most inspiring and splendid of companions. But we know this only by faith. The evidence is as vague as it is emphatic. Of the style and substance of not a few great talkers in the past we can piece together some more or less vivid and probably erroneous notion. But about Rossetti nothing has been recorded in such a way as to make

[8]Business man of the arts; Beerbohm is qualifying the snide allusion in Tupperossettine (see p. 1079 above).

him even faintly emerge. I suppose he had in him what reviewers seem to find so often in books: a quality that defies analysis. Listening to Watts-Dunton, I was always in hope that when next the long-lost turned up—for he was continually doing so—in the talk, I should *see* him, *hear* him, and share the rapture. But the revelation was not to be. You might think that to hear him called "Gabriel" would have given me a sense of propinquity. But I felt no nearer to him than you feel to the Archangel who bears that name and no surname.

It was always when Watts-Dunton spoke carelessly, casually, of some to me illustrious figure in the past, that I had the sense of being wafted right into that past and plumped down in the very midst of it. When he spoke with reverence of this and that great man whom he had known, he did not thus waft and plump me; for I, too, revered those names. But I had the magical transition whenever one of the immortals was mentioned in the tone of those who knew him before he had put on immortality. Browning, for example, was a name deeply honoured by me. "Browning, yes," said Watts-Dunton, in the course of an afternoon, "Browning," and he took a sip of the steaming whiskey-toddy that was a point in our day's ritual. "I was a great diner-out in the old times. I used to dine out every night in the week. Browning was a great diner-out, too. We were always meeting. What a pity he went on writing all those plays! He hadn't any gift for drama—none. I never could understand why he took to play-writing." He wagged his head, gazing regretfully into the fire, and added, "Such a *clever* fellow, too!"

Whistler, though alive and about, was already looked to as a hierarch by the young. Not so had he been looked to by Rossetti. The thrill of the past was always strong in me when Watts-Dunton mentioned—seldom without a guffaw did he mention—"Jimmy Whistler." I think he put in the surname because "that fellow" had not behaved well to Swinburne. But he could not omit the nickname, because it was impossible for him to feel the right measure of resentment against "such a funny fellow." As heart-full of old hates as of old loves was Watts-Dunton, and I take it as high testimony to the charm of Whistler's quaintness that Watts-Dunton did not hate *him*. You may be aware that Swinburne, in '88, wrote for one of the monthly reviews a criticism of the "Ten O'Clock" lecture. He paid courtly compliments to Whistler as a painter, but joined issue with his theories. Straightway there appeared in the *World* a little letter from Whistler, deriding "one Algernon Swinburne—outsider—Putney." It was not in itself a very pretty or amusing letter; and still less so did it seem in the light of the facts which Watts-Dunton told me in some such words as these: "After he'd published that lecture of his, Jimmy Whistler had me to dine with him at Kettner's or somewhere. He said 'Now, Theodore, I want you to do me a favour.' He wanted to get me to get Swinburne to write an article about his lecture. I said 'No, Jimmy Whistler, I can't ask Algernon to do that. He's got a great deal of work on hand just now—a great deal of work. And besides, this sort of thing wouldn't be at all in his line.' But Jimmy Whistler went on appealing to me. He said it would do him no end of good if Swinburne wrote about him. And—well, I half gave in: I said perhaps I *would* mention the matter to Algernon. And next day I did. I could see Algernon didn't want to do it at all. But—well, there, he said he'd do it to please *me*. And he did it. And then Jimmy Whistler published that letter. A very shabby trick— very shabby indeed." Of course I do not vouch for the exact words in which Watts-Dunton told me this tale; but this was exactly the tale he told me. I expressed my astonishment. He added that of course he "never wanted to see the fellow again after that, and never did." But presently, after a long gaze into the coals, he emitted a chuckle, as for earlier memories of "such a funny fellow." One quite recent memory he had, too. 'When I took on the name of Dunton, I had a note from him. Just this, with his butterfly signature: *Theodore! What's Dunton?* That was very good—very good. . . . But, of course," he added gravely, "I took no notice." And no doubt, quite apart from the difficulty of finding an answer in the same vein, he did well in not replying. Loyalty to Swinburne forbade. But I see a certain pathos in the unanswered message. It was a message from the hand of an old jester, but also, I think, from the heart of an old man—a signal waved jauntily, but in truth wistfully, across the gulf of years and estrangement; and one could wish it had not been ignored.

Some time after Whistler died I wrote for one of the magazines an appreciation of his curious skill in the art of writing. Watts-Dunton told me he had heard of this from Swinburne. "I myself," he said, "very seldom read the magazines. But Algernon always has a look at them." There was something to me very droll, and cheery too, in this picture of the illustrious recluse snatching at the current issues of our twaddle. And I was immensely pleased at hearing that my article had "interested him very much." I inwardly promised myself that as soon as I reached home I would read the article, to see just how it might have struck Swinburne. When in due course I did this, I regretted the tone of the opening sentences, in which I declared myself "no book-lover" and avowed a preference for "an uninterrupted view of my fellow-creatures." I felt that had I known my article would meet the eye of Swinburne I should have cut out that overture. I dimly remembered a fine passage in one of his books of criticism—something (I preferred not to verify it) about "the dotage of duncedom which cannot perceive, or the impudence of insignificance so presumptuous as to doubt, that the elements of life and literature are indivisibly mingled one in another, and that he to whom books are less real than life will assuredly find in men and women as little reality as in his accursed crassness he deserves to discover." I quailed, I quailed. But mine is a resilient nature, and I promptly reminded myself that Swinburne's was a very impersonal one: he would not think the less highly of me, for he never had thought about me in any way whatsoever. All was well. I knew I could revisit The Pines, when next Watts-Dunton should invite me, without misgiving. And to this day I am rather proud of having been mentioned, though not by name, and not consciously, and unfavourably, by Swinburne.

I wonder that I cannot recall more than I do recall of those hours at The Pines. It is odd how little remains to a man of his own past—how few minutes of even his memorable hours are not clean forgotten, and how few seconds in any one of those minutes can be recaptured. . . . I am middle-aged, and have lived a vast number of seconds. Subtract ½ of these, for one mustn't count sleep as life. The residual number is still enormous. Not a single one of those seconds was unimportant to me in its passage. Many of them bored me, of course; but even boredom is a positive state: one chafes at it and hates it; strange that one should afterwards forget it! And stranger still that of one's actual happinesses and unhappinesses so tiny and tattered a remnant clings about one! Of those hours at The Pines, of that past within a past, there was not a minute nor a second that I did not spend with pleasure. Memory is a great artist, we are told; she selects and rejects and shapes and so on. No doubt. Elderly persons would be utterly intolerable if they remembered *everything. Everything*, nevertheless, is just what they themselves would like to remember, and just what they would like to tell to *everybody*. Be sure that the Ancient Mariner, though he remembered quite as much as his audience wanted to hear, and rather more, about the albatross and the ghastly crew, was inwardly raging at the sketchiness of his own mind; and believe me that his stopping only one of three was the merest oversight. I should like to impose on the world many tomes about The Pines.

But, scant though my memories are of the moments there, very full and warm in me is the whole fused memory of the two dear old men that lived there. I wish I had Watts-Dunton's sure faith in meetings beyond the grave. I am glad I do not disbelieve that people may so meet. I like to think that some day in Elysium I shall—not without diffidence—approach those two and re-introduce myself. I can see just how courteously Swinburne will bow over my hand, not at all remembering who I am. Watts-Dunton will remember me after a moment: "Oh, to be sure, yes indeed! I've a great deal of work on hand just now—a great deal of work, but" we shall sit down together on the asphodel, and I cannot but think we shall have whiskey-toddy even there. He will not have changed. He will still be shaggy and old and chubby, and will wear the same frock-coat, with the same creases in it. Swinburne, on the other hand, will be quite, quite young, with a full mane of flaming auburn locks, and no clothes to hinder him from plunging back at any moment into the shining Elysian waters from which he will have just emerged. I see him skim lightly away into that element. On the strand is sitting a man of noble and furrowed brow. It is Mazzini, still thinking of Liberty. And anon the tiny young English amphibian comes ashore to fling himself dripping at the feet of the patriot and to carol the Republican ode he has composed in the course of his swim. "He's wonderfully active—active in mind and body," Watts-Dunton says to me. "I come to the shore now and then, just to see how he's getting on. But I spend most of my time inland. I find I've so much to talk over with Gabriel. Not that he's quite the fellow he was. He always had rather a cult for Dante, you know, and now he's more than ever under the Florentine influence. He lives in a sort of monastery that Dante has here; and there he sits painting imaginary portraits of Beatrice, and giving them all to Dante. But he still has his great moments, and there's no one quite like him—no one. Algernon won't ever come and see him, because that fellow Mazzini's as Anti-Clerical as ever and makes a principle of having nothing to do with Dante. Look!—there's Algernon going into the water again! He'll tire himself out, he'll catch cold, he'll—" and here the old man rises and hurries down to the sea's edge. "Now, Algernon," he roars, "I don't want to interfere with you, but I do think, my dear old friend,"—and then, with a guffaw, he breaks off, remembering that his friend is not deaf now nor old, and that here in Elysium, where no ills are, good advice is not needed.

DINNER AT THE PINES

Alfred Noyes

When I was at Oxford, between 1898 and 1902, undergraduates read a great deal of Swinburne. Before I left Oxford, when I was staying with one of my friends in London, we walked past Swinburne's house—"The Pines" on Putney Hill—and my companion, who was a great admirer of Swinburne, told me he always took off his hat as he passed the gate, which he did on this occasion, and observed: "I believe in Chaucer, Shakespeare, Shelley, Keats, and Swinburne." I felt that, too.

I wrote a poem for his seventieth birthday which was published in *The Fortnightly Review.* I didn't send it to him but I think the editor did, and I got a delightful letter from Swinburne consisting of one splendid Swinburnean sentence, which said: "I wish that my appreciation of your praise could give you half the pleasure that Victor Hugo's appreciation of my tributes repeatedly gave to me." I thought that the little distinction between praise and tributes in that one sentence was really a touch of exquisite courtesy in an older man to so young a writer. Of course, I had written to thank him for his letter, and shortly after that I got an invitation to dine at "The Pines."

You must remember that I was a very young man and very awestruck at going there, so I didn't exactly take notes; but there were pictures by Rossetti, and Morris wallpapers. The furniture was, I should say, rather

REPRINTED by permission of the author.

Victorian; but there were some articles of furniture which certainly were not—not Victorian at all. I think Swinburne really liked to feel that he was back in the Elizabethan days, and it was for that sort of reason that he liked to use candlelights rather than electricity or gas or any other modern lighting arrangements. I believe we had lamb and mint sauce, followed by a very ordinary sweet of some kind, but I really was so much more interested in Swinburne that I can't quite remember what I ate. He wore very neat clothes but there was a certain old-womanish look about some of his equipment. For instance, he wore elastic-sided boots, which was not at all what one expected of the poet of "Dolores" and "Hesperia."

There are many things that his biographers have said that didn't seem to me to be at all true. I never saw his hands twitching as Gosse described them, or any of those peculiar attitudes which the caricaturists were so fond of representing. But I did notice that he had rather delicate and weak fingers, because one of the amusing things that happened at that little dinner was that he tried to open one of those screw-top bottles of beer, and his fingers couldn't manage it. So he set it on the table in front of him and hissed at it. Nothing happened, of course, but I unscrewed it for him; then he was all the gracious host again, and before he had been a little sulphurous.

Of course he was an old man when I met him; he was over seventy. But there was a certain bird-like look about him. His shoulders sloped away in an extraordinarily bird-like way. The curious thing is that although he was a tiny little man with tiny little hands and tiny little feet, when he sat down he gave you the impression of being a biggish man: I don't know whether it was because he had a long body and a big head, but at the table he didn't look at all the little fellow that is always suggested by the descriptions of him.

The famous aureole, of course, had gone. It had been replaced by a fringe of grey hair surmounted by a very pink dome of bald head. It is curious that some people—Gosse included—have compared the shape of his head with that of Shakespeare. When I saw him at "The Pines" (and of course before I had read Gosse or Max Beerbohm) it did occur to me that there was a resemblance in his head to that of Shakespeare. But as he talked it lost that particular resemblance, and more than once it seemed to me that he might have been a younger brother of Walter Scott, who also had a very high forehead; and, curiously enough, it was when Swinburne was speaking of riding in the North Country, and sometimes of the sea, that the suggestion of Scott came into my mind.

I think that Gosse's description of the merciless expression of his eyes was true. It was a curious fact that although Swinburne made some very humorous remarks, I don't remember ever seeing a smile or hearing him laugh. There was a sort of fixed expression on his face, but there was something else which struck me as much more extraordinary: once or twice, when one was talking of some of his heroes, like Landor and Victor Hugo, a curious light came upon his face, which did suggest somehow—it seems perhaps a fantastic thing to say—that the light of immortality was shining upon it.

One of the first things I discovered when I went to see him was that it was unnecessary for me to say very much: I only had to be a good listener. There was a good deal of talking after dinner and Swinburne launched out into a wonderful description of a walk he had taken along the coast, which he also commemorated in a poem called "By the North Sea." He did, in his conversation, pour out a most extraordinary stream of what one might almost call jewelled ideas. His description of his walk by the North Sea was exactly that. It was a torrent of beautiful language and beautiful description. It was amazing because the walk took place about forty years earlier, and he remembered the most minute details of certain rock pools he had seen and described what he called "certain little lozenges of colour" in them.

He was mistaken for a merman once, you know, and some French fishermen picked him up; he was carried out to sea, a long way from shore. He couldn't really swim very well; he drifted about in the sea. He was picked up by these fishermen and astonished them by sitting on some nets in the stern of their boat and reciting Victor Hugo to them. He talked about Victor Hugo as if he were almost a god of his idolatry. Curiously enough, he talked most about Dickens. He worshipped Dickens, a curious thing because you would think that Dickens was entirely out of his realm. Swinburne was very much in the Rossetti and Burne-Jones and Pre-Raphaelite set in one sense, but when he talked of Dickens you felt somehow that he was a contemporary of Ford and Dekker and Ben Jonson and the Elizabethans. You felt somehow that he just fitted in with the "Mermaid" crew. He was a great traditionalist, and to him tradition did not mean the observance of dull conventions: it meant the handing on of the divine fire from the Greeks right down to the present day, and when he was attacked for what some of the mere conventionalists called his "daring," he was able to reply with true pride: "I write as others wrote, on Sunium's Height."

I think he almost called himself the "stormy petrel of English poetry," and it was just this independence which a more conventional age parodied —as, for instance, Owen Seaman in "Punch": a very delightful parody in which he imitated one of Swinburne's favourite metres:

> Far rolling my ravenous red eye,
> And lifting a mutinous lid,
> To all monarchs and matrons, I said I
> Would shock them, and did.

Shortly after I came to live in the Isle of Wight, about two or three miles from Bonchurch which was Swinburne's old home, I talked with the ancient sexton of the churchyard where the whole Swinburne family is buried—all his sisters, as well as his father and mother—and the sexton told me of an incident at the funeral of Swinburne's mother, Lady

Jane Swinburne. He said: "Mr. Swinburne, being an atheist, came down to his mother's funeral in a velvet coat and a slouch hat, and he wouldn't kneel down neither, by her grave. But his aunt was a big strong woman, caught hold of him by the shoulders and forced him down on to his knees and said: 'Kneel down, Algernon, kneel down!' And this was at the side of the grave, and if I hadn't been kneeling close behind Mr. Swinburne and caught a hold of his ankles, 'ead over 'eels into his mother's grave he would have gone."

One of the first and most startling things that Swinburne said to me was distinctly non-Victorian. Watts-Dunton had mentioned some gruesome newspaper sensation that had just come out about that time, and Swinburne stared straight at me and, as if he were challenging me to a duel, he said: "Christianity itself never conceived anything more ghastly." Swinburne in those days was looked upon as almost hermetically sealed off from the younger generation. There was a good deal of criticism at the time of the way in which Watts-Dunton protected Swinburne from the outside world. In fact, it was often suggested that he kept Swinburne like a kind of tropical bird in a cage. But that suggestion was almost entirely dispelled by what I saw that evening. It seemed to me that without Watts-Dunton he would have been a ship without a helm.

Watts-Dunton was almost as short as Swinburne; much more burly, and with rather a walrus moustache and a very deep voice. I did say what I thought were a few sensible things but neither of them heard because both Swinburne and Watts-Dunton were almost stone-deaf, so I just got comfortably accustomed to the idea that it didn't matter what I said or whether I said anything at all, and in a lull of the extremely interesting shouts which were exchanged by Swinburne and Watts-Dunton I did say something about the weather. I thought that I had to make my lips move as a sort of gesture anyway, and, to my horror, Swinburne noticed it and in a loud shout asked me what I'd said. I was rather stunned by this, and for the moment I was silent, and they both thought that I was deaf, too, so Swinburne shouted to Watts-Dunton, and Watts-Dunton relayed the enquiry to me with another shout, saying: "Swinburne wants to know what you said to him." I tried to tell the truth but it didn't get over, and this led to such an intensity of anxiety to know what I had said that I felt I had to improvise something sensible, so at the top of my voice I asked if Swinburne didn't think that Matthew Arnold owed a great deal to Keats, and happily Swinburne agreed with that.

I cannot quite account for the line that Gosse took about the association of Swinburne with Watts-Dunton, and I could never understand the way in which certain critics at that time talked as if they would have preferred Swinburne to die at an early age by drinking himself to death, and suggested that this would have been in the interests of his genius, because obviously his genius would have died simultaneously. It seems to me that anyone who realised the disasters that might have happened to Swinburne but for Watts-Dunton would see that he was doing the right thing. Gosse had a special delight in that peculiar type of literature which later on became associated with Lytton Strachey. He once said that he had modelled himself on the cat, so that he would at one moment be very pleasant and stretch out a velvet paw, and the next moment, before the victim was aware, he was receiving a pretty deep scratch. Barry Pain had no great opinion of Gosse as an expert on Swinburne, and in a letter to me enclosed some lines which expressed his feelings on a certain eulogy which Gosse had written on Swinburne after his death:

> Whatever ill our thorny path attends;
> May God Almighty save us from our friends!
> Or if His wisdom still ordains this cross,
> Spare us at least a eulogy from Gosse.

It seems to me really a sin against the integrity of literary history that Gosse and Wise should have omitted from the collected edition of Swinburne all the elaborate dedications to Watts-Dunton, except one very small one which they possibly overlooked. They omitted the twenty-page prose dedication which Swinburne gave as a preface to the collected edition published in his lifetime, and in which he called Watts-Dunton "his best and dearest friend"; they omitted his name from the dedication of another volume. They retained the poem in which the dedication was made, but they omitted the name of the dedicatee, although the last lines of that poem said—and they were perfectly true as a description of Watts-Dunton's protection of Swinburne:

> There is a friend, that as the wise man saith,
> Cleaves closer than a brother. Nor to me
> Hath time not shown through days like waves at strife
> This pearl, most precious found in all the sea,
> That washes towards your feet, these waifs of life.

That is exactly what Swinburne would have been himself if it had not been for Watts-Dunton: "a waif of life." As it was, he had a very happy life spent among his books, and he was able to produce—perhaps his greatest work—"Songs before Sunrise," which we should not have had if it hadn't been for Watts-Dunton. For instance, the world would be very unwilling to lose that great poem "In San Lorenzo," in which Swinburne invokes the marble figure of night by Michelangelo.

> Is thine hour come to wake, O slumbering Night?
> Hath not the Dawn a message in thine ear?
> Though thou be stone and sleep, yet shalt thou hear
> When the word falls from heaven—Let there be light.
> Thou knowest we would not do thee the despite
> To wake thee while the old sorrow and shame were near;
> We spake not loud for thy sake, and for fear
> Lest thou shouldst lose the rest that was thy right,

The blessing given thee that was thine alone,
The happiness to sleep and to be stone:
Nay, we kept silence of thee for thy sake
Albeit we knew thee alive, and left with thee
The great good gift to feel not nor to see;
But will not yet thine Angel bid thee wake?

A GIANT IN HER FIELD

Morton M. Hunt

Dr. Helaine Newstead, professor of English at Hunter College, is a scholar who specializes in tracing the origins of the characters, incidents, and minor details of the medieval Arthurian romances, starting with the earliest French texts and going back to their sources in Welsh and Irish legend, via the intermediate step of the bilingual Bretons of northern France—a task made no easier for her by the fact that not a trace remains of any Breton writing. In her intellectual life she resembles a foreigner in an obscure land; she is surrounded by people she cannot converse with, and her occasional meetings with one of her own countrymen are almost painfully sweet. "The number of people I can talk with about my work is extremely limited," she remarked rather wistfully the other day. Admittedly, she belongs to two organizations of similarly dedicated individuals—the Arthurian Romances group of the Modern Language Association of America and the Société Internationale Arthurienne—but the former, which has about two hundred members, meets only once a year, and the latter, which has about three hundred (many of the memberships, of course, overlap), meets only once every third year. Because she is so cut off, professionally, from the outside world, it can be readily understood how delighted she was a couple of years ago when she was invited to join a seminar of distinguished medievalists on the faculty of Columbia University who meet for dinner once a month at the Men's Faculty Club and then sit around the table talking shop. "It's wonderful, being with people like that," Miss Newstead told a group of non-medievalist acquaintances at a party during the holidays last December. "Why, there are fifteen of us, and we put in one whole year just discussing the subject of courtly love!" After disposing of courtly love, the seminar went on to other things, and in due time Miss Newstead was asked to read an after-dinner paper on King Mark's ears, which in some versions of the Tristan story are said to have been those of a horse. To have the undivided attention of fourteen persons who could comprehend what she was talking about was for Miss Newstead a heady experience indeed.

Permission the author; © 1957 The New Yorker Magazine, Inc.

As a humanist scholar—a scholar engaged in studying one of what Webster rather mincingly describes as "the branches of polite learning regarded as primarily conducive to culture"—Miss Newstead has more occasion than her colleagues in the branches of utilitarian learning to hear the bromidic taunt that the ideal member of her profession is "someone who knows more and more about less and less." In a sense, though hardly in the disparaging one intended, the characterization is warranted. This is especially true when it is applied to scholars interested in a subject like the Middle Ages—a field already raked over with such thoroughness that anyone eager to contribute something original must really scratch around to find a bit of unexplored territory. As a rule, the claim that the medieval scholar finally stakes out for himself is so remote, and the fragments of learning it yields are so arcane, that the whole project becomes unintelligible to the outsider, who thereupon tends to dismiss it as pointless.

Miss Newstead is not inclined to quibble with critics of this sort; indeed, to a certain extent she goes along with their more-and-more wheeze. Where she does differ with them is in the value she attaches to knowing more and more about anything—even about less and less. "Arthurian scholarship plays its part—a small part, to be sure—in preserving a record of man's cultural history," she gently informed a dinner companion a few months ago. "I admit that many people can see no point to it, and I also admit that it produces no immediate results, like engineering or medical research. Even some of the anthropologists—who, after all, aren't in the least utilitarian—don't understand us. In fact, one of the best of them told me that I ought to switch over to anthropology so that I could be dealing with something real. Well, my answer was, and is, that I *am* dealing with something real—the life history of a body of legend. Every new thing I learn about it tells us more about man himself. I suppose that's the final justification for scholarship. But personally I have never felt any need to justify it."

From the scholar's point of view, Arthurian literature is essentially a group of long romances—some of them in verse—written during the Middle Ages in any one of several languages and centering on the affairs of King Arthur and his court at Camelot. While these romances have the flavor of history, or at least of historical novels, they actually seem to have been almost entirely fictional. To be sure, it is a generally accepted hypothesis that there was a real Arthurian castle (possibly in Wales) and a real Arthur (a warrior but not a king), who in the late fifth or early sixth century led the Celts in their efforts to throw back the Teutonic invaders of England. But scholars have been able to find only one mention of the fellow before the eighth century—and that a mere phrase in a seventh-century Welsh poem "Gododdin," which tells of a Briton the ravens fed on, "though he was no Arthur." Tristan's Isolt was unknown to this Arthur, if he did exist, for it is certain that she didn't; no Lancelot was on hand to become Arthur's best friend and the seducer of his wife (who, assuming Arthur had one, was in all probability not named Guinevere); and Arthur almost surely never heard of the Holy Grail, which, as first conceived, is thought to have had no significance as a Christian symbol. Not being a medieval historian, Miss Newstead isn't the slightest bit interested in who or what the real Arthur was, or may have been, or who his associates were. "I'm not at all concerned with the facts of Arthur's life and deeds," she says. "I'm concerned only with the life story of the *legend*, and what it reveals about creative man." The legend reveals very little information about creative man until the twelfth century, when Arthur began to emerge in literature as a figure of prominence. As time passed, his stature grew, and writers, drawing on the old legends and other sources that are the particular province of Miss Newstead's studies, made him a king. Then they gave him his world-famous court and the Knights of the Round Table, and extended his rule to numerous domains; Tristan and Isolt entered the picture, along with Lancelot and Queen Guinevere, and the Holy Grail, now identified with the Last Supper, became one of the principal themes of the legend.

The Arthurian legend provided the most popular of the stories with which the members of the medieval aristocracy throughout Europe whiled away their spare time. Although these stories have lived on and have established a respectable place for themselves in the literature of all ages, very little is known about the writers responsible for them or about the sources of their inspiration. Arthurians feel a keen need to illuminate these dark areas, but for the most part their fellow-citizens do not share their sense of urgency in the matter and are content to let them do their illuminating on their own time and at their own expense. Miss Newstead's one great object in life has been to provide the needed light by means of tireless and painstaking study, and while her efforts have brought her some fame as one of the world's leading Arthurian scholars, they have brought her no fortune whatever. Indeed, if it were not for her salary from Hunter, where she has been on the faculty for twenty-nine years and where she conducts such routine courses as Freshman Composition, Medieval Literature, Chaucer, and History of English Literature, the already thin ranks of the Arthurians would probably be diminished by one.

A small woman of fifty, Miss Newstead has almost none of the physical attributes that have come to be popularly associated with the scholar. A somewhat receding chin, a prominent nose, and thick glasses combine to give her a pleasantly birdlike appearance; she wears her brown hair short, and her comfortable, middle-aged silhouette bears no hint of the ascetic. Unlike the cardboard scholar of the movies, she has been known to go swimming and to take a walk in the country; she frequently bustles around town after dark to attend poetry readings, plays, operas, and concerts (she is likely to anticipate such occasions with a visit to her hairdresser, where a friend recently discovered her sitting under the dryer deeply absorbed in a volume on Pictish archeology); and she sometimes accepts (but almost as often declines) invitations from her many friends to join them at Sunday dinner. About all that prevents her from being a typical maiden aunt is that, as an only child, she has no nieces or nephews. She is, however, known as Aunt Helaine to the children of several of her friends, and these youngsters think of her primarily as a genial lady who brings them presents now and then or stands treat for a lunch at Longchamps. But although no movie producer would type-cast Miss Newstead as a scholar, she has established herself as an almost perfect example of one. She is happiest when she is spending a long, silent evening or weekend in the untidy study of an otherwise extremely neat and comfortably furnished apartment on East Ninety-third Street, where she lives alone. There, surrounded by an array of books dealing with early myths, sagas, legends, and rituals of many lands, she may sit for hours poring over an antiquated Welsh genealogy or squinting through a magnifying glass at the crabbed letters in a photostatic copy of the text of some little-known medieval Latin narrative. Usually she spends her Christmas, spring, and summer vacations in the same way, but now and then she takes a summer trip to Europe. Even there the story is much the same; she does a little sightseeing and she calls on a few scholars, but she passes fully half her time in places like the Bodleian Library, at Oxford, and the University Library, at Cambridge, scrutinizing card indexes and collections of ancient manuscripts.

Once in a while in the course of her long and patient quest, Miss Newstead will come upon a scrap of previously overlooked evidence, indicating, perhaps, that an incident in one of the Arthurian stories bears a singular similarity to some happening in an old Irish myth, and then her excitement is such that she can't sleep that night. It may even be that she has found something important enough to warrant her writing an article about it for publication in one of the several scholarly journals that are edited for medievalists. Miss Newstead has had nine such articles published, and these stand out like multicolored mileposts along the normally neutral-toned path her life has taken. Each of them announces, in an almost impenetrably learned prose that in no way reflects her inner elation, the addition of one more tiny morsel to mankind's prodigious store of knowledge, and the fact that the morsel can be assimilated by fewer than five hundred persons throughout the world (Japan, incidentally, is a comparative hotbed of Arthurians) does not in the least diminish the excitement she derives from her accomplishment.

In the eyes of many competent teachers who just don't happen to care for scholarly research and the composition of learned papers, Miss Newstead is an exceedingly fortunate woman, since the sort of outside study and writing she revels in is a prerequisite for advancement—if not, indeed, for simple survival—in most colleges, where a would-be professor must heed the dictum "Publish or perish." There is no doubt that even if such pressures did not exist, Miss Newstead would be just as diligent in unearthing bits of knowledge and setting them down on paper, but at the same time she is fully aware of the material advantages that these undertakings have brought her. Since 1928, when she joined the Hunter faculty as a tutor in the English Department at a below-subsistence-level salary, her published writings, in addition to her nine articles, have consisted of one book, eight book reviews (another form of expression that greatly enhances a scholar's prestige), and a chapter apiece in three books edited by other scholars; moreover, she has delivered about a dozen lectures before various groups of medievalists. From none of this has she made a cent. But each year in making out a report to the President's office on her accomplishments during the past twelve months—a requirement imposed on all faculty members—she has not overlooked mentioning the writings she has published and the lectures she has delivered in that period, and it is safe to say that these professional cachets have had at least something to do with the fact that she has moved ahead, slowly but steadily, from rank to rank in the academic hierarchy, until in 1954 she became a full professor, at $7,850 a year. (Today, her salary is $10,750.) It is a commentary of sorts on the educational system that while at least some of her advancement almost certainly came about as a result of her study of Arthurian literature, she has never had an opportunity to teach a course in the subject, since none is included in the Hunter curriculum.

Studying the life history of a body of legend is not as fleshless a pursuit as might be imagined. An example of how earthy Arthurians can sometimes get is to be found in an energetic controversy Miss Newstead has been engaged in for nine years. The point at issue is whether two legendary characters—a young lady named Blancheflor and a young man named Perceval (also known as Parsifal)—behaved in a chaste or unchaste manner while spending a night together. In "Le Conte del Graal," a long, rhymed romance by the twelfth-century poet Chrétien de Troyes, Perceval stops off at a castle called Belrepaire, where he is welcomed and given a bed for the night. Presently he is awakened by the sound of someone weeping at his bedside; it is Blancheflor, the lady of the castle, who has come *en déshabillé*[1] from her bed to tell him her troubles (an enemy has been besieging her). Perceval comforts her and then invites her to spend the rest of the night with him, and the lady straightway crawls in. In the course of an exhaustive study of the characteristics common to besieged ladies in those days—published in the September, 1948, issue of *Publications of the Modern Language Association*, the most widely read of the learned journals she contributes to—Miss Newstead registered her disagreement with a scholar who had speculated that the couple's conduct was chaste. After all, she pointed out, the poet himself had clearly specified that they lay all night *"boche a boche, braz a braz."*[2]

So deliberate is the pace of scholarly argument that not until three years later did Miss Newstead learn that her stand on the matter had produced

---

[1]See the English word *dishabille*.

[2]Mouth to mouth, arm in arm. But notice that all the Latin and Old French passages are translated, very neatly, in the article.

a new adversary—Sister M. Amelia Klenke, a Dominican nun and professor of French in Columbus, Ohio. In 1951, addressing a group of scholars, including Miss Newstead, at a convention of the Modern Language Association, Sister Amelia vigorously asserted Blancheflor's purity. In all scholarly friendliness, Miss Newstead rose and learnedly dissented. A year later, an indignant article by Sister Amelia appeared in the 1952–53 winter issue of the periodical *Romance Philology*, in which she warned, "We must be alert and sensitive to his [Chrétien's] use of symbolism and to his mastery of the liturgy." Then, strewing references as prodigally as a baker strews flour, she held that the account of Perceval's night with Blancheflor was an artful portrayal of one step in his spiritual evolution and was not intended as realism at all. Furthermore, Sister Amelia observed, Perceval couldn't have had carnal contact with Blancheflor, because he didn't mention it in his subsequent confession to a hermit priest, and she topped this off by calling attention to a passage in which Chrétien himself specifically stated that Perceval enjoyed every comfort in bed except the love of woman—and of that, in the poet's own words, "he knew nothing at all, nor did he give it the slightest thought." Finally, Sister Amelia reminded her readers that under the medieval code of *l'amour courtois*[3] couples could engage in any sort of conduct and still be considered chaste, provided only that they avoided actual intercourse.

Having read this, Miss Newstead did not hurry to her desk, scribble a blistering retort, and shoot it right off to Sister Amelia. Instead, she went over Sister Amelia's article line by line, and spent many hours in libraries and in her study consulting half a hundred books and shorter treatises. Only then did she feel in a position to draft a suitable reply, which she did in the form of an article, bristling with erudition, that was printed in the 1953–54 winter issue of *Romance Philology*. In it, she dispassionately skewered Sister Amelia for the way she had used the quotation about Perceval's not giving a thought to the love of woman; in the poem, she observed, that passage precedes the account of Blancheflor's visit to the young man's bed—a sequence that Sister Amelia had neglected to mention. Miss Newstead also expressed the belief that in his confession Perceval might easily have overlooked any indiscretions with Blancheflor, since he was equally silent about having committed the worse sin of abandoning his mother. As for the business about *l'amour courtois*, it was her opinion that Chrétien would most likely not have invoked the code in connection with his hero, since the poet indicated elsewhere that he disapproved of the whole concept, and especially of its most bizarre manifestation, called *amor purus*, which, in the words of Andreas Capellanus, a twelfth-century cleric whom she quoted, ". . . *procedit autem usque ad oris osculum lacertique amplexum et verecundum amantis nudae contactum, extremo praetermisso solatio* . . ." What's more, she wrote, since St. Thomas Aquinas had ruled the libidinous kiss and touch to be mortal sins, how could anyone contend that all had been unsinful at Belrepaire

[3]Courtly love.

after reading Chrétien's description of the way the couple spent the night?
And she quoted it:

> *Et cil la beisoit,*
> *Qui an ses braz la tenoit prise,*
> *Si l'a soz le covertor mise*
> *Tot soavet et tot a eise;*
> *Et cele suefre qu'il la beise,*
> *Ne ne cuit pas qu'il li enuit.*
> *Einsi jurent tote la nuit,*
> *Li uns lez l'autre, boche a boche,*
> *Jusqu'au main que li jorz aproche.*
> *Tant li fist la nuit de solaz*
> *Que boche a boche, braz a braz,*
> *Dormirent tant qu'il ajorna.*

Miss Newstead's presentation of these two quotations—so tantalizing to
the layman because he can almost but not quite understand them—is characteristic of the way she and other Arthurian scholars communicate with
one another. It might be thought that prudishness dissuaded her from
translating the passages—obviously the most savory part of her argument
—but nothing could be further from the truth. Arthurian scholars expect
nobody to read their writings except other Arthurian scholars, and one and
all would have considered it a gratuitous insult to their intelligence if she
had provided translations. Miss Newstead could feel confident that any of
the readers she had in mind when she wrote her reply to Sister Amelia, no
matter what their native tongue or what part of the world they were living
in, would find Andreas's definition as clear as the prose in a grade-school
reader: "It [pure love] proceeds as far as the kiss and the embrace and the
modest contact with the nude lover, omitting the final solace." Moreover,
it would take an Arthurian less than thirty seconds to skim over the Chrétien quotation and realize that by St. Thomas's standards the couple were
unquestionably unchaste, for, as described by the poet, this is how they
spent the night:

> And he kissed her,
> Who held her clasped in his arms,
> And he placed her under the coverlet
> Quite softly and quite at ease;
> And she permitted him to kiss her,
> Nor do I believe that it displeased her.
> Thus they lay the whole night,
> The one beside the other, mouth to mouth,
> Until morning when the day approached.
> So much solace did he give her that night
> That mouth to mouth, arm in arm,
> They slept until day broke.

After Miss Newstead's broadside, the furor over just what went on that
night at Belrepaire Castle and how to classify it subsided for a couple of

years while Sister Amelia prepared for the next round. Her barrage came in the January, 1956, issue of a journal called *Studies in Philology*, in which she sharply scolded Miss Newstead and then, without offering much in the way of new evidence to support her all-was-well theory, defended Blancheflor as the very personification of chastity and interpreted Perceval's night with the lady as indicative of his growing love of continence. Miss Newstead got the impression that the tone of Sister Amelia's latest riposte was more personal than scholarly, and she now says that she intends to let it go unanswered. In the past few months, however, two other Arthurians have entered the dispute, taking her side against the doughty nun and leaving little reason to suppose that the controversy will not continue to flare fitfully for at least another nine years.

Non-Arthurian friends who have won Miss Newstead's confidence know that she regards the peccadilloes of the knights and ladies of King Arthur's court with tolerance and amusement. People who know her only through her writings, however—even the stanchest Arthurians—sometimes have a hard time sifting out this or any other attitude, owing to Miss Newstead's exuberant use of quotations in little-known ancient tongues. It is all very well, one of her colleagues observed not long ago, to define *amor purus* in Latin, a language that almost every student of the humanities is familiar with; the trouble is that Miss Newstead, an extraordinarily versatile linguist, is also capable of breaking out into Anglo-Norman, Middle High German, Early Italian, Old English, Middle English, Old Norse, Old French, Old Irish, and Early Dutch, as well as modern French, German, and Italian. In so doing, it appears, she makes a too generous estimate of her fellow-scholars' attainments, since few have the time, the inclination, or the capacity to learn such a string of languages. Miss Newstead's position on this point is not wholly consistent, though; she condescends to translate all her Welsh quotations because she happens to regard that language as a barbaric slag heap of agglomerated consonants and cemented-together syllables, very difficult for anybody to read.

To friends who marvel at her wide-ranging repertoire of languages, Miss Newstead explains casually that she "just picked them up" as she went along. And here again, pretty much by accident, her scholarship gives her added standing in workaday academic society. In such circles, each language mastered is comparable to a military decoration earned, while the appearance in a published paper of a lavish array of untranslated quotations from many discarded languages is much like the rows of ribbons on a hero's chest.

Another medium of communication among the small coterie of the enlightened is the scholarly footnote. To those people who, unindoctrinated but interested, hover uncertainly on the fringes of Miss Newstead's cerebral world, her expert use of the device gives her writing an impressively erudite hallmark. Even the most determined non-Arthurian can hardly help admiring her footnotes as exquisite little nuggets of the scholar's art.

Their charm lies not so much in the many familiar Latin signposts with which she peppers them (*viz., ib., loc. cit., cf., passim,* and so on) as in the way she is able to compress the results of prolonged study into an elegantly compact pill of information. The composition of footnotes takes up a good deal of Miss Newstead's time. Night after night, she sits in her study, with a portable typewriter on a table in front of her and books and back issues of her favorite journals precariously piled in heaps and windrows all around her—on the window sill, on the floor, on her desk, on the typewriter's cover, on a sofa—each with slips of paper inserted in it to mark appropriate passages. Boxes of her own notes stand open, with more slips of paper sticking out of key spots; masses of manuscripts, letters, and reprints of papers by her colleagues are stacked here and there in ink-soiled snowdrifts of learning. Presiding over this chaos—darting first right, then left, nibbling at one book after another, extracting a word or a phrase or a name or a date from some source near the window or near the door or beneath her chair—she may manage after an hour's work to compress the product of several weeks of research into a single footnote. In one of her most recent articles, "The Tryst Beneath the Tree: An Episode in the Tristan Legend," published in the February, 1956, issue of *Romance Philology,* she endeavors to track down the origins of an episode: King Mark has hidden in a tree to spy on Tristan and Isolt, but they see him there, and put him off the scent by pretending to hate each other. "One version [of this episode] current in the twelfth century," Miss Newstead's text reads, "is the Latin tale *Lidia,* composed about 1175 but based on an earlier French source.[47]" Here is footnote No. 47:

> G. Cohen, *La "Comédie" latine en France au XIIe siècle* (Paris, 1931), I, 213–246. This is evidently the source of Boccaccio's tale, *Decameron,* VII, 9. For analogues see A. C. Lee, *The Decameron, Its Sources and Analogues* (London, 1909), pp. 236–244. J. D. Bruce, *Evolution,* I, 187, suggested the "Pear Tree Story" as the source of the episode; but, as Mrs. Dempster has pointed out (W. F. Bryan and G. Dempster, *Sources and Analogues of the Canterbury Tales* [Chicago, 1941], pp. 341–356), one must distinguish between those versions, like Chaucer's *Merchant's Tale,* in which the blind husband's sight is restored, and the others, like *Lidia,* where the deceived husband's vision is normal. Cf. Bédier, *Les Fabliaux* (4th ed.; Paris, 1925), pp. 269 f.

As an academic bench mark, this is all that it should be—a condensed guide to the reader, telling him where to go if he wants to dig deeper. But as a work of art it is far more than that. It is the scholar's equivalent of a coloratura soprano's cadenza—an interpolation that flirts and trills as it swiftly and flawlessly skips through four reference sources, three original literary works, and two contrasting theories, and winds up by nonchalantly uncorking a fifth, and key, reference ("Cf. Bédier," etc.), much like the singer's bravura high D that ends the performance and brings down the house.

Footnote No. 47 represents many years of study, reflective thinking, and the orderly arrangement of knowledge, all distilled by Miss Newstead into a few lines of small type. It is one of sixty-seven footnotes appended to an article that, no doubt, will itself survive chiefly as a footnote to another article, by some future scholar. Thus does knowledge of the humanities accumulate, a grain at a time. Scholars absorbed in that branch of learning earnestly believe that the grains eventually compose a great bin of knowledge, from which present-day society can derive a better understanding of its antecedents and the development of its culture. Reward for contributing these grains must come principally from within, for present-day society seems to have put a rather low valuation on the privilege of finding out how it came to be what it is. Teachers of the humanities are not paid very well, and as a result there are relatively few of them—only twenty-eight thousand out of a total of about a hundred and fifty thousand men and women now teaching in American colleges and universities. A mere one and a half per cent of them are paid as much as ten thousand dollars a year, and the median annual salary for the group runs around five thousand—approximately what hourly workers in automobile factories and oil refineries receive. Unlike a teacher of chemistry, say, who may at any time be offered a better-paid job in industry, teachers of the humanities can have little hope of employment elsewhere.

Despite this bleak material outlook, however, and despite—or perhaps because of—a certain feeling of being cut off from the main stream of contemporary life, humanist scholars appear to be for the most part a reasonably contented lot. A substantial proportion of them are persons who, as adolescents, found that an afternoon spent alone exploring a library's stacks was more satisfying than sitting with a crowd in a football stadium or gossiping with classmates at a soda fountain. Miss Newstead counts herself one of this group. Possibly being an only child has something to do with the fact that as far back as she can remember she has been accustomed to solitude and to turning to books for relaxation. She was born in 1906, in an apartment house on Seventh Avenue near 113th Street—a neighborhood that is now part of Harlem and was then inhabited to a large extent by moderately successful Jewish businessmen and their families. Miss Newstead's father, Nathan, was a brewer's representative, and both he and his wife got just about all the intellectual stimulation they wanted from evenings of pinochle or small talk with friends, but they were determined to give their daughter the sort of background that would lead to a richer life—preferably as a concert pianist. (Mrs. Newstead had named her daughter Helaine—an Old French version of Helen—not because of any premonitory glimpse of the Arthurian future but simply because she wanted the child in every way to rise above the ordinary.) To this end, while Miss Newstead was attending Hunter College High School, on Lexington Avenue and Sixty-eighth Street, her parents practically insisted that she simultaneously put in a considerable number of hours a week at the Institute of Musical Art (now the Juilliard School of Music), where they hoped she would establish herself as a genius. Not only did she fail to achieve this end but her health nearly broke under the strain of attending two schools at once. She thereupon abandoned the idea of becoming a pianist, which gave her a lot more time for her real interest in life—reading books.

Never in her youth did Miss Newstead have much of a social life. As a child, she had no time for one because of her crowded educational schedule. She entered Hunter College in the fall of 1923, and soon began to distinguish herself in language and literature courses. Then excessive reading, coupled with a nutritional deficiency, brought on a painful eye inflammation that plagued her for more than a year. "There I was in college right in the middle of the roaring twenties," she recalled not long ago. "But I wasn't in any mood to go along on gin parties or wild automobile rides, even if someone had asked me. I was a longhair, and no doubt about it—constantly going to concerts and the theatre, and I guess I did pretty well in my classes, too." The satisfaction she derived from her classroom triumphs more than made up to her for any lack of gaiety in her way of living. "Helaine was a typical scholar even when she was an undergraduate," a former classmate of Miss Newstead's has said. "Before she was twenty, she already had a way of talking like a learned person. She never went in for idle girl-talk, like the rest of us." The elder Newsteads, recovered from their disappointment at their daughter's failure to become a musical genius, were delighted with the way things were turning out. It almost seemed that the less they understood about her intellectual interests the more they admired her.

In June, 1927, Miss Newstead graduated from Hunter *magna cum laude*, taking with her, in addition to her diploma, the assurance of Dr. Blanche Colton Williams, the chairman of the English Department, that if she would immediately go on to study for a Master's degree at Columbia, she would stand a good chance of landing a job on the Hunter teaching staff the following year. Accordingly, she went ahead and got an M.A. in English, and in 1928 was appointed a tutor at Hunter. "I was terrified of my students," she recalled the other day. "I was a scared little rabbit." For the next eleven years, she devoted her after-class hours to getting a Ph.D. at Columbia, where she studied under Professor Roger Sherman Loomis, now retired, who is generally regarded as the ranking Arthurian in the United States. A tall, erect, and intensely consecrated scholar, Loomis has long contended that, notwithstanding the claims of an opposition party based mostly in France and Germany, the Arthurian romances derive more of their substance from early Celtic story patterns than from the inventive imaginations of French poets and storytellers. The derivation of the romances is clearly a matter of fundamental concern to Arthurian scholars, and from the beginning of her postgraduate days Miss Newstead has been in Loomis's corner during every round of the dispute. He saw in her the makings of a scholar when, shortly after she had enrolled in a seminar he was conducting on the riddles that bedevil Arthurians, he asked if any of the group could read German easily. Miss Newstead said that she could, whereupon the Professor handed her a sheaf of German articles discussing the Mabinogion, a controversial collection of Welsh prose romances, and instructed her to summarize their contents. She turned in such a proficient performance that even Loomis, brusque and crusty by nature, could not restrain a cautious display of admiration. She has been his protégée ever since, now and then tagging along with him and his wife on trips to European caves and old castles that may have some bearing on the Arthurian legend. "I can kid Helaine about herself and her work but not about Loomis," a Columbia professor said recently. "That's the way it is with scholars. All the rest of their lives, they figuratively stand up whenever the man who started them off enters the room."

While working for her Ph.D. under Loomis, Miss Newstead made her first significant contribution to Arthuriana. Listening one day in the spring of 1934 as the Professor elaborated on the confusions arising from errors that medieval scribes made in copying manuscripts, she experienced one of those flashes of intuition whereby the murky becomes clear. It occurred to her that if, by any chance, the word "*cort*," meaning "court," as it appears at one point in a Chrétien romance called "Erec," had originally been "*cor*," meaning "horn," many small references in the text that seemed to make no sense would take their part in a logical pattern of thought. Strongly encouraged by Loomis, she spent an entire summer writing a paper on the subject, with such impressive results that she was invited to read it at the 1935 convention of the Modern Language Association, and the following year it was printed in *PMLA*.

The horn Miss Newstead discovered in "Erec" was the horn of Bran, an ancient Welsh sea-god, whose half-forgotten chronicle, truncated and mangled, lies buried in several twelfth-century Arthurian romances. Bran, she became convinced, was the original of the mysterious "Fisher King" of the romances, and for her doctoral dissertation she would disinter his bones from every Arthurian tale in which she could find a trace of them and thus strengthen the evidence that the Welsh did indeed make important contributions to the French romances about King Arthur. It was slow going, for her classes at Hunter took much of her time, but in 1937, with the help of a six-month leave of absence from teaching, during which she spent every weekday from nine to five in the Columbia library, she passed the oral examination for her doctorate and entered the home-stretch—completing the written dissertation. Nightly, she worked over her notes until nearly dawn, disregarding the entreaties of her gentle, devoted mother. (Mr. Newstead had died some years earlier.) Mrs. Newstead never asked what the dissertation was to be about; she knew it would make her daughter a Doctor of Philosophy, and that was all that mattered.

In 1939, climaxing eleven years of this kind of after-hours toil, Miss Newstead completed her dissertation and received her Ph.D. By then, she

had found resemblances to Bran embedded in twenty-two Arthurian characters (of whom the best known is the wounded Grail King Anfortas—or
Amfortas, as he appears in Wagner's "Parsifal") as well as echoes of his
exploits in a number of references to Arthurian feasts, battles, castles, and
miracles. Her dissertation, calling attention to these similarities, was published by the Columbia University Press under the title "Bran the Blessed
in Arthurian Romance," and bears the dedication "To My Mother." Those
three words and the title page were the only parts of the volume that Mrs.
Newstead ever tried to read, but her pride in the accomplishment was tremendous and, until her death five years ago, it surged up every time she
heard Helaine addressed as "Dr. Newstead."

As books go, "Bran the Blessed" is a short one—a mere fifty thousand
words—but it has an extremely high specific gravity: five hundred and
thirty-two footnotes, two hundred and fifty-eight listings in its bibliography, and two hundred and five quotations, both long and short, in
Latin, Old French, Anglo-Norman, Old German, and Welsh. The publishing of such a work bears about as much likeness to commercial publishing as the two-toed sloth does to the gazelle. A new novel has to sell anywhere from seven to ten thousand copies in order to break even, and if
after the first year its annual sales drop below a hundred or so, it is liable
to be remaindered and dumped on bargain counters in the vicinity of
Forty-second Street and Sixth Avenue, priced at around nineteen cents a
copy. In the rather different case of "Bran the Blessed," only five hundred
copies were run off, a printing order that was based on the most sanguine
estimate of the potential demand for copies; there was never any thought
of the book's breaking even financially. University-press managers look
forward calmly to losing money on all the works of rarefied scholarship
they publish, even if a whole edition should sell out. Their deficits are
covered by subsidies from the universities or from foundations, and it is
therefore hardly surprising that they find themselves publishing most of
the thousand or more scholarly books that appear each year. About a
tenth of these books, according to the rules of the game and the decisions
of the press's trustees, are paid for by the authors themselves. Painful
though this may be for struggling young students, most of them manage
to scare up enough money to back their manuscripts, stoically realizing
that it is all part of the business of making one's way as a scholar. Doctoral theses being within that unhappy tenth, the printing costs of "Bran
the Blessed"—a matter of nine hundred and ninety-three dollars—had to
be borne by Miss Newstead, and neither she nor anyone else had the
slightest expectation that she would recoup them. Seventy-five copies
were presented, free, to the Columbia library, in accordance with the
Ph.D. requirements then in effect. (Three typed copies and one micro-
filmed copy now suffice.) "You might call the other four hundred and
twenty-five copies our trade edition," Henry Wiggins, Manager of the
Publication Department of the Columbia University Press, told a visitor

a couple of months ago. Then he broke into an uneasy, slightly bitter spasm of laughter. "Trade edition!" he gasped. "Oh dear, oh dear!"

Mr. Wiggins went on to explain that sixty-six additional free copies of "Bran the Blessed" were sent to reviewers or to friends of Miss Newstead, and that the first year's actual sales, most of them to libraries, reached a trim total of fifty-nine copies, at two dollars and twenty-five cents apiece. During the second year, as might be expected, demand fell off somewhat, and fifteen copies were sold. Over the next eight years, annual sales ranged from two to ten copies. In 1949, inexplicably, they zoomed to a total of twenty-nine copies; then the yearly average dropped to four and a third until 1956, when the sales figure bounced modestly to thirteen. In all, a hundred and eighty-three copies have been sold, netting Miss Newstead $90.50 in royalties. Of a hundred and sixty-nine copies that Wiggins and his colleagues prudently did not bind, pending a call for them, a hundred and forty-four have been destroyed and twenty-five have been given to Miss Newstead, leaving seven bound copies still in stock. Now, seventeen years after the début of "Bran the Blessed," Wiggins, harassed by the trouble and expense of carrying such odds and ends on his inventory, would dearly love to throw out this lingering remnant of a publication that typifies what university-press people call, with mixed emotions, "a saleless wonder." But when he hinted to Miss Newstead that it might be well to dispose of the seven copies, she became so distressed that he didn't have the heart to proceed. "It's an important book," she told him. "And I'm not the only one who feels that a library anywhere in the world should be able to buy a copy as long as there are any left." Avarice definitely has nothing to do with Miss Newstead's position, since royalties from the seven copies would still leave her almost nine hundred dollars shy of getting back her original investment.

Desire to "add to the sum of human knowledge" (a favorite cliché in the trade) and eagerness to gain academic promotion neatly combine to bring forth annually a devastating quantity of scholarly literature. According to an authoritative estimate, nearly one out of every two college teachers of language and literature gets something into print every year. Arthurians do even better; in a single year, the Société Internationale Arthurienne has noted in its annual bibliography as many as two hundred and forty-six works, or almost one per member; to keep his head above water in these seas, a conscientious Arthurian would have to read nearly five treatises a week—a task impossible for body, spirit, and most budgets. Since 1922, when records started being kept, more than forty-six hundred additions to the sum of Arthurian knowledge have appeared. "Sometimes when I'm feeling tired, I think that at last the Arthurian field must be exhausted," Miss Newstead said a while ago. "But it never is. There's *so* much yet to do. Take one example—the thing I'm interested in right now. That's the need to disentangle the Wagnerian influence and reveal the original Tristan story in its true light. Most people, including many scholars, think of this legend as a solemn tragedy, with weighty moral significance. That's Wagner's fault. The real Tristan legend was a rattling good story—full of adventures, hair-raising escapes, and moments of low farce. That's what originally made it so popular." Miss Newstead has been working intermittently for eight years on a massive study of the Tristan legend, which she expects will clear away the Germanic under-brush that has grown up around a lusty medieval tale.

An auxiliary literary exercise that is rated highly among scholars—and one at which Miss Newstead excels—is reviewing books by other scholars in the pages of their favorite journals. This, too, can add a tidbit now and then to the sum of human knowledge, since a scholar's review of a scholarly book bears little similarity to an ordinary book review in that the reviewer is not content simply to offer a synopsis and evaluation of the book's contents but feels obliged to demonstrate that his own scholar-ship is at least as formidable as the author's. Bringing this off successfully is likely to entail a prolonged period of research. "Helaine Newstead may occasionally annoy an editor by excessively delaying a promised review but not by submitting one hastily written," says Professor Yakov Malkiel, of the University of California, at Berkeley, who himself edits *Romance Philology*. Miss Newstead admits that it has taken her as much as a year to do a book review, and when she describes the way she goes about it, one easily understands why. After reading the book, she goes over it again, checking every line for misquotations, misinterpretations, omissions, or other shortcomings. Then, with a perhaps quite damaging list of these at her elbow, she starts to write, and—in an effort to be fair to the author by thoroughly documenting her criticisms and to the reader by presenting a detailed background of the subject—she stirs in generous portions of quotation, citation, and parenthetical comment as she goes along, producing an extremely concentrated brew that outsiders are likely to find even more difficult to assimilate than her original writings. As if to make her reviews still less palatable to the general reader, she re-fuses to spice them, in the manner of some scholars, with injections of personal feeling. Among the reviews of her own "Bran the Blessed" is an excellent example of this sort of spice, provided by the late Dr. A. H. Krappe, of the University of Minnesota, who, after taking issue with her over a minor point, grumpily wrote in a footnote: "It is unnecessary to discuss the matter more fully; this was done, years ago, in my study 'Lancelot et Guinièvre,' *Revue Celtique*, XLVIII, 94-123, which I find nowhere quoted."

Like the university-press approach to books, the business of getting out the journals in which so many of the accretions to knowledge are printed defies all the rules of conventional publishing. A manuscript re-ceived by one of these journals is read by the editor, or editors, and then, if it seems to be on the right track, is sent on to a succession of experts for appraisal. Since neither the editors nor the experts are paid for this work, and since they have other jobs for which they *are* paid, the manuscript may lie around on any one of their desks for months before being read. After a year or two, the manuscript may be returned to its author, either rejected or with suggestions for extensive revisions that have been recommended by the experts. If the revisions are made, the new manuscript, after another long wait, may or may not be accepted, and even if it is, it probably won't be published for another year or two, or even three. When, at last, it does appear, its author becomes literally a contributor, since the learned journals cannot afford to pay anything for the material they accept. The generous ones give an author seventy-five free reprints of his article; the rest charge him for any he may request. Because of Miss Newstead's high standing, she gets treated a little better by the journals than the average scholar does. Not that she receives any payment for her articles; it is just that the handling of her manuscripts is expedited to such an extent that they often show up in print less than a year after being submitted.

None of the journals to which Miss Newstead contributes has a circulation that puts much of a strain on the presses. *PMLA*, which has published three of her articles, far out-strips the rest of the field by circulating some 10,500 copies of each issue, no doubt because it covers a wider range of interests than the others. The *Journal of English and Germanic Philology*, in which she has been represented once, has a more modest, and more characteristic, circulation of 702. *Romance Philology*, which served Miss Newstead as a forum during part of her duel with Sister Amelia, and which has since made her a member of its Advisory Council, sells 232 copies of each issue to libraries and 233 to individual subscribers, and gives away 78, for a grand total of 543. "Scholars write for journals, read journals, make their students read journals, but rarely, rarely support journals by actually subscribing to them," the editor of *PMLA* complained in the December, 1954, issue of that publication. While some of the journals receive a little financial help from universities or foundations, their principal means of keeping going is a heavy reliance on what in less genteel circles might be called exploitation, or even slave labor. Still, although most scholars enjoy griping about this state of affairs, those who, like Miss Newstead, have achieved recognition by long and patient acquiescence give the impression of being at heart not opposed to a system that so pointedly makes learning its own reward.

In Miss Newstead's case, a quarter of a century of acquiescence to the system, far from accentuating the meek and submissive qualities that marked her character at the outset of her career, has given her confidence and a certain amount of pride in the work she has done. In her early days as a member of the Hunter faculty, her annual reports on her accomplishments consisted of a few meagre, half-apologetic notations over a faint and microscopic signature. In recent years, her reports have grown fat with explicit and straightforward entries, listing her research activities, her contributions to journals, and the honors that have come her way—

among them the chairmanship of the Arthurian Romances group of the Modern Language Association (1956–57), the presidency of the Medieval Club of New York (1950–52), and a Guggenheim Fellowship (1948–49), which started her off on her investigation of the Tristan legend—and her signature has grown steadily larger and more self-assertive, to the point where today it looks almost bold. She is still by no means an aggressive person, but in her flat, precise speech only occasionally does a residual "um" or "ah" occur as a reminder of her former timidity. "It's hard for me to imagine Helaine's ever having been shy," a Columbia professor who first met Miss Newstead only a few years ago said the other day. "If she was—and people do claim she was—then it's all disappeared since she became a giant in her field." Miss Newstead's colleagues at Hunter concede that she is a giant, but most of them are willing to take her stature on faith. "We all admire her work, but only by hearsay" is the way a senior member of the faculty there has put it. "I don't believe any of us has read more than one of her papers. While we can't always understand what Helaine is up to, we certainly do like the way she goes about it."

Some of Miss Newstead's associates of long standing have remarked that she has lately seemed to be developing what they call "the light touch" in her writing. Most laymen must be alerted in advance to a bit of scholarly humor if they are to detect its fleeting presence. As an example of how "amusingly" Miss Newstead can handle difficult material, a fellow-Arthurian cites one of her articles in which, after discussing a possible connection between two ancient tales, she observes, "These two stories are so divergent that one might well doubt any relationship between them, were it not for the inconvenient presence of the Grail as the central element in both." Very, very rarely, in Miss Newstead's writing, does the sound of elfin laughter rise to the thunderous level of a whisper. Conceivably it does in an article of hers that summarizes the plot of a twelfth-century romance: A maiden allows her many suitors to pay for the privilege of spending the night with her and then outsmarts them as soon as they get into bed by putting them to sleep with the help of a magic feather. At last, one of the suitors, while rearranging his pillow, happens to brush the feather onto the floor. "Thus," Miss Newstead concludes, with the scholar's equivalent of wanton hilarity, "to the maiden's great astonishment, he is able to fulfill the requirements."

Lacing learned texts with such froth would have been unthinkable to Miss Newstead before she reached her present eminence and the sense of security that goes with it, for in the matter of humor scholars are much like businessmen; the boss makes the jokes and the junior executives do the laughing. It seems unlikely, however, that Miss Newstead will ever take more than a passing interest in making her juniors laugh. Intellectual adventure, rather than humor, is today, as it has always been, her mainstay, and it is significant that in summing up the excitement she derives from her work she now and then repeats a line from the writings of a fellow-scholar—Dr. Marjorie Nicolson, professor of English at Columbia —who speaks of "moments of splendid isolation when each of us has had the momentary experience of being the only living person to know something that the world has never known or long forgotten." After dinner at the home of a non-scholarly couple one night a couple of months ago, Miss Newstead, sitting in the living room with her host and hostess and two or three guests who were also outside the pale, lapsed into what was for her an unusually outspoken exposition of how deeply she feels about her career as an Arthurian explorer. "Majorie Nicolson put it in just the right words," she said, and quoted them. Then she went on, "The thrill in my work doesn't come from the possibility of finding a lost manuscript in someone's attic, or anything like that; I'm not hunting for lost manuscripts. And it's not a matter, either, of discovering, say, that Chrétien had two wives or an illegitimate daughter; there isn't that kind of gossipy information left over from the twelfth century. My discoveries are less dramatic, maybe, by Hollywood standards, but that doesn't make them any less dramatic to me. Take the Tristan story as told by the poet Béroul. There's a scene in it where Isolt is about to be turned over to a group of lepers by her jealous husband. Now, that's a curious detail, since it isn't in the original legend. How did it get it? Well, I thought about it and I studied everything that might have any bearing on it, and I finally discovered—and proved—that it was added because stories of wrongly accused queens were popular in the Middle Ages. To me, that was a thrilling thing to discover and to prove."

Pausing, Miss Newstead looked around her questioningly, in the manner of a person unused to taking others into her confidence. But the mood was on her, and now she began talking about the stirring days when she both made and reconstructed history with her revelations about Bran the Blessed. "Gradually, in my reading, I began to notice something," she said. "Gradually it became apparent to me that the shadowy figure of Perceval's father bore some traits of the early Welsh sea-god named Bran. No one had ever noticed the similarity before. I felt just as thrilled as if I *had* found a lost manuscript in an attic." Miss Newstead's listeners smiled and nodded in glassy admiration, and it was plain that she was again enjoying a moment of splendid isolation.

QUESTIONS

1. Describe the devices that Douglas uses to suggest the complexity of his attitude toward Lawrence.

2. Study the paragraph from Douglas that begins "I suppose he was not much concerned with the form of his novels." What material in it suggests that Douglas shared some of the attitudes and feelings of the group described in Keynes' "My Early Beliefs" (p. 1127)?

3. Analyze the structure from the paragraph beginning "I suppose he was not much concerned" through the one beginning "For the rest, the prevalent conception of Lawrence."

4. What is Douglas' tone and intention in this passage? "Scholars and men of the world will not find much inspiration in these novels. Lawrence opened a little window for the bourgeoisie. That is his life-work." Compare Frances Newman's discussion of Lawrence (p. 1223).

5. Apparently Swinburne was as upsetting a person as Lawrence, though no doubt in a very different way. How do their descriptions of Swinburne define the personalities of Noyes and Beerbohm?

6. Try to describe the tone or intonation that you catch as you read Beerbohm and Noyes. (Read a few paragraphs aloud.) How do the structure and movement of their sentences create the difference in effect?

7. What differences do you notice between Beerbohm the reminiscer or essayist and Beerbohm the daily reviewer?

8. Note the length of Beerbohm's second paragraph. How is it unified, or would you paragraph differently?

9. How do the details in Beerbohm's paragraph on Tennyson give you his opinion of the poet?

10. How does the first sentence of "A Giant in Her Field" give you Hunt's attitude toward Miss Newstead and her work?

11. What especially attracted Hunt in the controversy between Miss Newstead and Sister M. Amelia?

12. Would you agree that Hunt's last sentence is a rather sudden unkindness? Before answering, you have to decide what Hunt's tone is.

13. What kinds of sources did Hunt use?

14. Under what topics has Hunt organized his profile? (Note that the profile is not a short biography.) Or what kind of information does he give about his subject? What is the effect of the order he uses to present his information?

15. Discuss the organization of two or three of Hunt's longer paragraphs.

16. Read "You, Too, Can Write the Casual Style" by William H. Whyte, Jr., *Harper's*, October, 1953. How many of the devices listed by Whyte does Hunt use?

AUTOBIOGRAPHY: THE RISING OF BELIEFS

Here four interesting people describe and analyze some of the influences that helped to form their values. Perhaps their real subject is what it feels like to believe, or as in Santayana, what it feels like to be on the way to not believing. In the first two selections the authors reach the reader by the suggestion of their details, the accuracy of their observation of simple human behavior: there is not much analysis, though a good deal of thought went into the choosing of the details, of course. In the last two selections the points are made more abstractly and analytically.

PROFESSOR KILLS SANTA CLAUS

A. J. Liebling

A newspaper gives the reader the impression of being closer to life than a book, and he is likely to confuse what he has read in it with actual experiences he has not had.

"You should have seen Charlie White," a middle-aged bore may say to me in a bar. "*He* had a left hook."

I too know White had a left hook, because I read about it so often, but it is no more or less likely that the fellow talking saw him than that I saw Ty Cobb, about whose base-running I talk with the same knowing ease. I don't think I ever did see Cobb, personally, but I do know I saw Hans Wagner and Christy Mathewson in a game between the Pirates and Giants when I was small, and I can't remember what either of them looked like on that particular day or what he did. What I *know* about them, like what I know about Cobb, is simply the cumulative product of newspaper stories and newspaper photographs, and in that way I know as much about Cobb as I do about either.

In the same way, the first President I actually saw was Warren Gamaliel Harding, but he is a paler memory to me than the first Roosevelt, or Taft or Wilson. And it is incredible to me even now that I never saw Franklin

D. Roosevelt, who was nearly as much of a personal experience as my own father.

I cite these example of the suggestive power of newsprint because the principle applies also to ideas. You read a thesis set forth as a fact in the newspapers a certain number of times and you begin to think you have figured it out for yourself or at least had it at first hand from what the press would call an authoritative source.

A book has a less treacherous effect. Even its least wary reader is strongly conscious that there is a *man* at the other end of the process, telling him something. The studied impersonality of the newspaper, its simulation of photography in words, all soften the outline of the printed phrase as it blurs against the background of reality.

So when I went up to Dartmouth in the fall of 1920, lacking a month of being sixteen, I took it for granted that William Jennings Bryan was a crackpot and Nicholas Murray Butler a profound scholar, that the Reds in Europe were ravening beasts and Socialists here a bit touched in the head. I believed that all Allied failures in the then recent war had been well-conceived and ably conducted enterprises, doomed by circumstances beyond human control, and that the country would be forever prosperous if we let prosperous-looking people run it. All these notions I erroneously thought were the result of my own ratiocinations.

During the two years that followed the war, newspapers had begun to exert another sort of attraction upon me, one of which I was more conscious. I had become an admirer of the more literate columnists of the day, Don Marquis of the *Sun*, Christopher Morley of the *Post*, and Baird Leonard, a witty woman who wrote for the *Morning Telegraph*, which then was less exclusively a racing sheet than it has since become. The family continued to take the *Times* in the morning. The *Telegraph* in my teens was what the *Journal* had been in my years of dawning literacy, a secret, extramural indulgence. It gave me a glimpse, vicarious but convincing, into a world not even the Hearst papers covered, in which theatre people and horse trainers seemed as casually real as the fur merchants, lawyers, general agents for insurance companies, and cotton converters who formed the most numerous element in my parents' milieu.

I had arrived at the point in my own aesthetic development when I thought that Miss Leonard and Marquis and Morley were not only gay but important, and perhaps they were. Nobody writes stuff like theirs in newspapers today, and I sometimes wonder whether this marks a decline in the public's level of taste or the publishers'. It may denote a universal change in the type of thing people like to read about, or, it seems more likely to me, the quest for the common denominator which goes along with the consolidation of newspapers. There were more newspapers in the New York of 1920 than there are now, and they had more individualized clienteles for a writer to aim at. Nor was the mark of a columnist's eminence then his suitability for syndication to the back country. Syndicates have perhaps raised the reading standards of the provinces. San

Francisco, for example, can now enjoy George Sokolsky and Robert Ruark day and date with New York, instead of having to put up with some local chump like Ambrose Bierce. But the syndicates have taken the publishers' minds off the highly literate column hand-tailored for the New York trade.

There is not, in fact, in these days even a New York paper that *is* a New York paper. The biggest of the lot are either national institutions, like the *Times* and *Herald Tribune,* or show windows for national chains, like the *Daily News, Mirror, Journal-American,* and *World-Telegram.* The *Sun* is a suburban paper published on the island of Manhattan.

Most of my 623 classmates at Dartmouth were older than I, but I never heard one of them make any criticism of newspapers except that the Boston ones devoted a disproportionate amount of space to Harvard and Boston College football. The college was liberal; there was an exemplary freedom of thought and speech, but we never bothered to think or say anything more than "Hi" or "Howdy." Professor John Moffatt Mecklin told one of his classes that they were intellectual flappers, they had more freedom than they knew what to do with.

We weren't reactionary; the word wasn't even part of the current vocabulary. We were just indifferent. A certain number of students had served in the war, but they must have been convinced of its episodic quality. That was the autumn of Harding's presidential campaign for a "return to normalcy," and the concept seemed reasonable to our parents and us, although the English department sneered at the bastard word. We had not yet even arrived at the era of the campus aesthete, which was to be followed by that of the campus radical. F. Scott Fitzgerald, who had just published "This Side of Paradise," was the most heterodox prophet we listened to. If I go into this seemingly superfluous detail it is because I want to reconstruct for myself as well as for you the portrait of the paragon of newspaper readers I then was. I was as avid, unquestioning, and respectable as a piece of blotting paper with the name of the Guaranty Trust Company printed on the reverse side.

It was Professor Mecklin who continued the journalistic education that Carl Morris's downfall had begun. Professor Mecklin's arrival at Hanover had coincided with that of the class of 1924, to which I belonged. Journalism was not his subject; as I shall illustrate later, a course in journalism is the last place in which to look for journalistic education. Mecklin, who was then fifty years old, had left the chair of philosophy at the University of Pittsburgh as a fairly direct consequence of his sentiments and speeches in the great steel strike of 1919. He had come to Dartmouth as a professor of sociology. I didn't know anything about him or his past when, in the week between the Penn and Brown games—that was the way we measured time—I was summoned along with all my class to a lecture he was to deliver. This lecture was part of a survey and orientation course in the social sciences, which all freshmen had to take. I cannot remember anything else that happened in any other session of this course. This is an example of the charming grab-bag quality of a liberal-arts college education

—the items that will prove of subsequent value turn up in the most unexpected places. The lecture was a great event in Mecklin's life as well as mine, although I didn't learn this until much later, when I read the old man's autobiography, "My Quest for Freedom," published in 1945.

"Soon after my arrival at Dartmouth in 1920 I was asked to address the freshmen class on the great steel strike," he wrote. "The question at once arose in my mind as to whether I could tell the bald truth. I was assured, however, that I could talk frankly. I faced several hundred freshmen who had already been lectured into a state of incipient revolt. They were restless and noisy, but I had provided a map of the steel mills and as I began to state frankly the treatment of the workers by the "Cossacks" they began to listen. Within thirty minutes I had close attention. At the end, to make things concrete, I drew a parallel between the military methods of the steel barons and the militarism of Germany and stated that the strike was merely a crude effort by the strikers to do for the steel industry what Wilson sought to do in his struggle to "make the world safe for democracy." At the close a dozen or more rushed to the platform and insisted that I was talking "socialism." One boy with a white and tense face said that his father was in the steel business and he knew that what I said was false.

"This incident was to me more or less of an acid test of Dartmouth liberalism. So far as I could see it did not affect in the least my standing on the campus." Professor Mecklin stayed at Hanover the rest of his life, retiring as professor of philosophy and social ethics.

The part of Professor Mecklin's test-case talk that affected me most was not about the company police, whom he called Cossacks. It concerned newspapers. He has written, "The press in particular became utterly untrustworthy. We had to get the news as to what was going on in Pittsburgh from the Philadelphia and New York papers." But what he said was that of even the New York papers, the *World* was the only one that told the truth about the strike. After I heard him there was only one paper in the country I would have considered working on. That was the *World*.

The impact of the Mecklin lecture on me, which I am able to measure only after all these years, must have been directly connected with the nature of the man himself, although I never sought out his acquaintance afterward. I started reading "My Quest for Freedom" only when I began to write this book; my primary reason was to check on my recollection of the lecture and of the circumstances under which he left Pittsburgh. But it is evident from his autobiography that he must have been an impressive man in 1920. He had begun his life with a struggle against the Calvinism in which he had been reared as the son of a backwoods Presbyterian clergyman in Mississippi. Educated for the ministry himself, he had quit it after one year of self-torment in a small town in Georgia. He had made his definite break with Calvin after a controversy with the president of Lafayette College which had resulted in the resignation of both of them, in 1913, when Mecklin was forty-four. The Pittsburgh episode had followed. He had been a man all his life desperately trying to live at peace with authority, first spiritual and then temporal. But he had always been impelled in the end to speak out by the terrible Calvinist conscience he had inherited along with the God Who oppressed him. He was a most reluctant rebel, and I think this is what made him so convincing.

HERE WE ARE IN 1943

Gertrude Stein

And now it is June 1943 and two of the young men who are twenty-one have come to say good-bye, they hope they are not going to die right away but all who are twenty-one have to go to Germany as hostages to be put in a pen, they say to work in factories but there is no work, and if they go into hiding well it would be all right if it were not for the winter but will it be over before the winter, they ask me to tell them but can any one tell them, do I know, well anyway I can say that they might amuse themselves by learning and reading German and they might amuse themselves by saying that they are going traveling as students, and say they, if we do not consider them as enemies will the Americans like it, will they, might it not displease them, but said I you can learn their language and read their literature and contemplate them as if you were travelers and still know them to be enemies. Why not. Well said they why not. Anyway they said you have cheered us, and I kissed them each one of them and wished them well, and one of them came back to shake hands again and I kissed him again and said be prudent and he said I will and they went away up the hill. Oh dear me one cannot sleep very well.

But from fifteen on you can think about enemies, quite certainly think about enemies.

The idea of enemies is awful it makes one stop remembering eternity and the fear of death. That is what enemies are. Possessions are the same as enemies only less so, they too make one forget eternity and the fear of death.

So many things begin around fifteen. Money, possessions eternity, enemies, the fear of death, disappointments begin a long time before and sorrow, but around fifteen you can begin to write them down, which makes the depth and consolation of disappointment and sorrow. All this can and does begin around fifteen and then a little later came the Boer war, and war as no longer something that belonged to others and to history and to stories but something that was going on now and was a dis-

From *Wars I Have Seen* by Gertrude Stein. New York, Random House, 1945. Reprinted by permission of Alice B. Toklas. Title supplied by the editor.

illusion and disappointing. I did not know anybody who was fighting or
any of their relations, but it was the time when anglo-saxonism had come
in America to be a very conscious feeling. Dooley had made fun of it and
we all felt it and it was disappointing it was not what Kipling and the
describers of the Mutiny had made one feel was Anglo-Saxon it was something different it was only we did not know it it was the beginning of the
ending of the nineteenth century which now in 1943, is dying quite
quickly, but we who were active then we felt it because we already had
a beginning of the twentieth century and so although we did not know it
we felt that the Boer war was the first shot fired at the nineteenth century, and although we thought we were of it we knew inside that we were
not and we knew we should regret what the nineteenth century was but
we knew we did not regret it we wanted something else and we were to
have it.

In Shakespeare's Henry VI I just found that he said that Joan of Arc
and she was not yet dead not in the play in fact she was just beginning
and Shakespeare said that she would be the great French saint that she
would replace Saint Denis, and she was only made a saint very late, very
late indeed, just in time for the war of 1914 but she undoubtedly and
Shakespeare was right she undoubtedly is the great French saint and has
completely replaced Saint Denis. It is funny this business of being right.
Everybody wants to be right, even the one who said he would rather be
right than president. It is so natural to say and I was right was I not.

I am wondering if Laval and the rest of them think they are right now
in 1943, to be sure the Kiddie[1] wrote to me in 1942 and said that at the
end of 1942 there would be good news and in the spring of 1943 there
would be more good news than bad news and as the summer came on the
summer of 1943 the good news would be so good there would be no
letters in the newspaper printing presses big enough to make headlines to
celebrate them, and now the Italian islands are going one by one, one by
one and there is only one more water to cross, and everybody who knows
what an enemy was is now worried because and that is very strange,
everybody knowing that everything is coming to an end every neighbor
is denouncing every neighbor, for black traffic, for theft, for this and for
that, and there are so many being put in prison, poor Madame Berard said
it was so sad to see her husband going off between two policemen just as
if he was a criminal and to know that some of their neighbors were pleased
to see it. To be sure he had been killing meat and did he sell it or not or
only serve it in quantity in his restaurant and her boy has to go to Germany because he is twenty-one even though he is a great mathematician
and is to be a great man in the university of Lyon and the family were
always gentle and kindly and obliging and never charged too much even
when they might have and indeed it was all true they never did.

It is hard to know about enemies at fifteen it all begins, knowing every-

[1]W. G. Rogers, who met Gertrude Stein during the first World War. He is the author
of *When This You See Remember Me. Gertrude Stein In Person,* New York, 1948.

thing and never being happy again, excited yes but never happy again. And now Olympe has to go away and she knows what enemies are, they are Germans that is what enemies are and here there are none and she has to take a train and there she has to see them and the thought of it is making an old woman of her and she does not want to go, no no she does not want to go, but her mistress says the duty of a servant is to obey her mistress and not to follow her own changing fancy, but her fancy has never changed, she has always known what the enemy is what her enemies are, yes she has always known and more than ever since they have been in her home.

And so the Boer war was disagreeable but not really serious not even for the Boers, like all defeated people they got the best of it, it is better to be defeated and win than win and be defeated. Now here in 1943 it seems so strange to see the enemy weakening just slowly weakening, quickly weakening, not being defeated or anything but just weakening, the French do better, they get defeated but they do not weaken, while the Germans do not get defeated they weaken, and when they weaken enough to go out like a lamp with no oil, or with no wire, out, it does not die it just weakens to nothing. Until they weaken everybody says about them but they are still strong, and then they weaken. There you are, that is to say here we are 1943.

After the Spanish-American war there was the Boer war, and that was no longer fifteen that was older, I was in the medical school then the first year and I went out to San Francisco to see my brother Mike who had just been married.

The Spanish-American war was the first to me modern war. Modern is like realism, modern is always modern to some one as realism is always real to some one, not to some one but to a great many at one time. Modern, how nicely it is modern now then and when.

What was modern then was seeing all the middle western men, young men, boys too many, going out to San Francisco, and catching everything and then going off in boats to the Philippines. I was just reading Shakespeare's Henry the Fifth and I found it astonishing how easily they talked of transporting ten thousand, fifteen thousand even twenty thousand soldiers across the water from England to France. How when they had such comparatively little tonnage, did they get so many of them across, how did they, well anyway so they say they did. Call it modern if you like but soldiers any quantity of them at any time can be carried across the ocean, any quantity of them at any time and now here in June 1943, we are waiting for them, waiting for them, to bring us shoes and stockings and dental floss, here in the country we have plenty to eat although we would like more cake and sugar and butter but still here in the country having a goat and chickens we do have plenty to eat and fish, we do have plenty to eat. But one does get so tired of seeing everybody planting and growing vegetables you think how nice it will be to have those happy days come back when vegetables grew not in the ground but in tins. A vegetable garden in the beginning looks so promising and then after all little by little it grows nothing but vegetables, nothing, nothing but vegetables.

Well anyway the Spanish-American war was modern but it was completely nineteenth century, there was nothing but the question of sea power and whose sea power was it, we all read a book that told us it, but then we had known it anyway, because of Nelson, and now we were doing it again, and it was very exciting, we were all finding out about the difficulty of having to have two fleets a Pacific one and an Atlantic one, and we were all getting to feel that we were to be, well there it was still nineteenth century completely nineteenth century and we were not thinking about a twentieth century, and we were so excited that we were not realising that the nineteenth century was beginning to be over, not the least bit in the world. I was young then but I can still see those young men in San Francisco, those middle-western young men of twenty and twenty-one, with their undeveloped necks, their rather doughy faces, I see why they call them dough-boys, they are like that between twenty and twenty-one, they go to sleep anywhere sitting or standing, their heads and their mouths and their eyes can go to sleep anywhere, and open or not open, that is what it is to be twenty or twenty-one, and now here and now, it is just the same, the young of twenty-one, the young Frenchmen of twenty-one are all being deported to Germany, two came to see me to say good-bye to ask how I could encourage them and all I could say was try to study them and learn their language and get to know their literature, think of yourselves as a tourist and not as a prisoner, and they were worried and nervous and they said will the Americans like it if we think of them like that, sure I said all the Americans want is to make you free, and they said yes we know that. It makes me feel very very much like that, I used to say to any Frenchman or Frenchwoman who complained of anything, I said but every time I go out in the village of Bilignin there I see all your young men whatever is happening they are still there and that is everything that they are not gone. But now they are gone and going. Some of them betake themselves to the mountains others are conspiring, the son of our dentist a boy of eighteen has just been taken because he was helping and will he be shot or not. Oh dear. We all cry. But there is nothing to do but wait for us to come nothing to do. And they look so, I saw a train full of them, everybody was handing them up wine and bread, although nobody has much of it for themselves or to give them, and there they were with the gendarmes, going away. And they were awake then and pretty soon they will be tired out and go to sleep any way that it is possible to be sleeping, in a chair or standing or in any way.

It is funny but my memory of those middle-western boys going out to the Philippines was that they were just like these French boys twenty and twenty-one going off to Germany, as deported and held away from every one. Dear me.

So that was realism. Anything is realism but that certainly was realism. And it all made me remember the impression I have when I read Wyan-

dotte or The Hutted Knoll[2] which was about then, the shock I had in reading that book because for the first time I realised what it meant not to
know whether any one was loyal to you or not, did they or did they not
believe in you, were they interested in your interests and how can you
tell. I had read laments of great men and many novels but in some strange
way Wyandotte or The Hutted Knoll made me understand that you could
think that some one was devoted to you and loyal to you and really not at
all they were opposed to you and would if such a thing were necessary
denounce you. And now and again in June 1943 it is happening all
around one.

Well in the first place Olympe who knows who her enemies are, and
are they, could they become another thing or rather could those to whom
she was loyal could she stop being loyal to them, could she want so much
not to leave you and when she really did have it to leave you did she at
the last hour turn against you so as to prepare her mind to be attuned to
the other to whom she was going. Could she and did she. She did. Might
she and would she denounce the first one the second one or any one or
would she only prepare herself in case she had to do something and it
might be that something and would any one she was leaving realise that
she had not been very serviceable in fact that she had been rather useless
although everything made any one think that she was perfection and almost saintly as a character. Dear me. It is like a detective story particularly
as her sister Clothilde used a cheap enemy perfume to drown out the
smell of onions and cooking on her and does it came to be known that she
slept in her mistress' room. Dear me dear me.

How many mirrors there can be in a house when all the doors and the
doors are many and very wide and tall are filled with mirrors and what a
pleasure to see one's self in them. Expectedly and unexpectedly what a
pleasure.

And now in June 1943 something very strange is happening, every day
the feeling is strengthening that one or another has been or will be a
traitor to something and what do they do they send them a little wooden
coffin sometimes with a letter inside sometimes with a rope inside to tell
them to hang themselves, and sometimes it is sent by post or by railroad
and sometimes it is hung up in a tree and sometimes hung up in front of
the front door. Oh dear me. When this you see remember me is what they
mean because some of these people have told where young men of twenty-
one were hidden, and it was not necessary to tell they just did tell and so
somebody sent them a small wooden coffin. Of course they had to find a
reliable carpenter to make the coffins but they did find him.

So the Spanish-American war and seeing all those middle-western men
in San Francisco, made me realise what realism is.

Just to-night June 1943 I was out walking in the twilight in the mountain village of Culoz where I live now and my dog Basket was running
around and a young man in working clothes said he is a nice dog but I

[2]A novel by James Fenimore Cooper.

have been whistling to him and he wont come. Oh I said you have to do more than whistle, you have to talk English and he said my father could and I could too once but I now have forgotten. And I said but how is that not that you have forgotten but that your father talked English, that he said is very simple he is an American, ah I said yes, he came to France in the last war as a soldier he married a Frenchwoman, he got a good job at Chaumont and he stayed, and in '38 we intended to go away but my mother fell ill and we did not leave. And she, I said, oh she is dead, and he, oh he is in a concentration camp when America came into the war they came and took him, and you, we are four brothers and a sister, and the oldest is an actor in the Comedie Française and the second is a plumber and the third is head butcher in a camp of youth and here I am working for farmers and my name is Robert Nelson White and I looked as if I was not sure that all he said was so and he said here are my papers, they do not spell white right, but my name there is Robert White, I left out the Nelson all right. And it all made me feel a little funny anything these days these strange days can make you feel a little funny so I shook hands with him and we went up Basket and I up the hill and he Robert Nelson White went on down, down the hill.

Now all that made me feel all the more how different was that Spanish-American war. I asked Robert Nelson White if his father was a Frenchman by blood, if his grandfather or grandmother either one was French but no he said he was always American his people never had been anything but American and his little sister of fourteen was at school and he and his brother had crossed the lines at night to come into the free zone and here he was.

In the Spanish-American war romance was simple and realistic like the young Californians who went to the war and General King wrote novels about it and in one he said and I threw the bridle of my horse to my orderly Ned Hanford, and it was Ned Hanford and when he read these simple words, he had a thrill he always had a thrill. That was the way it was then in the Spanish-American war. It was then that they began to think about realism. The Red Badge of Courage by Crane, and any simple description of war as done by the Russians, later on a naval battle in the next war, the Russo-Japanese war, which described it just as it was not as it felt or looked. But anyway there they were the middle-western boys in San Francisco, and there was Chinatown and there was the French quarter, and there were the Lurline baths and there was everything that they never had seen before. It is always that way in war, always.

And now in June 1943, it is trying, there are so many sad things happening, so many in prison, so many going away, our dentist's son and he was only eighteen and he should have been taking his entrance university examinations and he with others in a camion took shoes and clothes and weapons to give to the young men who had taken themselves to the mountains, to avoid being sent away and what has happened to him and to them. I have just met a very charming woman courageous and lives in an old castle and has five children and the youngest one is twenty-one and he has gone, she has never lost any money but life is always dearer and she and her children have worked very hard to keep their castle sheared their own sheep, and everything, and now she said, of course she would not mind Christian's going away, that is to say not to mind if it were not the times are so uncertain and so troubling, and he is very sweet and he is big and tall and very winning and since he was born there have never been three months without their seeing him, never and now, well I said he hopes to come back for the vintage and she had clear eyes very wide open and she said yes.

And all that makes one think more and more of the strangeness and the unreality of those middle-western boys who were naturally called dough-boys, being in San Francisco, and then going to the Philippines, when they got to the Philippines and back again I never saw them so I do not really know what happened to them, by that time we were all interested in real-ism in literature, and that kind of went on until 1938, when it was all over, there was an end of the nineteenth century and realism was the last thing the nineteenth century did completely. Anybody can understand that there is no point in being realistic about here and now, no use at all not any, and so it is not the nineteenth but the twentieth century, there is no realism now, life is not real it is not earnest, it is strange which is an entirely different matter.

During the Spanish-American war there were food scandals, and in the Boer war there were concentration camps where they had nothing to eat, and all that is natural enough. The concentration camps for the Boers ex-cited us all, nobody knew then how everybody was finally that is every-body in Europe was finally not going to have anything to eat. There was famine in China even in Russia and there was famine in India and every one then in the time of the Boer war and before and after was very much excited about it but now here in 1943 not having anything to eat enough to eat, having what you can eat, buying eating black, that is black traffic, thinking about eating, everybody on the road bicycling or walking with a pack on their back or a basket in the hand, or a big bundle on the bicycle, hoping for provisions, somewhere in the country there would be an egg or something or something, and perhaps you will get that something. One day I was out walking, well naturally I had a basket and big prospects and hopes and I met a nice gentle little bourgeoise from Belley, and it was spring time and she had a very charming and quite large bouquet of flowers very beautifully arranged in her hand and I said what a charming bouquet of flowers, yes she said eyeing the bouquet carefully, yes, I have been in the country to visit some relations, and I had hoped, I had hoped perhaps for an egg, perhaps even perhaps for a chicken, and she heaved a little breath they gave me these flowers. They are very charming flowers I said, yes she said, and we said good-bye and went each one on our way. There are so many people in prison because they sell what they should not sell, and yet, well and yet, I met Roselyn I said you are looking very well, the restrictions do not seem to have had any effect on you, well said Roselyn, one finds things. Roselyn, I said, you indulging in black traffic, mais non, she said of course I would not, to find something is one thing, to indulge in black traffic is quite another thing. Explain the difference to me I said Well said Roselyn, to find is when you find a small amount any day at a reasonable price which will just augment your diet and keep you healthy. Black traffic is when you pay a very large sum for a large amount of food, that is the difference. And she is right that is a difference and we all all day and every day go about and in every way we do or do not find something that helps the day along. As Madame Pierlot said, you do not buy now-a-days only with money you buy with your personality. Jo David-son used to say that you always had to sell your personality, but now it is not a question of selling it is a question of buying by personality. Nothing is sadder these days than people who never make friends, they poor dears have nothing to eat, neither do the indiscreet, and yet almost everybody does eat. Almost everybody, almost, it comes hardest on mid-dle aged men, not women they resist better but middle aged men, without wine and cheese, they get thinner and thinner and thinner. We women of a certain age, we reduce to a certain place and then we seem to get along all right, but the middle aged men get thin, and thinner and thinner. Naturally those that had been fat. Oh dear me.

So the Boer war was the first time we really realized that war made them thin that is the civilian population, it must have been true in the civil war, but at that time, there were so many pioneers and pioneers are always thin, and Boers were fat, and the Boer war made them thin just like that.

I just heard a nice story about a farmer's wife. She complained that her cow could not live because she had no hay. Some one who had a large house and a lot of land heard her and said I will give you two thousand pounds of hay that is a load of hay as a present if you will sell me every day a litre of milk. And said the farmer's wife what will I do having so much less butter. No not at all said the farmer's wife. The Boer war might be like that just like that and so is 1943.

And so there was the Spanish-American war. So much happened in the Spanish-American war, to us and to me to the United States and to us, something to Spain too and to any Spaniard but then that was a habit, they always had these things happen in Europe. But with us although in a kind of a way in our short history it had very frequently happened still it was not a habit.

To-day we were at Aix-les-Bains, end of June 1943 when this you see remember me, and in a kind of way it was different but in a kind of way it was the middle-western dough boys in San Francisco. We were at the station it was the first of July and there were many trains and many peo-ple, on one track where our train should have been it was not. And then a train came along, all trains go very slowly now, the engineers are used up the track is used up and the coal is bad so therefore there are a fair num-ber of trains moving they move at a walk. This train that came along and kept moving and did not stop had on it tanks and trucks which did not look very strong, as they were not armored and seated on them and seated in the open cars placed on trucks and seated anywhere were Germans all naked except a little trouser nothing on their heads and sitting there and the train went on slowly and all the French people were as if they were at a theatre that was not interesting and the train went on slowly and then our train came in and I got on it with my white dog Basket and the French people were pleased, Basket was the real circus, he was a theatre that they found interesting and they were interested and they said so, and nobody had noticed the train full of Germans except four young Frenchmen from the camp de Jeunesse and they like all young fellows of that age laughed, which reminded me of the dough boys in San Francisco, in the midst of the San Francisco public. Which ones. Those Germans.

It is funny funny in the sense of strange and peculiar and unrealisable, the fact that so many are prisoners, prisoners, prisoners every where, and now Berard where we used to lunch is in prison, for black traffic, and an Alsatian and his wife and his son, because of the younger son who went to the funeral of his fiancée and on his way he was taken and he escaped and they were in prison and now they are out and he is in safety but where. Anywhere. And whole countries in prison and now we have a feeling that they who put everybody in prison are now in prison they feel themselves in prison, they feel imprisoned. They have just told us that our friends the American consul and vice-consul although in prison and are very free and amusing themselves and have flowers in their rooms and play tennis and send messages and make excursions. Oh dear me, when this you see, but after all, when this you see, and after all you would imagine that with all that I would not any longer want to read mystery stories and spy stories and all that but not at all I want to read them more than ever, to change one reality for another, one unreality for another and so the Spanish-American war made us Americans conscious of being a world power, conscious of the school of realism, conscious of England being nineteenth century, with Kipling and the white man's burden, was in a way for me the beginning of killing the nineteenth century, which is now not any longer dying but dead and the little coffins that are being sent to all pro-Germans are part of the funeral. French people like New Englanders like funerals, they are a peaceful occupation, nice and quiet, and certain. Ah say the French before all this we were so happy but we did not appreciate our good fortune.

Realism.

After all there has to be realism realism in romance and in novels and the reason why is this. Novels have to resemble something and in order that they do there must be realism. Of course all writers had had realism, writers and readers always have a realism, after all living is in a way always real, that is to say what one hears and sees, even what one feels is in a way always real, but the realism of the present seems new because the realism of the past is no longer real.

And so just at the time of the Spanish-American war, there commenced the difference between Kipling's realism, which was romanticism, but real enough, and the French and Russian realism, which was so real that it was real enough. Was it real as anybody could know realism, or was it not. Just at the time of the Spanish-American war and later the Russo-Japanese war this question of realism was becoming the vital question for Americans who having a land with a clear light manufacturing light and resistant steel, their life needed a clean and resistant realism but at the same time they needed to move around and you cannot keep moving around without feeling romantic. The nineteenth century was then in its full strength and everybody knew it, and everybody knew that when a thing is like that you have to begin to try to forget it, and they all began to they all began to begin to forget it.

MY EARLY BELIEFS

John Maynard Keynes

I can visualise very clearly the scene of my meeting with D. H. Lawrence in 1914 (Bunny seems to suggest 1915, but my memory suggests that it may have been earlier than that) of which he speaks in the letter from which Bunny quoted at the last meeting of the Club. But unfortunately I cannot remember any fragments of what was said, though I retain some faint remains of what was felt.

It was at a breakfast party given by Bertie Russell in his rooms in Nevile's Court. There were only the three of us there. I fancy that Lawrence had been staying with Bertie and that there had been some meeting or party the night before, at which Lawrence had been facing Cambridge. Probably he had not enjoyed it.[1] My memory is that he was morose from the outset and said very little, apart from indefinite expressions of irritable dissent, all the morning. Most of the talk was between Bertie and me, and I haven't the faintest recollection of what it was about. But it was not the sort of conversation we should have had if we had been alone. It was *at* Lawrence and with the intention, largely unsuccessful, of getting him to participate. We sat round the fireplace with the sofa

FROM *Two Memoirs* by John Maynard Keynes. Reprinted by permission of the publisher, Rupert Hart-Davis Ltd.

[1]Professor G. E. Moore tells me that he sat next Lawrence in Hall that night and found nothing to say to him, but that afterwards Lawrence was introduced to Professor Hardy, the mathematician, and there was a friendly general discussion. The end of the evening was a great success. Professor Moore's diary shows it was the night of March 7th, 1915. D. G. [The people mentioned in this essay can be identified by consulting *Who's Who* or *Who Was Who.* Bunny: David Garnett; Ottoline: Lady Ottoline Morell; Ludwig: Ludwig Wittgenstein; Bob Trevy: R. C. Trevelyan. (Editor)]

drawn across. Lawrence sat on the right-hand side in rather a crouching position with his head down. Bertie stood up by the fireplace, as I think I did, too, from time to time. I came away feeling that the party had been a failure and that we had failed to establish contact, but with no other particular impression. You know the sort of situation when two familiar friends talk *at* a visitor. I had never seen him before, and I never saw him again. Many years later he recorded in a letter, which is printed in his published correspondence, that I was the only member of Bloomsbury who had supported him by subscribing for *Lady Chatterley*.

That is all I *remember*. But Bunny's story suggests some inferences to me. In the passage of his life which Bunny has described I think that Lawrence was influenced by two causes of emotional disturbance. One of them centred round Ottoline. As always, Ottoline was keeping more than one world. Except for Bertie, the Cambridge and Bloomsbury world was only just beginning to hold her. Lawrence, Gertler, Carrington were a different strand in her furbelows. Lawrence was jealous of the other lot; and Cambridge rationalism and cynicism, then at their height, were, of course, repulsive to him. Bertie gave him what must have been, I think, his first glimpse of Cambridge. It overwhelmed, attracted and repulsed him—which was the other emotional disturbance. It was obviously a civilisation, and not less obviously uncomfortable and unattainable for him—very repulsive and very attractive. Now Bunny had come into his life quite independently, neither through Ottoline nor from Cambridge and Bloomsbury; he was evidently very fond of Bunny; and when he saw *him* being seduced by Cambridge, he was yet more jealous, just as he was jealous of Ottoline's new leanings that way. And jealousy apart, it is impossible to imagine moods more antagonistic than those of Lawrence and of pre-war Cambridge.

But when all that has been said, was there something true and right in what Lawrence felt? There generally was. His reactions were incomplete and unfair, but they were not usually baseless. I have said that I have forgotten what the conversation was about. But I expect it was pretty brittle stuff—not so brittle as Frankie Birrell's—but pretty brittle all the same. And although it was silly to take it, or to estimate it, at its face value, did the way of responding to life which lay behind it lack something important? Lawrence was oblivious of anything valuable it may have offered—it was a *lack* that he was violently apprehending. So Bunny's memoir has thrown my mind back to reflections about our mental history in the dozen years before the war; and if it will not shock the Club too much, I should like in this contribution to its proceedings to introduce for once, mental or spiritual, instead of sexual, adventures, to try and recall the principal impacts on one's virgin mind and to wonder how it has all turned out, and whether one still holds by that youthful religion.

I went up to Cambridge at Michaelmas 1902, and Moore's *Principia Ethica* came out at the end of my first year. I have never heard of the present generation having read it. But, of course, its effect on *us*, and the talk which preceded and followed it, dominated, and perhaps still dominate, everything else. We were at an age when our beliefs influenced our behaviour, a characteristic of the young which it is easy for the middle-aged to forget, and the habits of feeling formed then still persist in a recognisable degree. It is those habits of feeling, influencing the majority of us, which make this Club a collectivity and separate us from the rest. They overlaid, somehow, our otherwise extremely different characters—Moore himself was a puritan and precisian, Strachey (for that was his name at that time) a Voltairean, Woolf a rabbi, myself a nonconformist, Sheppard a conformist and (as it now turns out) an ecclesiastic, Clive a gay and amiable dog, Sydney-Turner a quietist, Hawtrey a dogmatist and so on. Of those who had come just before, only MacCarthy and Ainsworth, who were much influenced by their personal feelings for Moore, came under his full influence. We did not see much of Forster at that time; who was already the elusive colt of a dark horse. It was only for us, those who were active in 1903, that Moore completely ousted McTaggart, Dickinson, Russell. The influence was not only overwhelming; but it was the extreme opposite of what Strachey used to call *funeste;* it was exciting, exhilarating, the beginning of a renaissance, the opening of a new heaven on a new earth, we were the forerunners of a new dispensation, we were not afraid of anything. Perhaps it was because we were so brought up that even at our gloomiest and worst we have never lost a certain resilience which the younger generation seem never to have had. They have enjoyed, at most, only a pale reflection of something, not altogether superseded, but faded and without illusions.

Now what we got from Moore was by no means entirely what he offered us. He had one foot on the threshold of the new heaven, but the other foot in Sidgwick and the Benthamite calculus and the general rules of correct behaviour. There was one chapter in the *Principia* of which we took not the slightest notice. We accepted Moore's religion, so to speak, and discarded his morals. Indeed, in our opinion, one of the greatest advantages of his religion, was that it made morals unnecessary—meaning by "religion" one's attitude towards onself and the ultimate and by "morals" one's attitude towards the outside world and the intermediate. To the consequences of having a religion and no morals I return later.

Even if the new members of the Club know what the religion was (do they?), it will not do any of us any harm to try and recall the crude outlines. Nothing mattered except states of mind, our own and other people's of course, but chiefly our own. These states of mind were not associated with action or achievement or with consequences. They consisted in timeless, passionate states of contemplation and communion, largely unattached to "before" and "after." Their value depended, in accordance with the principle of organic unity, on the state of affairs as a whole which could not be usefully analysed into parts. For example, the value of the state of mind of being in love did not depend merely on the nature of one's own emotions, but also on the worth of their object and on the reciprocity and nature of the object's emotions; but it did not depend, if I remember rightly, or did not depend much, on what happened, or how one felt about it, a year later, though I myself was always an advocate of a principle of organic unity through time, which still seems to me only sensible. The appropriate subjects of passionate contemplation and communion were a beloved person, beauty and truth, and one's prime objects in life were love, the creation and enjoyment of aesthetic experience and the pursuit of knowledge. Of these love came a long way first. But in the early days under Moore's influence the public treatment of this and its associated acts was, on the whole, austere and platonic. Some of us might argue that physical enjoyment could spoil and detract from the state of mind as a whole. I do not remember at what date Strachey issued his edict that certain Latin technical terms of sex were the correct words to use, that to avoid them was a grave error, and, even in mixed company, a weakness, and the use of other synonyms a vulgarity. But I should certainly say that this was later. In 1903 those words were not even esoteric terms of common discourse.

Our religion closely followed the English puritan tradition of being chiefly concerned with the salvation of our own souls. The divine resided within a closed circle. There was not a very intimate connection between "being good" and "doing good"; and we had a feeling that there was some risk that in practice the latter might interfere with the former. But religions proper, as distinct from modern "social service" pseudo-religions, have always been of that character; and perhaps it was a sufficient offset that our religion was altogether unworldly—with wealth, power, popularity or success it had no concern whatever, they were thoroughly despised.

How did we know what states of mind were good? This was a matter of direct inspection, of direct unanalysable intuition about which it was useless and impossible to argue. In that case who was right when there was a difference of opinion? There were two possible explanations. It might be that the two parties were not really talking about the same thing, that they were not bringing their intuitions to bear on precisely the same object, and, by virtue of the principle of organic unity, a very small difference in the object might make a very big difference in the result. Or it might be that some people had an acuter sense of judgment, just as some people can judge a vintage port and others cannot. On the whole, so far as I remember, this explanation prevailed. In practice, victory was with those who could speak with the greatest appearance of clear, undoubting conviction and could best use the accents of infallibility. Moore at this time was a master of this method—greeting one's remarks with a gasp of incredulity—*Do* you *really* think *that*, an expression of face as if to hear such a thing said reduced him to a state of wonder verging on imbecility, with his mouth wide open and wagging his head in the negative so violently that his hair shook. *Oh!* he would say, goggling at you as if either you or he must be mad; and no reply was possible. Strachey's methods were different; grim silence as if such a dreadful observation was beyond comment and the less said about it the better, but almost as effective for disposing of what he called death-packets. Woolf was fairly good at indicating a negative, but he was better at producing the effect that it was useless to argue with *him* than at crushing *you*. Dickinson knew how to shrug his shoulders and retreat unconvinced, but it was retreat all the same. As for Sheppard and me we could only turn like worms, but worms who could be eventually goaded into voluble claims that worms have at least the *right* to turn. Yet after all the differences were about details. Broadly speaking we all knew for certain what were good states of mind and that they consisted in communion with objects of love, beauty and truth.

I have called this faith a religion, and some sort of relation of neoplatonism it surely was. But we should have been very angry at the time with such a suggestion. We regarded all this as entirely rational and scientific in character. Like any other branch of science, it was nothing more than the application of logic and rational analysis to the material presented as sense-data. Our apprehension of good was exactly the same as our apprehension of green, and we purported to handle it with the same logical and analytical technique which was appropriate to the latter. Indeed we combined a dogmatic treatment as to the nature of experience with a method of handling it which was extravagantly scholastic. Russell's *Principles of Mathematics* came out in the same year as *Principia Ethica*; and the former, in spirit, furnished a method for handling the material provided by the latter. Let me give you a few examples of the sort of things we used to discuss.

If A was in love with B and believed that B reciprocated his feelings, whereas in fact B did not, but was in love with C, the state of affairs was certainly not so good as it would have been if A had been right, but was it worse or better than it would become if A discovered his mistake? If A was in love with B under a misapprehension as to B's qualities, was this better or worse than A's not being in love at all? If A was in love with B because A's spectacles were not strong enough to see B's complexion, did this altogether, or partly, destroy the value of A's state of mind? Suppose we were to live our lives backwards, having our experiences in the reverse order, would this affect the value of our successive states of mind? If the states of mind enjoyed by each of us were pooled and then redistributed, would this affect their value? How did one compare the value of a good state of mind which had bad consequences with a bad state of mind which had good consequences? In valuing the consequences did one assess them at their actual value as it turned out eventually to be, or their probable value at the time? If at their probable value, how much evidence as to possible consequences was it one's duty to collect before applying the calculus? Was there a separate objective standard of beauty? Was a beautiful thing, that is to say, by definition that which it was good to contemplate? Or was there an actual objective quality "beauty," just like "green" and "good"? And knowledge, too, presented a problem. Were all truths equally good to pursue and contemplate?—as for example the number of grains in a given tract of sea-sand. We were disposed to repudiate very strongly the idea that useful knowledge could be preferable to useless knowledge. But we flirted with the idea that there might be some intrinsic quality—though not, perhaps, quite on a par with "green" and "good" and "beautiful"—which one could call "interesting," and we were prepared to think it just possible that "interesting" knowledge might be better to pursue than "uninteresting" knowledge. Another competing adjective was "important," provided it was quite clear that "important" did not mean "useful." Or to return again to our favourite subject, was a violent love affair which lasted a short time better than a more tepid one which endured longer? We were inclined to think it was. But I have said enough by now to make it clear that the problems of mensuration, in which we had involved ourselves, were somewhat formidable.

It was all under the influence of Moore's method, according to which you could hope to make essentially vague notions clear by using precise language about them and asking exact questions. It was a method of discovery by the instrument of impeccable grammar and an unambiguous dictionary. "What *exactly* do you mean?" was the phrase most frequently on our lips. If it appeared under cross-examination that you did not mean *exactly* anything, you lay under a strong suspicion of meaning nothing whatever. It was a stringent education in dialectic; but in practice it was a kind of combat in which strength of character was really much more valuable than subtlety of mind. In the preface to his great work, bespattered with the numerous italics through which the reader who knew him could actually hear, as with Queen Victoria, the vehemence of his utterance, Moore begins by saying that error is chiefly "the attempt to answer questions, without first discovering precisely *what* question it is which you desire to answer. . . . Once we recognise the exact meaning of the two questions, I think it also becomes plain exactly what kind of reasons are relevant as arguments for or against any particular answer to them." So we spent our time trying to discover *precisely what* questions we were asking, confident in the faith that, if only we could ask precise questions, everyone would know the answer. Indeed Moore expressly claimed as much. In his famous chapter on "The Ideal" he wrote:

> "Indeed, once the meaning of the question is clearly understood, the answer to it, in its main outlines, appears to be so obvious, that it runs the risk of seeming to be a platitude. By far the most valuable things, which we know or can imagine, are certain states of consciousness, which may be roughly described as the pleasures of human intercourse and the enjoyment of beautiful objects. No one, probably, who has asked himself the question, has ever doubted that personal affection and the appreciation of what is beautiful in Art or Nature, are good in themselves; nor if we consider strictly what things are worth having *purely for their own sakes,* does it appear probable that any one will think that anything else has *nearly* so great a value as the things which are included under these two heads."

And then there was the question of pleasure. As time wore on towards the nineteen-tens, I fancy we weakened a bit about pleasure. But, in our prime, pleasure was nowhere. I would faintly urge that if two states of mind were similar in all other respects except that one was pleasurable and the other was painful there *might* be a little to be said for the former, but the principle of organic unities was against me. It was the general view (though not quite borne out by the *Principia*) that pleasure had nothing to do with the case and, on the whole, a pleasant state of mind lay under grave suspicion of lacking intensity and passion.

In those days X. had not taken up women, nor Woolf monkeys, and they were not their present blithe selves. The two of them, sunk deep in silence and in basket chairs on opposite sides of the fireplace in a room which was at all times pitch dark, would stop sucking their pipes only to murmur that all good states of mind were extremely painful and to imply that all painful states of mind were extremely good. Strachey seconded them—it was only in his second childhood that Lytton took up pleasure—though his sorrow was more fitful than their settled gloom. But with Sheppard and myself cheerfulness could not but break through, and we were in great disgrace about it. There was a terrible scene one evening when we turned insubordinate and reckless and maintained that there was nothing wrong in itself in being cheerful. It was decided that such low habits were particularly characteristic of King's as opposed to the austerity of Trinity.

Socrates had persuaded Protarchus that pure hedonism was absurd. Moore himself was only prepared to accept pleasure as an enhancement of a state of affairs otherwise good. But Moore hated evil and he found a place in his religion for vindictive punishment. "Not only is the pleasantness of a state *not* in proportion to its intrinsic worth; it may even add positively to its vileness. . . . The infliction of pain on a person whose state of mind is bad may, if the pain be not too intense, create a state of things that is better *on the whole* than if the evil state of mind had existed unpunished. Whether such a state of affairs can ever constitute a *positive* good is another question." I call attention to the qualification "if the pain be not too intense." Our Ideal was a merciful God.

Thus we were brought up—with Plato's absorption in the good in itself, with a scholasticism which outdid St Thomas, in calvinistic withdrawal from the pleasures and successes of Vanity Fair, and oppressed with all the sorrows of Werther. It did not prevent us from laughing most of the time and we enjoyed supreme self-confidence, superiority and contempt towards all the rest of the unconverted world. But it was hardly a state of mind which a grown-up person in his senses could sustain literally. When MacCarthy came down for a week-end, he would smile affectionately, persuade Moore to sing his German Lieder at the piano, to hear which we all agreed was a very good state of mind indeed, or incite Bob Trevy to deliver a broken oration which was a frantic travesty of the whole method, the charm of it lying in the impossibility of deciding whether Bob himself meant it, half at least, seriously or not.

It seems to me looking back, that this religion of ours was a very good one to grow up under. It remains nearer the truth than any other that I know, with less irrelevant extraneous matter and nothing to be ashamed of; though it is a comfort to-day to be able to discard with a good conscience the calculus and the mensuration and the duty to know *exactly* what one means and feels. It was a purer, sweeter air by far than Freud cum Marx. It is still my religion under the surface. I read again last week Moore's famous chapter on "The Ideal." It is remarkable how wholly oblivious he managed to be of the qualities of the life of action and also of the pattern of life as a whole. He was existing in a timeless ecstasy. His way of translating his own particular emotions of the moment into the language of generalised abstraction is a charming and beautiful comedy. Do you remember the passage in which he discusses whether, granting that it is mental qualities which one should chiefly love, it is important that the beloved person should also be good-looking? In the upshot good looks win a modest victory over "mental qualities." I cannot forbear to quote this sweet and lovely passage, so sincere and passionate and careful:

"I think it may be admitted that wherever the affection is most valuable, the appreciation of mental qualities must form a large part of it, and that the presence of this part makes the whole far more valuable than it could have been without it. But it seems very doubtful whether this appreciation, by itself, can possess as much value as the whole in which it is combined with an appreciation of the appropriate *corporeal* expression of the mental qualities in question. It is certain that in all actual cases of valuable affection, the bodily expressions of character, whether by looks, by words, or by actions, do form a part of the object towards which the affection is felt, and that the fact of their inclusion appears to heighten the value of the whole state. It is, indeed, very difficult to imagine what the cognition of mental qualities *alone*, unaccompanied by *any* corporeal expression, would be like; and, so far as we succeed in making this abstraction, the whole considered certainly appears to have less value. I therefore conclude that the importance of an admiration of admirable mental qualities lies chiefly in the immense superiority of a whole, in which it forms a part, to one in which it is absent, and not in any high degree of intrinsic value which it possesses by itself. It even appears to be doubtful, whether, in itself, it possesses so much value as the appreciation of mere corporeal beauty undoubtedly does possess; that is to say, whether the appreciation of what has great intrinsic value is so valuable as the appreciation of what is merely beautiful.

"But further if we consider the nature of admirable mental qualities, by themselves, it appears that a proper appreciation of them involves a reference to purely material beauty in yet another way. Admirable mental qualities do, if our previous conclusions are correct, consist very largely in an emotional contemplation of beautiful objects; and hence the appreciation of them will consist essentially in the contemplation of such contemplations. It is true that the most valuable appreciation of persons appears to be that which consists in the appreciation of their appreciation of other persons: but even here a reference to material beauty appears to be involved, *both* in respect of the fact that what is appreciated in the last instance may be the contemplation of what is merely beautiful, *and* in respect of the fact that the most valuable appreciation of a person appears to *include* an appreciation of his corporeal expression. Though, therefore, we may admit that the appreciation of a person's attitude towards other persons, or, to take one instance, the love of love, is far the most valuable good we know, and far more valuable than the mere love of beauty, yet we can only admit this if the first be understood to *include* the latter, in various degrees of directness."

The New Testament is a handbook for politicians compared with the unworldliness of Moore's chapter on "The Ideal." I know no equal to it in literature since Plato. And it is better than Plato because it is quite free from *fancy*. It conveys the beauty of the literalness of Moore's mind, the pure and passionate intensity of his vision, *un*fanciful and *un*dressed-up. Moore had a nightmare once in which he could not distinguish propositions from tables. But even when he was awake, he could not distinguish love and beauty and truth from the furniture. They took on the same definition of outline, the same stable, solid, objective qualities and common-sense reality.

I see no reason to shift from the fundamental intuitions of *Principia Ethica*; though they are much too few and too narrow to fit actual experience which provides a richer and more various content. That they furnish a justification of experience wholly independent of outside events has become an added comfort, even though one cannot live to-day secure in the undisturbed individualism which was the extraordinary achievement of the early Edwardian days, not for our little lot only, but for everyone else, too.

I am still a long way off from D. H. Lawrence and what he might have been justified in meaning when he said that we were "done for." And even now I am not quite ready to approach that theme. First of all I must explain the other facet of our faith. So far it has been a question of our attitude to ourselves and one another. What was our understanding of the outside world and our relation to it?

It was an important object of Moore's book to distinguish between goodness as an attribute of states of mind and rightness as an attribute of actions. He also has a section on the justification of general rules of conduct. The large part played by considerations of probability in his theory of right conduct was, indeed, an important contributory cause to my spending all the leisure of many years on the study of that subject: I was writing under the joint influence of Moore's *Principia Ethica* and Russell's *Principia Mathematica*. But for the most part, as I have said, we did not pay attention to this aspect of the book or bother much about it. We were living in the specious present, nor had begun to play the game of consequences. We existed in the world of Plato's *Dialogues*; we had not reached the *Republic*, let alone the *Laws*.

This brought us one big advantage. As we had thrown hedonism out of the window and, discarding Moore's so highly problematical calculus, lived entirely in present experience, since social action as an end in itself and not merely as a lugubrious duty had dropped out of our Ideal, and, not only social action, but the life of action generally, power, politics, success, wealth, ambition, with the economic motive and the economic criterion less prominent in our philosophy than with St Francis of Assisi, who at least made collections for the birds, it follows that we were amongst the first of our generation, perhaps alone amongst our generation, to escape from the Benthamite tradition. In practice, of course, at least so far as I was concerned, the outside world was not forgotten or forsworn. But I am recalling what our Ideal was in those early days when the life of passionate contemplation and communion was supposed to oust all other purposes whatever. It can be no part of this memoir for me to try to explain why it was such a big advantage for us to have escaped from the Benthamite tradition. But I do now regard that as the worm which has been gnawing at the insides of modern civilisation and is responsible for its present moral decay. We used to regard the Christians as the enemy, because they appeared as the representatives of tradition, convention and hocus-pocus. In truth it was the Benthamite calculus, based on an over-valuation of the economic criterion, which was destroying the quality of the popular Ideal.

Moreover, it was this escape from Bentham, joined with the unsurpassable individualism of our philosophy, which has served to protect the whole lot of us from the final *reductio ad absurdum* of Benthamism known as Marxism. We have completely failed, indeed, to provide a substitute for these economic bogus-faiths capable of protecting or satisfying our successors. But we ourselves have remained—am I not right in saying *all* of us?—altogether immune from the virus, as safe in the citadel of our ultimate faith as the Pope of Rome in his.

This is what we gained. But we set on one side, not only that part of Moore's fifth chapter on "Ethics in relation to Conduct" which dealt with the obligation so to act as to produce by causal connection the most probable maximum of eventual good through the whole procession of future ages (a discussion which was indeed riddled with fallacies), but also the part which discussed the duty of the individual to obey general rules. We entirely repudiated a personal liability on us to obey general rules. We claimed the right to judge every individual case on its merits, and the wisdom, experience and self-control to do so successfully. This was a very important part of our faith, violently and aggressively held, and for the outer world it was our most obvious and dangerous characteristic. We repudiated entirely customary morals, conventions and traditional wisdom. We were, that is to say, in the strict sense of the term, immoralists. The consequences of being found out had, of course, to be considered for what they were worth. But we recognised no moral obligation on us, no inner sanction, to conform or to obey. Before heaven we claimed to be our own judge in our own case. I have come to think that this is, perhaps, rather a Russian characteristic. It is certainly not an English one. It resulted in a general, widespread, though partly covert, suspicion affecting ourselves, our motives and our behaviour. This suspicion still persists to a certain extent, and it always will. It has deeply coloured the course of our lives in relation to the outside world. It is, I now think, a justifiable suspicion. Yet so far as I am concerned, it is too late to change. I remain, and always will remain, an immoralist.

I am not now concerned, however, with the fact that this aspect of our code was shocking. It would have been not less so, even if we had been perfectly right. What matters a great deal more is the fact that it was flimsily based, as I now think, on an *a priori* view of what human nature is like, both other people's and our own, which was disastrously mistaken.

I have said that we were amongst the first to escape from Benthamism. But of another eighteenth-century heresy we were the unrepentant heirs and last upholders. We were among the last of the Utopians, or meliorists as they are sometimes called, who believe in a continuing moral progress by virtue of which the human race already consists of reliable, rational, decent people, influenced by truth and objective standards, who can be safely released from the outward restraints of convention and traditional standards and inflexible rules of conduct, and left, from now onwards, to their own sensible devices, pure motives and reliable intuitions of the good. The view that human nature is reasonable had in 1903 quite a long history behind it. It underlay the ethics of self-interest—rational self-interest as it was called—just as much as the universal ethics of Kant or Bentham which aimed at the general good; and it was because self-interest was *rational* that the egoistic and altruistic systems were supposed to work out in practice to the same conclusions.

In short, we repudiated all versions of the doctrine of original sin, of there being insane and irrational springs of wickedness in most men. We were not aware that civilisation was a thin and precarious crust erected by the personality and the will of a very few, and only maintained by rules and conventions skilfully put across and guilefully preserved. We had no respect for traditional wisdom or the restraints of custom. We lacked reverence, as Lawrence observed and as Ludwig with justice also used to say—for everything and everyone. It did not occur to us to respect the extraordinary accomplishment of our predecessors in the ordering of life (as it now seems to me to have been) or the elaborate framework which they had devised to protect this order. Plato said in his *Laws* that one of the best of a set of good laws would be a law forbidding any young man to enquire which of them are right or wrong, though an old man remarking any defects in the laws might communicate this observation to a ruler or to an equal in years when no young man was present. That was a *dictum* in which we should have been unable to discover any point or significance whatever. As cause and consequence of our general state of mind we completely misunderstood human nature, including our own. The rationality which we attributed to it led to a superficiality, not only of judgment, but also of feeling. It was not only that intellectually we were pre-Freudian, but we had lost something which our predecessors had without replacing it. I still suffer incurably from attributing an unreal rationality to other people's feelings and behaviour (and doubtless to my own, too). There is one small but extraordinary silly manifestation of this absurd idea of what is "normal," namely the impulse to *protest*—to write a letter to *The Times*, call a meeting in the Guildhall, subscribe to some fund when my presuppositions as to what is "normal" are not fulfilled. I behave as if there really existed some authority or standard to which I can successfully appeal if I shout loud enough—perhaps it is some hereditary vestige of a belief in the efficacy of prayer.

I have said that this pesudo-rational view of human nature led to a thinness, a superficiality, not only of judgment, but also of feeling. It seems to me that Moore's chapter on "The Ideal" left out altogether some whole categories of valuable emotion. The attribution of rationality to human nature, instead of enriching it, now seems to me to have impoverished it. It ignored certain powerful and valuable springs of feeling. Some of the spontaneous, irrational outbursts of human nature can have a sort of value from which our schematism was cut off. Even some of the feelings associated with wickedness can have value. And in addition to the values arising out of spontaneous, volcanic and even wicked impulses, there are many objects of valuable contemplation and communion beyond those we knew of—those concerned with the order and pattern of life amongst communities and the emotions which they can inspire. Though one must ever remember Paley's *dictum* that "although we speak of communities as of sentient beings and ascribe to them happiness and misery, desires, interests and passions, nothing really exists or feels but *individuals*," yet we carried the individualism of our individuals too far.

And as the years wore on towards 1914, the thinness and the superficiality, as well as the falsity, of our view of man's heart became, as it now seems to me, more obvious; and there was, too, some falling away from the purity of the original doctrine. Concentration on moments of communion between a pair of lovers got thoroughly mixed up with the, once rejected, pleasure. The pattern of life would sometimes become no better than a succession of permutations of short sharp superficial "intrigues," as we called them. Our comments on life and affairs were bright and amusing, but brittle—as I said of the conversation of Russell and myself with Lawrence—because there was no solid diagnosis of human nature underlying them. Bertie in particular sustained simultaneously a pair of opinions ludicrously incompatible. He held that in fact human affairs were carried on after a most irrational fashion, but that the remedy was quite simple and easy, since all we had to do was to carry them on rationally.

A discussion of practical affairs on these lines was really very boring. And a discussion of the human heart which ignored so many of its deeper and blinder passions, both good and bad, was scarcely more interesting. Indeed it is only states of mind that matter, provided we agree to take account of the pattern of life through time and give up regarding it as a series of independent, instantaneous flashes, but the ways in which states of mind can be valuable, and the objects of them, are more various, and also much richer, than we allowed for. I fancy we used in old days to get round the rich variety of experience by expanding illegitimately the field of aesthetic appreciation (we would deal, for example, with all branches of the tragic emotion under this head), classifying as aesthetic experience what is really human experience and somehow sterilising it by this mis-classification.

If, therefore, I altogether ignore our merits—our charm, our intelligence, our unworldliness, our affection—I can see us as water-spiders, gracefully skimming, as light and reasonable as air, the surface of the stream without any contact at all with the eddies and currents underneath. And if I imagine us as coming under the observation of Lawrence's ignorant, jealous, irritable, hostile eyes, what a combination of qualities we offered to arouse his passionate distaste; this thin rationalism skipping on the crust of the lava, ignoring both the reality and the value of the vulgar passions, joined to libertinism and comprehensive irreverence, too clever by half for such an earthy character as Bunny, seducing with its intellectual *chic* such a portent as Ottoline, a regular skin-poison. All this was very unfair to poor, silly, well-meaning us. But that is why I say that there may have been just a grain of truth when Lawrence said in 1914 that we were "done for."

9th September 1938.

COLLEGE STUDIES

George Santayana

With my return to Harvard, a fortnight late, from the journey to Spain, my College studies may be said to have begun. They did not begin well. I had failed in one subject—a half course in algebra—which I was obliged to pass later, as Freshman work was prescribed and no substitutions were permitted. I had done well enough in the rest of the prescribed mathematics, analytic geometry, which I had had some grounding in at school, and also in the physics, which interested me immensely: and even in the algebra there were points that struck my imagination, as for instance the possibility and advantages of duo-decimal notation: our decimal system being founded only on the stupid reason that we have ten fingers and ten toes. If my teachers had begun by telling me that mathematics was pure play with presuppositions, and wholly in the air, I might have become a good mathematician, because I am happy enough in the realm of essence. But they were over-worked drudges, and I was largely inattentive, and inclined lazily to attribute to incapacity in myself or to a literary temperament that dullness which perhaps was due simply to lack of initiation. With a good speculative master I might have been an eager pupil and cried at once: *Introibo ad altare Dei.*[1]

I began badly also in not having a fixed plan of study. President Eliot's elective system was then in the ascendant. We liked it, I liked it; it seemed to open a universal field to free individuality. But to be free and cultivate individuality one must first exist, one's nature must be functioning. What was I, what were my powers and my vocation? Before I had discovered that, all freedom could be nothing but frivolity. I had chosen to go on with Latin and Greek, but disregarded the requirements for second-year honors in the classics, because those requirements involved Greek composition, which I couldn't attempt. I consciously continued my reading as an amateur, not as a scholar, I wasn't going to *teach* Greek or Latin. In this way I illustrated the complementary vices of the elective system: I was a smatterer, because things were arranged for the benefit of professionals.

So superficial was my study that I hardly remember what Latin authors I read or who was the professor. I read Lucretius, in a pocket edition without notes given me by a friend, somewhat pathetically, because he was leaving College. I couldn't properly understand the text, many a word was new to me, and I had to pass on, reading as I did at odd moments, or in the horse cars. But the general drift was obvious, and I learned the great passages by heart. Even the physical and biological theories seemed instructive, not as scientific finalities, if science could be final, but as serving to dispel the notion that anything is non-natural or miraculous. If the theory suggested were false, another no less naturalistic would be true: and this presumption recommended itself to me and has become one of my first principles: not that a particular philosophy called naturalism must be true *a priori*, but that nature sets the standard of naturalness. The most miraculous world, if it were real, would subdue the teachable mind to its own habit, and would prove that miracles were—as they are in the Gospels—the most ordinary and most intelligible of events. It made me laugh afterwards to read in pedantic commentators that Lucretius abandoned his atomism whenever he was poetical, and contradicted himself in invoking Venus, when Epicurus maintains that the gods do not trouble about human affairs. On the contrary, Lucretius might perfectly well have invoked Jupiter or Fate (as Leopardi constantly invokes Fate); for Fate, Jupiter, or Venus are names for the whole or some part of the life of na-

[1]The first words of the Mass: I shall go in unto the altar of God.

ture. There is no incompatibility in these various appellations, if they are understood sympathetically as the ancients understood them. They were not gaping phenomenalists, but knew that our senses, no less than our poetry and myth, clothe in human images the manifold processes of matter. By these hidden processes they lived, before them they trembled, the promise and potency of them they sought to prophesy. Matter was the ancient plastic substance of all the gods.

I also took a half course in Latin composition which I audaciously neglected, "cutting" all the lectures except the first, but doing the prescribed exercises and taking the examinations. I passed with a mark of ninety per cent.

In Greek I did as badly as at school. Here again this was not the teacher's fault. He was the amiable Louis Dyer, who had studied at Balliol, married a Miss Macmillan, and later lived in Oxford, where I often saw him. He gave me his *Gods of Greece*, nicely bound, a book that had a great influence over me. Perhaps Matthew Arnold moved in the background and inspired us. But I was thirsting for inspiration, and Greek grammar and prosody didn't hold my attention. We were supposed to read the *Ajax*, but though in this case I went to all the lectures, I didn't study the text. The *Bacchæ*, however, was a revelation. Here, before Nietzsche had pointed it out, the Dionysiac inspiration was explicitly opposed to the Apollonian; and although my tradition and manner are rather Apollonian, I unhesitatingly accept the Dionysiac inspiration as also divine. It comes from the elemental god, from the chaotic but fertile bosom of nature; Apollo is the god of measure, of perfection of humanism. He is more civilized, but more superficial, more highly conditioned. His worship seems classic and established forever, and it does last longer and is more often revived than any one form of Dionysiac frenzy: yet the frenzy represents the primitive wild soul, not at home in the world, not settled in itself, and merging again with the elements, half in helplessness and half in self-transcendence and mystic triumph.

I have taken for a motto a phrase out of one of Euripides' choruses: Τὸ σοφὸν οὐ σοφία. It was this phrase, in that year, 1884, that led me to write my first sonnet, printed a year or two later, and reappearing as Sonnet III in my *Poems;* the first two having been composed afterwards on purpose to frame in the earlier ones and bring the argument to a head. I translated the dictum of Euripides in the rather thin and prosaic line: "It is not wisdom to be only wise"; and then, given that sentiment and that rhyme, I built the whole sonnet round them. Even when I wrote it, this sonnet was belated. I was twenty years old, and that sentiment was what I had felt at sixteen. But I still recognized, as I recognize now at nearly eighty, the legitimacy of that feeling.

The chief difference is that when, at sixteen or even at twenty, I said "faith," I meant the Catholic faith; and when now I oppose "faith" to reason I mean faith in the existence and order of nature, a faith in the assumptions made inevitably in daily life; yet I see far more clearly than I did in my youth that pure reason, a reason that is not based on irrational postulates and presuppositions, is perfectly impotent. It is not "smoky" or indistinct: on the contrary, it is mathematically precise, but abstract and in the air. What I had in mind then when I spoke of "knowledge" was the common sense and science of the day, which in fact were uncritically based on animal faith and empirical presumption, and which I, with a solipsistic breath, could at once reduce to a dream, not to say a nightmare. For that reason I called them "smoky," at once ugly, obscure, and unsubstantial. But it was immature of me to wish, lackadaisically and hopelessly, to substitute a religious myth for that sensuous obsession. And the rest of those twenty youthful sonnets pointed out well enough where a mature solution might be found: in obedience to matter for the sake of freedom of mind.

As to William James on Taine's *De l'Intelligence,* I am not conscious of any intellectual residuum, only of a few graphic memories touching his aspects and ways, which at that time were distinctly medical. He was impatient of the things he didn't like in philosophy; his latent pragmatism appeared only in its negative germ, as scorn of everything remote or pretentious; and his love of lame ducks and neglected possibilities, which later took the form of charity and breadth of mind, then seemed rather the doctor's quick eye for bad symptoms, as if he had diagnosed people in a jiffy and cried: "Ah, *you* are a paranoiac! Ah, *you* have the pox!" I remember his views better in another set of lectures on Herbert Spencer, or rather against him. James detested any system of the universe that professed to enclose everything: we must never set up boundaries that exclude romantic surprises. He retained the primitive feeling that death *might* open new worlds to us—not at all what religions predict but something at once novel and natural; also the primitive feeling that invisible spirits *might* be floating about among us, and might suddenly do something to hurt or to help us. Spencer was intolerable for shutting out such possibilities: he was also intolerable for his verbose generalities and sweeping "principles." There were no "principles," except in men's heads: there were only facts. James did not stop to consider whether this assertion was not itself a principle that might describe a fact.

Herbert Spencer, I think, taught me nothing. I agreed with his naturalism or materialism, because that is what we all start with: the minimum presupposition of perception and action. But I agreed with James about Spencer's theory of evolution: It was a tangle of words, of loose generalities that some things might sometimes suggest to us, and that, said properly, it might have been *witty* to say, but that had absolutely no value as "laws" or "causes" of events. Such "principles" might serve an "objective idealist," not a naturalist or a scientific man. James was characteristically masculine and empirical in his wrath at the "scandalous vagueness" of Spencer's ideas. For instance, what did it mean to say that things passed from the indefinite to the definite? Nothing can be indefinite. Make a blot of ink at random on a piece of paper. The spot is not indefinite: it has precisely the outline that it has.[2] But James, though trenchant, was short-winded in argument. He didn't go on, for instance to consider on this occasion how, if there be nothing indefinite, the notion of the indefinite comes into existence. Suppose that having made a random blot, shapeless as we call it in spite of its perfectly definite shape, I at once folded the paper in two. The blot would become two symmetrical blots, or a larger blot bilaterally symmetrical. It might resemble an oak leaf. It would then cease to have a nameless shape, but would become Platonically or humanly specific. We should say it had a definite shape, one that we could recognize and reproduce. Spencer, if we interpret him critically and progressively, was therefore saying that things change from forms that for our senses and language would not be recognizable or namable into forms that we can distinguish and name. This happens sometimes not because things grow more definite, but because our senses and imagination have a limited range and can arrest one form of things rather than another; so that the world grows definite *for us* when we are able to perceive more parts of it and their relations. Nature thereby has changed but only intelligence has advanced; change is called evolution when sense and language are thereby enabled better to distinguish their objects. The notion that nature first acquired form as an animal mind may gradually grow less stupid, belongs to the age of fable. Spencer, unlike Lucretius and Spinoza, had no speculative power. He meant to be a naturalist, but language and the hypostasized idea of progress turned him into an idealistic metaphysician.

I will not attempt to describe here the many lessons that I learned in the study of Spinoza, lessons that in several respects laid the foundation of my philosophy. I will only say that I learned them from Spinoza himself, from his *ipsissima verba*,[3] studied in the original in all the crucial passages; as a guide and stimulus I had Sir Frederick Pollock's sympathetic book, with good renderings, and not much modern interpretation. It was a work, as he told me himself forty-five years later, at the Spinoza commemoration at the Hague, of his youth; and perhaps the science was emphasized at the expense of the religion. Yet that the object of this religion was *Deus sive Natura*[4]—the universe, whatever it may be, of which we are a part—was never concealed or denaturalized. Royce himself seemed to suffer less from the plague of idealistic criticism in this case than usual; for instance, about the saying of Spinoza's that the mind of God resembled the mind of man as the Dog Star resembles the barking animal. Royce said only that this was too materialistic, without caring or daring to broach the question as to the diffusion or concentration of that cosmic "mind." The unified "universal thought" that Royce posited would not be

---

[2]Here was a hint of my "essences" given by an unintended shot, that hit the bull's-eye without seeing it. Forms are infinite in multitude and each perfectly concrete. James's radical empiricism was undoubtedly a guide to me in this matter. Also Berkeley's nominalism. [Author's note]

[3]Very own words.   [4]God or Nature.

a "cogitation" but only a truth, the total *system* of cogitations that may accompany the total movement of matter. If it were one actual intuition it would not *accompany* the movement of matter but either describe and command it from afar or merely imagine it. Royce had a powerful and learned mind, and it was always profitable, if not pleasant, to listen to him: not pleasant because his voice was harsh, his style heavy, repetitious and pedantic, and his monotonous preoccupation with his own system intolerable. To listen was profitable nevertheless because his comfortless dissatisfaction with every possible idea opened vistas and disturbed a too easy dogmatism: while the perversity and futility of his dialectic threw one back in the end on the great certainties and the great possibilities, such as made the minds of the great philosophers at once sublime and sane.

As I have said elsewhere, I regard Spinoza as the only modern philosopher in the line of orthodox physics, the line that begins with Thales and culminates, for Greek philosophy, in Democritus. Orthodox physics should inspire and support orthodox ethics; and perhaps the chief source of my enthusiasm for Spinoza has been the magnificent clearness of his orthodoxy on this point. Morality is something natural. It arises and varies, not only psychologically but prescriptively and justly, with the nature of the creature whose morality it is. Morality is something relative; not that its precepts in any case are optional or arbitrary; for each man they are defined by his innate character and possible forms of happiness and action. His momentary passions or judgments are partial expressions of his nature, but not adequate or infallible; and ignorance of the circumstances may mislead in practice, as ignorance of self may mislead in desire. But there is a fixed good relative to each species and each individual; so that in considering the moral ideal of any philosopher, two questions arise. First, does he, like Spinoza, understand the natural basis of morality, or is he confused and superstitious on the subject? Second, how humane and representative is his sense for the good, and how far, by his disposition or sympathetic intelligence, does he appreciate all the types of excellence towards which life may be directed?

James and Royce were then the "young" professors of philosophy, they represented the dangers and scandals of free thought, all the more disquieting in that their free thought enveloped religion. But Harvard possessed safe, sober old professors also and oldest of all, "Fanny" Bowen. He was so old that to be old, self-repeating, dogmatic, rheumatic, and querulous had become picturesque in him, and a part of his dramatic personage. He was a dear old thing, and an excellent teacher. Between his fits of coughing, and his invectives against all who were wrong and didn't agree with Sir William Hamilton, he would impress upon us many an axiom, many an argument belonging to the great traditions of philosophy: and when after spitting into the vast bandanna handkerchief that he carried for the purpose, he would drop it on the desk with a gesture of combined disgust and relief, he expressed vividly to the eye the spirit in which philosophic and religious sects have always refuted and denounced one another. History sat living before us in this teacher of history. Descartes, Leibniz and Spinoza would be quoted verbatim, and expounded (especially the first two) on their own presuppositions and in their own terms. It was not criticism but it was instruction. Spinoza was rather beyond Bowen's range; yet even here the words of the master would be repeated, and could be remembered in their terseness, while the professor's refutations would blow by like dead leaves. Unfortunately old Bowen did not always preach to his text. Sometimes he would wander into irrelevant invectives against John Stuart Mill, who in a footnote had once referred to Bowen (who was then editor of a reputable review) as "an obscure American."

We had another right-thinking and edifying teacher, no less thoroughly well baked in all his opinions and mannerisms, but younger in years and following a later fashion in philosophy. Professor Palmer practised all the smooth oratorical arts of a liberal parson or headmaster; he conciliated opponents, plotted (always legally) with friends, and if things went against him, still smiled victoriously and seemed to be on the crest of the wave. He was the professor of ethics. His lectures were beautifully prepared, and exactly the same year after year. He had been professor of Greek also, and made anodyne translations from Homer and Sophocles in "rhymic" and sleepy prose. In his course on English moralists he brought out his selected authors in dialectical order; each successive view appeared fresh and plausible, but not sensational. They came in a subtle crescendo, everything good, and everything a little better than what went before, so that at the end you ought to have found yourself in the seventh heaven. Yet we, or at least I, didn't find ourselves there. I felt cheated. The method was Hegelian adapted to a Sunday School: all roses without thorns. All defects in doctrine (why not also in conduct?) were stepping-stones to higher things. We began with pungent, mannish, violent theories: Hobbes and Mandeville. We passed onward to something more feminine and refined, to Shaftesbury. From this we dialectically reacted, landing in the apparently solid, liberal, political reformer, John Stuart Mill: but no, that was not our divine destination. A breath of higher philosophy somehow blew over us. We levitated; and we knew not how or why, utilitarianism dissolved, lost in the distant valleys beneath us, and we realized the providential utility of utilitarianism in carrying us so far above it. "Purring pussy Palmer," my sporting friend "Swelly" Bangs used to call him: yet Palmer was a benign influence. The crude, half-educated, conscientious, ambitious young men who wished to study ethics gained subtler and more elastic notions of what was good than they had ever dreamt of: and their notions of what was bad became correspondingly discriminating and fair. Palmer was like a father confessor, never shocked at sin, never despairing of sinners. There must be a little of everything in the Lord's vineyard. Palmer was a fountain of sweet reasonableness. That his methods were sophistical and his conclusions lame didn't really matter. It was not a question of discovering or deciding anything final: the point was to become more cultivated and more intelligent. You could then define your aims and your principles for yourself. I found the authors read in Palmer's course, especially Hobbes, valuable in themselves; and Palmer's methods of exposition and criticism, sly and treacherous as they were, gave me a lesson in dialectic, and a warning against it. I began to understand that the cogency of dialectic is merely verbal or ideal, and its application to facts, even to the evolution of ideas, entirely hypothetical and distorting. If ideas created themselves (which they don't) or succeeded one another in the mind or in history by logical derivation (as again they don't), evolution might be dialectical: but as it is, dialectic merely throws a verbal net into the sea, to draw a pattern over the fishes without catching any of them. It is an optical illusion.

Dialectic didn't show its other, its honest, side to me until many years later, when I read Plato and knew Bertie Russell. Honest logicians never apply dialectic to history, and only in play to cosmology. Events are derived from one another materially and contingently. This is no less true when events are mental than when they are physical. It is *external* insights and interests that transform one system of philosophy into another, Socrates into Plato, Locke into Berkeley, Kant into Schopenhauer and Hegel. Each system remains logically and morally stable, like a portrait of its author. A philosophy that is radical and consistent cannot evolve. That which evolves is only the immature, the self-contradictory; and if circumstances do not permit it to ripen according to its inner potentialities, it withers and dissolves into dust, leaving no progeny. Each fact, each group of ideas, in fusion with other facts, passes into a new natural form, not evolved from the previous forms dialectically, but created by nature out of their matter and occasion, at each juncture with a fresh result.

I also studied Locke, Berkeley, and Hume under William James. Here there was as much honest humanity in the teacher as in the texts, and I think I was not impervious to the wit and wisdom of any of them. Hume was the one I least appreciated: yet Palmer once said that I had Hume in my bones. In reality, whether through my immaturity only, or through James's bewilderment also, I seem to have gathered no clear lesson from those authors or from James himself. Verbally I understood them well enough; they were not superficially obscure; but critically, as to their presuppositions, their categories and their places in history, I understood nothing. Even when four years later I gave that very course, I didn't advance beyond a friendly literary interpretation of their meaning and of the psychological cosmos that they seemed to posit. I hardly questioned their ambiguous units, their "perceptions" or "ideas," but accepted them, as James then accepted them, as representing total scattered moments of "experience" or "life." This was historically just. This philosophy is purely literary and autobiographical. It sees "experience" as composed of the high lights that language and memory find in it retrospectively. It hypostasizes the description into the object. But such hypostasis is an indefensible trick of memory, a poetical or mythical substitution of images for events and of verbal for dynamic elements. It is as if I pretended, in writing this book, to have discovered the fundamental reality and total composition of myself, of my family, of Spain, America, Germany, England, and Italy. A monstrous trick of verbal legerdemain, a sophistical curiosity.

The only solid foundation for all my play with this subject was supplied by the sturdy but undeveloped materialism of Hobbes, powerfully supported by the psychology of Spinoza and insecurely by the early medical psychology of James: to which in Germany my passing enthusiasm for Schopenhauer may be added, because by that time I was able to discount the language of a system and perceive from what direction it drew its inspiration. The "Will" in Schopenhauer was a transparent mythological symbol for the flux of matter. There was absolute equivalence between such a system, in its purport and sense for reality, and the systems of Spinoza and Lucretius. This was the element of ancient sanity that kept me awake and conscious of the points of the compass in the subsequent wreck of psychologism. Such wrecks are not fatal. Psychologism lives, and must always live, in literature and history. In these pursuits we are living as we imagine others might have lived, and seeing things as they might have seen them. We are dramatically enlarging our experience. What was lost in that moral tempest was only the illusion that such play of imagination revealed any profound truth or dislodged Nature to put Experience in her place.

An event that had important consequences in the future course of my life occurred silently and almost unnoticed during my Senior year. A young man named Charles Augustus Strong—there was already something royal and German about that "Augustus" and that "Strong," though the youth was modesty and Puritanism personified—came from the university of his native Rochester, New York, to study philosophy for a year at Harvard. As I too was taking all the advanced courses in that subject, we found ourselves daily thrown together, gradually began to compare notes, and to discuss the professors and their opinions; and finally we founded a philosophical club, in order to discuss everything more thoroughly with the other embryonic philosophers in the place. Towards the end of the year we both became candidates for the Walker Fellowship, usually awarded to graduates who wished to study philosophy in Germany. This was a rivalry that I disliked and also feared; because, if I had the advantage of being a Harvard man and better known to the professors, and also of being more glib and more resourceful in examinations, he had the decisive advantage of inspiring professional confidence. When you learned that his father and his brother were Baptist clergymen, you recognized at once that he too was a Baptist clergyman by nature and habit, only that some untoward influence had crossed his path and deflected him from his vocation. He had lost his faith in revelation. Modernist compromises and ambiguities were abhorrent to his strict honesty and love of precision. You mustn't preach what you don't believe.

He turned therefore to the nearest thing to being a clergyman that he could be sincerely, which was to be a professor of philosophy. He was already, in aspect, in manner, in speech, in spirit, thoroughly professional. Moreover, for studying in Germany he was far better prepared than I in that he spoke German perfectly. He had been at school in Germany, in a Gymnasium at Güteslohe, and had received that strict training in all subjects which was not to be expected in free America. He was slow but accurate, and his zeal in the pursuit of truth was unflagging. He had the memory and solidity of the head boy of the class. Besides, when you observed him afresh, you saw that he was very good-looking, tall, firm, with curly black hair and noble features. It was only his shyness, reserve, and lack of responsive sympathy that obscured these advantages. Perhaps if he found his proper element and were happy they would shine out again.

How about me? Was I professional? Should I ever make a professor of philosophy? Everybody doubted it. I not only doubted it myself, but was repelled by the idea. What I wanted was to go on being a student, and especially to be a travelling student. I loved speculation for itself, as I loved poetry, not out of worldly respect or anxiety lest I should be mistaken, but for the splendor of it, like the splendor of the sea and the stars. And I knew I should love living obscurely and freely in old towns, in strange countries, hearing all sorts of outlandish marvellous opinions. I could have made a bargain with Mephistopheles, not for youth but for the appearance of youth, so that with its tastes but without its passions, I might have been a wandering student all my life, at Salamanca, at Bologna, in Oxford, in Paris, at Benares, in China, in Persia. Germany would be a beginning. If I never became a professor, so much the better. I should have seen the world, historical and intellectual: I should have been free in my best years.

Now my mother was going to assign me a permanent allowance of $500 a year, the sum that she received from "Uncle Russell" or that symbolically represented the $10,000 she had once received from "Uncle Robert," which she retained and meant to leave to me. The Walker Fellowship amounted to another $500. The two would make a neat sum, yet I knew that in Europe I could easily get on with less. From things that Strong had dropped in conversation, I had gathered that he was much in the same case. His father was well off and he too had an allowance. Perhaps he didn't need the whole Fellowship. I therefore did a sly thing. I asked him if he would be willing to agree that whoever of us got the Fellowship should divide it with the other. Then we should both be sure of going to Germany for the next year. He consented at once. I think he liked the idea of having me with him. Our discussions enlivened him. I should serve as a useful pace-maker in the pursuit of absolute truth.

Nevertheless my conscience was a bit uneasy. I felt in my bones that Strong would get the appointment, and I was simply robbing him of half his stipend. So I made a second proposal. Before agreeing to this plan, let us lay it before Professor Palmer, professional moralist and Head of the Department, practically the man who would decide between us. Let us ask him if he thought well of it. We went to see him together. I acted as spokesman, having the readier tongue. I said we supposed we were the only likely candidates for the Fellowship, that we both wanted it very much, and that we both had small allowances from our families, so that we could get on with less than the whole amount of the Fellowship. Would it be a fair thing for us to agree, whoever got it, to divide it between us?

Professor Palmer bit his lips, thought for a moment, and decided to be sympathetic. He saw no objection. The action would be equally unselfish in both of us. I knew it was not unselfish in me, yet Palmer's cant set me at rest. They must have been undecided about the choice in the Committee, otherwise Palmer would not have agreed to the division. Now they would give the Fellowship to Strong, knowing that I was to get half the money; so that really they would be voting half the money to me. Not quite satisfactory this, but excusable and rather ingenious.

I think this is the only occasion in my life when I have done something a little too clever in order to get money. Yet the result might have encouraged a person inclined to trickery, because I not only got what I wanted, but in consequence made a great haul, not exactly in money, but precisely in what I cared for more than for money, in travel, in residence in foreign parts, in a well-paved path open to all sorts of intellectual pleasures. Strong, for a family reason that I shall mention later, gave up the Fellowship at the end of one year. It was then awarded to me for two successive years. Later, Strong went to live in Europe, in Paris, in Fiesole. He had got used to having me to talk with. I was often his guest for long periods; and that division of his $500 let me into a series of favors that I was positively begged to receive. Strong had become rich, he was married and had a young daughter: yet his life was strangely solitary. He was no less bored than when he was younger. He would actually have paid me, as he paid one or two others, to live near him so as to have stated hours for philosophical discussions. He once expressly offered to guarantee me an income of $2,500 if I would give up my professorship and go and live with him in Paris. I didn't accept that offer; I waited before retiring until I had money enough of my own to make me independent; but I did make his apartment in Paris my headquarters for some years; which for me at that time was a great convenience and economy. I had a lodging at will, gratis, and I paid for food and service only when I was alone in the apartment or when we dined in restaurants, as we did every evening. At first on these occasions each paid for both on alternate days; later each always paid for what he ordered. Our tastes were becoming more different.

There was always a latent tension between us, because our reasons for living together were mixed and not the same in both of us. In both there was real sympathy up to a point and a real interest in the same philosophical problems and political and social matters; and our views if not identical were cooperative. They played round the same facts in the same speculative spirit. Yet we were not intimate friends. We were more like partners in the same business. And our motive for forming this partnership was in neither of us personal affection but in both only private interest. Strong wanted a philosophical friend to talk with; at first mainly for the sake of company and stimulation, later rather in the hope of forcing his views and confirming himself in them by convincing someone else of their truth. I, on the other hand, wanted a material pied-à-terre, a place and a person or persons that should take the place of a home; and Strong offered these in a most acceptable form, especially when he lived in Paris. He was free from almost all the bonds from which I wished to be free; he was less entangling socially and financially than such attachments as I might have found in Spain or in England. Besides, I lived with him only at certain seasons, seldom longer than for a month or two at a time; and there was no pledge that our arrangement should be permanent. In fact, I constantly went off by myself, to Spain, to Oxford, to Rome, or even to other lodgings in Paris: because I found writing difficult, both materially and psychologically, when we lived together. His hours were inflexible, also his determination to revert daily to the same discussions; the limitations that had become tyrannical over him became tyrannical over others also. In this way, while the friendly partnership originally formed by us in dividing the Walker Fellowship accompanied us through life, the mixed motives that had prompted it accompanied us also. Strong was always being cheated, and a victim that complained of not being victimized enough; and I was always being punished by a sense of unnecessary dependence and constraint, when it was freedom and independence that I had sought.

These observations anticipate events that lay far in the future. For the moment I was plunged in work, more wholeheartedly perhaps than ever again, because I saw my future and my studies in an undivided prospect: my whole inner life would be in those studies, while those studies in turn would determine my career. And my bad beginning as a student at Harvard was redeemed by an honorable end. I received my bachelor's degree *summa cum laude*. In spite of mediocre standing in some subjects, my teachers thought that my speculative vocation and my understanding of the great philosophers entitled me to a first place. This was a repetition with a difference, of my career at the Latin School. There I had, as a person, carried the day against a middling record as a pupil: now at Harvard I carried the day against the same handicap by force of personal abilities in a special half-artistic direction.

I didn't wait, however, to receive my degree in person at Commencement. Herbert Lyman took the parchment in charge and brought it to me in Germany. On taking my last examination, I had sailed without knowing what would be the result. I took a German ship, not that I was bound directly to Germany, but that it touched at Cherbourg whence second class this time, I could travel leisurely to Avila and see a lot of cathedral towns: Caen, Le Mans, Angers, Poitiers, Angoulême, Bordeaux, and Burgos. The expense, stopping one night at each place, was not greater than in going first class through Paris. I was to spend the summer quietly in Avila, and in the autumn to join Herbert Lyman in Dresden and Strong in Berlin.

The curtain drops here, to rise presently on those other scenes.

QUESTIONS

1. Find some evidence to illustrate what Liebling calls the "studied impersonality of a newspaper, its simulation of photography in words." Look especially at the editorials, but don't overlook the news.

2. On p. 1116 Liebling speaks about "the charming grab-bag quality of a liberal-art college education—the items that will prove of subsequent value turn up in the most unexpected places." Does he mean, "It's what you learn outside of class that counts"?

3. Check what your composition book has to say on coherence or on transitions between paragraphs. Then analyze how Liebling's piece is held together.

4. Explain Liebling's title.

5. If you ever need a topic for a library paper, the passing of the old *World* should be a good one.

6. What details and episodes make the most effective contribution to the central effect or the atmosphere of "Here We Are in 1943"? How does Gertrude Stein let the reader know what her important ideas are?

7. What qualities of Gertrude Stein's style might justify a reader who thinks "she sounds like half of a morning telephone conversation between a couple of gabbling housewives"?

8. What is your opinion of Keynes' definition of morals and religion? How does it compare with Santayana's?

9. How would Professor Mecklin (in Liebling's "Professor Kills Santa Claus," page 1116) have fitted in with the academics and men of letters that Keynes is talking about? What was the Santa Claus of this group?

10. Would it be fair to say that Lawrence had roughly the same effect on Keynes and Douglas?

11. What tone does Santayana get in his first three sentences in the paragraph on G. H. Palmer? Can you tell whether it is Bowen or Palmer he approves?

12. Santayana's analysis of dialectic is an important point for any college student. You should be able to explain it in your own words, especially the wonderful figure of the fish net.

13. What is the difference between a verbal and a critical understanding of a text?

14. What kinds of material does Santayana have in this selection? Is there some logical or dramatic principle to unify them?

15. Compare Sanayana and Whitehead on the use of the classics.

INFORMATIONAL ESSAYS: WHAT THE WORLD MEANS

These selections are the stuff of history. Their mixture of fact, opinion, analysis, conjecture, and, no doubt, prejudice will be the evidence that a future historian (perhaps one less of a polemicist than Barraclough) uses in describing the climate of our times. The selections also illustrate one of the most popular of modern forms of exposition: the article that analyzes a current situation from a fairly limited perspective. (This may be slightly unfair to Barraclough, since he does attempt to view Soviet-Western relations from the distance of history.) Actually (excepting Barraclough's) the analysis in these articles, as is typical of the form, is hardly more than description; and one often wonders how self-conscious about their own thinking and the forces that operate in society the authors of such pieces are. Stylistically Holmes is pretty artful. Schickel and Reichley are rather academic; the flat rhythms and relatively neutral diction justify the adjective, even if one did not know that they were graduate students when they wrote. Snow's is clear and pleasant, there is even some tone to it; but it is hardly the most distinctive prose. Once upon a time the piece by Dickens would have been called an informal essay, but except that it is rather theatrical or indeed sentimental, it is not much different from what we call a feature story. Sidney Smith's review contains a good deal of evidence of what the world was like in the great days of the nineteenth century; I include it also because the quotations from the Select Committee Reports often reproduce sentences pretty much as they must have been said.

THE ISLAND
OF THE PRESENT

Richard Schickel

My generation might properly be called "the analyzed generation." Sometimes it seems as if nearly every prominent magazine, editorial writer, and columnist has had a crack at trying to explain the admittedly odd behavior of the current college-age group.

As early as 1951 historian Oscar Handlin was wondering (in *The Atlantic*) "why is this generation which has been so ill-used, which has so

FROM *The Progressive*. Reprinted by permission.

many grievances—why is it so lacking in youthful energies?" *Time,* with its usual irritating finality, said that "today's generation either through fear, passivity, or conviction is ready to conform."

Irritating or not, *Time's* sentiments have been echoed by almost everyone who has observed today's younger generation. The liberal journals have told us we are "silent" because we have been made timid by the doings of McCarthy and his friends. From the right comes the cry that the New Deal's welfare measures have sapped us of our individuality. We have been called "the beat generation," "a generation of jellyfish," "the vacuum-tube generation," and so on.

On one point everyone seems to agree: My generation does not fit the traditional stereotype of youth. Young people are supposed to burn with idealism, lust after adventure, be prepared for any sort of radical excitement. Obviously today's collegian does not fit this pattern. In fact, most of his observers agree that he is, in his outlook, prematurely middle-aged. He seems set in his ways, world-weary (if not worldly-wise), and highly unreceptive to change.

His father contrasts his memories of the moral and social upheaval of the twenties, in which he was more participant than observer, to the ordered world and orderly behavior of today's youth, and we have to admit that, despite the seeming stability we have found, we suffer by comparison. The thirties, with the Oxford petition, the peace strikes, the warm-hearted (if wrong-headed) enthusiasm over Marxism, the social consciousness of the era, seem, to the young liberals of today, to have been times in which they could have reveled.

But it is a mistake to compare the behavior of one younger generation to that of another. I have been making that mistake for the last four years, as have, I think, the writers of all those "generation" articles. Youth in every era is faced with the problem of getting on in a world it did not make. And, in the Twentieth Century, each new generation finds the world it inherits radically different from the world its fathers found. It attempts to solve the new problems of this world in new ways which defy comparison to the ways a previous generation met its problems.

II

It is foolish, of course, to generalize about anything as heterogeneous as a "generation." For every Fitzgeraldian character of the twenties, there was undoubtedly some youth quietly preparing to be an outstanding scholar. For every member of the Young Communist League in the thirties, there were, no doubt, several young men beginning careers in investment banking. But younger generations, seen in perspective, have an unfortunate habit of taking on, correctly or not, the hues in which those we regard as their chief spokesmen have painted them.

I do not have the temerity to pretend to be setting forth the views of a "chief spokesman" for my generation, but I do think I can offer a fairly reasonable explanation for the colors in which it has been painted. It seems hardly necessary to ask the reader to remember that I am writing about a climate of opinion, not about the fresh breezes which alter, for a day or two, the prevailing weather.

Modern America, from 1920 to, roughly, 1950, presents a fairly consistent picture of growth. The rise of the large corporation began considerably earlier than 1920, to be sure, but by that year it had reached adolescence. By 1950 it had reached the position of community elder statesman. Mass media, after a rapid period of growth, reached a position of vigorous maturity (technically, and in terms of power, if not in content) around 1950 when television began to come into its own. Labor, after causing its parents considerable worry over its early radical flings, had shucked off most of its youthful reputation; by the end of World War II it had gained middle-class respectability. And with the Wallace debacle in 1948, America apparently had rejected what seemed to be radical political ideas and ideals. By 1950 both major political parties were paying lip service, and were in the process granting respectability, to the leftist ideas which seemed to offer to all men at least a measure of material comfort and security.

In short, America was settling down, in the postwar years, to the business of consolidating the somewhat haphazard growth of its great industrial era. Into this land of giants came the "new" college generation, replacing the more liberally oriented veterans on the college campuses. But this new group, lacking the depression experiences of the veterans, saw the giants as benevolent rulers. They were not going to chop down any of their beanstalks. Rather they decided that, as long as it was possible to obtain a suburban nirvana by attaching themselves to the court of one of the giants, that's what they would do.

If on the one hand America was "consolidating" its material growth, on the other it was speculatively balancing a globe labeled "new world." What it saw in that clouded crystal was frightening. On the international scene it was one of two principal contestants for control of the entire world. The awesome prospect of atomic war confronted it. At home, the Far Right was violently questioning the liberal democratic values which the depression and the war had finally succeeded in at least introducing to the general conscience.

To college students the future, because of the Cold War, no longer looked like an extension of the familiar world in which they had grown up. Like most of the rest of America, the student found his faith in Progress shaken. Progress, it seemed, had certainly brought him remarkable comforts—but it had also brought his world closer to the possibility of total destruction.

What does one do in such a situation? He may try, as many students have tried, to avert his eyes from the menacing future. Or he may try to shut out the future by concentrating on the present, by resisting change, by clinging desperately to the familiar. Consider Eric Hoffer's remarks in his brilliant little book, *The True Believer:*

"Patriotism, racial solidarity, and even the preaching of revolution find a more ready response among people who see limitless opportunities spread out before them than among those who move within the fixed limits of a familiar, orderly, and predictable existence."

This seems to me to describe the situation of today's college student rather more cogently than anything else. He is not going to be a radical when his radicalism might lead him to a future nowhere near so desirable as the present—even though he is aware that his present world is not all that it might be. And, as Thornton Wilder has noted, there is no longer the need for "shocking" his parents there once was. This generation's parents, with an assist from the generation of the thirties, accomplished the revolution in morals (and manners) necessary for the transition from the Victorian to the newer industrial epoch. The generation of the thirties, as previously noted, witnessed a shift in the national climate of opinion in the realms of politics and economics to a view fairly consistent with modern democratic and humanitarian values.

Today's college student, although he realizes that he could extend and bring up to date the work begun twenty and thirty years ago, lacks the confidence to do so. His predecessors had that confidence. In the twenties disillusion with old values combined with a confidence in the boom that would never bust. In the thirties no one was afraid of the better world he was working for. After all, it couldn't be much worse than the one in which he was living, could it? To today's collegian, however, it is conceivable that a new world could be worse—much worse.

And, while he is beset by his fears for the future, the college student has his natural love for the current order reinforced by the colleges themselves, who counsel "adjustment." Consider the statement of a man who should know, economic historian and Columbia Dean Louis Hacker:

"Increasingly a good part of college administration has fallen into the hands of non-academic people who are stressing services and activities which have nothing to do with learning. The socially adjusted boy or girl, the fully rounded youngster, the outgoing young person: This is the college ideal . . .

"Presidents and deans justify all this by saying 'adjustment to life' is one of their responsibilities."

The trouble with all this is that, by the time he graduates, today's student may find that he has adjusted to a life that no longer exists. But the people who grant the endowments and pay the taxes on which universities are run are the same people who give job trainees batteries of personality tests and who expect today's graduate to be a well-adjusted (that word again) youth capable of playing ball on the "team." Small wonder the colleges quickly adjust to the idea of producing "adjusted" students.

But this is, perhaps, too harsh a judgment to pass on the universities. Adjustment might have come even without outside pressure, as an answer to the felt necessities of many students. As everyone knows, higher education has become increasingly democratized. It is no longer the haven for an intellectual elite. The majority of students come to college looking for the know-how that will enable them to live a comfortable suburban existence. They want to adjust to the material values held by the most vocal segment of the population. The student intellectual, faced with his fears for the future, and not wishing to disturb the order of the present, tends more and more, as he looks with some disgust at the non- (if not anti-) intellectuals who surround him, even in the classroom, to retreat. His retreat may lead him into a pedantic scholarship (like the new criticism which so attracts young writers today) or into a mystic embrace with an ancient religion, or, perhaps, even into the writing of science fiction.

Perhaps no other recent cultural manifestation bespeaks so clearly America's fear of the future as science fiction. Utopia, from More to Bellamy, has, until recently, reflected man's faith in the future, in Progress which would bring him to a heaven on earth. Now Utopia has become (to use Karl Meyer's word, in an excellent article in *The Reporter*) "futopia." In his fear the writer has created a future which is ruled by vast totalitarian states, complete with the most scientific methods of thought control—as in Orwell's *1984*.

In our times almost as many intellectuals are reading science fiction as are reading the lives of the Saints. This is especially true of college students.

But what of the student liberal, who is not quite of the vanished breed he is thought to be? Although he exists, his ideas are no longer as exciting to his contemporaries as they were in the confident years when the future still seemed to promise a Utopia. Hence his audience is now smaller and less easily stirred than it once was. It is difficult to say whether the fault lies with the liberal or the audience.

Once liberalism seemed to offer both a clear view of a new (and better) world and the ideas with which to meet its challenge. But liberal thought today has been busy with the fight to keep us from regressing or, to put it more positively, to preserve the hard won social gains of this century. It has scarcely had time to fulfill its traditional role as a guide to future action. More importantly, the solutions liberalism has offered for the present international predicament (which, after all, has given birth to our fears for the future) have been mainly clichés. Support the U.N., liberals say. But how does one make it into a truly effective force for peace? And what does one do about the Know-Nothings and the China lobbies and the Clarence Manions at home? How does one achieve a working relationship with Russia, or break through the fear and misunderstanding of the United States in underdeveloped areas?

There have been, of course, many liberal answers to these and other questions, but none has appealed to the nation as a clear-cut and decisive one. Like the adult liberal, the student liberal can only offer his fellows phrases which have gone platitudinous with the passage of time, phrases whose appeals are gone with the past. Happily, their opponents on the right are in much the same quandary.

Like the adult, the student liberal can only hope to go on searching for the answers which will appeal to the nation—answers which may not be found.

So the college student, neither strongly attracted nor strongly repelled by either pole of opinion, goes his rather directionless, apolitical way, trying to "adjust" as best he can to the precarious present, and trying not to look too searchingly at the future.

III

I wish I could close my report from "inside" today's college generation on a more optimistic note, but I share with my generation a feeling of helplessness in the face of powerful, inexorable forces. I am aware of both present and future dangers, but I don't know what to do about them. I said before that each college generation tries, as best it can, to get on in a world it never made. My generation has chosen to ride out a storm on what seems to be the safe island of the present. I, along with many others, think we should move off it, before the island is inundated. I don't know where to go, though; I only know the sea wall doesn't look very safe.

A GENERATION ON ICE

James Reichley

The post-war generation—my generation—has gone conservative. This fact, though perhaps not generally recognized by the young themselves, has achieved virtually the status of an axiom in the highbrow press. Liberals and intellectuals of the World War I and Depression generations have begun to complain that nobody understands them anymore, and almost all of them assume that reaction is certain to master American society for some years to come. E. V. Walter wrote in *Partisan Review* that intellectual conservatism "has swept this generation."

If this be true, what kind of conservatism has captured the young man's fancy? And how did the young man get that way? I am not sure of the answers to these questions, but I think that a brief examination of the way in which ideological problems manifested themselves during the years in which we—the generation born too late for World War II but just in time for Korea—were growing up will contribute something to their solution.

All children are born conservative, and most of them remain conservative

FROM *The Progressive*. Reprinted by permission.

as long as they can. Their interests are entirely selfish. They are suspicious of, and frightened by, change, and they seek protection from the ever-threatening outside world by enclosing themselves in the conservative institutions of the family and the gang. Their hostilities and aggressions are usually released against those members of the community who are marked as being outside the group.

In the time of my childhood—the relatively balmy pre-war days of the thirties—these natural tendencies were re-enforced in that citadel of conservative ideology, "The Movies," where every Saturday afternoon we were instructed in the Galahad tradition which divides the human race into gentle knights and common clods—and makes it clear that the gentle knight is always loved by the clods, knocks hell out of the egoistic bully, and wins the hand of the princess.

This conservative bent which most children carry at least as far as adolescence used to be undone in a number of ways. (That is, for those for whom it was undone at all. It is hardly necessary to say that in every generation there are large numbers of children who pass into their fullest maturity without breathing any but a conservative breath.) First of all, many children are simply thrown out of the conservative camp. Members of minority groups, for instance, were ordinarily given the choice between virtually endorsing their own persecution or putting up some kind of revolt.

Second, painful experience with the effects of the economic system often made pragmatic converts to the opposition.

Finally—and from this source came the old core of middle-class liberals —there were those who left the conservative camp primarily for reasons of the spirit. They were moved by natures which might express themselves in terms which were egoistic (like Scott Fitzgerald) or moral (like the early New Dealers) or both—egoistic in that they were in revolt against all kinds of authority which seemed to frustrate their desire for a fuller life, and moral in that they responded to an ethical ideal which they held to be of higher validity than the practical rules and regulations of industrial society. In my generation, this source has dried up.

II

For those of us born around 1930, unable to remember a Republican President in the White House and too young to have suffered much first-hand knowledge of the Great Depression, the political labels and slogans reported on the radio and in the newspapers had a somewhat different significance from what they must have had during the thirty preceding years.

Power to us was identified with liberalism, and society at large—the great threatening society which always seems determined to throw ice water on the dreams of adolescence—went by the name of Democracy. The whole sense of overpowering bigness which is such a constant aspect of industrialized, super-urbanized America seemed to stem from hypothetical hordes of big city labor rather than from equally hypothetical bankers or business tycoons.

Wall Street, which for decades had appeared to be the ultimate seat of worldly authority, inscrutable and absolute, became a shell without substance, like a god that frightened one age of men and has been found by the next to be but the sighing of the wind.

In its place, the new idol discerned in newsreels and news broadcasts and in the conversations of our elders, sprang the federal bureaucracy, pervasive, snooping, its heart in a filing cabinet, sweeping up bits of personal idiosyncrasy into an uncongenial Mass. It has been this idea of Mass, this danger of being reduced to a number on a social security card, this authority in horn-rimmed glasses against which rebellious youth in my generation has been most likely to rebel.

This rebellion, such as it is, has usually taken personal rather than social forms. It is reflected, on various cultural levels, in hoodlumism such as the thrill killings in Brooklyn last summer, in the odd night-club nihilism of the fifties and in the intensification of interest in the arts (which, however, has been channeled more into the construction of a New Alexandria in the graduate schools of our great universities than into original creative activity). And yet this rebellion, in any of its forms, has not had much steam. Mine is not a rebellious generation.

Rebellion, after all, is a spiritual luxury, and we came of age in a time when only material luxuries could be permitted. By the forties—when we had reached high school and college age—the United States had plunged into a time of international troubles. The nation was in danger, and no decent citizen would have thought of criticizing or even examining its dogmas.

The national ethos intercepted and engaged the rebellious enthusiasms which might otherwise have been given social or personal expression. For approximately four years, and into the final fizz of peace, it kept those enthusiasms suspended in undischarged tension, giving us time while we were still very young to acquire the tough shell of cynicism and apathy which is the only possible means of dealing with boredom with an ideal one continues to acknowledge.

After the war there was some slight relaxation of the pressure for conformity, but not much and not for long. The international rivalry with Soviet Russia and her allies—involving a real and pressing danger to our physical survival unknown to the United States since the Civil War—began around 1947 to create in the national consciousness a demand for enforcement of loyalty to the ethos at least as strict as that which had been necessary in this country during either of the great wars of the Twentieth Century. This is not to say that many young Americans, coming shakily of age in the time of the aspirin and the atom, did not in their hearts anxiously question the ethics and values of industrialized and urbanized society.

William McKinley, it turned out, still hulked sturdily at the center of the American spirit, which was not to be tinkered with for the duration of the emergency. But spotlighted and tricked out in neon was not Old William, really now, a peculiar looking guy? Did he not become tiresome when reduced to a phonographic squawk? How did he make out in a duplex apartment (which had succeeded the log cabin as an outpost on the frontier of terror and of hope)? How did he stack up against the other voices from other worlds which were being heard in American universities and the American press?

But we did not ask these questions too loudly—it was not a time for dissent. Generally, we decided to go along. Generally, we kept our mouths shut, we put no rocks in our snowballs, we joined no crusades (not, I think, as some of us have contended, because we were afraid for our jobs or for some day appearing on an Attorney General's list, but because we were afraid for our souls, because it was not a time for dissent). Generally, we quietly signed on at the nearest country club, took short views, and, when the time came, voted Republican.

III

But what had become of liberalism? What had become of the body of social idealism, which, aside from any personal rebellion, had for a century exerted a kind of ethical imperative over the minds and hearts of morally sensitive young men and women? The fact was that liberalism had largely won its fight and, in so doing, had, for a time at least, become irrelevant. Orthodoxy itself had been enlarged to the extent that it almost tediously insisted on racial equality, collective bargaining, and social security.

My generation has never known a period of serious unemployment. There were few occasions on which we could receive the kind of moral and emotional shocks that had sent the members of earlier generations onto permanent posts at the political barricades. Civil liberties remained the one ground of practical dispute on which liberalism might appeal for supporters. But this issue was clouded by the actual danger of world communism and by the fact that few of the old liberals seemed to operate with much confidence when dealing with its contemporary aspects.

The way of the egghead, as Adlai Stevenson has remarked, is hard, and to pursue it without a passionate heart is impossible. In the fifties liberalism was arousing few passions. The flurry of enthusiasm in the 1952 campaign was mainly confined to the middle-aged veterans of the New Deal and before. Actually, there was little real choice between Stevenson and Eisenhower.

The Old Guard Republicans were quite right in contending that they represented only slightly different shades of opinion in a common ideology, but what the Old Guard did not choose to admit was that this ideology was entirely orthodox. The considerable heat generated by the Stevenson campaign was, I think, largely a result of the friction caused among his supporters by the effort of the will to believe that he *must* stand for something of real significance.

Liberalism during the thirties had become largely committed to some kind of economic analysis of society, and in the fifties the economic analysis of society seemed pretty much beside the point. Our economic problems were not too pressing—there were few of us, at least, who were actually hungry or ever remembered being hungry—but we still had problems.

These problems did not seem to be social in nature. It was hard for most of us to identify with or even understand the shadowy figures who appeared before Senator McCarthy's committee. We sympathized and were indignant, but we did not feel that we were in danger. The possibility of atomic extinction was, of course, a real problem, but the international situation was so fearful and so complex and seemed so utterly beyond our power to control that most of us simply did not think about it.

It seemed possible, then, that our problems, the real eye-blinkers, were personal and moral (as distinguished from the personal and egoistic problems to which emancipation had been the characteristic solution, and to the social and moral problems to which liberalism had been the characteristic solution). The key question of my generation is not "What is pleasant?" nor "What is right?" but "What is good?" Among a generation in this frame of mind, some philosophy that is armed with universals is bound to reap a harvest.

Political conservatism is only one of the ideological aspirants currently trying to fill this role. (Modern psychiatry and organized religion, for instance, have not hesitated to rush into the breach. The doctors are busily rebuilding the moral temple, and the pastors—from Graham to Peale to Sheen—are promoting an ever more personal experience of religion.) The conservatives are themselves split into several wings. The McCarthyites are fumbling toward a gross and fantastic variety of nationalism; intellectuals like Peter Viereck are interested chiefly in the cultivation of cultural values in democratic society; Russell Kirk, who seems to appeal most strongly to young men of my acquaintance, longs nostalgically for the revival of a hierarchical feudal community.

All, however, share one common preoccupation: an attempt to evaluate and proscribe individual conduct by some kind of extra-human value. They try, that is, to rally personal emotional experience around a morally significant standard. The standards which they have suggested have, it is true, so far seemed to be meaningless or absurd. Kirk turns out to be the prophet of the mores of a portion of upper-middle-class Eighteenth Century British society, Viereck of the "Graeco-Roman-Christian-Hebraic tradition," and McCarthy, apparently, of McCarthy. The point is that all three, keenly intuitive men whatever else they may be, have felt it worth their while to make the effort, and a considerable number of the young men and women of my generation have felt that their effort was at least relevant to the problems with which we are most deeply concerned.

By a considerable number I do not mean a majority. The majority of my generation continue, pretty much by default, to give assent to the McKinley-Eisenhower-Stevenson orthodoxy. The startling aspect of the situation is that the most formidable dissent just now being raised by the young to this orthodoxy is neither individualistic nor liberal but *conservative*. This poses an obvious paradox—the idea of conservatives dissenting from orthodoxy—and suggests that the name conservative may be a misnomer. I think that it may be. What is currently calling itself conservatism is, I suspect, a symptom of a kind of force, as yet inarticulate, thrashing toward consciousness among the nominally orthodox as well as among the dissenting conservatives.

IV

We can not yet guess what form—destructive or constructive, good or evil—this force will take. No one can yet predict what will be the nature of the age that it is certain to shape. The politics of the new age have not begun, the religion has not been announced, the poems are still being fitted together inside the poet's head, the philosophy is on some pillow waiting for the morning sun. These, in their own time, will reveal to us much that is now mysterious and dimly perceived. I, for one, await their message with anxiety and impatience but without dismay. The challenges of the age of which we will be masters will be great, the chances will be long, but the possibilities will be rich, richer in certain ways than any since the days of the last Roman emperor. I believe that we will make them good.

THIS IS THE BEAT
GENERATION

Clellon Holmes

Several months ago, a national magazine ran a story under the heading "Youth" and the subhead "Mother Is Bugged at Me." It concerned an 18-year-old California girl who had been picked up for smoking marijuana and wanted to talk about it. While a reporter took down her ideas in the uptempo language of "tea," someone snapped a picture. In view of her contention that she was part of a whole new culture where one out of every five people you meet is a user, it was an arresting photograph. In the pale, attentive face, with its soft eyes and intelligent mouth, there was no hint of corruption. It was a face which could only be deemed criminal through an enormous effort of righteousness. Its only complaint seemed to be "Why don't people leave us alone?" It was the face of a Beat Generation.

That clean young face has been making the newspapers steadily since the war. Standing before a judge in a Bronx court house, being arraigned for stealing a car, it looked up into the camera with curious laughter and no guilt. The same face, with a more serious bent, stared from the pages of Life magazine, representing a graduating class of ex-GI's, and said that as it believed small business to be dead, it intended to become a comfortable cog in the largest corporation it could find. A little younger, a little more bewildered, it was this same face that the photographers caught in Illinois when the first non-virgin club was uncovered. The young copywriter, leaning down the bar on Third Avenue, quietly drinking himself into relaxation, and the energetic hot-rod driver of Los Angeles, who plays Russian roulette with a jalopy, are separated only by a continent and a few years. They are the extremes. In between them fall the secretaries wondering whether to sleep with their boy friends now or wait; the mechanics, beering up with the guys and driving off to Detroit on a whim; the models studiously name-dropping at a cocktail party. But the face is the same. Bright, level, realistic, challenging.

Any attempt to label an entire generation is unrewarding, and yet the generation which went through the last war, or at least could get a drink easily once it was over, seems to possess a uniform, general quality which demands an adjective. It was John Kerouac, the author of a fine, neglected novel "The Town and the City," who finally came up with it. It was several years ago, when the face was harder to recognize, but he has a sharp, sympathetic eye, and one day he said, "You know, this is really a *beat* generation." The origins of the word "beat" are obscure, but the meaning is only too clear to most Americans. More than mere weariness, it implies the feeling of having been used, of being raw. It involves a sort of nakedness of mind, and, ultimately, of soul; a feeling of being reduced to the bedrock of consciousness. In short, it means being undramatically pushed up against the wall of oneself. A man is beat whenever he goes for broke and wagers the sum of his resources on a single number; and the young generation has done that continually from early youth.

Its members have an instinctive individuality, needing no bohemianism or imposed eccentricity to express it. Brought up during the collective bad circumstances of a dreary depression, weaned during the collective uprooting of a global war, they distrust collectivity. But they have never been able to keep the world out of their dreams. The fancies of their childhood inhabited the half-light of Munich, the Nazi-Soviet pact and the eventual blackout. Their adolescence was spent in a topsy-turvy world of war bonds, swing shifts and troop movements. They grew to independent mind on beachheads, in ginmills and U. S. O.'s, in past-midnight arrivals and pre-dawn departures. Their brothers, husbands, fathers or boy friends turned up dead one day at the other end of a telegram. At the four trembling corners of the world, or in the home town invaded by factories and lonely servicemen, they had intimate experience with the nadir and the zenith of human conduct, and little time for much that came between. The peace they inherited was only as secure as the next headline. It was a cold peace. Their own lust for freedom, and their ability to live at a pace that kills, to which war had adjusted them, led to black markets, bebop, narcotics, sexual promiscuity, hucksterism and Jean-Paul Sartre. The beatness set in later.

It is a post-war generation, and, in a world which seems to mark its cycles by its wars, it is already being compared to that other post-war generation, which dubbed itself "lost." The Roaring Twenties, and the generation that made them roar, are going through a sentimental revival, and the comparison is valuable. The Lost Generation was discovered in a roadster, laughing hysterically because nothing meant anything any more. It migrated to Europe, unsure whether it was looking for the "orgiastic future" or escaping from the "puritanical past." Its symbols were the flapper, the flask of bootleg whiskey, and an attitude of desperate frivolity best expressed by Noel Coward's line: "Tennis, anyone?" It was caught up in the romance of disillusionment, until even that became an illusion. Every act in its drama of lostness was a tragic or an ironic third act, and T. S. Eliot's "The Wasteland" was more than the dead-end statement of a perceptive poet. The pervading atmosphere was an almost objectless sense of loss, through which the reader felt immediately that the cohesion of things had disappeared. It was, for an entire generation, an image which expressed, with dreadful accuracy, its own spiritual condition.

But the wild boys of today are not lost. Their flushed, often scoffing, always intent faces elude the word, and it would sound phony to them. For this generation conspicuously lacks that eloquent air of bereavement which made so many of the exploits of the Lost Generation symbolic actions. Furthermore, the repeated inventory of shattered ideals, and the laments about the mud in moral currents, which so obsessed the Lost Generation, does not concern young people today. They take it frighteningly for granted. They were brought up in these ruins and no longer notice them. They drink to "come down" or to "get high," not to illustrate anything. Their excursions into drugs or promiscuity come out of curiosity, not disillusionment.

Only the most bitter among them would call their reality a nightmare and protest that they have indeed lost something, the future. But ever since they were old enough to imagine one, that has been in jeopardy anyway. The absence of personal and social values is to them, not a revelation shaking the ground beneath them, but a problem demanding a day-to-day solution. *How* to live seems to them much more crucial than *why*. And it is precisely at this point that the copywriter and the hot-rod driver meet, and their identical beatness becomes significant, for, unlike the Lost Generation, which was occupied with the loss of faith, the Beat

Generation is becoming more and more occupied with the need for it. As such, it is a disturbing illustration of Voltaire's reliable old joke: "If there were no God, it would be necessary to invent Him." Not content to bemoan His absence, they are busily and haphazardly inventing totems for Him on all sides.

For the giggling nihilist, eating up the highway at ninety miles an hour, and steering with his feet, is no Harry Crosby, the poet of the Lost Generation who flew his plane into the sun one day because he could no longer accept the modern world. On the contrary, the hot-rod driver invites death only to outwit it. He is affirming the life within him in the only way he knows how, at the extreme. The eager-faced girl, picked up on a dope charge, is not one of those "women and girls carried screaming with drink or drugs from public places," of whom Fitzgerald wrote. Instead, with persuasive seriousness, she describes the sense of community she has found in marijuana, which society never gave her. The copywriter, just as drunk by midnight as his Lost Generation counterpart, probably reads "God and Man at Yale" during his Sunday afternoon hangover. The difference is this almost exaggerated will to believe in something, if only in themselves. It is a *will* to believe, even in the face of an inability to do so in conventional terms. And that is bound to lead to excesses in one direction or another.

The shock that older people feel at the sight of this Beat Generation is, at its deepest level, not so much repugnance at the facts, as it is distress at the attitudes which move it. Though worried by this distress, they most often argue or legislate in terms of the facts rather than the attitudes. The newspaper reader, studying the eyes of young dope addicts, can only find an outlet for his horror and bewilderment in demands that passers be given the electric chair. Sociologists, with a more academic concern, are just as troubled by the legions of young men whose topmost ambition seems to be to find a secure berth in a monolithic corporation. Contemporary historians express mild surprise at the lack of organized movements, political, religious or otherwise, among the young. The articles they write remind us that being one's own boss and being a natural joiner are two of our most cherished national traits. Everywhere, people with tidy moralities shake their heads and wonder what is happening to the younger generation.

Perhaps they have not noticed that, behind the excess on the one hand, and the conformity on the other, lies that wait-and-see detachment that results from having to fall back for support more on one's human endurance than on one's philosophy of life. Not that the Beat Generation is immune to ideas; they fascinate it. Its wars, both past and future, were and will be wars of ideas. It knows, however, that in the final, private moment of conflict a man is really fighting another man, and not an idea. And that the same goes for love. So it is a generation with a greater facility for entertaining ideas than for believing in them. But it is also the first generation in several centuries for which the act of faith has been an obsessive problem, quite aside from the reasons for having a particular faith or not having it. It exhibits on every side, and in a bewildering number of facets, a perfect craving to believe.

Though it is certainly a generation of extremes, including both the hipster and the "radical" young Republican in its ranks, it renders unto Caesar (i. e., society) what is Caesar's, and unto God what is God's. For in the wildest hipster, making a mystique of bop, drugs and the night life, there is no desire to shatter the "square" society in which he lives, only to elude it. To get on a soapbox or write a manifesto would seem to him absurd. Looking out at the normal world, where most everything is a "drag" for him, he nevertheless says: "Well, that's the Forest of Arden after all. And even it jumps if you look at it right." Equally, the young Republican, though often seeming to hold up Babbitt as his culture hero, is neither vulgar nor materialistic, as Babbitt was. He conforms because he believes it is socially practical, not necessarily virtuous. Both positions, however, are the result of more or less the same conviction—namely that the valueless abyss of modern life is unbearable.

A generation can sometimes be better understood by the books it reads, than by those it writes. The literary hero of the Lost Generation should have been Bazarov, the nihilist in Turgenev's "Fathers and Sons." Bazarov sat around, usually in the homes of the people he professed to loathe, smashing every icon within his reach. He was a man stunned into irony and rage by the collapse of the moral and intellectual structure of his world.

But he did nothing. The literary hero of the Beat Generation, on the other hand, might be Stavrogin, that most enigmatic character in "The Possessed" by Dostoevski. He is also a nihilist, or at least intimately associated with them.

But there is a difference, for Stavrogin, behind a facade very much like Bazarov's, is possessed by a passion for faith, almost any faith. His very atheism, at its extreme, is metaphysical. But he knows that disbelief is fatal, and when he has failed in every way to overcome it, he commits suicide because he does not have what he calls "greatness of soul." The ground yawned beneath Bazarov, revealing a pit into which he fell; while Stavrogin struggled at the bottom of that pit, trying feverishly to get out. In so far as it resembles Stavrogin, there have been few generations with as natural and profound a craving for convictions as this one, nor have there been many generations as ill-equipped to find them.

For beneath the excess and the conformity, there is something other than detachment. There are the stirrings of a quest. What the hipster is looking for in his "coolness" (withdrawal) or "flipness" (ecstasy) is, after all, a feeling of somewhereness, not just another diversion. The young Republican feels that there is a point beyond which change becomes chaos, and what he wants is not simply privilege or wealth, but a stable position from which to operate. Both have had enough of homelessness, valuelessness, faithlessness.

The variety and the extremity of their solutions is only a final indication that for today's young people there is not as yet a single external pivot around which they can, as a generation, group their observations and their aspirations. There is no single philosophy, no single party, no single attitude. The failure of most orthodox moral and social concepts to reflect fully the life they have known is probably the reason, but because of it each person becomes a walking, self-contained unit, compelled to meet the problem of being young in a seemingly helpless world in his own way, or at least to endure.

More than anything else, this is what is responsible for this generation's reluctance to name itself, its reluctance to discuss itself as a group, sometimes its reluctance to be itself. For invented gods invariably disappoint those who worship them. Only the need for them goes on, and it is this need, exhausting one object after another, which projects the Beat Generation forward into the future and will one day deprive it of its beatness.

Dostoevski wrote in the early Eighteen Eighties that, "Young Russia is talking of nothing but the eternal questions now." With appropriate changes, something very like this is beginning to happen in America, in an American way; a re-evaluation of which the exploits and attitudes of this generation are only symptoms. No simple comparison of one generation against another can accurately measure effects, but it seems obvious that a Lost Generation, occupied with disillusionment and trying to keep busy among the broken stones, is poetically moving, not very dangerous. But a Beat Generation, driven by a desperate craving for belief and as yet unable to accept the moderations which are offered it, is quite another matter. Thirty years later, after all, the generation of which Dostoevski wrote, was meeting in cellars and making bombs.

This generation may make no bombs; it will probably be asked to drop some, and have some dropped on it, however, and this fact is never far from its mind. It is one of the pressures which created it and will play a large part in what will happen to it. There are those who believe that in generations such as this there is always the constant possibility of a great new moral idea, conceived in desperation, coming to life. Others note the self-indulgence, the waste, the apparent social irresponsibility, and disagree.

But its ability to keep its eyes open, and yet avoid cynicism; its ever-increasing conviction that the problem of modern life is essentially a spiritual problem; and that capacity for sudden wisdom which people who live hard and go far, possess, are assets and bear watching. And, anyway, the clear, challenging faces are worth it.

THE CORRIDORS OF POWER

C. P. Snow

I was about seventeen, walking down a street in Leicester after a chess match. I was walking with a middle-aged man who was always agreeable to be with. He was gentle, fond of books, contented with an uneventful life, obliquely humorous, the sort of oddity it was fun to know at my age in a provincial town. Somehow we had got to talking about the French Revolution.

"I hope you realise who were behind that?" said my acquaintance.

"No?" I said. "The Rosicrucians," he said. "What made it worse, the inner circle of the Rosicrucians. It would never have happened if it hadn't been for them."

I thought he was joking. But he was not joking in the slightest. His expression, which was usually amiable and slightly teasing, had become fixed in a kind of fascinated hate. The Rosicrucians, or rather, in his view, a secret conspiracy of their leaders, had not only produced the French Revolution but also the Russian one. He had a vision of a handful of men, meeting with mysterious ceremony in darkened rooms. He found the vision, I think, both horrifying and obscurely romantic. They were still at it, he thought, still plotting with diabolical efficiency. They did it all, he was convinced, out of sheer malevolence and love of power.

That was one idea of how the world ticks; a mildly eccentric one, most people would agree. But most people have their own idea of how the world ticks. It usually is not as cranky as my old acquaintance's, but it bears a certain family resemblance. It is not easy to get the feel of how the machinery of a modern society works at all. Most of us tend to make lurid pictures of power and those who hold the power. Those pictures seem to be made up of all the secret societies, all the gray eminences, we have ever heard of: Lenin's sealed train, the atomic spies, Harry Hopkins at the White House, the Yalta Conference—such pictures can be exciting, they may even be true, but they do not make it easier to understand the world we are living in. The working truth is a good deal more difficult, nothing like as lurid, and quite as interesting.

The most characteristic picture of modern power is nothing at all sinister. It is no more or less remarkable than an office—I mean, an office building. Office buildings are much the same all over the world. Down the corridor of one of these offices, of any of them, a man is walking briskly. He is carrying a folder of papers. He is middle-aged and well-preserved, muscular, and active. He is not a great tycoon but he is well above the middle of his particular ladder. He meets someone in the corridor not unlike himself. They are talking business. They are not intrigu-

REPRINTED by permission of the author. From *The Listener*.

ing. One of them says: "This is going to be a difficult one"—meaning a question on which, in a few minutes, they are going to take different sides. They are off to a meeting of a dozen similar bosses. They will be at it for hours.

That is the face of power in a society like ours, a simple and unassuming face. By "a society like ours" I am not thinking of political forms. Certainly in societies which are as industrially and technically highly organised as, say, the United States, ourselves, and Sweden, there are a number of people making decisions, taking choices, which, to all intents and purposes, are identical. I am thinking of the higher officials, the factory managers, the upper bureaucrats, the cost accountants, the personnel officers, the chief designers, the people who are springing up because our societies cannot get on without them. Let me borrow a word from James Burnham, and call them "the managers" of the modern world. It is not a perfect term, but it will do. In the whole world, there are not a large number of these managers at the level I am thinking of. The number is, perhaps, something like 100,000, a little smaller, say, than the population of a town like Norwich. So far as anyone possesses power in the modern world, these do.

More Competent, less Speculative

What are they like? The short answer is, much like you and me. In a large number of people doing different jobs all over the world one is bound to find all sorts of persons, and it is foolish to make generalisations. But, foolish as it is, I am going to risk it. I believe there are some respects in which, on the average, the managers of this world are significantly a little different from you and me. To begin with, they like managing. They like responsibility—that is what the managers say. They like power—that is what the managed say. In any case, it is right that they should, if they are going to do their jobs at all. They like to see something practical for their efforts, to see the machines coming off the production line or the milk safely distributed on each doorstep. They are considerably more competent than the rest of us and rather less speculative. They do not question much the value of what they are doing and they are totally loyal to whatever society they happen to be working for. That is, the English and American managers are absolutely solid for the western way of life: the Russian managers seem to be just as solid for their own. Yet, if they meet and discuss their daily jobs, they have a great deal of fellow feeling, they know the others are pretty sensible chaps doing pretty sensible things. It is the greatest mistake to think of the managers as desiccated. They have learned to guard their tongues—that is part of their job: but they are masculine, vigorous characters. A friend of mine, meeting a group of them for the first time, described them as "savage-looking, reputable men."

There comes to my mind someone who always seemed to me a very good type-specimen of the manager. He flourished not in official or industrial life but in academic life. He was a powerful man physically—that is true of a great many managers—short and thick; taking decisions was the breath of life to him. Almost any kind of decision: pulling down a wall, altering the time of a lecture, electing a Chancellor. He had a great aptitude for power; and, of course, he got it, even though colleagues who were not so able grumbled that he was not an intellectual at all, which was, in a sense, true. Nevertheless, he got all the practical jobs that were going. He did them very well. Then, again like so many managers, he died in full career.

Working Model of Managerial Society

These men are human enough. They are not even specially mysterious. Watch with attention the machinery of a local football club or an amateur dramatic society. Notice who gets the power, how they get it, and what they do with it. If you do that, you will have a good working model of managerial society. Men do not alter much because they are operating on a bigger scale. It is important that we should get an understanding of what our managers are like and how their society works. It is important we should if the world is to be livable in. Most people, I think, are frightened off for one of three reasons.

The first reason really amounts to a hatred of the managerial society itself. It is rather like Dickens and the Circumlocution Office, pretending that men's social condition would be infinitely improved if we had no official relations at all and substituted simple instinctive relations of fortunate men to unfortunate men. It is a nice dream: we have all had it. The only serious objection is that it is utterly untrue. The whole point of the managerial society is to save us from simple instinctive relations of fortunate men to unfortunate men. Sometimes those relations are very beautiful: sometimes they are not so beautiful: for an example, recent in time and near at home, read Cecil Woodham Smith's account of the Anglo-Irish landlords' behaviour to their tenants in the great Irish famine. All over the world, men in their collective wisdom have decided that the non-beautiful examples are a hundred times more likely than the beautiful examples, and men in their collective wisdom are right. Out of official relations, one cannot in the nature of things get generosity—only fairness; but the fairness is more than most men have ever had. That is why the managerial society is in the long run men's best source of social hope.

The second reason why people are uneasy with the managers has a little more in it. It is that they take on rather too much of the "padding" of power; that they talk as though they were always in the right; that they become too kind to themselves. This is the occupational risk of managers everywhere. Take one example: I suppose about a hundred times in my life, in all sorts of groups, I have heard remarks of this nature: "I feel we oughtn't to give X this award just yet, in his own best interests . . .," or else: "Aren't we all agreed that it wouldn't be in the man's own best interests to say 'yes' to his request?" "In his own best interests . . ."; as I say, I have heard that ominous phrase at least a hundred times, and each time it meant that some unlucky chap was being dished—far more often than not for perfectly good reasons, but it is one thing to stop a man getting what he wants, and another to congratulate yourselves on what a good turn you are doing him. That is part of the "cant" of power; and we have too much of it. Meanwhile, if you hear anyone talking to you about your own best interests, look out for yourself.

Dangerous Power

But there is only one really good reason for regarding the managers with distrust. That is, they possess power: and we all feel deep in our hearts that it is dangerous for anyone, it doesn't matter who he is, to have any power at all. Anyone who doubts it has only to ask himself what he would be like if he had the power. Some would feel jolly at the thought and sincerely believe that they would be nothing but splendid and benevolent. They are the ones who ought to be kept away from it at all costs. Yet, someone has to keep society going. In the long run, someone has to have some power: and, of all the people who have ever possessed it, the managers of modern society are probably as well-intentioned as any.

That leads me to a dilemma which will probably worry the western world more in the next twenty years, not less. We are frightened of power and those who possess it; so we have invented a good many safeguards, and checks and balances. That is wise; it is a defence against the worst in human nature; it makes the western countries more tolerable to live in. But on the other hand, in some directions at least we ought to give our managers their heads. Let me take two examples: one of them is more or less local to this country, one which is true all over the western world. The local example is atomic power.

To give this country a real chance in the next generation, we cannot waste a year now. The managers know what they want to do—shall we let them? Or will the checks and balances be too strong? In something the same way, if the western world next century is to compete with Russia and China, it must re-shape a great deal of its education. We must become far more scientific. Plenty of managers in the United States and this country and France agree on what we should try to do. Will it happen? We are faced with a dilemma about those active men walking down the corridors. It is a very old dilemma, and I do not pretend there is an easy answer to it. How are we going to prevent them having dangerous power, and, at one and the same time, let them have enough power to see us through?

THE CONTINUITY
OF EUROPEAN TRADITION

Geoffrey Barraclough

During the years since 1945 the clarification of the principles upon which civilisation rests has become one of the major preoccupations of thoughtful people.[1]

Scarcely a day goes by without our reading or hearing of "our inherited cultural tradition," the "typical values of western civilisation," "the idea of European coherence"—or, more simply, "our western tradition," "our western values," "our western culture." No set of ideas has become more commonplace, none been more assiduously drummed into our ears, since the end of the war. In part, this new emphasis on the inherited traditions of our civilisation is a reflection of our awareness of crisis; it shows a tardy realization on our part that the dangers confronting the contemporary world—in particular, the dangers springing from the terrifying control which humanity now exercises over the material forces of destruction—can only be averted if they are counterbalanced by a far more intensive knowledge than our generation seems yet to possess, of the enduring elements upon which the structure of civilisation rests. And that is all to the good. What is more dubious is the implication that the enduring values and traditions of civilisation are linked, in some unique way, with western Europe. That view not only underestimates the importance of the independent civilisations of the Orient, but it also introduces an ominous division in Europe between the countries of east and west, with Germany as a sort of "no-man's land" lying in between. For there is little room for doubt that the intention is to contrast "western" values with the outlook and traditions of eastern Europe, and in particular with the ideology of Soviet Russia. In the background lies the idea, deliberate or unconscious, of providing a broad ideological foundation for the "western" conception of democracy, in its conflict with that other conception of democracy which predominates wherever Soviet influence is strong.

The theory of an "inherited cultural tradition," common to western Europe, is a platitude which has been familiar to historians for generations. It was erected on the basis of the great liberal historical tradition of the nineteenth century—the tradition of Ranke and Giesebrecht, of Bryce and Acton—but it was only in the aftermath of the second world war that it

REPRINTED from *History in a Changing World* by Geoffrey Barraclough, published by University of Oklahoma Press. Used by permission.

[1]Adapted from an article first printed in *Humanitas* I (1947), No. 4; I have incorporated some passages from an article, "Is there a Western Tradition?", which appeared in *The Listener* in August, 1947. [Author's note]

passed into wider currency, and emerged, detached from its historical setting, as a dogma or creed or article of faith. This significant transformation—familiar throughout the history of ideas—is to be explained by the fact that what, in an earlier phase, was an intellectual conviction, devoid of political implications (hence the failure of generations of historians to impress on society the elements of truth and salvation it indisputably contains), has now become the vehicle of organised political forces, charged with political content; it has come into its own as an ideological smoke-screen behind which the more militant upholders of "western tradition" are preparing to manoeuvre into position the compelling artillery of the atomic bomb.

But the theory of the unity of "western European culture" and of the continuity of European civilisation is in the last resort an interpretation of historical fact, which stands or falls with the history upon which it is based; and as such it falls within the proper sphere of historical criticism. It is noteworthy that it has emerged as a dogmatic assertion precisely at the moment when, notwithstanding the respect which all historians to-day feel for the extraordinary powers of synthesis of their nineteenth-century predecessors, the interpretation of history upon which it is based has been shattered by historical criticism and discarded by historical scholarship; and it is perhaps still more noteworthy that the weakening and under-mining by professional historians of the historical premises underlying the theory has failed to detract from its effectiveness as a political dogma, or to break the spell which, constantly reiterated and rarely criticised, it patently exerts over public opinion.

That the theory of a common "western tradition" should exercise a powerful influence over our minds is not difficult to understand. It is, after all, a stirring battle-cry in a distracted age, this appeal from the divisions of the present to the unity of "western European culture" and the continuity of western European civilisation; it links us in a chain with the great men of the past and sustains us with their faith. It makes us partakers in the greatness of Rome and Athens, "defendants" (as Gilbert Murray recently said) "of the Hellenic culture and Roman empire," with "a magnificent heritage to keep alive." For what, in the last analysis, is the warp and woof of this "western tradition"? Its constituent elements, we are told, are "the values of the Hellenic and Christian civilisations in which our own has its roots." What has "served to establish as a reality in the human mind the idea of European coherence," is, above all else, "the ideas of the Roman empire, of the papacy and more distantly of Athens."[2] "Europe," the argument runs, "owes its political existence to the Roman empire and its spiritual unity to the Catholic church," and for its "intellectual culture" it is indebted to a third factor—"the Classical tradition." These "are the true foundations of European unity"; but—the theory

[2]Cf. the essay on "The Idea of Europe" by Charles Morgan—perhaps the most influential of the popular exponents of the theory of "coherence"—in *Reflections in a Mirror* (1944), 36. [Author's note]

continues—"they do not of themselves constitute Europe. They are the formative influences which have shaped the material of our civilisation, but the material itself is to be found elsewhere"—namely, in the barbarian invaders who, in the fourth or fifth centuries, migrated into Europe and settled on the soil of the Roman empire. It was they "who provided the human material out of which Europe has been fashioned"; and this fashioning was the work of the middle ages. The fall of the Roman empire in the west left "a chaotic mixture of barbarian and Roman elements, which as yet possessed no spiritual unity"; and it was only in the middle ages—first of all in the empire of Charlemagne—that Europe emerged as a coherent whole. "Carolingian unity," it is said, "may be regarded without exaggeration as the foundation and starting-point of the whole development of western civilisation."[3]

What is immediately clear, if we examine this view of history in detail, is the fact that it attributes the highest importance to the middle ages as a key link between classical and western culture. The Latin language itself appears as the "ark which carried the seed of Hellenic culture through the deluge of barbarism"; but more important still is Christianity which, with an unerring instinct scarcely (some may think) to be explained without the inscrutable guidance of Providence, seized—it is not explained how—"upon what was vital in the Roman world," thus allowing the Catholic church to become at once "the heir and representative of the old Roman culture and the teacher and guide of the new barbarian peoples." "It was civilisation struggling for survival"; and "in the struggle between a world which was civilised and latinised and barbarians who were just then coming out of the darkness of their native forests . . . civilisation"—which "meant Latin and Rome"—"was bound to conquer." Through the idea of "a universal empire" and "parallel to a universal empire . . . a universal church, no less dependent on Roman traditions," through Roman law and above all through the unifying and civilising bond of the Latin language, "the forces of continuity" prevailed and the foundations of the "western tradition" and of "the edifice of European culture" were laid.

There is no doubt that this story of the compounding of a new civilisation from the classical heritage, the Latin language, and the Christian religion is an impressive construction; it raises the Middle Ages to a new dignity, providing the highest justification for their intensive study; it attracts no less because of its inherent simplicity than through the comforting sense of unbroken purpose which it engenders. Yet for the historian who tries to stand apart from the west and view the wide panorama of the past with impartiality—and who would deny that such should be his endeavour?—what is it but "parochial" history, throwing the past into the

---

[3]Cf. C. Dawson, *The Making of Europe* (1934), 48, 67, 286. It is perhaps right to add that, if I cite Mr. Dawson above all others for the views which (it seems to me) stand in need of criticism, it is because he is in my view the most able and persuasive of his school, for whose powers of interpretation I have the greatest admiration. [Author's note]

mould which best flatters our predilections "instead of liberating the mind from provincialism by widening the intellectual horizon"?

Let us pass over, in the first place, the difficulty (of which every schoolboy is aware) that the Roman empire, with its centre of gravity in the Mediterranean—and increasingly, as time passed, in the eastern basin of the Mediterranean—drew its sustenance from eastern and non-European lands, and was therefore scarcely more appropriate, as a model for an "idea of European coherence," than is the British empire to-day. Let us pass over also the mistranslation of the Latin word, *barbari*, which underlies this whole conception of European history; for *barbari* did not mean "barbarians," and since the substantial works of Alfons Dopsch passed into common currency, every undergraduate (if not every schoolboy) knows that the accession to power of the "barbarian" peoples was no catastrophe, and that the revolt against Roman political hegemony was not accompanied by a frontal attack on Roman civilisation.[4] More insidious (because less easily combatted) is the deprecatory, almost contemptuous attitude towards the Eastern empire, which this attitude implies, as though Roman "traditions" of empire, instead of passing to the "New Rome" on the Bosphorus, remained tied down for all time in the west. There is a famous dictum that "all history is contemporary history," in the sense that our picture of the past reflects our own outlook on the world, our ideology and our predispositions; and for me, the interpretation of the past outlined above is a reflection of the liberal ideology which perished, as an effective force, in the war of 1914–18; it is a sort of comforting hang-over from the rather resplendent prosperity of the late nineteenth century.

It puts a premium, in the first place, on "culture," as though culture were the essence instead of the last refinement of civilisation—the sugaricing (as it were) on the top of the cake. It flatters, because it shows western Europe, through the intermediacy of the Catholic church, as the heir of Rome, forgetting that there was also an Eastern church with traditions equally strong, and that the direct heir of Rome was not the west but Byzantium, where Roman civilisation and the very structure of the Roman state continued—changing, of course, but in unbroken succession—down to the fall of Constantinople in 1453. It is comforting, because it inculcates a sense of continuity, forgetting that continuity (as one acute historian has observed) "is by no means the most conspicuous feature of history," and that "the connexion of one civilisation with another is often obscure," "a matter of faith rather than of sight." It was one of the protagonists of the continuity of western European civilisation who incautiously admitted that, in order to appreciate the process by which in the Middle Ages western European civilisation was compounded, "it is best to look at the process in its complex entirety rather than in its thousand details"; and it is unquestionably true that when we descend to detail, much that seemed

[4] Cf. A. Dopsch, *The Economic and Social Foundations of European Civilisation* (1937); p. 89 sqq. on the word *barbari*, p. 30 sqq. on the myth of the "primeval forest." [Author's note]

obvious (and even significant) becomes a matter for legitimate doubt and questioning. In short, this whole conception—with its progressive, liberal flavour—is open to criticism in detail; and it is arguable that criticism in detail can shatter the whole structure, and force us to seek a new interpretation.

Consider, in the first place, the idea of a "classical tradition," which, handed down in unbroken succession from Rome, has (it is said) "been the constant foundation of western letters and western thought." At first glance such a statement sounds plausible. But it is a commonplace that by the third century A.D., when ancient civilisation was falling into decay, what is known as the "classical spirit" was extinct in Rome, swamped by strong currents flowing in from the Orient and from the Germanic world. It is a commonplace that the admirable spirit of rational enquiry, so vigorous six centuries earlier, had given way to superstition and mystical cults; that creative literary activity had ceased; and that even in architecture "the Greek laws of proportion had lost their meaning." When we are told that the evidence of the Christian arts can be "relied upon to prove the continuity of tradition," it is well to remember that such was not the conclusion of Max Dvořák, the founder of the modern study of art history, who on the contrary expressly defined their character as "unclassical" or even "anti-classical." Or consider, again, the theory that the Latin fathers were "the heirs of the western tradition," and that the Latin church, in the fifth century, became at once the repository of the "old Roman culture." In fact, what is remarkable about the church of that day is how little it rested on specifically Roman or western European foundations. Far from "seizing upon what was vital in the Roman world," we find the church—as represented (for example) by Tertullian and Jerome, by St. Ambrose and St. Augustine—filled with antipathy to Roman traditions, which it regarded as the work of anti-Christ. The places that really mattered in the early Christian centuries were not in Europe at all, but were cities like Alexandria and Carthage in Africa, or Nicaea and Cappadocia in Asia Minor; and even as late as the seventh and eighth centuries half the popes in Rome were Greeks or Syrians by birth. It is a commonplace that the language of the church, even in the west, was in the first place Greek, and that Christianity failed for the first two centuries of its history to produce a Latin literature. But even in the following century—although intellectual leadership still remained with the Eastern churches—the first stirrings of Christian thought outside the Eastern churches took place not in western Europe but in North Africa. It has even been suggested that it was in Africa, and not in Rome, that the cardinal dogma of papal primacy was fabricated.

Considerations such as these should warn us against exaggerating the Latin element in western Christianity. As the late Dr. Coulton once remarked, "Cardinal Newman's vision of the mediaeval monk as a classical scholar is largely imaginary." Nor is it easy, if we approach the question from the opposite angle, to visualize the precise process by which the

Catholic church transmitted the classical traditions to the western peoples. Much has been made, in this respect, of the services of the Latin language both as a vehicle of tradition and as a bond of unity; but Traube, whose authority remains unimpaired, speaks with greater caution, asserting in the first place that the maintenance of the Roman tongue has no intrinsic connexion with Catholicism, and passing on to the observation that any attempt to treat mediaeval Latin as a universal language must be taken with a pinch of salt. When we find, for example, that in 1222, out of seventeen livings in the diocese of Salisbury, five were held by priests unable to construe even the opening words of the first prayer in the Canon of the Mass, we may well wonder how deep a tradition confined to the Latin language really penetrated. Rightly Traube emphasizes the contrast between the possibilities of a rich and unitary culture, which Latin offered, and the historical reality; underlines the atrocious barbarism of Latin usage even in the schools at the Carolingian court; points out that the existence of a manuscript is no proof that it was read; and that not even mention or imitation of classical work is evidence that it was understood. This is true of Charles the Great himself, whose love of Augustine is not necessarily a proof of appreciation of Augustinian thought; it is true even of Alcuin, whose typically mediaeval exegesis of Plato the latter would scarcely have understood. Where there is continuity, in short, it is formal in character, not a persistence of classical modes of thought, but a repetition of classical phrases, selected, isolated and re-interpreted, to which a new meaning has been attributed; and many arguments can be adduced to support the view that this process of adaptation was less the maintenance of tradition than the creation of something new. That is true of Aristotelian philosophy, which on its rediscovery in the west was crudely misinterpreted and refashioned through misinterpretation, and it is true of the inheritance of Roman law. Few who have had the opportunity to study in detail the civil law of the middle ages would hesitate to endorse Hermann Kantorowicz's dictum, that "it was only the form which was provided by the Roman law, while the substance . . . was rooted in the contemporary social structure."

Fundamentally more important than any of this, however, is the question of the validity of the conception of "mediaeval unity"—that "feeling of the unity of western civilisation" which (it is said) "we inherit from the middle ages." That unity, if it existed at all, was either spiritual (and as such represented by the church), or it was material (and as such represented by a supra-national empire); but from either point of view it is a conception hard to reconcile with the known facts.

Much of the apparent unity of thought is due primarily to the fact that Catholicism extirpated its opponents and burnt the literature in which they expressed their ideals; it is due also to the fact that the clergy had for many centuries a monopoly of writing, and that the surviving evidence of a non-clerical ethos is sparse and usually indirect. But it is clear enough to-day that anti-Catholic thought was extraordinarily vigorous and its diffusion extraordinarily widespread; and the existence of this hostile tradition—the tradition (it is often called) of "Christian dualism"—is alone a challenge to the theory of spiritual unity. Nor is it clear that there was general acceptance, even within the organised church, of the idea of the ecclesiastical coherence of western Christendom under the direction of the pope. We know, for example, that an anonymous ecclesiastic, commonly associated with York, who was writing in the early years of the twelfth century, was vigorously rejecting the pope's primacy on doctrinal grounds, and protesting against Roman attempts to introduce uniformity; we know of equally trenchant criticism in Italy around the year 1180; and we know that similar convictions were strongly held in the French church in the middle of the thirteenth century. Can we, in face of such facts, really maintain that the unity for which the papacy stood was a characteristic feature even of the two centuries when the papacy was most influential, to say nothing of the centuries preceding and following, when the tendency to division into "national" or territorial churches is admitted on all sides to have been strong?

The other approach to this question is from the standpoint of the empire, for next to the papacy the empire is usually described as the symbol and embodiment of mediaeval unity. And yet from this point of view the most obvious feature of the Middle Ages is not unity but dichotomy. From the time of Charlemagne, there were always two empires, the western empire and the Byzantine empire; and we shall never understand the development of mediaeval Europe if we ignore their interaction and concentrate exclusively on the west.

In the second place, it is essential to bear in mind that the western empire itself was never the equivalent of western, or Latin, Christendom; it excluded Britain, it excluded Scandinavia, and it excluded Spain. Furthermore, the "Roman" character of the mediaeval empire, which was a matter of faith to the generation of Bryce, is to-day in hot dispute, and as the pawns move forward to the attack, some of the major pieces are already in evident danger of falling. At most it was the Roman aristocracy which (for political reasons in no need of explanation) preserved some sense of Roman imperial traditions; but their empty claims were met by Frederick I with the contempt they deserved, and it would be hard to prove that they reverberated beyond the confines of the city. Even the papal theory of the empire, as it developed after the pontificate of Gregory the Great, showed little sympathy with the imperialism of antiquity, and elsewhere—for example, at the Frankish court—there were palpable manifestations of hostility. Not only was the Frankish empire not a revival of the Roman empire; it was not even conceived of as a new Roman empire.

And what is true of the Frankish empire, can be demonstrated even more easily of its successors in the west. It is easy to think of the mediaeval empire as a "supra-national unity," and it is perfectly true that many theories were devised to imbue it with an œcumenical character; but in fact its sphere was limited (like that of modern empires) to the constituent lands within its boundaries. If we wish to discover the positive influence of Roman imperial traditions anywhere in the mediaeval world, then we should turn not to the west, but to Byzantium which—unlike the western empire—was both the linear descendant of Rome and (in Sir Maurice Powicke's words) for eight hundred years "the chief Christian state in the world." And this is a fact of the greatest historical significance; for when Constantinople, the "second Rome," fell to the Turks in 1453, it was to Russia that the imperial and Christian tradition of Byzantium passed. After 1453 Russia emerged as heir to the Byzantine inheritance. The Russian ruler was hailed as the "new Constantine," legitimate successor to the "Roman emperor and czar who ruled the whole world," and Moscow established the proud claim to be the "third Rome." "Two Romes have fallen," proclaimed the monk, Philotheus of Pskov, "but the third is standing; and there shall be no fourth." In this way the imperial mission of Rome was transmitted through the Orthodox church from Byzantium to Holy Russia.

We have here, I think, the best indication of any that the west has no monopoly of the Roman or of the Christian tradition. There is, in fact, no sense in which it can be claimed that the Carolingian empire was the successor of the Roman empire in the west, in which it cannot be claimed that Russia was the successor of the Roman empire in the east; and it would be hard to think of any way in which the Christian religion has served as a spiritual bond between the western peoples, in which it has not equally effectively served as a bond of union among the peoples of eastern Europe. The fundamental traditions in both cases are the same; and we should bear this fact in mind before we use historical arguments in support of the present tendency to oppose the "western European traditions" of "Latin Christendom" to the "eastern European traditions" of the Slav world. I am well aware that in the hands of St. Ambrose, St. Leo and St. Augustine western Christianity took shape as something different from the orthodox faith of the east; but when it is asserted that this difference, consisting in the "assimilation" or adoption of "Roman culture," marked a decisive break, I find it difficult—considering the unity maintained for centuries thereafter between the Greek and Latin churches, and the degree to which the Western church was permeated with Greek thought—to avoid scepticism. Anything such as this should, it seems to me, be resisted—no matter from which side it comes—as an unwarrantable attempt "to divest the notion of civilisation of its universal content."

* * *

I have thought it necessary to offer some criticism of a current theory which is at once so plausible and so congenial to our present frame of mind that it is in danger of passing unchallenged; but I would not have my criticism misunderstood. I am not so foolish as to suppose that it is my vocation to demolish in a few sentences a powerful synthesis which has engrossed and often enchanted the best brains of many generations; still less do I suppose that a problem of this magnitude can be solved with a simple affirmation or negation. I am only concerned lest—as that penetrating English scholar, J. Horace Round, once hinted with reference to a different but intrinsically similar question—we should confuse words and things. The problem of continuity or discontinuity in history is, as Traube observed, one of the most important in our whole civilisation, and it would be folly to ignore that such a theme, even if it carries us back to the fourth and fifth centuries of the Christian era, is more "actual," nearer to contemporary life, than (let us say) the history of sanitation and street-lighting in Bolton or the unedifying annals of eighteenth-century diplomacy. But for that very reason it must be insisted—unless we accept the nominalist heresy that victorious regimes make their own history—that the truth of such theories as I have attempted to criticise cannot be established by the staccato (and scarcely disinterested) reiteration of political propaganda. On the contrary, their elucidation requires the devoted labour of acute and accurate scholarship; and it is no credit to modern historical scholarship that it tends to take refuge from the enduring but controversial themes of history in abstruse research, leaving "the amateurs and the propagandists in possession of the field."

To-day, as in the past, it remains one of the great tasks of historical scholarship—in which the mediaeval historian is called upon to play a leading role—to investigate the persistence of classical traditions and their share in the formation of modern civilisation. But such results as are won will only carry a valid message if we remain aware of their limiting conditions. The connexion with classical antiquity is there, obvious and undeniable; for the garment of Clio (as we all know) is a seamless web, and there was no break or sudden reorientation of men's lives in 476. What is at issue is, therefore, not the existence of continuity of some sort, but rather its character; and it is here, as it seems to me, that the attempt to establish anything in the way of a direct connexion between "western European" and classical civilisation is both unhistorical and dangerous. It carries within it the risk of creating an artificially closed system, derived from the myth of a common mediaeval civilisation "when all civilised men spoke the same tongue, thought the same thoughts, and agreed in a common faith and in common ideals." In fact there was no time when all civilised men spoke the same tongue, or thought the same thoughts, or agreed in a common faith and ideals. Hence we shall rightly remain sceptical when we are told that "the ultimate foundation of our culture is not the national state but the European unity." As Dr. Coulton showed us, this transcendental unity, even when supported—as, for example, during the Albigensian crusades—by the harsh regimentation of military power, was never real or strong enough to override more fundamental differences, and such demonstrations of European disunity should not be lightly disregarded. It is for that reason that I am sceptical whether history, if we really analyse its processes in detail, provides a valid argument for the existence of a "common Latin culture" or of a "common western European tradition," creating bonds (or potential bonds) of unity between England and France (for example) or France and Spain, different in their nature from the bonds (or potential bonds) existing between England or France and Russia, which also through Byzantium is heir to the classical tradition. No doubt the circumstances in the instances mentioned are very different, and distance or proximity alone have counted for much; but, as Dr. Coulton has said, it is upon common interests, personal contacts, and "the slow attrition of facts" that the bonds between peoples are based, not upon transcendental unities which are not facts but hypotheses or ideals.

It will, therefore, be clear (I hope) that I am concerned not to deny the reality of the classical tradition and of its formative influence in western European history, but rather to keep it within measurable bounds, lest it should swell into a monstrous, cloudy phantom, obscuring not only our view of history as a whole, in which western Europe is but a fraction, but also our approach to the problems of the present. It is when we have established the formal continuity of tradition from classical antiquity through the middle ages to our own times that our real task begins; and it is at this stage, I think, that the current view of western European civilisation unduly simplifies the issues. Such a view is, of course, not altogether incorrect; but (to adopt one of Hans Hirsch's telling phrases) it fails to satisfy in so far as it presents only the external aspects of the problem. The process of history is not merely a compounding of pre-existing "factors"; rather I believe, with Max Dvořák, that we must consider historical change not as the tracing of a single, unbroken line of development, but as an organic process establishing at every stage new conditions of individual creative activity and releasing at all stages new branches from which new developments unfold.

Viewed from this angle the problem of continuity and tradition will seem infinitely more complex and yet infinitely more lifelike, for it will not be subordinated to a single overriding pattern. I am convinced, for example, that even within the mediaeval western church, at the height of its development in the thirteenth century, there was wide diversity, that the unifying force of Roman canon law and of the doctrine of *plenitudo potestatis*[5] was only one factor in the situation, and that the terms *ecclesia Anglicana, ecclesia Gallicana,*[6] were not merely geographical expressions, devoid of substantive content. And so I am led to question the historical justification for the assumption of the existence of a specifically western European civilisation, differentiating or even separating western Europe as an historic unity from the Slavonic east. Rather history points, if it points at all, in the opposite direction, revealing to the searcher not impatient of detail or craving for a unitary scheme, how different peoples in different regions at different stages took different elements in different

[5]Fullness of power.
[6]Reference to the national Churches of England and France, as opposed to the Universal (Roman) Church.

proportions, and created therefrom the heterogeneous cultures—only painfully reduced to any semblance of unity or uniformity or even harmony—which are the reality behind the abstraction generically termed "mediaeval and modern civilisation."

The conception of European unity certainly is a high ideal, worthy of effort and sacrifice; but it draws its strength from our hopes for the future and not from our interpretation of the past. If it is to become a reality, it will be through our determination to grapple realistically with the hard facts of the present, as we find them, and not through the revival of the illusory unity of an imaginary golden age; and not least among the dangers, as I see them, of the cult of a common western European civilisation, which is so rife to-day, is the fact that, far from promoting European unity, it is visibly in danger of becoming an ideological obstacle to the attainment of that measure of unity which a practical, non-ideological approach to contemporary problems still has to offer.

NIGHT WALKS

Charles Dickens

Some years ago, a temporary inability to sleep, referable to a distressing impression, caused me to walk about the streets all night, for a series of several nights. The disorder might have taken a long time to conquer, if it had been faintly experimented on in bed; but, it was soon defeated by the brisk treatment of getting up directly after lying down, and going out, and coming home tired at sunrise.

In the course of those nights, I finished my education in a fair amateur experience of houselessness. My principal object being to get through the night, the pursuit of it brought me into sympathetic relations with people who have no other object every night in the year.

The month was March, and the weather damp, cloudy, and cold. The sun not rising before half-past five, the night perspective looked sufficiently long at half-past twelve: which was about my time for confronting it.

The restlessness of a great city, and the way in which it tumbles and tosses before it can get to sleep, formed one of the first entertainments offered to the contemplation of us houseless people. It lasted about two hours. We lost a great deal of companionship when the late public-houses turned their lamps out, and when the potmen thrust the last brawling drunkards into the street; but stray vehicles and stray people were left us, after that. If we were very lucky, a policeman's rattle sprang and a fray turned up; but, in general, surprisingly little of this diversion was provided. Except in the Haymarket, which is the worst kept part of London, and about Kent Street in the Borough, and along a portion of the line of the Old Kent Road, the peace was seldom violently broken. But, it was always the case that London, as if in imitation of individual citizens belonging to it, had expiring fits and starts of restlessness. After all seemed quiet, if one cab rattled by, half a dozen would surely follow; and Houselessness even observed that intoxicated people appeared to be magnetically attracted towards each other: so that we knew when we saw one drunken object staggering against the shutters of a shop, that another drunken object would stagger up before five minutes were out, to fraternise or fight with it. When we made a divergence from the regular species of drunkard, the thin-armed, puff-faced, leaden-lipped gin-drinker, and encountered a rarer specimen of a more decent appearance, fifty to one but that specimen was dressed in soiled mourning. As the street experience in the night, so the street experience in the day; the common folk who come unexpectedly into a little property, come unexpectedly into a deal of liquor.

At length these flickering sparks would die away, worn out—the last veritable sparks of waking life trailed from some late pie-man or hot-potato man—and London would sink to rest. And then the yearning of the houseless mind would be for any sign of company, any lighted place, any movement, anything suggestive of any one being up—nay, even so much as awake, for the houseless eye looked out for lights in windows.

Walking the streets under the pattering rain, Houselessness would walk and walk and walk, seeing nothing but the interminable tangle of streets, save at a corner, here and there, two policemen in conversation, or the sergeant or inspector looking after his men. Now and then in the night— but rarely—Houselessness would become aware of a furtive head peering out of a doorway a few yards before him, and, coming up with the head, would find a man standing bolt upright to keep within the doorway's shadow, and evidently intent upon no particular service to society. Under a kind of fascination, and in a ghostly silence suitable to the time, Houselessness and this gentleman would eye one another from head to foot, and so, without exchange of speech, part, mutually suspicious. Drip, drip, drip, from ledge and coping, splash from pipes and water-spouts, and by and by the houseless shadow would fall upon the stones that pave the way to Waterloo Bridge; it being in the houseless mind to have a halfpenny worth of excuse for saying "Good night" to the toll-keeper, and catching a glimpse of his fire. A good fire and a good great-coat and a good woollen neck-shawl, were comfortable things to see in conjunction with the toll-keeper; also his brisk wakefulness was excellent company when he rattled the change of halfpence down upon that metal table of his, like a man who defied the night, with all its sorrowful thoughts, and didn't care for the coming of dawn. There was need of encouragement on the threshold of the bridge, for the bridge was dreary. The chopped-up murdered man, had not been lowered with a rope over the parapet when those nights were; he was alive, and slept then quietly enough most likely, and undisturbed by any dream of where he was to come. But the river had an awful look, the buildings on the banks were muffled in black shrouds, and the reflected lights seemed to originate deep in the water, as if the spectres of suicides were holding them to show where they went down. The wild moon and clouds were as restless as an evil conscience in a tumbled bed, and the very shadow of the immensity of London seemed to lie oppressively upon the river.

Between the bridge and the two great theatres, there was but the distance of a few hundred paces, so the theatres came next. Grim and black within, at night, those great dry Wells, and lonesome to imagine, with the rows of faces faded out, the lights extinguished, and the seats all empty. One would think that nothing in them knew itself at such a time but Yorick's skull. In one of my night walks, as the church steeples were shaking the March winds and rain with strokes of Four, I passed the outer boundary of one of these great deserts, and entered it. With a dim lantern in my hand, I groped my well-known way to the stage and looked over the orchestra—which was like a great grave dug for a time of pestilence—into the void beyond. A dismal cavern of an immense aspect, with the chandelier gone dead like everything else, and nothing visible through mist and fog and space, but tiers of winding-sheets. The ground at my feet where, when last there, I had seen the peasantry of Naples dancing among the vines, reckless of the burning mountain which threatened to overwhelm them, was now in possession of a strong serpent of engine-hose, watchfully lying in wait for the serpent Fire, and ready to fly at it if it showed its forked tongue. A ghost of a watchman, carrying a faint corpse candle, haunted the distant upper gallery and flitted away. Retiring within the proscenium, and holding my light above my head towards the rolled-up curtain—green no more, but black as ebony—my sight lost itself in a gloomy vault, showing faint indications in it of a shipwreck of canvas and cordage. Methought I felt much as a diver might, at the bottom of the sea.

In those small hours when there was no movement in the streets, it afforded matter for reflection to take Newgate in the way, and, touching its rough stone, to think of the prisoners in their sleep, and then to glance in at the lodge over the spiked wicket, and see the fire and light of the watching turnkeys, on the white wall. Not an inappropriate time either, to linger by that wicked little Debtors' Door—shutting tighter than any other door one ever saw—which has been Death's Door to so many. In the days of the uttering of forged one-pound notes by people tempted up from the country, how many hundreds of wretched creatures of both sexes —many quite innocent—swung out of a pitiless and inconsistent world, with the tower of yonder Christian church of Saint Sepulchre monstrously before their eyes! Is there any haunting of the Bank Parlour, by the remorseful souls of old directors, in the nights of these later days, I wonder, or is it as quiet as this degenerate Aceldama of an Old Bailey?

To walk on to the Bank, lamenting the good old times and bemoaning the present evil period, would be an easy next step, so I would take it, and would make my houseless circuit of the Bank, and give a thought to the treasure within; likewise to the guard of soldiers passing the night there, and nodding over the fire. Next, I went to Billingsgate, in some hope of market-people, but it proving as yet too early, crossed London Bridge and got down by the waterside on the Surrey shore among the buildings of the great brewery. There was plenty going on at the brewery; and the reek, and the smell of grains, and the rattling of the plump dray horses at their mangers, were capital company. Quite refreshed by having mingled with this good society, I made a new start with a new heart, setting the old King's Bench prison before me for my next object, and resolving, when I should come to the wall, to think of poor Horace Kinch, and the Dry Rot in men.

A very curious disease the Dry Rot in men, and difficult to detect the beginning of. It had carried Horace Kinch inside the wall of the old King's Bench prison, and it had carried him out with his feet foremost. He was a likely man to look at, in the prime of life, well to do, as clever as he needed to be, and popular among many friends. He was suitably married, and had healthy and pretty children. But, like some fair-looking houses or fair-looking ships, he took the Dry Rot. The first strong external revelation of the Dry Rot in men, is a tendency to lurk and lounge; to be at street-corners without intelligible reason; to be going somewhere when met; to be about many places rather than at any; to do nothing tangible, but to have an intention of performing a variety of intangible duties to-morrow or the day after. When this manifestation of the disease is observed, the observer will usually connect it with a vague impression once formed or received, that the patient was living a little too hard. He will scarcely have had leisure to turn it over in his mind and form the terrible suspicion "Dry rot," when he will notice a change for the worse in the patient's appearance: a certain slovenliness and deterioration, which is not poverty, nor dirt, nor intoxication, nor ill-health, but simply Dry Rot. To this, succeeds a smell as of strong waters, in the morning; to that, a looseness respecting money; to that, a stronger smell as of strong waters, at all times; to that, a looseness respecting everything; to that, a trembling of the limbs, somnolency, misery, and crumbling to pieces. As it is in wood, so it is in men. Dry Rot advances at a compound usury quite incalculable. A plank is found infected with it, and the whole structure is devoted. Thus it had been with the unhappy Horace Kinch, lately buried by a small subscription. Those who knew him had not nigh done saying, "So well off, so comfortably established, with such hope for him—and yet, it is feared, with a slight touch of Dry Rot!" when lo! the man was all Dry Rot and dust.

From the dead wall associated on those houseless nights with this too common story, I chose next to wander by Bethlehem Hospital; partly, because it lay on my road round to Westminster; partly, because I had a night fancy in my head which could be best pursued within sight of its walls and dome. And the fancy was this: Are not the sane and the insane equal at night as the sane lie a dreaming? Are not all of us outside this hospital, who dream, more or less in the condition of those inside it, every night of our lives? Are we not nightly persuaded, as they daily are, that we associate preposterously with kings and queens, emperors and empresses, and notabilities of all sorts? Do we not nightly jumble events and personages and times and places, as these do daily? Are we not sometimes troubled by our own sleeping inconsistencies, and do we not vexedly try to account for them or excuse them, just as these do sometimes in respect of their waking delusions? Said an afflicted man to me, when I was last in a hospital like this, "Sir, I can frequently fly." I was half ashamed to reflect that so could I—by night. Said a woman to me on the same occasion, "Queen Victoria frequently comes to dine with me, and her Majesty and I dine off peaches and maccaroni in our nightgowns, and his Royal Highness the Prince Consort does us the honour to make a third on horseback in a Field-Marshal's uniform." Could I refrain from reddening with consciousness when I remembered the amazing royal parties I myself had given (at night), the unaccountable viands I had put on table, and my extraordinary manner of conducting myself on those distinguished occasions? I wonder that the great master who knew everything, when he called Sleep the death of each day's life, did not call Dreams the insanity of each day's sanity.

By this time I had left the Hospital behind me, and was again setting towards the river; and in a short breathing space I was on Westminster Bridge, regaling my houseless eyes with the external walls of the British Parliament—the perfection of a stupendous institution, I know, and the admiration of all surrounding nations and succeeding ages, I do not doubt, but perhaps a little the better now and then for being pricked up to its work. Turning off into Old Palace Yard, the Courts of Law kept me company for a quarter of an hour; hinting in low whispers what numbers of people they were keeping awake, and how intensely wretched and horrible they were rendering the small hours to unfortunate suitors. Westminster Abbey was fine gloomy society for another quarter of an hour; suggesting a wonderful procession of its dead among the dark arches and pillars, each century more amazed by the century following it than by all the centuries going before. And indeed in those houseless night walks—which even included cemeteries where watchmen went round among the graves at stated times, and moved the tell-tale handle of an index which recorded that they had touched it at such an hour—it was a solemn consideration what enormous hosts of dead belong to one old great city, and how, if they were raised while the living slept, there would not be the space of a pin's point in all the streets and ways for the living to come out into. Not only that, but the vast armies of dead would overflow the hills and valleys beyond the city, and would stretch away all round it, God knows how far.

When a church clock strikes, on houseless ears in the dead of the night, it may be at first mistaken for company and hailed as such. But, as the spreading circles of vibration, which you may perceive at such a time with great clearness, go opening out, for ever and ever afterwards widening perhaps (as the philosopher has suggested) in eternal space, the mistake is rectified and the sense of loneliness is profounder. Once—it was after leaving the Abbey and turning my face north—I came to the great steps of St. Martin's church as the clock was striking Three. Suddenly, a thing that in a moment more I should have trodden upon without seeing, rose up at my feet with a cry of loneliness and houselessness, struck out of it by the bell, the like of which I never heard. We then stood face to face looking at one another, frightened by one another. The creature was like a beetle-browed hare-lipped youth of twenty, and it had a loose bundle of rags on, which it held together with one of its hands. It shivered from head to foot, and its teeth chattered, and as it stared at me—persecutor, devil, ghost, whatever it thought me—it made with its whining mouth as if it were snapping at me, like a worried dog. Intending to give this ugly object money, I put out my hand to stay it—for it recoiled as it whined and snapped—and laid my hand upon its shoulder. Instantly, it twisted out of its garment, like the young man in the New Testament, and left me standing alone with its rags in my hands.

Covent Garden Market, when it was market morning, was wonderful company. The great waggons of cabbages, with growers' men and boys lying asleep under them, and with sharp dogs from market-garden neighbourhoods looking after the whole, were as good as a party. But one of the worst night sights I know in London, is to be found in the children who prowl about this place; who sleep in the baskets, fight for the offal, dart at any object they think they can lay their thieving hands on, dive under the carts and barrows, dodge the constables, and are perpetually making a blunt pattering on the pavement of the Piazza with the rain of their naked feet. A painful and unnatural result comes of the comparison one is forced to institute between the growth of corruption as displayed in the so much improved and cared for fruits of the earth, and the growth of corruption as displayed in these all uncared for (except inasmuch as ever-hunted) savages.

There was early coffee to be got about Covent Garden Market, and that was more company—warm company, too, which was better. Toast of a very substantial quality, was likewise procurable: though the towzled-headed man who made it, in an inner chamber within the coffee-room, hadn't got his coat on yet, and was so heavy with sleep that in every interval of toast and coffee he went off anew behind the partition into complicated cross-roads of choke and snore, and lost his way directly. Into one of these establishments (among the earliest) near Bow Street, there came one morning as I sat over my houseless cup, pondering where to go next, a man in a high and long snuff-coloured coat, and shoes, and, to the best of my belief, nothing else but a hat, who took out of his hat a large cold meat pudding; a meat pudding so large that it was a very tight fit, and brought the lining of the hat out with it. This mysterious man was known by his pudding, for on his entering, the man of sleep brought him a pint of hot tea, a small loaf, and a large knife and fork and plate. Left to himself in his box, he stood the pudding on the bare table, and, instead of cutting it, stabbed it, overhand, with the knife, like a mortal enemy; then took the knife out, wiped it on his sleeve, tore the pudding asunder with his fingers, and ate it all up. The remembrance of this man with the pudding remains with me as the remembrance of the most spectral person my houselessness encountered. Twice only was I in that establishment, and twice I saw him stalk in (as I should say, just out of bed, and presently going back to bed), take out his pudding, stab his pudding, wipe the dagger, and eat his pudding all up. He was a man whose figure promised cadaverousness, but who had an excessively red face, though shaped like a horse's. On the second occasion of my seeing him, he said huskily to the man of sleep, "Am I red to-night?" "You are," he uncompromisingly answered. "My mother," said the spectre, "was a red-faced woman that liked drink, and I looked at her hard when she laid in her coffin, and I took the complexion." Somehow, the pudding seemed an unwholesome pudding after that, and I put myself in its way no more.

When there was no market, or when I wanted variety, a railway terminus with the morning mails coming in, was remunerative company. But like most of the company to be had in this world, it lasted only a very short time. The station lamps would burst out ablaze, the porters would emerge from places of concealment, the cabs and trucks would rattle to their places (the post-office carts were already in theirs), and, finally, the bell would strike up, and the train would come banging in. But there were few passengers and little luggage, and everything scuttled away with the greatest expedition. The locomotive post-offices, with their great nets—as if they had been dragging the country for bodies—would fly open as to their doors, and would disgorge a smell of lamp, an exhausted clerk, a guard in a red coat, and their bags of letters; the engine would blow and heave and perspire, like an engine wiping its forehead and saying what a run it had had; and within ten minutes the lamps were out, and I was houseless and alone again.

But now, there were driven cattle on the high road near, wanting (as cattle always do) to turn into the midst of stone walls, and squeeze themselves through six inches' width of iron railing, and getting their heads down (also as cattle always do) for tossing-purchase at quite imaginary dogs, and giving themselves and every devoted creature associated with them a most extraordinary amount of unnecessary trouble. Now, too, the conscious gas began to grow pale with the knowledge that daylight was coming, and straggling work-people were already in the streets, and, as waking life had become extinguished with the last pieman's sparks, so it began to be rekindled with the fires of the first street-corner breakfast-sellers. And so by faster and faster degrees, until the last degrees were very fast, the day came, and I was tired and could sleep. And it is not, as

I used to think, going home at such times, the least wonderful thing in London, that in the real desert region of the night, the houseless wanderer is alone there. I knew well enough where to find Vice and Misfortune of all kinds, if I had chosen; but they were put out of sight, and my house-lessness had many miles upon miles of streets in which it could, and did, have its own solitary way.

CHIMNEY SWEEPERS

Sidney Smith

Account of the Proceedings of the Society for superseding the Necessity of Climbing Boys. Baldwin, &c. London, 1816.

An excellent and well-arranged dinner is a most pleasing occurrence, and a great triumph of civilised life. It is not only the descending morsel, and the enveloping sauce—but the rank, wealth, wit, and beauty which surround the meats—the learned management of light and heat—the silent and rapid services of the attendants—the smiling and sedulous host, proffering gusts and relishes—the exotic bottles—the embossed plate—the pleasant remarks—the handsome dresses—the cunning artifices in fruit and farina! The hour of dinner, in short, includes every thing of sensual and intellectual gratification which a great nation glories in producing.

In the midst of all this, who knows that the kitchen chimney caught fire half an hour before dinner!—and that a poor little wretch, of six or seven years old, was sent up in the midst of the flames to put it out? We could not, previous to reading this evidence, have formed a conception of the miseries of these poor wretches, or that there should exist, in a civilised country, a class of human beings destined to such extreme and varied distress. We will give a short epitome of what is developed in the evidence before the two Houses of Parliament.

Boys are made chimney sweepers at the early age of five or six.

Little boys for small flues, is a common phrase in the cards left at the door by itinerant chimney sweepers. Flues made to ovens and coppers are often less than nine inches square; and it may be easily conceived, how slender the frame of that human body must be, which can force itself through such an aperture.

"What is the age of the youngest boys who have been employed in this trade, to your knowledge? About five years of age: I know one now between five and six years old; it is the man's own son in the Strand: now there is another at Somers Town, I think, said he was between four and five, or about five; Jack Hall, a little lad, takes him about.—Did you ever know any female children employed? Yes, I know one now. About two years ago there was a woman told me she had climbed scores of times, and there is one at Paddington now whose father taught her to climb: but I have often heard talk of them when I was apprentice, in different places.—What is the smallest-sized flue you have ever met with in the course of your experience? About eight inches by nine; these they are always obliged to climb in this posture (*describing it*), keeping the arms up straight; if they slip their arms down, they get jammed in; unless they get their arms close over their head they cannot climb."— *Lords' Minutes*, No. 1, p. 8.

The following is a specimen of the manner in which they are taught this art of climbing chimneys.

"Do you remember being taught to climb chimneys? Yes.—What did you feel upon the first attempt to climb a chimney? The first chimney I went up, they told me there was some plum-pudding and money up at the top of it, and that is the way they enticed me up; and when I got up, I would not let the other boy get from under me to get at it, I thought he would get it; I could not get up, and shoved the pot and half the chimney down into the yard.—Did you experience any inconvenience to your knees, or your elbows? Yes, the skin was off my knees and elbows too, in climbing up the new chimneys they forced me up.— How did they force you up? When I got up, I cried out about my sore knees.—Were you beat or compelled to go up by any violent means? Yes, when I went to a narrow chimney, if I could not do it, I durst not go home; when I used to come down, my master would well beat me with the brush; and not only my master, but when we used to go with the journeymen, if we could not do it, they used to hit us three or four times with the brush."—*Lords' Minutes*, No. 1. p. 5.

In practising the art of climbing, they are often crippled.

"You talked of the pargetting to chimneys; are many chimneys pargetted? There used to be more than are now; we used to have to go and sit all a-twist to parge them, according to the floors, to keep the smoke from coming out; then I could not straighten my legs; and that is the reason that many are cripples,—from parging and stopping the holes." —*Lords' Minutes*, No. 1. p. 17.

They are often stuck fast in a chimney, and, after remaining there many hours, are cut out.

"Have you known, in the course of your practice, boys stick in chimneys at all? Yes, frequently.—Did you ever know an instance of a boy being suffocated to death? No; I do not recollect any one at present, but I have assisted in taking boys out when they have been nearly exhausted.—Did you ever know an instance of its being necessary to break open a chimney to take the boy out? O yes.—*Frequently? Monthly I might say;* it is done with a cloak, if possible, that it should not be discovered: a master in general wishes it not to be known, and therefore speaks to the people belonging to the house not to mention it, for it was merely the boy's neglect; they often say it was the boy's neglect.—Why do they say that? The boy's climbing shirt is often very bad; the boy coming down, if the chimney be very narrow, and numbers of them are only nine inches, gets his shirt rumpled underneath him, and he has no power after he is fixed in that way (*with his hand up*).—Does a boy frequently stick in the chimney? Yes; I have known more instances of that the last twelvemonth than before.—Do you ever have to break open in the inside of a room? Yes, I have helped to break through into a kitchen chimney in a dining room."—*Lords' Minutes*, p. 34.

To the same effect is the evidence of John Daniels (*Minutes*, p. 100.), and of James Ludford (*Lords' Minutes*, p. 147.).

"You have swept the Penitentiary? I have.—Did you ever know a boy stick in any of the chimneys there? Yes, I have.—Was it one of your boys? It was.—Was there one or two that stuck? Two of them.—How long did they stick there? Two hours.—How were they got out? They were cut out.—Was there any danger while they were in that situation? It was the core from the pargetting of the chimney, and the rubbish that the labourers had thrown down, that stopped them, and when they got it aside them, they could not pass.—They both stuck together? Yes."
—*Lords' Minutes*, p. 147.

One more instance we shall give, from the Evidence before the Commons.

"Have you heard of any accidents that have recently happened to climbing boys in the small flues? Yes; I have *often* met with accidents myself when I was a boy; there was lately one in Mary-le-bone where the boy *lost his life* in a flue, a boy of the name of Tinsey, (his father was of the same trade); that boy I think was about eleven or twelve years old.—Was there a coroner's inquest sat on the body of that boy you mentioned? Yes, there was; he was an apprentice of a man of the name of Gay.—How many accidents do you recollect, which were attended with loss of life to the climbing boys? I have heard talk of many more than I know of; I never knew of more than three since I have been at the trade, but I have heard talk of many more.—Of twenty or thirty? I cannot say; I have been near losing my own life several times."—
Commons' Report, p. 53.

We come now to burning little chimney sweepers. A large party are invited to dinner—a great display is to be made;—and about an hour before dinner, there is an alarm that the kitchen chimney is on fire! It is impossible to put off the distinguished personages who are expected. It gets very late for the soup and fish—the cook is frantic—all eyes are turned upon the sable consolation of the master chimney sweeper—and up into the midst of the burning chimney is sent one of the miserable little infants of the brush! There is a positive prohibition of this practice, and an enactment of penalties in one of the acts of Parliament which respect chimney sweepers. But what matter acts of Parliament, when the pleasures of genteel people are concerned? Or what is a toasted child, compared to the agonies of the mistress of the house with a deranged dinner?

"Did you ever know a boy get burnt up a chimney? Yes.—Is that usual? Yes, I have been burnt myself, and have got the scars on my legs; a year ago I was up a chimney in Liquor Pond Street; I have been up *more than forty chimneys where I have been burnt.*—Did your master or the journeymen ever direct you to go up a chimney that is on fire? Yes, it is a general case.—Do they compel you to go up a chimney that is on fire? Oh yes, it was the general practice for two of us to stop at home on Sunday to be ready in case of a chimney being a-fire.—You say it is general to compel the boys to go up chimneys on fire? Yes, boys get very ill treated if they do not go up."—*Lords' Minutes*, p. 34.

"Were you ever forced up a chimney on fire? Yes, I was forced up one once, and, because I could not do it, I was taken home and well hided with a brush by the journeyman.—Have you frequently been burnt in ascending chimneys on fire? Three times.—Are such hardships as you have described common in the trade with other boys? Yes, they are."—*Ibid.* p. 100.

"What is the price for sending a boy up a chimney badly on fire? The price allowed is five shillings, but most of them charge half a guinea.— Is any part of that given to the boy? No, but very often the boy gets half a crown; and then the journeyman has half, and his mistress takes the other part to take care of against Sunday.—Have you never seen water thrown down from the top of a chimney when it is on fire? Yes.— Is not that generally done? Yes; I have seen that done twenty times, and the boy in the chimney; at the time when the boy has hallooed out, 'It is so hot I cannot go any further'; and then the expression is, with an oath, 'Stop, and I will heave a pail of water down.' "—*Ibid.* p. 39.

Chimney sweepers are subject to a peculiar sort of cancer, which often brings them to a premature death.

"He appeared perfectly willing to try the machines everywhere? I must say the man appeared perfectly willing; he had a fear that he and his family would be ruined by them; but I must say of him, that he is very different from other sweeps I have seen; he attends very much to his own business; he was as black as any boy he had got, and unfortunately in the course of conversation he told me he had got a cancer; he was a fine healthy strong-looking man; he told me he dreaded having an operation performed, but his father died of the same complaint, and that his father was sweeper to King George the Second."—*Lords' Minutes*, p. 84.

"What is the nature of the particular diseases? The diseases that we particularly noticed, to which they were subject, were of a cancerous description.—In what part? The scrotum in particular, &c.—Did you ever hear of cases of that description that were fatal? No, I do not think them as being altogether fatal, unless they will not submit to the operation; they have such a dread of the operation that they will not submit to it, and if they do not let it be perfectly removed they will be liable to the return of it.—To what cause do you attribute that disease? I think it begins from a want of care: the scrotum being in so many folds or crevices, the soot lodges in them and creates an itching, and I conceive that, by scratching it and tearing it, the soot gets in and creates the irritability; which disease we know by the name of the chimney sweeper's cancer, and is always lectured upon separately as a distinct disease. —Then the Committee understands that the physicians who are entrusted with the care and management of those hospitals think that disease of such common occurrence, that it is necessary to make it a part of surgical education? Most assuredly; I remember Mr. Cline and Mr. Cooper were particular on that subject.—Without an operation there is no cure? I conceive not; I conceive without the operation it is death; for cancers are of that nature that unless you extirpate them entirely they will never be cured."—*Commons' Rep.* p. 60, 61.

In addition to the life they lead as chimney sweepers, is superadded the occupation of nightmen.

"(*By a Lord.*) Is it generally the custom that many masters are likewise nightmen? Yes; I forgot that circumstance, which is very grievous; I have been tied round the middle and let down several privies, for the purpose of fetching watches and such things; it is generally made the practice to take the smallest boy, to let him through the hole without taking up the seat, and to paddle about there until he finds it; they do not take a big boy, because it disturbs the seat."—*Lords' Minutes*, p. 38.

The bed of these poor little wretches is often the soot they have swept in the day.

"How are the boys generally lodged; where do they sleep at night? Some masters may be better than others, but I know I have slept on the soot that was gathered in the day myself.—Where do boys generally sleep? Never on a bed; I never slept on a bed myself while I was apprentice.—Do they sleep in cellars? Yes, very often; I have slept in the cellar myself on the sacks I took out.—What had you to cover you? The same.—Had you any pillow? No further than my breeches and jacket under my head.—How were you clothed? When I was apprentice we had a pair of leather breeches and a small flannel jacket.—Any shoes and stockings? Oh dear no; no stockings.—Had you any other clothes for Sunday? Sometimes we had an old bit of a jacket, that we might wash out ourselves, and a shirt."—*Lords' Minutes*, p. 40.

Girls are occasionally employed as chimney sweepers.

"Another circumstance, which has not been mentioned to the Committee, is, that there are several little girls employed; there are two of the name of Morgan at Windsor, daughters of the chimney sweeper who is employed to sweep the chimneys of the Castle; another instance at Uxbridge, and at Brighton, and at Whitechapel (which was some years ago), and at Hadley near Barnet, and Witham in Essex, and elsewhere." —*Commons' Report*, p. 71.

Another peculiar danger to which chimney sweepers are exposed, is the rottenness of the pots at the top of chimneys;—for they must ascend to the very summit, and show their brushes above them, or there is no proof that the work is properly completed. These chimney-pots, from their exposed situation, are very subject to decay; and when the poor little wretch has worked his way up to the top, pot and boy give way together, and are both shivered to atoms. There are many instances of this in the evidence before both Houses. When they outgrow the power of going up a chimney, they are fit for nothing else. The miseries they have suffered lead to nothing. They are not only enormous, but unprofitable: having suffered, in what is called the happiest part of life, every misery which an human being can suffer, they are then cast out to rob and steal, and given up to the law.

Not the least of their miseries, while their trial endures, is their exposure to cold. It will easily be believed that much money is not expended on the clothes of a poor boy stolen from his parents, or sold by them for a few shillings, and constantly occupied in dirty work. Yet the nature of their occupations renders chimney sweepers peculiarly susceptible of cold. And as chimneys must be swept very early, at four or five o'clock of a winter morning, the poor boys are shivering at the door, and attempting by repeated ringings to rouse the profligate footman; but the more they ring the more the footman does not come.

"Do they go out in the winter time without stockings? Oh yes.—Always? I never saw one go out *with* stockings; I have known masters make their boys pull off their leggings, and cut off the feet, to keep their feet warm when they have chilblains.—Are chimney sweepers' boys peculiarly subject to chilblains? Yes; I believe it is owing to the weather: they often go out at two or three in the morning, and their shoes are generally very bad.—Do they go out at that hour at Christmas? Yes; a man will have twenty jobs at four, and twenty more at five or six.—Are chimneys generally swept much about Christmas time? Yes; they are in general; it is left to the Christmas week.—Do you suppose it is frequent that, in the Christmas week, boys are out from three o'clock in the morning to nine or ten? Yes, further than that; I have known that a boy has been only in and out again directly all day till five o'clock in the evening.—Do you consider the journeymen and masters treat those boys generally with greater cruelty than other apprentices in other trades are treated? They do, most horrid and shocking."—*Lords' Minutes*, p. 33.

The following is the reluctant evidence of a master.

"At what hour in the morning did your boys go out upon their employment? According to orders.—At any time? To be sure; suppose a nobleman wished to have his chimney done before four or five o'clock in the morning, it was done, or how were the servants to get their things done?—Supposing you had an order to attend at four o'clock in the morning in the month of December, you sent your boy? I was generally with him, or had a careful follower with him.—Do you think those early hours beneficial for him? I do; and I have heard that 'early to bed and early to rise, is the way to be healthy, wealthy, and wise.'—Did they always get in as soon as they knocked? No; it would be pleasant to the profession if they could.—How long did they wait? *Till the servants please to rise.*—How long might that be? According how heavy they were to sleep.—How long was that? It is impossible to say; ten minutes at one house, and twenty at another.—Perhaps half an hour? *We cannot see in the dark how the minutes go.*—Do you think it healthy to let them stand there twenty minutes at four o'clock in the morning in the winter time? He has a cloth to wrap himself in like a mantle, and keep himself warm."—*Lords' Minutes*, pp. 138, 139.

We must not forget sore eyes. Soot lodges on their eyelids, produces irritability, which requires friction; and the friction of dirty hands of course increases the disease. The greater proportion of chimney sweepers are in consequence blear-eyed. The boys are very small, but they are compelled to carry heavy loads of soot.

"Are you at all lame yourself? No; but I am "knapped-kneed" with carrying heavy loads when I was an apprentice.—That was the occasion of it? It was.—In general, are persons employed in your trade either stunted or knock-kneed by carrying heavy loads during their childhood? It is owing to their masters a great deal; and when they climb a great deal it makes them weak."—*Commons' Report*, p. 58.

In climbing a chimney, the great hold is by the knees and elbows. A young child of six or seven years old, working with knees and elbows against hard bricks, soon rubs off the skin from these bony projections, and is forced to climb high chimneys with raw and bloody knees and elbows.

"Are the boys' knees and elbows rendered sore when they first begin to learn to climb? Yes, they are, and pieces out of them.—Is that almost generally the case? It is; *there is not one out of twenty who is not;* and they are sure to take the scars to their grave: I have some now.—Are they usually compelled to continue climbing while those sores are open? *Yes;* the way they use to make them hard is that way.—Might not this severity be obviated by the use of pads in learning to climb? Yes; but they consider in the business, learning a boy, that he is never thoroughly learned until the boys' knees are hard after being sore; then they consider it necessary to put a pad on, from seeing the boys have bad knees;

the children generally walk stiff-kneed.—Is it usual among the chimney sweepers to teach their boys to learn by means of pads? No; they learn them with nearly naked knees.—Is it done in one instance in twenty? No, nor one in fifty."—*Lords' Minutes,* p. 32.

According to the humanity of the master, the soot remains upon the bodies of the children, unwashed off, for any time from a week to a year.

"Are the boys generally washed regularly? No, unless they wash themselves.—Did not your master take care you were washed? No.— Not once in three months? No, *not once a year.*—Did not he find you soap? No; I can take my oath on the Bible that he never found me one piece of soap during the time I was apprentice."—*Lords' Minutes,* p. 41.

The life of these poor little wretches is so miserable, that they often lie sulking in the flues, unwilling to come out.

"Did you ever see severity used to boys that were not obstinate and perverse? Yes.—Very often? Yes, very often. The boys are rather obstinate; some of them are; some of them will get half-way up the chimney, and will not go any further, and then the journeyman will swear at them to come down, or go on; but the boys are too frightened to come down; they halloo out, we cannot get up, and they are afraid to come down; sometimes they will send for another boy, and drag them down; sometimes get up to the top of the chimney, and throw down water, and drive them down; then, when they get them down, they will begin to drag, or beat, or kick them about the house; then, when they get home, the master will beat them all round the kitchen afterwards, and give them no breakfast perhaps."—*Lords' Minutes,* pp. 9, 10.

When a chimney boy has done sufficient work for the master, he must work for the man; and he thus becomes for several hours after his morning's work a perquisite to the journeyman.

"It is frequently the perquisite of the journeyman, when the first labour of the day on account of the master is finished, to 'call the streets,' in search of employment on their own account, with the apprentices, whose labour is thus unreasonably extended, and whose limbs are weakened and distorted by the weights which they have to carry, and by the distance which they have to walk. John Lawless says, 'I have known a boy to climb from twenty to thirty chimneys for his master in the morning; he has then been sent out instantly with the journeyman, who has kept him out till three or four o'clock, till he has accumulated from six to eight bushels of soot.' "—*Lords' Report,* p. 24.

The sight of a little chimney sweeper often excites pity: and they have small presents made to them at the houses where they sweep. These benevolent alms are disposed of in the following manner:—

"Do the boys receive little presents of money from people often in your trade? Yes, it is in general the custom.—Are they allowed to keep that for their own use? Not the whole of it,—the journeymen take what they think proper. The journeymen *are entitled to half* by the master's orders; and whatever a boy may get, if two boys and one journeyman are sent to a large house to sweep a number of chimneys, and after they have done, there should be a shilling, or eighteen-pence given to the boys, the journeyman has his full half, and the two boys in general have the other.—Is it usual or customary for the journeyman to play at chuck farthing or other games with the boys? Frequently.—Do they win the money from the boys? Frequently; the children give their money to the journeymen to screen for them.—What do you mean by screening? Such a thing as sifting the soot. The child is tired, and he says, "Jem, I will give you twopence if you will sift my share of the soot"; there is sometimes twenty or thirty bushels to sift.—Do you think the boys retain one quarter of that given them for their own use? No."—*Lords' Minutes.* p. 35.

To this most horrible list of calamities is to be added the dreadful deaths by which chimney sweepers are often destroyed. Of these we once thought of giving two examples; one from London, the other from our own town of Edinburgh: but we confine ourselves to the latter.

"James Thomson, chimney sweeper.—One day in the beginning of June witness and panel (that is, the master, the party accused), had been sweeping vents together. About *four* o'clock in the afternoon, the panel proposed to go to Albany Street, where the panel's brother was cleaning a vent, with the assistance of Fraser, whom he had borrowed from the panel for the occasion. When witness and panel got to the house in Albany Street, they found Fraser, who had gone up the vent, *between eleven and twelve* o'clock, not yet come down. On entering the house they found a mason making a hole in the wall. Panel said, what was he doing? I suppose he has taken a lazy fit. The panel called to the boy, "What are you doing? what's keeping you?" The boy answered that he could not come. The panel worked a long while, sometimes persuading him, sometimes threatening and swearing at the boy, to get him down. Panel then said, "I will go to a hardware shop and get a barrel of gunpowder, and blow you and the vent to the devil, if you do not come down." Panel then began to slap at the wall—witness then went up a ladder, and spoke to the boy through a small hole in the wall previously made by the mason—but the boy did not answer. Panel's brother told witness to come down, as the boy's master knew best how to manage him. Witness then threw off his jacket, and put a handkerchief about his head, and said to the panel, "Let me go up the chimney to see what's keeping him." The panel made no answer, but pushed witness away from the chimney, and continued bullying the boy. At this time the panel was standing on the grate, so that witness could not go up the chimney; witness then said to panel's brother, "There is no use

for me here," meaning, that panel would not permit him to use his services. He prevented the mason making the hole larger, saying, Stop, and
I'll bring him down in five minutes' time. Witness then put on his jacket,
and continued an hour in the room, *during all which time the panel continued bullying the boy.* Panel then desired witness to go to Reid's
house to get the loan of his boy Alison. Witness went to Reid's house,
and asked Reid to come and speak to panel's brother. Reid asked if panel
was there? Witness answered he was; Reid said he would send his boy
to the panel, but not to the panel's brother. Witness and Reid went to
Albany Street; and when they got into the room, panel took his head
out of the chimney and asked Reid if he would lend him his boy; Reid
agreed; witness then returned to Reid's house for his boy, and Reid
called after him, "Fetch down a set of ropes with you." By this time
witness had been ten minutes in the room, during which time panel
was swearing, and asking "What's keeping you, you scoundrel?" When
witness returned with the boy and ropes, Reid took hold of the rope,
and, having loosed it, gave Alison one end, and directed him to go up
the chimney, saying, "Do not go farther than his feet, and when you get
there fasten it to his foot." Panel said nothing all this time. Alison went
up, and having fastened the rope, Reid desired him to come down; Reid
took the rope and pulled, but did not bring down the boy; the rope
broke! Alison was sent up again with the other end of the rope, which
was fastened to the boy's foot. When Reid was pulling the rope, panel
said, "You have not the strength of a cat"; he took the rope into his own
hands, *pulling as strong as he could.* Having pulled *about a quarter of
an hour,* panel and Reid fastened the rope round a crow bar, which they
applied to the wall as a lever, and both *pulled with all their strength for
about a quarter of an hour longer,* when it broke. During this time witness heard the boy cry, and say, "My God Almighty!" Panel said, "If
I had you here, I would God Almighty you." Witness thought the cries
were in agony. The master of the house brought a new piece of rope,
and the panel's brother spliced an eye on it. Reid expressed a wish to
have it fastened on both thighs, to have greater purchase. Alison was
sent up for this purpose, but came down, and said he could not get it
fastened. Panel then began to slap at the wall. After striking a long
while at the wall he got out a large stone; he then put in his head and
called to Fraser, "Do you hear, you sir?" but got no answer: he then
put in his hands, and threw down deceased's breeches. He then came
down from the ladder. At this time the panel was in a state of perspira-
tion: he sat down on a stool, and the master of the house gave him a
dram. Witness did not hear panel make any remarks as to the situation
of the boy Fraser. Witness thinks, that, from panel's appearance, he
knew the boy was dead."—*Commons' Report,* pp. 136-138.

We have been thus particular in stating the case of the chimney sweepers, and in founding it upon the basis of facts, that we may make an answer to those profligate persons who are always ready to fling an air of
ridicule upon the labours of humanity, because they are desirous that

what they have not virtue to do themselves, should appear to be foolish and romantic when done by others. A still higher degree of depravity than this, is to want every sort of compassion for human misery, when it is accompanied by filth, poverty, and ignorance,—to regulate humanity by the income tax, and to deem the bodily wretchedness and the dirty tears of the poor a fit subject for pleasantry and contempt. We should have been loath to believe, that such deep-seated and disgusting immorality existed in these days; but the notice of it is forced upon us. Nor must we pass over a set of marvellously weak gentlemen, who discover democracy and revolution in every effort to improve the condition of the lower orders, and to take off a little of the load of misery from those points where it presses the hardest. Such are the men into whose heart Mrs. Fry has struck the deepest terror,—who abhor Mr. Bentham and his penitentiary; Mr. Bennet and his hulks; Sir James Mackintosh and his bloodless assizes; Mr. Tuke and his sweeping machines,—and every other human being who is great and good enough to sacrifice his quiet to his love for his fellow creatures. Certainly we admit that humanity is sometimes the veil of ambition or of faction; but we have no doubt that there are a great many excellent persons to whom it is misery to see misery, and pleasure to lessen it; and who, by calling the public attention to the worst cases, and by giving birth to judicious legislative enactments for their improvement, have made, and are making, the world somewhat happier than they found it. Upon these principles we join hands with the friends of the chimney sweepers, and most heartily wish for the diminution of their numbers, and the limitation of their trade.

We are thoroughly convinced there are many respectable master chimney sweepers; though we suspect their numbers have been increased by the alarm which their former tyranny excited, and by the severe laws made for their coercion: but even with good masters the trade is miserable,—with bad ones it is not to be endured; and the evidence already quoted shows us how many of that character are to be met with in the occupation of sweeping chimneys.

After all, we must own that it was quite right to throw out the bill for prohibiting the sweeping of chimneys by boys—because humanity is a modern invention; and there are many chimneys in old houses which cannot possibly be swept in any other manner. But the construction of chimneys should be attended to in some new building act; and the treatment of boys be watched over with the most severe jealousy of the law. Above all, those who have chimneys accessible to machinery, should encourage the use of machines,[1] and not think it beneath their dignity to take a little trouble, in order to do a great deal of good. We should have been very glad to have seconded the views of the Climbing Society, and to have pleaded for the complete abolition of climbing boys, if we could conscientiously have done so. But such a measure, we are convinced from the evidence, could not be carried into execution without great injury to

[1] The price of a machine is fifteen shillings. [Author's note]

property, and greatly increased risk of fire. The Lords have investigated the matter with the greatest patience, humanity, and good sense; and they do not venture, in their Report, to recommend to the House the abolition of climbing boys.

QUESTIONS

1. Pick out passages in Holmes which would justify calling him a "writer," and passages in Schickel and Reichley which would justify calling them "academic writers," if not amateurs.

2. How many of the values mentioned by Schickel, Reichley, and Holmes can you recognize as among your own? Have you any significantly different values or problems? (The question applies to you, not to what you think about your generation.)

3. Prove that for Schickel the determining forces that mold his generation are on the whole external to the person (social or political) whereas for Reichley they are internal (moral or psychological, if not psychoanalytical). Where does Holmes find his causes?

4. What do Schickel, Reichley, and Holmes consider to be the most important events of the period between the wars. Compare those of Forster.

5. Study Holmes's paragraph beginning "It is a post-war generation." List the formal transitional devices, then try to trace the rhythmic organization of the paragraph.

6. Make a list of the devices that Snow uses to make us feel comfortable with the power he is describing, to domesticate it.

7. What can you think of in your own experience that is comparable to the Rosicrucians of Snow's middle-aged friend? What theory of history did the friend believe, according to Snow, that is?

8. All of Snow's novels are examinations of the ways of the higher bureaucracy, of which he himself is a member. But *The Masters,* which deals with the academic bureaucracy, or *The New Men,* which deals with the bureaucracy of the atomic scientists, might be the most interesting to you.

9. What is the tone of the paragraph (p. 1173) beginning "That the theory of a common 'western tradition' "? How is the paragraph developed, held together?

10. What is the proper translation of *barbari?*

11. Make a list of Barraclough's facts, of his statements based on authority, of his interpretations. Does your list lead to any conclusions about his general argument?

12. List the sections of Barraclough's essay (or the stages of his argument). Show how these develop his thesis. How does he emphasize or mark off the separate stages?

13. What characteristics make Barraclough's style distinctly formal? Can you tell what parts of the article might come from the talk mentioned in his first footnote?

14. What qualities of Dickens' style tone down the effect of the scenes he describes?

15. What is the effect of the last paragraph of Sidney Smith's review?

CRITICAL ESSAYS:
A CAT MAY LOOK
AT A KING

Once upon a time Wodehouse's article might have been called an informal essay, though perhaps it is a little sharper, a little less decorous than those ever were; today it is a feature story. The change of name doesn't change the form, a short reflection on an important subject that tries to find something light or amusing either in the subject or in the approach to it. Incidentally, don't let Wodehouse's tone obscure the usefulness of his point; and compare Shaw on Shakespeare. The three reviews prove that journalists write cleanly and decently, indeed (in the case of Beerbohm) with some conventionally literary flourishes.

WILLIAM SHAKESPEARE
AND ME

P. G. Wodehouse

What with this summer's activities at Stratford-on-Housatonic, the movie of "Richard the Third" and Orson Welles having a pop at "King Lear," Shakespeare has been a good deal in the news of late. And when I say Shakespeare, do not run away with the idea that I am not perfectly aware that it may have been Shakespere, Shakspere or even Shikspur. Spelling was his weak spot, and to the end of his life he never could get it right. But, as he said himself, what's in a name?

It is too bad that we have so little information about this great writer. Nobody seems to know where he lived, whom he married and what he looked like. He is generally supposed to have married Anne Hathaway, but there is an entry in an existing register relating to the wedding of "William Shakespeare" and "Annam Whately de Temple Grafton." One can only suppose that the clerk was a poorer speller than the bridegroom himself and that this was his plucky, though scarcely successful, attempt

REPRINTED with the permission of *The New York Times Book Review* and of the author's agent Scott Meredith Literary Agency, Inc.

at writing "Anne Hathaway." At that, it would not have been at all a bad shot for those times.

As regards his appearance, there are sixteen portraits of him in the book of reference which I have consulted, and except that they are all solid on the fact that he never shaved, each is absolutely different from the others. Of course, it must have been difficult to paint Shakespeare's portrait. He was always working on a new play in the room in the theatre marked "No Admittance," and you had to get the best view of him you could through the keyhole. It is, indeed, possible that, absorbed in his work, he had to have himself painted by the correspondence method, describing by letter what he thought he looked like and leaving the rest to the artist.

The reason I am bringing him up now is that the press-clipping agency to which I subscribe has just sent me an extract from one of the English morning papers which seems to me to open up a rather interesting line of thought. It is a letter to Ye Ed from a woman living in Wortleberry-below-the-Hill, near Market Bumpstead, Salop, and in it she says that she considers Shakespeare "grossly materialistic and much overrated" and "greatly prefers P. G. Wodehouse."

Well, it is not for me to say whether she is right or not. One cannot arbitrate in these matters of taste. Shakespeare's stuff is different from mine, but that is not necessarily to say that it is inferior. There are passages in Shakespeare to which I would have been quite pleased to put my name. That "To be or not to be" thing. Some spin on the ball there. The man may have been grossly materialistic, but he could line them out all right when in midseason form. I doubt, too, if I have ever done anything much better than Falstaff. Let's leave it at this—Bill's good, I'm good. Both good eggs, is the way I look at it. (Still, awfully glad you like my stuff, old thing, and I hope you don't just get it out of the library. Even if you do, 'At-a-girl, and cheers.)

One of the things people should remember when they compare Shakespeare with me and hand him the short straw, is, that he did not have my advantages. I have privacy, he did not. When I write a novel I sit down on the old trouser-seat and write it. I may have to break off at intervals to let the dog out and let the cat in and let the cat out and let the dog in and interview young men who are working their way through college by selling magazine subscriptions and then let the cat in and let the dog out and go and answer wrong numbers on the telephone, but I don't have Burbage breathing down my neck all the time and asking haven't I for God's sake finished that thing yet.

Burbage must have been a perpetual pain in the neck to Shakespeare. Even today a dramatic author suffers from managers—Feuer and Martin, for instance, think nothing of grabbing you by the seat of the pants and throwing you out of the theatre—but in the Fifteen Nineties anyone who got mixed up with the writing end was like somebody in a slave camp. Burbage was the fellow who was putting on the show and he felt that that entitled him to treat the Swan of Avon like a juvenile delinquent.

In those days a good run for a play was one night. Two was sensational, and if you did three Variety called it a socko. Shakespeare would dash off "Romeo and Juliet," say, for production on Monday, and on Tuesday morning at 6 o'clock along would come Burbage in a great state of excitement and wake him with a wet sponge.

"Asleep!" Burbage would say, seeming to address an invisible friend on whose sympathy he knew he could rely. "Six o'clock in the morning and he's still asleep! Six by golly o'clock and still wallowing in hoggish slumber! Don't I get no service or cooperation? Is this a system? Good heavens, Bill, why aren't you up and working?"

Shakespeare sits up and rubs his eyes.

"Oh, hello, Burb. That you? How are the notices?"

"Never mind the notices. Don't you realize we've got to give 'em something tomorrow night?"

"What about 'Romeo'?"

"Came off last night. Hell's bells, how long do you expect these charades to run? If you haven't something to follow, we'll have to close the theatre. Got anything?"

"Not a thing."

"Then what do you suggest?"

"Bring on the bears."

"They don't want bears, they want a play, and stop groaning like that. Groaning won't get us anywhere."

So Shakespeare would heave himself out of bed, and dig down in the box where he kept other people's plots, and by lunchtime, with Burbage popping in all the while he would somehow manage to turn out "Othello," and Burbage would skim through it and say "It'll need work," but he supposed it would have to do.

A playwright cannot give of his best under these conditions, and this, I think, accounts for a peculiarity in Shakespeare's work which has escaped the notice of many critics—to wit, the fact that while his stuff sounds all right, it generally doesn't mean anything. There can be little doubt that, when he was pushed for time (and when wasn't he?), William Shakespeare just shoved down anything and trusted to the charity of the audience to pull him through.

"What on earth does 'abroach' mean?" Burbage would ask, halting the rehearsal of "Romeo and Juliet."

"It's something girls wear," Shakespeare would say. "You know. Made of diamonds and fastened with a pin."

"But you say 'Who set this ancient quarrel new abroach?', and it don't seem to me to make sense."

"Oh, it's all in the acting," Shakespeare would say. "Just speak the line quick and nobody will notice anything."

And that would be that, till they were putting on "Pericles, Prince of Tyre" and somebody had to say to somebody else "I'll fetch thee with a wanion." Shakespeare would get around that by pretending that a wanion was the latest court slang for cab, but this gave him only a brief respite, for the next moment they would be asking him what a "geck" was or a "loggat" and wanting to know what he meant by saying a character had become "frampold" or "rawly." It was a wearing life, and though Shakespeare would try to pass it off jocularly by telling the boys at the Mermaid that it was all in a lifetime and the first hundred years were the hardest and all that sort of thing, there can be little doubt that he felt the strain and that it affected the quality of his work.

Nevertheless, I stick to it that he was good. I would definitely place him in the Wodehouse class. I would say that the principal difference between Shakespeare and myself is not that he is grossly materialistic while I, as everybody knows, am so spiritual that it hurts, but purely a matter of treatment. We get our effects differently. Take, for instance, the familiar farcical situation of the man who doesn't know that something unpleasant is standing behind him. Here is how Shakespeare handles it ("The Winter's Tale," Act. 3, Scene 3):

> *Farewell!*
> *The day frowns more and more. . . . I never saw*
> *The heavens so dim by day.*
> *A savage clamor!*
> *I am gone for ever!*
> *(Exit, pursued by a bear)*[1]

I should have adopted a somewhat different approach. Thus:
I gave the man one of my looks.
"Touch of indigestion, Jeeves?"
"No, sir."
"Then why is your tummy rumbling like that?"
"Pardon me, sir, the noise to which you allude does not emanate from my interior but from that of the animal that has just joined us."
"Animal? What animal?"
"A bear, sir. If you will turn your head, you will observe that a bear is standing in your immediate rear, inspecting you in a somewhat menacing manner."

I pivoted the loaf. The honest fellow was perfectly correct. It was a bear, and not a small bear either. One of the large economy size. And it was certainly giving me an extremely dirty look. One could see at a g. that there was little or no chance of starting a beautiful friendship.

"Advise me, Jeeves," I yipped. "What do I do for the best?"
"I fancy it might be advisable if you were to exit, sir."
I did, closely followed by the dumb chum. And that, boys and girls, is how your grandfather clipped six seconds off Roger Bannister's mile.
Who can say which method is the superior?

---

[1]This is not quite what Shakespeare wrote, but close enough for Wodehouse's purpose. [Editor]

TOP

Robert Benchley

In the midst of the acclaim with which Eugene O'Neill is being so justly hailed for his latest and most gigantic *tour de force*, "Mourning Becomes Electra," and in the confusion of cross-references to the Greek dramatists from which he derived his grim and overpowering story, are we not forgetting one very important source of his inspiration, without which he might perhaps have been just a builder of word-mountains? Was there not standing in the wings of the Guild Theatre, on that momentous opening night, the ghost of an old actor in a white wig, with drawn sword, who looked on proudly as the titanic drama unfolded itself, scene by scene, and who murmured, with perhaps just the suggestion of a chuckle: "That's good, son! Give 'em the old Theatre!"? The actor I refer to needs no introduction to the older boys and girls here tonight—Mr. James O'Neill, "The Count of Monte Cristo" and the father of our present hero.

Let us stop all this scowling talk about "the inevitability of the Greek tragedy" and "O'Neill's masterly grasp of the eternal verities" and let us admit that the reason we sat for six hours straining to hear each line through the ten-watt acoustics of the Guild Theatre was that "Mourning Becomes Electra" is filled with good, old-fashioned, spine-curling melodrama. It is his precious inheritance from his trouper-father, his father who counted "One," "Two," "Three" as he destroyed his respective victims, one at the curtain to each act; it is his supreme sense of the Theatre in its most elementary appeal, which allows Eugene O'Neill to stand us on our heads (perhaps our heads would have been more comfortable) and keep us there from five in the afternoon until almost midnight. In this tremendous play he gives us not one thing that is new, and he gives us nothing to think about (unless we are just beginning to think), but he does thrill the bejeezus out of us, just as his father used to, and that is what we go to the theatre for.

Just run over in your mind the big scenes in "Mourning Becomes Electra." A daughter upbraiding her mother for adultery, the mother plotting with her lover the murder of her husband, the poisoning of the husband and the discovery of the tablets in the fainting mother's hand, the placing of the tablets on the breast of the corpse to frighten the mother into a confession (and what a scene *that* was!), the brother and sister peering down the hatch of a sailing ship to spy on the mother and later to murder her lover, and the tense moments of waiting for the offstage shots which would tell of the successive suicides of the mother and the brother. Greek tragedy, my eye! The idea may have been the Greeks', but the hand is the hand of Monte Cristo. If the Greek idea of revenge, murder, incest, and suicide is so thrilling, why isn't Margaret Anglin busier than she is? "Mourning Becomes Electra" is just the old Greek story put into not particularly convincing New England talk, but it is a hundred times better show than "Electra" because O'Neill has a God-given inheritance of melodramatic sense. So let's stop kidding ourselves about the Verities and the Unities and take a grand, stupendous thriller when we find it and let it go at that.

In the face of such an overwhelming victory over Time, Space, and the Daily Press as that which Mr. O'Neill has won, it is perhaps puny in a single commentator to admit such a personal reaction as fatigue during the last of the three sections of the drama (for they are *not* three plays, as advertised, but one play in fourteen successive acts). But, willing as the spirit may be to take punishment, the human frame is not equipped for such a session as that which is imposed upon it in the Guild Theatre (at any rate, mine isn't, and I have a pretty good equipment), and, starting with a pretty bad scene (go ahead, strike me dead, Jove!) of comic relief at the beginning of the section called "The Haunted," I began to be cushion-conscious. This uneasiness was heightened as I saw approaching that margin of Diminishing Returns in Tragedy which I alone seem to be conscious of in O'Neill's dramas, when one more fell swoop of Fate, one more killing, one more father in love with one more daughter, or one more sister in love with one more brother, and the whole thing becomes just a bit ridiculous. It was when I saw those magnificent scenes of the middle section becoming confused with a grand finale of bad comedy, incest, and extra suicide that Miss Brady's agonized cry, "I couldn't bear another death!," struck home, and I began to realize that, for me personally, "Mourning Becomes Electra" was getting to be just about one hour too long. I know that this is a purely individual and unworthy reaction, quite out of place in what should be a serious review of a great masterpiece, but, as this page is nothing if not personal, I am setting it down. And the final scene of all, in which Electra, or Lavinia, closes herself up in the great New England Greek temple for the rest of her unhappy life, content that mourning is her *métier*, made up for everything.

And now we come to Miss Brady and to Alla Nazimova and to all the rest of the splendid cast which the Theatre Guild has assembled to do homage to Mr. O'Neill's *magnum opus*. Without them, and without Robert Edmond Jones' superb settings, I am not so sure just how effective this drama would be. I can imagine its being pretty bad, as a matter of fact, if only moderately well done. We thrill to the scenes between the mother and daughter on the steps of the cold New England mansion, but how much credit do we give to Mr. Jones and to Mr. Moeller, who gave us this picture of two women in black on the white steps of a Greek temple? (It may have been so nominated in the 'script, but without Mr. Jones to give it being, it might have remained just a stage-direction.) Alice Brady has at last come into her own, in voice and bearing the perfect Electra, and Nazimova, in spite of her Russian accent, which rings so strangely in Suffolk County, made so much of the sinning Clytemnestra that the drama lost much when she withdrew into the shades of the House of Mannon never to return. Earle Larimore, too, as Orin-Orestes, gave the role a human quality which could hardly have been expected in the writing, and Thomas Chalmers, with an opera-trained speaking voice, not only overcame the trick sound currents of the theatre but gave a healthy robustness to the rather murky proceedings which was reassuring, as long as it lasted. Lee Baker, the first of a long string of entries to die, may have seemed a little stiff, but I suspect that it was a rather stiff part. In short, Philip Moeller in his direction, and the cast in their interpretation, and especially Mr. Jones in his settings, all did more than their share to raise Mr. O'Neill to the undisputed, and probably for a long time uncontested, eminence of the First Dramatist of Our Time. Not that he wasn't there already, but it is good to be sure.

But while we are on our feet, let us drink once again to the Count of Monte Cristo.

DOOM

Wolcott Gibbs

People of hypercritical or frivolous disposition are bound to find a great deal to complain about in Eugene O'Neill's massive "Long Day's Journey Into Night," at the Helen Hayes. It is approximately twice the normal length, not because so much time was really necessary to develop and explain the four tragic figures involved but simply because its author chose to repeat himself endlessly and also to drag in a lot of material neither particularly fascinating in itself nor perceptibly relevant to the story he had to tell. A moderately competent editor would have had little difficulty in cutting the manuscript in half, and the result would almost certainly have been an improvement. The play is often as barbarously written as it is possible for the work of a major writer to be. Somewhere in the course of the evening, the young man who represents Mr. O'Neill on the stage says of himself, "Stammering is the native eloquence of us fog people," and there is a considerable amount of stammering, not to mention a considerable amount of humor that has a very labored air, and of original poetry—as distinguished from the abundant quotations from Swinburne, Wilde, Baudelaire, and Dowson—that would have been rejected as vacant and pretentious by any judicious publisher. In answer to the obvious inference here, it might be said that neither the jokes nor the lyrical passages are fumbling by intention, as a means of indicating some poverty or vulgarity

PERMISSION the author; © 1956 The New Yorker Magazine, Inc.

of the characters' minds. There are a few such, but for the most part the offending samples occur in the speeches delivered by two young men who are presented as authentic ironists and—potentially, at least—original and sensitive masters of the language. The failure is a curious one, and perhaps it can be explained only on the ground that while Mr. O'Neill clearly thought of himself as strongly linked with the Irish dramatists, he was almost totally lacking in their wit and their feeling for poetic speech, and his attempts to incorporate these qualities into his work were generally unfortunate.

Finally, it is hard to deny that the assorted dooms that close in on the Tyrones during the sixteen hours covered by the play may stir a customer here and there to some emotion other than the appropriate pity and terror. The mistress of the house has come to what seems the inevitable end of a twenty-three-year struggle against morphine addiction; her younger son is discovered to have consumption and is about to be packed off to a cheap sanatorium, presumably to die; the elder, a drunken failure, cries out that—with half his heart—he has always hated his brother and worked to destroy him as he has destroyed himself; and old Tyrone, an actor who has betrayed his talent for the sake of popular success, comes at last to confront the fact that the miserliness he learned in the frightful poverty of his youth started them all on their various paths to ruin. Every family, of course, has its vicissitudes, but the epic scale of calamity here, the simultaneous termination of four major tragedies, is so far beyond common experience that some may find it too shocking to accept at all, and others —the cynical, who are always with us—may regard it only as a dramatist's instinctive heightening and rearrangement of life into a form too recognizable as magnificently expert theatre to be deeply affecting.

In spite of all these objections, most of which strike me as reasonably valid, I think "Long Day's Journey Into Night" is an impressive play. It was written, as you doubtless know, in 1940, when the author was fifty-two, and it deals with things that happened to him and his family twenty-eight years before that. In essence, it is a man's desperate effort to recall and explain the past, to reduce it to some ultimate comprehensible order, to understand and consequently forgive. In the play, it is suggested that to a certain extent this understanding and forgiveness existed in him at the time—that he understood when he was twenty-three the strange insecurity, the passion for owning land, that made his father save money by employing only the cheapest quacks for his family, and thus condemn his wife to a lifetime of drug-taking and his sons, conceivably, to death; the destructive balance of love and hostility in his brother's heart; and even all the mingled factors, including an early devotion to the Catholic Church, that made his mother's addiction incurable practically from the start. It is hard to believe that a boy of such an age and so situated would know anything but hatred and despair, and it seems likely that Mr. O'Neill gave his younger self quite a lot of extra penetration, but that is a minor point, as is the overskillful telescoping of many years of suffering into a single day. The play, I think, accomplishes its purpose. In a dedication in the printed version, the author expresses his gratitude for having been able to face his dead at last, and write of them with pity and forgiveness. He has done that, and he has made them understandable and pitiable to us, too. In the face of a formidable body of opinion to the contrary, I seriously question whether "Long Day's Journey Into Night" will survive as a major contribution to the drama of our time, but it is a courageous one, and I hope its writing gave its author peace.

The four principal performers are Fredric March, as Tyrone; Florence Eldridge, as his wife; Jason Robards, Jr., as the elder son; and Bradford Dillman, as his brother and, of course, the character representing O'Neill himself. All these parts are extremely difficult and exhausting, the Tyrones having been a singularly volatile family, even without the assistance of drugs and alcohol, and I can only say that every one is handled superbly. José Quintero, who directed "The Iceman Cometh" so brilliantly downtown last spring, has done equally brilliant work here, and David Hays' set, a living room hideous even by suburban 1912 standards, is a fitting graveyard for all mortal hopes.

MR. SHAW CRESCENT

Max Beerbohm

January 26, 1901

Having regard to the commonweal, Mr. Shaw bemoans the existence of "reputations" in art, and vents a hope that the attractive specimen acquired by himself will decay quickly. If he is sincere in this protestation, he must change his tactics. He is not going the right way about the business. His new book[1] will increase the bulk of his reputation, and will make it more durable. In these "Three Plays for Puritans" he has made a perceptible advance from the point he occupied in those "Plays, Pleasant and Unpleasant."

When a well-known writer is, like Mr. Shaw, in his forty-fifth year, people are apt to assume that he cannot further advance. He may, it is thought, increase his reputation by repeating himself, but cannot increase it by doing anything better than, or in kind different from, what he has done before. And usually this popular assumption is quite correct. Nine lustres exhaust from a writer any vital stuff that may be in him. The question is not of the amount he has to express, but simply of the time during which he has tried to express it. The small writer aged 30 will have rela-

[1]"Three Plays for Puritans." By Bernard Shaw. (Grant Richards.)

tively as much left in him as the great writer aged 30; and neither will have anything to express fifteen years later. Be there never so great an amount of vital stuff in a man—in other words, if he be a genius—he will, nevertheless, be on the shelf (however devoutly he may believe himself to be *sur le tapis*[2]) so soon as his ninth lustre is fulfilled. But to this rule there are, here and there, a few glaring exceptions, and Mr. Shaw happens to be one of them. I care not that he is in his forty-fifth year: he is, I assure you, a young writer; he is still in an early state of development. I will not try to determine whether he be a great writer or otherwise. But I do insist that you should regard him as a young one. Perhaps it will help you if I venture for a moment into that first-personal manner which Mr. Shaw himself has used to such effect. I am, I believe, regarded as a young writer. On the other hand, you think you know all about Mr. Shaw. You think his ideas and his methods are fixed, and that he, as a writer, must continue to be exactly what he already is. Now let me give you a striking proof of your error. Mr. Shaw and I, as writers, are exactly connate. Thirteen years ago, when the writing-instinct first stirred in me, one of my relatives was writing a weekly "London Letter" for a well-known journal in Scarborough. I implored that I might be allowed to write it for him, claiming no reward. He assented. I well remember that the first paragraph I wrote was in reference to the first number of "The Star," which had just been published. Mr. T. P. O'Connor, in his editorial pronunciamento, had been hotly philanthropic. "If," he had written, "we enable the charwoman to put two lumps of sugar in her tea instead of one, then we shall not have worked in vain." My comment on this was that if Mr. O'Connor were to find that charwomen did not take sugar in their tea, his paper would, presumably, cease to be issued. I believe the paragraph had a great success, in Scarborough. Recalling it, I do not think much of it. I quote it merely to show that I, who am still regarded as a young writer, am exactly as old as Mr. Shaw. For it was in this very number of "The Star" that Mr. Shaw, as "Corno di Bassetto," made his first bow to the public. Thitherto he had confined himself to speaking on platforms, talking to his friends, reading books. He had never, before the year 1888, been induced to express himself in writing. And thus he is as young a writer as I am. He is still perched on the lap of the gods. Almost every man who has a vocation to writing takes to his pen, as I did, when he is fifteen years old. Mr. Shaw did not take to his before he was twenty-eight. As I have already suggested, the amount that a writer has still to express, and the possibility of novelty in its expression, depends entirely on the time during which he has been writing. Thus, since the writer who begins at the normal age becomes barren at the age of forty-five, Mr. Shaw, glaring exception that he is, will have celebrated his fifty-eighth birthday before we can pass any definite judgment on his powers. If his future progress in dramaturgy be in ratio to his progress during the past three years, he will leave behind him an immortal name. So I advise him to "slow down" at once.

[2]Talked about.

When he published his "Plays, Pleasant and Unpleasant," I, knowing him to be quite young and malleable, thought it well to urge him not to go in for serious drama. "Arms and the Man" and "You Never Can Tell" seemed to me much better, much more sincere and genuine, as comedic farces than were "Mrs. Warren's Profession" and the rest as serious plays. Nor has my opinion changed in the meantime. In his serious plays Mr. Shaw was not himself. He was still the youth groping his way to self-expression, and groping, as so many youths do, in the wrong direction, under the wrong master. Hanging on to the coat-tails of even the wrong master is healthy exercise for a youth; it strengthens his muscles, and so forth. But such exercise must not be overdone. Mr. Shaw has loosened his hold on Ibsen's coat-tails not too soon. I admit that his serious plays were exceeding good *pastiches* of Ibsen, and that in time he could have written serious plays to which one could have given higher praise than that. Nevertheless, he was not born to write serious plays. He has too irresponsible a sense of humour. This sense he never could have suppressed so utterly as to prevent it from marring his plays; and, as it is his greatest gift, one does not wish him to suppress it at all. Again, he is (though he may deny that he is) incapable of portraying satisfactorily those human passions which must form the basis of serious drama. In all his serious plays, he tried (and tried very cleverly) to reproduce Ibsen's women. These creatures are tolerable and admirable because they are warmly human, warmly alive. But Mr. Shaw never could get further than their surface-characteristics. And the result was that his heroines were quite appalling. They were just dowdy and ill-conditioned shrews—wasps without waists. I am glad to think that I have seen the last of them. Now that Mr. Shaw has got clean away from the Ibsen formula, and makes no attempt at dealing seriously with the great issues of human life, his heroines are quite delightful and (as far as they go) quite real.

The first of the plays in this book is a melodrama, the second an extravagant historical comedy, the third a romantic "adventure." In fact, the *form* of them is quite frivolous. Seriousness enters into them now and again, but inheres in them never. In "Mrs. Warren" and the rest it was the form that was serious, and the frivolity that could not be kept out. The change in Mr. Shaw's method is welcome because he himself is a jester with serious interludes, not an occasionally jocular seer. The new method is for him the artistic method. All three plays are presented on a large, loose scale which is about as far as anything could be from the strait, strict form of his early plays—as far from it as Mr. Shaw's true self is from Ibsen's. And Mr. Shaw uses this large, loose scale in a thoroughly masterly way, having found it for himself by the light of nature, and not having imposed it on himself as a duty. I admit that the last play, "Captain Brassbound's Conversion," is not masterly. The admission is, indeed, wrung from me by the fact that I elaborately disparaged the play in these columns a few short weeks ago. Nevertheless, it marks a distinct advance from the serious plays: it is much more capable than were they of being treated with respect. Of the first play, "The Devil's Disciple," I have also written here, and, reading it, I have nothing to subtract from the praises I heaped on it after seeing it acted. The second play, "Cæsar and Cleopatra," is quite new to me. It is, I think, far the best thing Mr. Shaw has yet done. Every scene in it is delicious. Most of the scenes are mere whimsical embroidery, a riotous sequence of broadly humorous incidents. But some of them, very cleverly woven in, are true psychological comedy. Both Cæsar and Cleopatra are perfectly credible studies. Of course, if Mr. Shaw had tried to portray Cæsar in some really serious love affair, or to give us Cleopatra in the Antonine phase, he would have failed utterly. But here, merely, is Cæsar as an important public man who knows that a little chit of a girl-queen has taken a fancy to him, and is tickled by the knowledge, and behaves very kindly to her, and rather wishes he were young enough to love her. This kind of emotion Mr. Shaw can delineate sharply and truly. Nor could the kittenish admiration of Cleopatra for her hero have been more sympathetically shown to us. I wish very much that this play could be produced. But it would cost many thousands of pounds, and managers are coy of a vast production which is not the setting of some vast dramatic motive. Indeed, there is, as I have more than once demonstrated, an artistic, besides a financial, objection to such a production. Nevertheless, if I were a very rich manager, I should produce the play, if only to watch how a modern British audience would be affected by the early Briton whom Mr. Shaw has foisted into his play. Mr. Alfred Bishop would be engaged by me for this part. He would be immense in it.

I am not sure that Mr. Shaw's prefaces, notes, and stage-directions are not even more delightful than the plays themselves. In them, too, I find that Mr. Shaw has made real progress. He has always had a "style," in the sense that he has always been able to express accurately, in a live manner, the thoughts that are in him. But now he is evidently beginning to realise that a style may be beautiful, and ought to be beautiful, in itself. In one of the prefaces, especially, in which he describes the career and character of Mr. Cunninghame Graham, he introduces some really graceful and charming prose. The Puritan, paying homage to the Cavalier, decks himself with some of the Cavalier's own plumes, and looks, I am bound to say, very well in them. But I hope Mr. Shaw will not, like so many of our young writers, pay attention to manner at the expense of matter. I notice, with misgiving, his use of the word "stupent." He must beware the fascination of archaisms. On the other hand, I am glad to find in his prefaces evidence that he has just been reading Plato. To quote Plato freely, as he does, is a very proper habit in a young writer.

QUESTIONS

1. What is the meaning of Wodehouse's allusion to Feuer and Martin? Look them up in the *New York Times Index* and see what the references say.

2. What old stage convention, familiar in Shakespearean plays, is alluded to in this passage? " 'Asleep!' Burbage would say, seeming to address an invisible friend on whose sympathy he knew he could rely." (Who was Burbage?)

3. At what points does Wodehouse seem closest to parody?

4. Discuss the colloquialisms and slang in the reviews by Gibbs and Benchley. Can you arrange the four selections in a series from formal to familiar?

5. What does *tour de force* mean as Benchley uses it?

6. Do you gather that Benchley points to O'Neill's sense of theater because of some characteristics of the plays or because his own taste is un-literary?

7. Does Benchley belong to the "hypercritical or frivolous" people who, Gibbs says, find a lot to complain about in O'Neill?

8. Do these two reviews suggest anything about the fate of O'Neill's reputation in the fifteen years between them?

9. Look over all the selections from *The New Yorker* that have been included in this book. What common characteristics of attitude and style have they?

10. Compare Benchley's and Gibbs's reviews with the newspaper reviews of the same plays. Note especially the tone as well as the stated opinions. How are all the reviews organized?

11. What evidence can you find in *Candida* to justify Beerbohm's remark, "Nevertheless, [Shaw] was not born to write serious plays. He has too irresponsible a sense of humor."

12. Why would Shaw have failed if he "had tried to portray Caesar in some really serious love affair, or to give us Cleopatra in the Antonine phase [that is, in a serious affair of her own and older]"?

13. How well does Beerbohm obey his warning against using archaisms? The point of this question is to have you find out how many of Beerbohm's words, here and in "No. 2. The Pines," which you think are odd are really archaic too.

CRITICAL ESSAYS: GOODLY STATES AND KINGDOMS

The essays here are somewhat more formal than those in the preceding section; indeed Frances Newman's style will bear at least one sense of the adjective baroque. *Forster's is a lecture (compare Hutchins' speech) and rather chatty, but it is still somewhat less personal than the criticisms in the preceding section, in which the authors were admittedly giving their hasty reactions or feelings. Presumably Forster's remarks involve some careful thought and analysis. All three essays are admirable examples of the relation between opinion and evidence. Notice that all three authors assume a literary audience; in Whitehead's case, the assumption is so strong that he takes for granted agreement with his opinion of Latin classics.*

ENGLISH PROSE BETWEEN 1918 AND 1939

E. M. Forster

This is a period between two wars—the Long Week-End it has been called—and some of the books published in it look backward—like Siegfried Sassoon's *Memoirs of an Infantry Officer*—and try to record the tragedy of the past; others look forward and try to avert or explain the disaster which overtook Europe in the thirties. And even when they are not directly about a war—like the works of Lytton Strachey or Joyce or Virginia Woolf—they still display unrest or disillusionment or anxiety, they are still the products of a civilisation which feels itself insecure. The French lady, Madame de Sévigné, writing letters during the wars of the late seventeenth century, can feel tranquil. The English lady, Jane Austen, writing novels in the Napoleonic wars, can feel tranquil. Those wars were not total. But no one can write during or between our wars and escape their influence. There, then, is one obvious characteristic of our prose. It is the product of people who have war on their mind. They need not be gloomy or hysterical—often they are gay and sane and brave—but if they have any sensitiveness they must realise what a mess the world is in, and if they have no sensitiveness they will not be worth reading.

We can conveniently divide the long week-end into two periods—the 1920's and the 1930's. The division is not hard and fast, still it is helpful. The twenties react after a war and recede from it, the thirties are apprehensive of a war and are carried towards it. The twenties want to enjoy life and to understand it: the thirties also want to understand but for a special purpose: to preserve civilisation. They are less detached. In *Life among the English* Rose Macaulay contrasts the two periods neatly:

> The twenties were, as decades go, a good decade: gay, decorative, intelligent, extravagant, cultured. There were booms in photography, Sunday films and theatre clubs, surrealism, steel furniture, faintly obscure poetry, Proust, James Joyce, dancing, rink-skating, large paintings on walls of rooms.
>
> The next decade was more serious, less cultured, less esthetic, more political. The slump blew like a cold draught at its birth, war stormed like forest fire at its close: between these two catastrophes Communists and Fascists battled and preached, and eyes turned apprehensively across the north sea towards the alarming menace which had leaped up like a strident jack-in-the-box from a beer-cellar to more than a throne.

Rose Macaulay is a wise guide, tolerant, generous-minded, liberal, courageous, cheerful, and her judgments of society and social values are always sound. She sums up the two decades very well.

But of course there is more to say. There are influences in this world more powerful than either peace or war. And we cannot get a true idea of our period and the books it produces until we look deeper than fashions or politics or the achievements and failures of generals. For one thing, there is a huge economic movement which has been taking the whole world, Great Britain included, from agriculture towards industrialism. That began about a hundred and fifty years ago, but since 1918 it has accelerated to an enormous speed, bringing all sorts of changes into national and personal life. It has meant organisation and plans and the boosting of the community. It has meant the destruction of feudalism and relationship based on the land, it has meant the transference of power from the aristocrat to the bureaucrat and the manager and the technician. Perhaps it will mean democracy, but it has not meant it yet, and personally I hate it. So I imagine do most writers, however loyally they try to sing its praises and to hymn the machine. But however much we detest this economic shift we have to recognise it as an important influence, more important than any local peace or war, which is going on all the time and transforming our outlooks. It rests on applied science, and as long as science is applied it will continue. Even when a writer seems to escape it, like T. E. Lawrence, he is conditioned by it. T. E. Lawrence hated the progress of industrialism, he hated what your city of Glasgow and my city of London stand for. He fled from it into the deserts of Arabia and the last of the romantic wars, in the search of old-time adventure, and later on into the deserts of his own heart. I think he was right to fly, because I believe that a writer's duty often exceeds any duty he owes to society, and that he often ought to lead a forlorn retreat. But of course the flight failed. Industrialism did T. E. Lawrence in in the long run, and it was not by the spear of an Arab but by a high-power motor-bike that he came to his death.[1] We must face the unpleasant truths that normal life today is a life in factories and offices, that even war has evolved from an adventure into a business, that even farming has become scientific, that insurance has taken the place of charity, that status has given way to contract. You will see how disquieting all this is to writers, who love, and ought to love, beauty and charm and the passage of the seasons, and generous impulses, and the tradition of their craft. And you will appreciate how lost some of them have been feeling during the last quarter of a century, and how they have been tempted to nostalgia like Siegfried Sassoon, or to disgust like Evelyn Waugh and Graham Greene.

But this economic movement, from the land to the factory, is not the only great movement which has gathered strength during our period. There has been a psychological movement, about which I am more enthusiastic. Man is beginning to understand himself better and to explore his own contradictions. This exploration is conveniently connected with the awful name of Freud, but it is not so much in Freud as in the air. It has brought a great enrichment to the art of fiction. It has given subtleties and depths to the portrayal of human nature. The presence in all of us of the subconscious, the occasional existence of the split personality, the persistence of the irrational especially in people who pride themselves on their reasonableness, the importance of dreams and the prevalence of daydreaming—here are some of the points which novelists have seized on and which have not been ignored by historians. This psychology is not new, but it has newly risen to the surface. Shakespeare was subconsciously aware of the subconscious, so were Emily Brontë, Herman Melville and others. But conscious knowledge of it only comes at the beginning of the century, with Samuel Butler's *The Way of All Flesh,* and only becomes general after 1918—partly owing to Freud. It gathers strength now, like the economic movement, and, like it, is independent of war or peace. Of course, writers can be stupid about it, as about anything else, they can apply it as a formula instead of feeling it as a possibility; the stupid psychologist who applies his (or her) formula in season or out and is always saying "you think you don't but you do" or "you think you do but you don't" can be absolutely maddening. But the better minds of our age— what a rich harvest they have reaped! Proust in France to begin with;

[1]See Christopher Caudwell, *Studies in a Dying Culture;* a brilliant criticism of the period from a communist standpoint. [Author's note]

Gertrude Stein and her experiments in uninhibited talk—not too successful in her own case but influential: Dorothy Richardson's novels, another pioneer in this country: the later work of D. H. Lawrence, the novels of Virginia Woolf, Joyce, de la Mare, Elizabeth Bowen. History too has profited. This new method of examining the human individual has helped to reinterpret the past. Aldous Huxley's *Grey Eminence* is one example— it gives a fresh view of Cardinal Richelieu and his adviser Father Joseph —a fresh view of their insides. Livingston Lowes' *The Road to Xanadu* is another example: a fresh view of the genius and make-up of Coleridge. And then there is the great work of a Christian historian, Arnold Toynbee, *A Study of History*, which regards history as a record of what men think and feel as well as of what they assert and achieve, and tries, with this extra material, to account for the rise and fall of civilisations. Professor Toynbee comes to the conclusion that they rise and fall in accord with a religious law, and that except the Lord build the house their labour is but lost that build it; or, if you prefer the language of Freud to that of the Old Testament, that the conscious must be satisfactorily based on the subconscious.

So though we are justified in thinking of our period as an interval between two wars we must remember that it forms part of larger movements where wars become insignificant: part of an economic movement from agriculture to industrialism, and of a psychological movement which is reinterpreting human nature. Both these movements have been speeded up, and writers have in my judgment been worried by the economic shift but stimulated by the psychological. Remember too, in passing, another factor, and that is the shift in physics exemplified by the work of Einstein. Can literary men understand Einstein? Of course they cannot—even less than they can understand Freud. But the idea of relativity has got into the air and has favoured certain tendencies in novels. Absolute good and evil, as in Dickens, are seldom presented. A character becomes good or evil in relation to some other character or to a situation which may itself change. You can't measure people up, because the yard-measure itself keeps altering its length. The best exponent of relativity in literature known to me is Proust, though there are instances in English too. Most of Proust's people are odious, yet you cannot have the comfort of writing any of them off as bad. Given the circumstances, even the most odious of them all, Madame Verdurin, can behave nobly. Proust and others have this attitude—not because they know anything about science, but because the idea of relativity, like the idea of the subconscious self, has got about and tinged their outlook.

A word must now be said on the special character of prose. Prose, unlike poetry, does two things. It serves us in daily life and it creates works of art. For instance, I travelled from Euston to Glasgow on prose, I am talking prose now, and, like M. Jourdain, I am astonished at finding myself doing so. For prose, besides serving our practical ends, also makes great literature.

Now, one of the problems which a critic has to tackle is that these two uses of prose are not water-tight, and one of these is as it were constantly slopping over into the other. The practical popular prose is always getting into the deliberate artistic prose which makes books. Indeed, if it didn't, the artistic prose couldn't live very long as it would get stale and stuffy. It has to be replenished by contemporary speech. And in this period of ours there has been a great deal of this replenishment. New words and phrases—and, what is more important, the new habits of thought expressed by them—are rapidly absorbed by authors and put into books. That is one tendency of our period, and it may be called, for want of a better word, the popular tendency. The writer feels himself part of his people. He enters or wants to enter into their ways. And he wants to be understood by them, and so he tries to be informal and clear. I'll give several examples of it. Here is a little example, taken from letter-writing. In 1918, if I had had a letter from a stranger it would certainly have begun "Dear Sir." Today, if I have a letter from a stranger, it will probably begin "Dear Mr. Forster." One form of address doesn't mean more than another, but the convention is a more friendly one. I expect it came in, like other speakeasies, from America. It shows which way the wind of words is blowing. Another sign is the speeches of public men. Public men are becoming less formal—some of them because of the influences of the radio, for they know if they broadcast too pompously listeners will switch off. Others are informal by instinct, like Winston Churchill, whose speeches sound and read more democratic than those of the Prime Ministers of the last war. Novelists too—they practise the friendly unpatronising tone; Christopher Isherwood's *Mr. Norris changes Trains* is an example of this. Isherwood—who is extremely intelligent—always writes as if the reader were equally intelligent. He is an example of democratic good manners. He trusts his public. Another novelist—Ernest Hemingway—introduces a new technique of conversation. Another straw which shows which way this wind is blowing is the tendency of official notices and proclamations to become more intelligible. They do so reluctantly, for the bureaucrat who gives his meaning clearly is afraid he may be giving something else away too. Still they do it. They tend to issue orders which we understand. And since we live under orders, this is a good thing.

I could continue this list of the popular tendencies in prose. We have had an example in the demand from high quarters for Basic English—and I expect it is a useful commercial idea though I cannot see what it has to do with literature, or what it can do to literature, except impoverish it. I'll conclude with an example of another kind, a reference to the English of the Authorised Version of the Bible. This, the great monument of our seventeenth-century speech, has constantly influenced our talk and writing for the last three hundred years. Its rhythm, its atmosphere, its turns of phrase, belonged to our people and overflowed into our books. Bunyan, Johnson, Blake, George Eliot, all echo it. About ten years ago an edition of the Bible came out called *The Bible Designed to Be Read as Literature.*

Its publication gave some of us a shock and caused us to realise that the English of the Authorised Version had at last become remote from popular English. This was well put in a review by Somerset Maugham. The English of the Bible, he agreed, is part of our national heritage, but it is so alien to our present idiom that no writer can study it profitably. I shall soon be quoting from a writer who has studied it, still Somerset Maugham is right on the whole, and there is now an unbridgeable gulf between ourselves and the Authorised Version as regards style, and the gulf widened about 1920, when those other influences we have discussed became strong. Quotations from the Bible still occur, but they support my contention: they are usually conventional and insensitive, introduced because the author or speaker wants to be impressive without taking trouble. Listen to the following advertisement of "Cable and Wireless" in *The Times* of July 28th, 1943. The advertisement is reporting a speech made by a cabinet minister, Colonel Oliver Stanley, at a "Cable and Wireless" staff lunch:

> When the end comes, when victory is won, then history will begin to assess merit. We shall all of us be searching our conscience. . . . We shall be discussing who succeeded and who failed . . . I have no doubt at all, when we come to discuss the part that "Cable and Wireless" has played, what the verdict of the nation will be—"Well done, thou good and faithful servant."

No doubt "Cable and Wireless" has done and deserved well, but I do not feel it can be suitably congratulated in the words of St. Matthew's Gospel, and if the English of the Bible had been in Colonel Stanley's blood instead of in his cliché-box I do not think he would have used such words. It is an example of insensitiveness to the Authorised Version and of the complete divorce between Biblical and popular English. (A similar example, this time of insensitiveness to Milton, was the slogan "They also serve" on a war-workers' poster.)

So much for this popular tendency in prose. I have suggested that it takes various forms, bringing freshness and informality and new usages and democratic good manners into literature, but also bringing vulgarity and flatness. Now for the other tendency to which I will attach the name esoteric; the desire on the part of writers—generally the more distinguished writers—to create something better than the bloodshed and dullness which have been creeping together over the world. Such writers are often censured. You may complain that Lytton Strachey, Virginia Woolf, James Joyce, D. H. Lawrence and T. E. Lawrence have done little to hearten us up. But you must admit they were the leading writers of our age. It is an age that could not produce a Shakespeare or even a Madame de Sévigné or a Jane Austen: an age in which sensitive people could not feel comfortable, and were driven to seek inner compensation: an age similar in some ways to that which caused St. Augustine to write *The City of God*. St. Augustine, though he looked outside him, worked within. He too was esoteric. These writers look outside them and find their material lying about in the world. But they arrange it and recreate it within, temporarily sheltered from the pitiless blasts and the fog.

A further word on T. E. Lawrence. *The Seven Pillars of Wisdom* is a most enigmatic book. Lawrence made good in the world of action and was what most of us regard as a hero—brave, selfless, modest, and kind by nature yet ruthless at need, loyal and the inspirer of loyalty, magnetic, a born leader of men, and victorious at Damascus in the last of the picturesque wars. Such a man, even if not happy, will surely be true to type. He will remain the man of action, the extrovert. But when we read the *Seven Pillars* we find beneath the gallant fighting and the brilliant description of scenery—sensitiveness, introspection, doubt, disgust at the material world. It is the book of a man who cannot fit in with twentieth-century civilisation, and loves the half-savage Arabs because they challenge it. This comes out in the following quotation: note in the final sentence the hit at "vested things"; at the innate commercialism of the west which ruined the peace of Versailles.

> Their mind [the Arabs'] was strange and dark, full of depressions and exaltations, lacking in rule, but with more of ardour and more fertile in belief than any other in the world. They were a people of starts, for whom the abstract was the strongest motive, the process of infinite courage and variety, and the end nothing. They were as unstable as water, and like water would perhaps finally prevail. Since the dawn of life, in successive waves, they had been dashing themselves against the coasts of flesh. Each wave was broken, but, like the sea, wore away ever so little of the granite on which it failed, and some day, ages yet, might roll unchecked over the place where the material world had been, and God would move over the face of those waters. One such wave (and not the least) I raised and rolled before the breath of an idea till it reached its crest, and toppled over and fell at Damascus. The wash of this wave, thrown back by the resistance of vested things, will provide the matter of the following wave, when in fullness of time the sea shall be raised once more.

The *Seven Pillars* for all its greatness is too strange a book to be typical of a period, and the same applies to another curious masterpiece, James Joyce's *Ulysses*. For a typical example I'd take Lytton Strachey's *Queen Victoria*. This is important for several reasons. It came out at the beginning of our period, it is an achievement of genius, and it has revolutionised the art of biography. Strachey did debunk of course; he hated pomposity, hypocrisy and muddle-headedness, he mistrusted inflated reputations, and was clever at puncturing them, and he found in the Victorian age, which had taken itself very, very seriously, a tempting target for his barbed arrows. But he was much more than a debunker. He did what no biographer had done before: he managed to get inside his subject. Earlier biographers, like Macaulay and Carlyle, had produced fine and convincing pictures of people; Lytton Strachey makes his people move; they are alive, like characters in a novel: he constructs or rather reconstructs them from within. Sometimes he got them wrong; his presentation of General Gordon has been questioned, so has his brilliant later work on Elizabeth and Essex. But even when they are wrong they seem alive, and in the *Queen Victoria* his facts have not been seriously challenged; and, based on dry documents, a whole society and its inhabitants rise from the grave, and walk about. That was his great contribution. He was a historian who worked from within, and constructed out of the bones of the past something more real and more satisfactory than the chaos surrounding him. He is typical of our period, and particularly of the twenties—throughout them his influence is enormous; today it has declined, partly because people are again taking themselves very, very seriously, and don't like the human race to be laughed at, partly because Strachey had some tiresome imitators, who have brought his method into discredit. However that doesn't matter. Reputations always will go up and down. What matters is good work, and *Queen Victoria* is a masterpiece. It is a pageant of the historical type, but as the grand procession passes we—you and I, we little readers, are somehow inside the procession, we mingle unobserved with royalty and statesmen and courtiers and underlings, and hear their unspoken thoughts.

Even a frivolous passage, like the one about the Boy Jones, has its historical function. Lytton Strachey was a gay person who loved fun and nonsense, and he knew how to make use of them in his work. Through the episode of the enigmatic Boy Jones, an undersized youth who repeatedly entered Buckingham Palace and hid there in the year 1840, was discovered under sofas, and confessed that he had "helped himself to soup and other eatables, sat upon the throne, seen the Queen, and heard the Princess Royal squall," Strachey recreates the domestic confusion existing there, and makes the period come alive. Then he passes on to more serious topics.

What was he serious about? Not about political ideals or social reform. Like T. E. Lawrence, he was disillusioned though in another way. He believed, however, in wit and aristocratic good manners, and he was implacable in his pursuit of truth. He believed, furthermore, in fidelity between human beings. There, and there only, the warmth of his heart comes out. He is always moved by constant affection, and the Queen's love for the Prince Consort, and for his memory, makes the book glow and preserves it from frigidity. Strachey's belief in affection, like his fondness for fun, is too often forgotten. Here is the famous passage describing the Queen's death, with which the book closes. He begins by being the dignified historian; then he dismisses his subject tenderly, and launches the Queen as it were on an ebbing tide, carrying her backwards through the manifold joys of life till she vanishes in the mists of her birth.

By the end of the year the last remains of her ebbing strength had almost deserted her; and through the early days of the opening century it was clear that her dwindling forces were kept together only by an effort of will. On January 14, she had at Osborne an hour's interview with Lord Roberts, who had returned victorious from South Africa a few days before. She inquired with acute anxiety into all the details of the war; she appeared to sustain the exertion successfully; but, when the audience was over, there was a collapse. On the following day her medical attendants recognised that her state was hopeless; and yet, for two days more, the indomitable spirit fought on; for two days more she discharged the duties of a Queen of England. But after that there was an end of working; and then, and not till then, did the last optimism of those about her break down. The brain was failing, and life was gently slipping away. Her family gathered round her; for a little more she lingered, speechless and apparently insensible; and, on January 22, 1901, she died.

When, two days previously, the news of the approaching end had been made public, astonished grief had swept over the country. It appeared as if some monstrous reversal of the course of nature was about to take place. The vast majority of her subjects had never known a time when Queen Victoria had not been reigning over them. She had become an indissoluble part of their whole scheme of things, and that they were about to lose her appeared a scarcely possible thought. She herself, as she lay blind and silent, seemed to those who watched her to be divested of all thinking—to have glided already, unawares, into oblivion. Yet, perhaps, in the secret chambers of consciousness, she had her thoughts, too. Perhaps her fading mind called up once more the shadows of the past to float before it, and retraced, for the last time, the vanished visions of that long history—passing back and back, through the cloud of years, to older and ever older memories—to the spring woods at Osborne, so full of primroses for Lord Beaconsfield—to Lord Palmerston's queer clothes and high demeanour, and Albert's face under the green lamp, and Albert's first stag at Balmoral, and Albert in his blue and silver uniform, and the Baron coming in through a doorway, and Lord M. dreaming at Windsor with the rooks cawing in the elm-trees, and the Archbishop of Canterbury on his knees in the dawn, and the old King's turkey-cock ejaculations, and Uncle Leopold's soft voice at Claremont, and Lehzen with the globes, and her mother's feathers sweeping down towards her, and a great old repeater-watch of her father's in its tortoise-shell case, and a yellow rug, and some friendly flounces of sprigged muslin, and the trees and the grass at Kensington.

You'll remember what I said before about the new psychology being in the air, and this last long lovely drifting sentence, with its imaginings of the subconscious, could not have been created at an earlier date.

A word on the authors whom I have mentioned. I have kept to those who may be said to belong to our period, who were formed by it, and received its peculiar stamp. Authors like Arnold Bennett, Galsworthy, Wells, Belloc, Chesterton, Frank Swinnerton, Norman Douglas, Bertrand Russell, Lowes Dickinson, George Moore, Max Beerbohm, did good work after

1920, and some of them are still active. But they got their impressions and formed their attitudes in an earlier period, before the first of the two world-wars. D. H. Lawrence presents a special difficulty. Does he come in or not? His finest novels, *The White Peacock* and *Sons and Lovers,* were published round about 1912 and he displays all his life a blend of vision and vituperation which seems to date him further back still—right back to Carlyle. On the other hand, he was alive to the new economics and the new psychology, and well aware, when he died in 1930, that the war to end war had ended nothing but the Victorian peace. My own feeling is that he does come into our survey.

To sum up my remarks. Our period: a long week-end between two wars. Economic and psychological changes already in existence intensify. Writers are intimidated by the economic changes but stimulated by the psychological. Prose, because it is a medium for daily life as well as for literature, is particularly sensitive to what is going on, and two tendencies can be noted: the popular, which absorbs what is passing, and the esoteric, which rejects it, and tries to create through art something more valuable than monotony and bloodshed. The best work of the period has this esoteric tendency. T. E. Lawrence, though heroic in action, retreats into the desert to act. Lytton Strachey is disillusioned, except about truth and human affection.

As for assessing the value of our period, I am disposed to place it high, and I do not agree with those numerous critics who condemn it as a failure, and scold mankind for enjoying itself too much in the twenties and for theorising too much in the thirties. We are plunged in a terrific war, and our literary judgments are not at their best. All our criticism is or ought to be tentative. And tentatively I suggest that the long week-end did valuable work, and I ask you to pause before you yield to the prevalent tendency to censure it.

THE FREUDIAN PRIMITIVES

Frances Newman

If Gogol and Turgenev had not written the first stories that are truly Russian stories, Chekhov undoubtedly would not have found the road to his Russian perfection so short. But if he had written Gogol's Overcoat, which is becoming as inaccurately celebrated as The Necklace, he would not have brought the ghost of poor Akaky Akakyevich back to revenge

FROM *The Short Story's Mutations* by Frances Newman. Copyright 1924 by B. W. Huebsch, Inc. Reprinted by permission of the Viking Press, Inc., New York. (Title supplied by the editor.)

himself by stripping court councillors of their overcoats—and if he had found any psychological or physiological reason for Akaky Akakyevich to die of losing his beautiful new overcoat and of the proper authorities' lack of interest in his loss, Chekhov would almost certainly have ended his story when a new clerk who was taller than Akaky Akakyevich sat in his seat and copied documents of state in letters that slanted more than Akaky Akakyevich's letters. And The Overcoat would have been a much better story and a much more Russian story. Tolstoi seems to have given himself and every one else a great deal more trouble about his style than Chekhov did, but no other Russian, so far as one may read them and judge them in the western languages, had the fastidiousness of a Racine or a Flaubert about words and the fastidiousness of a Mérimée or a Maupassant about form that Chekhov showed in his letters to Gorki and to the publisher Suvorin. If Conrad got very little for the inconvenience of being a Slav and Dostoevski got rather too much, Tolstoi and Chekhov got just enough—if Tolstoi got rather too much for a husband and a father, his genius and his beautifully scrupulous craftmanship made it just enough for a writer, and if Chekhov might have gotten rather too little, judging from his letters, his critical eye for his own defects and his own excellencies, and for the defects and the excellencies of Tolstoi and Turgenev and Dostoevski and Gorki and even of Bourget joined with the advantage of a doctor's exact knowledge and made it just enough.

Chekhov never spoke of Freud, so far as I know, though there is no reason why he should not have heard his theories, and his prose never suffered the blight of the Freudian vocabulary even in such a story as The Nervous Breakdown. But in one of his letters he said that no surgeon could dissect a human body without seeing that the mind was a part of the body and without seeing that there was no place for a soul, and in another letter he drew a diagram of the broken fall of the Russian spirit—of the extreme excitement, the feeling of guilt, and the exhaustion which are peculiarly Russian and which explain some of the Russian's difference from the unexcited German and the eternally and normally excited Frenchman. He knew the souls that his characters have in spite of the soul's organic improbability, and he knew when they were healthy souls and when they were unhealthy souls. But Olenka did not know that only what are called feminine women have no opinions of their own about bottles and rain and peasants in carts, and Olga Mihailovna, who slipped away from her husband's name-day party to think about the little creature who would be born in another two months did not know why she did not care when the little creature did not come after all, and the spectacled little officer called Ryabovich who had sloping shoulders and whiskers like a lynx's did not know why he thought for two months of the house where he was accidentally kissed and then went to bed in his hut and refused to struggle against life's incomprehensible, aimless jests when he came back to the house again—and none of them knew whether his soul was healthy or unhealthy. That is, perhaps, the distinctive difference between the psychology of Chekhov and the psychoanalysis of all the Freudian primitives.

The stories of Lawrence and Joyce and Sherwood Anderson are far enough from being the mere charts of neurotic cases that Beresford and Ludovici and Rebecca West and May Sinclair sometimes write, but they do not often forget the modern Joseph who interprets all his dreams with due regard to his renunciation of Potiphar's wife. Lawrence's Gudruns and Ursulas and Hildas and Hermiones and Alvinas never forget him and Lawrence is the only one of the three geniuses among this generation of primitives who has publicly cried out that the unconscious is the soul and that the mysterious stream of consciousness is the stream which undermined his adolescence, but if that mysterious stream did not undermine the adolescence of Anderson and Joyce, the knowledge of the unconscious has flowed through it into the blood of every character they have created and it has assisted nature in denying all of them the grace of humour which is not often a quality of the poetic genius.

Anderson and Lawrence and Joyce are all primitives because none of them writes as the men who will always have known their unconscious will write. But Anderson is the only one of them who is Gothic—his genius is the genius which could create tales that would become folklore in an age that had not learned the art of printing from movable type, or in an age that had forgotten it. Chekhov worked out his problems by arithmetic because they were problems for arithmetic and because he was a Russian, not because his father was born a serf, and Anderson works out his problems with hardly more than addition and subtraction because his problems are problems for addition and subtraction. When Anderson meets Chekhov on the neutral ground of German or even of French they may be alike, but in English they are alike only in a beautiful kindness towards their characters—a kindness that comes from belonging to the two nations which are at once the kindest and the cruellest in what is called the civilized world—and in a perfection of simplicity that leaves no one excellence projecting from the smooth edges of an extraordinary evenness of character, of style, and of theme. Anderson writes of the Ohio he has always known, and of the George Willards and Ray Pearsons and the boys who want to know why and the boys who know they are fools—of the men and the boys he has known, perhaps the men and the boys he has been. They are not very different, I suppose, from the men and the boys the other Mid-Americans write of; but Anderson is the only Mid-American writer who can be explained only by the possession of that extreme degree of human intelligence called genius, and he is the only one whose form is created by the knowledge that these people can not be looked at from the outside—that they must be allowed to write themselves down in their own virgin vulgarity unless they are seen through the very depths of another mind. He is Gothic in the same way that Giotto was Gothic—Gothic with the discovery of the bones and sinews of the American mind and with the struggle of killing the smooth conventionalism of the story America inherited from England. A year or two ago he wrote the story of a man who was seen through the very depths of a doctor's mind—the story of a man who wanted one woman for a lifetime and another woman for a night, and he called it The Other Woman. Thirty years before Richard Harding Davis had written the story of a man who wanted one woman for a lifetime and another woman for a month, and he had called his story The Other Woman—Davis's young Latimer and his Ellen and his bishop are so many wax-works from the Eden Musée, and his America and Anderson's America look at each other across a stream wider than the unconscious and do not know each other. But the boys who want to know why and the boys who know they are fools know the boys who were created by Mark Twain, even across the stream of the unconscious and even though Mark Twain saw them only from outside even when they wrote themselves down.

Anderson is less admirably Gothic when he masses three words between the halves of an infinitive with something less than the deliberation and the elegance of Henry James, when he drops a heavy word into a phrase that will not bear its weight, when he writes the English *one* in a phrase where the familiar American *you* would be less perceptible, and when he speaks of Van Gogh and Picasso as if he had heard their names just as he was sitting down to write. When Lawrence speaks of Botticelli and Hippolytus he seems to have heard their names yesterday or the day before, but Lawrence is romantic, and he is romantic because he gave grace and style and brilliance to the unconscious even though he is a snarling romantic. He tears dark secrets from the dark blood current of his lyrical creatures and throws them on his pages in a prose that is not often prose except in the manner of its printing. If some critic who found Women in Love sufficiently magnificent or sufficiently hideous to make such a research agreeable would count the number of similes and metaphors and synechdoches and metonymies in that mænadic tale, he would doubtless discover that Lawrence uses fewer unfigurative speeches than any other man who was ever called a prose writer. Everything in nature and out of nature looks like something else in or out of nature to him, and if an impressionist painter is a painter who reproduces the impression the external world has made on his spirit, Lawrence's stories are all impressionist paintings. A writer's similes are always a record of his life and what are called his allusions are always a record of his learning, but every story is not signed with the latitude and longitude of its creation as Lawrence's are—his phrases were always hot from his own unconscious, but his prose did not burst with the richness of seeds more pregnant than Annunzio's until he felt the blazing beauty of Italy, and it did not fade like a pomegranate broken from its stem until he left Italy for Australia and America.

Joyce is the same man in Dublin and in Trieste and in Paris, and Ulysses is Two Gallants and Grace and Ivy Day in the Committee Room and all of the other stories in Dubliners with a stethoscope held to the current of Celtic consciousness and reported in a language that jeers at itself in its own mirror. He is classic because he is as Roman a Catholic as Thomas Aquinas, no matter what he believes or disbelieves—classic because everything that he knows has become part of what he has always known, what his fathers have known before him, and what his Church has always known and will know forever, even when his knowledge is the knowledge of Mallarmé and Cours la Reine and Goethe and nighttown with Bella Cohen looking like Minnie Hauck in Carmen. Whether the future of his method is art or science and whether or not even genius can hold a stethoscope to any consciousness except its own, only genius can hold a stethoscope even to its own consciousness; but Joyce is the only one of these primitives who has an erudition, a magnificence of intellect and a solemn subtle cleverness which could almost explain his stories without forcing his critics to fall helplessly back on the miracle of genius.

THE PLACE OF CLASSICS
IN EDUCATION

Alfred North Whitehead

The future of classics in this country is not going mainly to be decided by the joy of classics to a finished scholar, and by the utility of scholarly training for scholarly avocations. The pleasure and the discipline of character to be derived from an education based mainly on classical literature and classical philosophy has been demonstrated by centuries of experience. The danger to classical learning does not arise because classical scholars now love classics less than their predecessors. It arises in this way. In the past classics reigned throughout the whole sphere of higher education. There were no rivals; and accordingly all students were steeped in classics throughout their school life, and its domination at the universities was only challenged by the narrow discipline of mathematics. There were many consequences to this state of things. There was a large demand for classical scholars for the mere purposes of tuition; there was a classical tone in all learned walks of life, so that aptitude for classics was a synonym for ability; and finally every boy who gave the slightest promise in that direction cultivated his natural or acquired interest in classical learning. All this is gone, and gone for ever. Humpty Dumpty was a good egg so long as he was on the top of the wall, but you can never set him up again. There are now other disciplines each involving topics of wide-

FROM *The Aims of Education*, by Alfred North Whitehead. New York, The Macmillan Company. Reprinted by permission of the publisher.

spread interest, with complex relationships, and exhibiting in their development the noblest feats of genius in its stretch of imagination and its philosophic intuition. Almost every walk of life is now a learned profession, and demands one or more of these disciplines as the substratum for its technical skill. Life is short, and the plastic period when the brain is apt for acquirement is still shorter. Accordingly, even if all children were fitted for it, it is absolutely impossible to maintain a system of education in which a complete training as a classical scholar is the necessary preliminary to the acquirement of other intellectual disciplines. As a member of the Prime Minister's Committee on the Place of Classics in Education it was my misfortune to listen to much ineffectual wailing from witnesses on the mercenary tendencies of modern parents. I do not believe that the modern parent of any class is more mercenary than his predecessors. When classics was the road to advancement, classics was the popular subject for study. Opportunity has now shifted its location, and classics is in danger. Was it not Aristotle who said that a good income was a desirable adjunct to an intellectual life? I wonder how Aristotle, as a parent, would have struck a headmaster of one of our great public schools. From my slight knowledge of Aristotle, I suspect that there would have been an argument, and that Aristotle would have got the best of it. I have been endeavouring to appreciate at its full value the danger which besets classics in the educational curriculum. The conclusion that I draw is that the future of classics will be decided during the next few years in the secondary schools of this country. Within a generation the great public schools will have to follow suit, whether they like it or not.

The situation is dominated by the fact that in the future ninety per cent. of the pupils who leave school at the age of eighteen will never again read a classical book in the original. In the case of pupils leaving at an earlier age, the estimate of ninety per cent. may be changed to one of ninety-nine per cent. I have heard and read many a beautiful exposition of the value of classics to the scholar who reads Plato and Virgil in his armchair. But these people will never read classics either in their armchairs or in any other situation. We have got to produce a defence of classics which applies to this ninety per cent. of the pupils. If classics is swept out of the curriculum for this section, the remaining ten per cent. will soon vanish. No school will have the staff to teach them. The problem is urgent.

It would, however, be a great mistake to conclude that classics is faced with a hostile opinion either in the learned professions or from leaders of industry who have devoted attention to the relation between education and efficiency. The last discussion, public or private, on this subject at which I have been present was a short and vigorous one at one of the leading committees of a great modern university. The three representatives of the Faculty of Science energetically urged the importance of classics on the ground of its value as a preliminary discipline for scientists. I mention this incident because in my experience it is typical.

We must remember that the whole problem of intellectual education is controlled by lack of time. If Methuselah was not a well-educated man, it was his own fault or that of his teachers. But our task is to deal with five years of secondary school-life. Classics can only be defended on the ground that within that period, and sharing that period with other subjects, it can produce a necessary enrichment of intellectual character more quickly than any alternative discipline directed to the same object.

In classics we endeavour by a thorough study of language to develop the mind in the regions of logic, philosophy, history and of æsthetic apprehension of literary beauty. The learning of the languages—Latin or Greek —is a subsidiary means for the furtherance of this ulterior object. When the object has been obtained, the languages can be dropped unless opportunity and choice lead to their further pursuit. There are certain minds, and among them some of the best, for which the analysis of language is not the avenue of approach to the goal of culture. For these a butterfly or a steam-engine has a wider range of significance than a Latin sentence. This is especially the case where there is a touch of genius arising from vivid apprehensions stimulating originality of thought. The assigned verbal sentence almost always says the wrong thing for such people, and confuses them by its trivial irrelevance.

But on the whole the normal avenue is the analysis of language. It represents the greatest common measure for the pupils, and by far the most manageable job for the teachers.

At this point I must cross-question myself. My other self asks me, Why do you not teach the children logic, if you want them to learn that subject? Wouldn't that be the obvious procedure? I answer in the words of a great man who to our infinite loss has recently died, Sanderson, the late headmaster of Oundle. His phrase was, They learn by contact. The meaning to be attached to this saying goes to the root of the true practice of education. It must start from the particular fact, concrete and definite for individual apprehension, and must gradually evolve towards the general idea. The devil to be avoided is the cramming of general statements which have no reference to individual personal experiences.

Now apply this principle to the determination of the best method to help a child towards a philosophical analysis of thought. I will put it in more homely style, What is the best way to make a child clear-headed in its thoughts and its statements? The general statements of a logic book have no reference to anything the child has ever heard of. They belong to the grown-up stage of education at—or not far from—the university. You must begin with the analysis of familiar English sentences. But this grammatical procedure, if prolonged beyond its elementary stages, is horribly dry. Furthermore, it has the disadvantage that it only analyses so far as the English language analyses. It does nothing to throw light upon the complex significance of English phrases, and words, and habits of mental procedure. Your next step is to teach the child a foreign language. Here you gain an enormous advantage. You get away from the nauseating formal drill for the drill's sake. The analysis is now automatic, while the pupil's attention is directed to expressing his wants in the language, or to understanding someone who is speaking to him, or to making out what an author has written. Every language embodies a definite type of mentality, and two languages necessarily display to the pupil some contrast between their two types. Common sense dictates that you start with French as early as possible in the child's life. If you are wealthy, you will provide a French nursery-governess. Less fortunate children will start French in a secondary school about the age of twelve. The direct method is probably used, by which the child is immersed in French throughout the lesson and is taught to think in French without the intervention of English between the French words and their significations. Even an average child will get on well, and soon acquires the power of handling and understanding simple French sentences. As I have said before, the gain is enormous; and, in addition, a useful instrument for after life is acquired. The sense for language grows, a sense which is the subconscious appreciation of language as an instrument of definite structure.

It is exactly now that the initiation of Latin is the best stimulus for mental expansion. The elements of Latin exhibit a peculiarly plain concrete case of language as a structure. Provided that your mind has grown to the level of that idea, the fact stares you in the face. You can miss it over English and French. Good English of a simple kind will go straight into slipshod French, and conversely good French will go into slipshod English. The difference between the slipshod French of the literal translation and the good French, which ought to have been written, is often rather subtle for that stage of mental growth, and is not always easy to explain. Both languages have the same common modernity of expression. But in the case of English and Latin the contrast of structure is obvious, and yet not so wide as to form an insuperable difficulty.

According to the testimony of schoolmasters, Latin is rather a popular subject; I know that as a schoolboy I enjoyed it myself. I believe that this popularity is due to the sense of enlightenment that accompanies its study. You know that you are finding out something. The words somehow stick in the sentences in a different way to what they do either in English or French, with odd queer differences of connotation. Of course in a way Latin is a more barbaric language than English. It is one step nearer to the sentence as the unanalysed unit.

This brings me to my next point. In my catalogue of the gifts of Latin I placed philosophy between logic and history. In this connection, that is its true place. The philosophic instinct which Latin evokes, hovers between the two and enriches both. The analysis of thought involved in translation, English to Latin or Latin to English, imposes that type of experience which is the necessary introduction to philosophic logic. If in after life your job is to think, render thanks to Providence which ordained that, for five years of your youth, you did a Latin prose once a week and daily construed some Latin author. The introduction to any subject is the process of learning by contact. To that majority of people for whom the language is the readiest stimulus to thought-activity, the road towards enlightenment of understanding runs from simple English grammar to French, from French to Latin, and also traverses the elements of Geometry and of Algebra. I need not remind my readers that I can claim Plato's authority for the general principle which I am upholding.

From the philosophy of thought we now pass to the philosophy of history. I again recur to Sanderson's great saying, They learn by contact. How on earth is a child to learn history by contact? The original documents, charters and laws and diplomatic correspondence, are double Dutch to it. A game of football is perhaps a faint reflection of the Battle of Marathon. But that is only to say that human life in all ages and circumstances has common qualities. Furthermore, all this diplomatic and political stuff with which we cram children is a very thin view of history. What is really necessary is that we should have an instinctive grasp of the flux of outlook, and of thought, and of æsthetic and racial impulses, which have controlled the troubled history of mankind. Now the Roman Empire is the bottleneck through which the vintage of the past has passed into modern life. So far as European civilisation is concerned the key to history is a comprehension of the mentality of Rome and the work of its Empire.

In the language of Rome, embodying in literary form the outlook of Rome, we possess the simplest material, by contact with which we can gain appreciation of the tides of change in human affairs. The mere obvious relations of the languages, French and English, to Latin are in themselves a philosophy of history. Consider the contrast which English presents to French: the entire break of English with the civilised past of Britain and the slow creeping back of words and phrases of Mediterranean origin with their cargoes of civilised meaning: in French we have continuity of development, amid obvious traces of rude shock. I am not asking for pretentious abstract lectures on such points. The thing illustrates itself. An elementary knowledge of French and Latin with a mother-tongue of English imparts the requisite atmosphere of reality to the story of the racial wanderings which created our Europe. Language is the incarnation of the mentality of the race which fashioned it. Every phrase and word embodies some habitual idea of men and women as they ploughed their fields, tended their homes, and built their cities. For this reason there are no true synonyms as between words and phrases in different languages. The whole of what I have been saying is merely an embroidery upon this single theme, and our endeavour to emphasise its critical importance. In English, French, and Latin we possess a triangle, such that one pair of vertices, English and French, exhibits a pair of diverse expressions of two chief types of modern mentality, and the relations of these vertices to the third exhibit alternative processes of derivation from the Mediterranean civilisation of the past. This is the essential triangle of literary culture, containing within itself freshness of contrast, embracing both the present and the past. It ranges through space and time. These are the grounds by which we justify the assertion, that in the acquirement of French and Latin is to be found the easiest mode of learning by contact the philosophy of logic and the philosophy of history. Apart from some such intimate experience, your analyses of thought and your histories of actions are mere sounding brasses. I am not claiming, and I do not for a moment believe, that this route of education is more than the simplest, easiest route for the majority of pupils. I am certain that there is a large minority for which the emphasis should be different. But I do believe that it is the route which can give the greatest success for the largest majority. It has also the advantage of having survived the test of experience. I believe that large modifications require to be introduced into existing practice to adapt it for present needs. But on the whole this foundation of literary education involves the best understood tradition and the largest corps of experienced scholarly teachers who can realise it in practice.

The reader has perhaps observed that I have as yet said nothing of the glories of Roman literature. Of course the teaching of Latin must proceed by the means of reading Latin literature with the pupils. This literature possesses vigorous authors who have succeeded in putting across the footlights the Roman mentality on a variety of topics, including its appreciation of Greek thought. One of the merits of Roman literature is its comparative lack of outstanding genius. There is very little aloofness about its authors, they express their race and very little which is beyond all differences of race. With the exception of Lucretius, you always feel the limitations under which they are working. Tacitus expressed the views of the Die-hards of the Roman Senate, and, blind to the achievements of Roman provincial administration, could only see that Greek freedmen were replacing Roman aristocrats. The Roman Empire and the mentality which created it absorbed the genius of Romans. Very little of Roman literature will find its way into the kingdom of heaven, when the events of this world will have lost their importance. The languages of heaven will be Chinese, Greek, French, German, Italian, and English, and the blessed Saints will dwell with delight on these golden expressions of eternal life. They will be wearied with the moral fervour of Hebrew literature in its battle with a vanished evil, and with Roman authors who have mistaken the Forum for the footstool of the living God.

We do not teach Latin in the hope that Roman authors, read in the original, may be for our pupils companions through life. English literature is so much greater: it is richer, deeper, and more subtle. If your tastes are philosophic, would you abandon Bacon and Hobbes, Locke, Berkeley, Hume, and Mill for the sake of Cicero? Not unless your taste among the moderns would lead you to Martin Tupper. Perhaps you crave for reflection on the infinite variety of human existence and the reaction of character to circumstance. Would you exchange Shakespeare and the English novelists for Terence, Plautus, and the banquet of Trimalchio? Then there are our humorists, Sheridan, Dickens, and others. Did anyone ever laugh like that as he read a Latin author? Cicero was a great orator, staged amid the pomp of Empire. England also can show statesmen inspired to expound policies with imagination. I will not weary you with an extended catalogue embracing poetry and history. I simply wish to justify my scepticism as to the claim for Latin literature that it expresses with outstanding perfection the universal element in human life. It cannot laugh, and it can hardly cry.

You must not tear it from its context. It is not a literature in the sense that Greece and England have produced literatures, expressions of universal human feeling. Latin has one theme and that is Rome—Rome, the mother of Europe, and the great Babylon, the harlot whose doom is described by the writer of the Apocalypse:

"Standing afar off for the fear of her torment, saying, Alas, alas, that great city Babylon, that mighty city! for in one hour is thy judgment come. And the merchants of the earth shall weep and mourn over her; for no man buyeth their merchandise any more:

"The merchandise of gold, and silver, and precious stones, and of pearls, and fine linen, and purple, and silk, and scarlet, and all thyine wood, and all manner vessels of ivory, and all manner vessels of most precious wood, and of brass, and iron, and marble;

"And cinnamon, and odours, and ointments, and frankincense, and wine, and oil, and fine flour, and wheat, and beasts, and sheep, and horses, and chariots, and slaves, and souls of men."

This is the way Roman civilisation appeared to an early Christian. But then Christianity itself is part of the outcrop of the ancient world which Rome passed on to Europe. We inherit the dual aspect of the civilisations of the eastern Mediterranean.

The function of Latin literature is its expression of Rome. When to England and France your imagination can add Rome in the background, you have laid firm the foundations of culture. The understanding of Rome leads back to that Mediterranean civilisation of which Rome was the last phase, and it automatically exhibits the geography of Europe, and the functions of seas and rivers and mountains and plains. The merit of this study in the education of youth is its concreteness, its inspiration to action, and the uniform greatness of persons, in their characters and their staging. Their aims were great, their virtues were great, and their vices were great. They had the saving merit of sinning with cart-ropes. Moral education is impossible apart from the habitual vision of greatness. If we are not great, it does not matter what we do or what is the issue. Now the sense of greatness is an immediate intuition and not the conclusion of an argument. It is permissible for youth in the agonies of religious conversion to entertain the feeling of being a worm and no man, so long as there remains the conviction of greatness sufficient to justify the eternal wrath of God. The sense of greatness is the groundwork of morals. We are at the threshold of a democratic age, and it remains to be determined whether the equality of man is to be realised on a high level or a low level. There was never a time in which it was more essential to hold before the young the vision of

Rome: in itself a great drama, and with issues greater than itself. We are now already immersed in the topic of æsthetic appreciation of literary quality. It is here that the tradition of classical teaching requires most vigorous reformation for adaptation to new conditions. It is obsessed with the formation of finished classical scholars. The old tradition was remorselessly to devote the initial stages to the acquirement of the languages and then to trust to the current literary atmosphere to secure enjoyment of the literature. During the latter part of the nineteenth century other subjects encroached on the available time. Too often the result has been merely time wasted in the failure to learn the language. I often think that the ruck of pupils from great English schools show a deplorable lack of intellectual zest, arising from this sense of failure. The school course of classics must be planned so that a definite result is clearly achieved. There has been too great a product of failures on the road to an ambitious ideal of scholarship.

In approaching every work of art we have to comport ourselves suitably in regard to two factors, scale and pace. It is not fair to the architect if you examine St. Peter's at Rome with a microscope, and the Odyssey becomes insipid if you read it at the rate of five lines a day. Now the problem before us is exactly this. We are dealing with pupils who will never know Latin well enough to read it quickly, and the vision to be illumed is of vast scale, set in the history of all time. A careful study of scale and pace, and of the correlative functions of various parts of our work, should appear to be essential. I have not succeeded in hitting upon any literature which deals with this question with reference to the psychology of the pupils. Is it a masonic secret?

I have often noticed that, if in an assembly of great scholars the topic of translations be introduced, they function as to their emotions and sentiments in exactly the same way as do decent people in the presence of a nasty sex-problem. A mathematician has no scholastic respectability to lose, so I will face the question.

It follows from the whole line of thought which I have been developing, that an exact appreciation of the meanings of Latin words, of the ways in which ideas are connected in grammatical constructions, and of the whole hang of a Latin sentence with its distribution of emphasis, forms the very backbone of the merits which I ascribe to the study of Latin. Accordingly any woolly vagueness of teaching, slurring over the niceties of language defeats the whole ideal which I have set before you. The use of a translation to enable the pupils to get away from the Latin as quickly as possible, or to avoid the stretch of mind in grappling with construction, is erroneous. Exactness, definiteness, and independent power of analysis are among the main prizes of the whole study.

But we are still confronted with the inexorable problem of pace, and with the short four or five years of the whole course. Every poem is meant to be read within certain limits of time. The contrasts, and the images, and the transition of moods must correspond with the sway of rhythms in the human spirit. These have their periods, which refuse to be stretched beyond certain limits. You may take the noblest poetry in the world, and, if you stumble through it at snail's pace, it collapses from a work of art into a rubbish heap. Think of the child's mind as he pores over his work: he reads "as when," then follows a pause with a reference to the dictionary, then he goes on—"an eagle," then another reference to the dictionary, followed by a period of wonderment over the construction, and so on, and so on. Is that going to help him to the vision of Rome? Surely, surely, common sense dictates that you procure the best literary translation you can, the one which best preserves the charm and vigour of the original, and that you read it aloud at the right pace, and append such comments as will elucidate the comprehension. The attack on the Latin will then be fortified by the sense that it enshrines a living work of art.

But someone objects that a translation is woefully inferior to the original. Of course it is, that is why the boy has to master the Latin original. When the original has been mastered, it can be given its proper pace. I plead for an initial sense of the unity of the whole, to be given by a translation at the right pace, and for a final appreciation of the full value of the whole to be given by the original at the right pace. Wordsworth talks of men of science who "murder to dissect." In the past, classical scholars have been veritable assassins compared to them. The sense of beauty is eager and vehement, and should be treated with the reverence which is its due. But I go further. The total bulk of Latin literature necessary to convey the vision of Rome is much greater than the students can possibly accomplish in the original. They should read more Virgil than they can read in Latin, more Lucretius than they can read in Latin, more history than they can read in Latin, more Cicero than they can read in Latin. In the study of an author the selected portions in Latin should illumine a fuller disclosure of his whole mind, although without the force of his own words in his own language. It is, however, a grave evil if no part of an author be read in his own original words.

The difficulty of scale is largely concerned in the presentation of classical history. Everything set before the young must be rooted in the particular and the individual. Yet we want to illustrate the general characters of whole periods. We must make students learn by contact. We can exhibit the modes of life by visual representations. There are photographs of buildings, casts of statues, and pictures from vases or frescoes illustrating religious myths or domestic scenes. In this way we can compare Rome with the preceding civilisation of the eastern Mediterranean, and with the succeeding period of the Middle Ages. It is essential to get into the children's minds how men altered, in their appearance, their dwellings, their technology, their art, and their religious beliefs. We must imitate the procedure of the zoologists who have the whole of animal creation on their hands. They teach by demonstrating typical examples. We must do likewise, to exhibit the position of Rome in history.

The life of man is founded on Technology, Science, Art and Religion. All four are inter-connected and issue from his total mentality. But there are particular intimacies between Science and Technology, and between Art and Religion. No social organisation can be understood without reference to these four underlying factors. A modern steam-engine does the work of a thousand slaves in the ancient world. Slave-raiding was the key to much of the ancient imperialism. A modern printing-press is an essential adjunct to a modern democracy. The key to modern mentality is the continued advance of science with the consequential shift of ideas and progress of technology. In the ancient world Mesopotamia and Egypt were made possible by irrigation. But the Roman Empire existed by virtue of the grandest application of technology that the world had hitherto seen: its roads, its bridges, its aqueducts, its tunnels, its sewers, its vast buildings, its organised merchant navies, its military science, its metallurgy, and its agriculture. This was the secret of the extension and the unity of Roman civilisation. I have often wondered why Roman engineers did not invent the steam-engine. They might have done it at any time, and then how different would have been the history of the world. I ascribe it to the fact that they lived in a warm climate and had not introduced tea and coffee. In the eighteenth century thousands of men sat by fires and watched their kettles boil. We all know of course that Hiero of Alexandria invented some slight anticipation. All that was wanted was that the Roman engineers should have been impressed with the motive force of steam by the humble process of watching their kettles.

The history of mankind has yet to be set in its proper relation to the gathering momentum of technological advance. Within the last hundred years, a developed science has wedded itself to a developed technology and a new epoch has opened.

Similarly about a thousand years before Christ the first great literary epoch commenced when the art of writing was finally popularised. In its earlier dim origins the art had been used for traditional hieratic formulæ and for the formal purposes of governmental record and chronicle. It is a great mistake to think that in the past the full sweep of a new invention has ever been anticipated at its first introduction. It is not even so at the present day, when we are all trained to meditate on the possibilities of new ideas. But in the past, with its different direction of thought, novelty slowly ate its way into the social system. Accordingly writing, as a stimulus to the preservation of individual novelty of thought, was but slowly grasped on the borders of the eastern Mediterranean. When the realisation of its possibilities was complete, in the hands of the Greeks and the Hebrews, civilisation took a new turn; though the general influence of Hebrew mentality was delayed for a thousand years till the advent of Christianity. But it was now that their prophets were recording their inward thoughts, when Greek civilisation was beginning to take shape.

What I want to illustrate is that in the large scale treatment of history necessary for the background and the foreground of the vision of Rome, the consecutive chronicle of political events on the scale traditional to our histories absolutely vanishes. Even verbal explanations partly go into the background. We must utilise models, and pictures, and diagrams, and charts to exhibit typical examples of the growth of technology and its impact on the current modes of life. In the same way art, in its curious fusion with utility and with religion, both expresses the actual inward life of imagination and changes it by its very expression. The children can see the art of previous epochs in models and pictures, and sometimes the very objects in museums. The treatment of the history of the past must not start with generalised statements, but with concrete examples exhibiting the slow succession of period to period, and of mode of life to mode of life, and of race to race.

The same concreteness of treatment must apply when we come to the literary civilisations of the eastern Mediterranean. When you come to think of it, the whole claim for the importance of classics rests on the basis that there is no substitute for first-hand knowledge. In so far as Greece and Rome are the founders of European civilisation, a knowledge of history means above all things a first-hand knowledge of the thoughts of Greeks and Romans. Accordingly, to put the vision of Rome into its proper setting, I urge that the pupils should read at first hand some few examples of Greek literature. Of course it must be in translation. But I prefer a translation of what a Greek actually said, to any talk about the Greeks written by an Englishman, however well he has done it. Books about Greece should come after some direct knowledge of Greece.

The sort of reading I mean is a verse translation of the Odyssey, some Herodotus, some choruses of plays translated by Gilbert Murray, some lives of Plutarch, especially the part about Archimedes in the life of Marcellus, and the definitions and axioms and one or two propositions from Euclid's Elements in the exact scholarly translation of Heath. In all this, just enough explanation is wanted to give the mental environment of the authors. The marvellous position of Rome in relation to Europe comes from the fact that it has transmitted to us a double inheritance. It received the Hebrew religious thought, and has passed on to Europe its fusion with Greek civilisation. Rome itself stands for the impress of organization and unity upon diverse fermenting elements. Roman Law embodies the secret of Roman greatness in its Stoic respect for intimate rights of human nature within an iron framework of empire. Europe is always flying apart because of the diverse explosive character of its inheritance, and coming together because it can never shake off that impress of unity it has received from Rome. The history of Europe is the history of Rome curbing the Hebrew and the Greek, with their various impulses of religion, and of science, and of art, and of quest for material comfort, and of lust of domination, which are all at daggers drawn with each other. The vision of Rome is the vision of the unity of civilisation.

QUESTIONS

1. Comment on the underlined passages in the following sentences (from Forster):

He [T. E. Lawrence] fled from it into the deserts of Arabia and the last of the romantic wars, in the search of old-time adventure, and later on into the deserts of his own heart.

Industrialism did T. E. Lawrence in in the long run, and it was not by the spear of an Arab but by a high-power motor-bike that he came to his death.

2. How does Frances Newman think Chekhov's method differed from Gogol's?

3. What is the topic sentence (or the topic) of her first paragraph?

4. Analyze the allusion in "but they [Lawrence, Joyce, Anderson] do not often forget the modern Joseph who interprets all his dreams with due regard to his renunciation of Potiphar's wife." How does its effect suggest Frances Newman's feeling about the Freudian primitives?

5. What is the effect of the allusion to Humpty Dumpty in the first paragraph of Whitehead's essay? Find examples of comparable devices elsewhere in the essay. What is the argument of the paragraph? How does Whitehead give the paragraph coherence? Analyze several other of his long paragraphs.

6. If you wanted to criticize Whitehead's main argument, how would you proceed?

7. In how many places does Whitehead seem to disagree with Barraclough?

8. Show that learning by contact is basic to Whitehead's whole description of proper teaching.

9. What interpretation of history lies behind Whitehead's explanation of the Roman failure to invent the steam engine?

⁞ ARGUMENT: NEWSPAPERS
⁞ AND THE FOURTH ESTATE

A speech to a convention and a column; what forms of exposition are more typical of our time? (For that matter, Hutchins and De Voto are pretty typical too.) Both selections are written with decisive rhythms and intonations, one can hear the voices of men of convictions, who are not much given to qualifying, except, perhaps, in the next column or speech. Both men write with some pleasure in the good fight, fully aware that it still goes on, that the side they speak for can, at most, win a skirmish here or there, sometimes perhaps even a battle, but never the war itself. Notice the wide range of allusions in De Voto's column; Hutchins's may be some-what more restricted, as might be expected from an academician.

FREEDOM AND THE RESPONSIBILITY OF THE PRESS: 1955

Robert M. Hutchins

In 1930, some twenty-five years ago, I last had the honor of confronting the American Society of Newspaper Editors. The quarter of a century between has been the longest in history. That was a different world, before the Depression, before the New Deal, before the Newspaper Guild, before the suburbs, before they charged for newsprint, before the atom, before television. It was a world in which the press was powerful and numerous. Though the press is powerful still, some eight hundred papers that were alive then are gone now. Twenty-five years hence, when I am eighty-one, where will the press be?

When last here, I said: "The greatest aggregation of educational foundations is the press itself . . . Indeed I notice that in spite of the frightful lies you have printed about me I still believe everything you print about other people . . . If the American press does not need or cannot get the leadership of some endowed newspapers, we must fall back on the long process of education through educational institutions, hoping that in the long run we may produce a generation that will demand better things of you. This process will be tedious and difficult, because of the power of the press itself over the minds and habits of those whom the educational institutions produce."

Though I am neither prophet nor preacher, my words were not attended. I would merely remind you that a great many men who paid no attention then are not here now.

I joined in another effort in your behalf in 1947, when the Report of the Commission on the Freedom of the Press appeared. The Commission felt a little sad. It said, "The outstanding fact about the communications industry today is that the number of its units has declined." It expressed a high opinion of your role in life, for it said, "Freedom of speech and free-

REPRINTED by arrangement with Meridian Books, Inc., from its volume, *Freedom Education, and the Fund,* copyright 1956 by Robert M. Hutchins.

dom of the press are moral rights which the state must not infringe." And again, "We must recognize that the agencies of mass communication are an educational instrument, perhaps the most powerful there is."

You were furious. Your president issued a statement in six paragraphs, in three of which he said that the members of the Commission were "left-wing," and in all of which he stated his conviction that, since most of the members of the Commission were professors without experience in the newspaper business, nothing they said could be of any importance, although it might be dangerous. At the meeting of this society in 1947, to which I had expected to be invited to receive your congratulations, the only thing that saved me from condemnation was the expressed unwillingness of your committee to "dignify" me by such action.

All over the country you attacked the Report. I hope you will read it sometime. But for fear you won't, I shall quote a passage from it that will give you the main idea: "If modern society requires great agencies of mass communication, if these concentrations become so powerful that they are a threat to democracy, if democracy cannot solve the problem simply by breaking them up—then those agencies must control themselves or be controlled by government. If they are controlled by government, we lose our chief safeguard against totalitarianism—and at the same time take a long step toward it."

A kind of neurotic sensitivity is characteristic of the press throughout the English-speaking world. The British papers were outraged by the report of the Royal Commission on the Press, which was almost as mild as ours. I don't know what makes the press feel this way. After all, in this country there is a special amendment to the Constitution, and the first one at that, protecting it. Perhaps it is this special dignity that sometimes leads newspapers to confuse their private interests with those of the public. One of the most celebrated managing editors in the country told our Commission that the only threat to the freedom of the press was the Newspaper Guild and that all we had to do was to adopt a resolution denouncing the Guild and go home. Most papers saw Marshall Field's suit against the AP as the end of freedom of the press. All he wanted to do to the AP was to join it. About once a week you break out in exasperation against anybody who tries to keep anything from you, for reasons of state or for any reason at all. You are the only uncriticized institution in the country. You will not criticize one another, and any suggestion that anybody else might do so sets you to muttering about the First Amendment.

I know that lately life has been hard for you. And it may get even worse; for it may turn out that reading is an anachronism. When I was a boy, reading was the only established and available path to knowledge, information, or even entertainment. But the other day in Hollywood I met a man who was putting the Great Books on records. Everything else has already been put on records or films. One glance at the children making for the television set on their return from school is enough to show that this is a different world. The habit of reading, which my generation fell into because there was not much else to do, may now not be formed at all; it may have too much competition.

The competition may win. Gresham's Law of Culture is that easy stuff drives out hard. It is harder to read, even after Dr. Flesch has finished with the printed page, than it is to look and listen. I do not believe that newspapers can do what comic books, picture magazines, motion pictures, and television can do in glorious technicolor. Since they can do this kind of thing better, why should you do it at all?

You may say it is the only way to survive. John Cowles suggests it may be a way to die. In his Sigma Delta Chi speech he said newspapers have realized that complete and fair coverage builds circulation. With few exceptions, he said, those newspapers which "have had the heaviest circulation losses are not papers that regard full and fair news presentation as their primary function and reason for existence." If so good a businessman as Mr. Cowles can think there is *any* chance that sensationalism and entertainment are not good for business, a layman may perhaps be forgiven for being impressed.

Emboldened by his example, I will say that newspapers should do as well as they can the things that they can do best, and they should leave to others the responsibility of entertaining the public. If you are worried about who is going to discharge that responsibility, read the March 21, 1955 issue of *Newsweek*, which says that television is abandoning "Johns Hopkins Science Review," "Princeton, '55," and "The Search." These programs have won many honors and audiences that look large to people who do not work in advertising agencies.

A couple of years ago Henry Luce was discussing the monopoly newspaper. He said the argument against it was that it deprived the community of differing presentations of news and opinions. He went on, "Like so many high-brow discussions about newspapers (I notice that journalists invariably use the word 'high-brow' when referring to criticisms of the press, even when, as in this case, the truth of the criticism is self-evident to the merest moron) this one is fine, except that it ignores the actual nature of a newspaper. Does any one feel strongly that a city ought to have several newspapers in order to offer the community a greater variety of comic strips, breakfast menus, and cheesecake?" If this is the actual nature of a newspaper, the fewer papers the better. Certainly the special constitutional protection thrown about them seems no more warranted than such protection would be for acrobats, chefs, beauty parlor operators, and astrologers.

What the framers of the First Amendment had in mind was debate, a great continuing debate, with the people hearing all sides and getting all the facts. If government could be kept from interfering with this debate, nothing could interfere with it; for a man who differed with the existing papers could start one of his own. The Founding Fathers did not foresee that 94 per cent of American cities and eighteen American states would be without competing papers. In the overwhelming majority of communities there can now be no debate among rival editors. The editor in a one-paper town has the only voice there is, and the only one there is likely to be. The debate has become a soliloquy.

Talk about the virtues of monopoly is the flimsiest rationalization, as is shown by the poor quality of the papers in many monopoly towns. Monopoly cannot be a good thing. At its best it can be like a benevolent despotism, good while the benevolence lasts, but an accident in any case. Monopoly may in the present state of affairs be a necessary evil, but let us not pretend that it is not an evil.

Rising costs have put the publisher in the driver's seat, where he has no business to be. The First Amendment was not instituted to give a preferred position to people who were making money out of papers as against those who were making money out of other articles of commerce. The Amendment was to protect the content of the press, not the cash return from it. The reason the publisher is in the driver's seat is that it costs so much money to own and operate a newspaper, and more all the time. If the soliloquy is that of one of the richest men in town, it is more than likely that it will sound the same political note as other soliloquies in other towns, rendered by other rich men. This is the basis of the phrase, "a one-party press."

Of course we have a one-party press in this country, and we shall have one as long as the press is big business, and as long as people with money continue to feel safer on the Republican side. For sheer psalm-singing sanctimoniousness no statement in recent years has surpassed that of Charles F. McCahill, president of the American Newspaper Publishers Association, when he was asked to comment on Adlai Stevenson's polite remarks on a one-party press. Mr. McCahill said, and I quote him: "It is the responsibility of the individual editor and publisher to decide what is printed in a particular newspaper. Fortunately, there is no power in this country to standardize the editorial views of any editor or publisher." Here in two sentences Mr. McCahill managed (1) to say what everybody knew already; (2) to be completely irrelevant; and (3) to prove Mr. Stevenson's point for him by making the partisan insinuation that Mr. Stevenson wanted the power to standardize editorial opinion. How you get along with these publishers is more than I can understand.

Lord Beaverbrook, when he was asked by the Royal Commission on the Press what his purpose in life was, replied under oath: "I run the paper purely for the purpose of making propaganda, and with no other motive." (There is apparently less cant among publishers in England than we are accustomed to here.) Lord Beaverbrook's propaganda collides wherever it goes with the counter-propaganda of numerous local and national voices. The popular press in Britain is the most sensational in the world, but an Englishman who doesn't want a sensational newspaper does not have to take the *Mirror*. Because of the geography of England he can get anywhere, inexpensively, and usually with his breakfast, a presentation of the news as fair as an editor can make it and as full as the restrictions on newsprint will allow, together with serious commentary upon it.

In the absence of some new technological revolution the number of papers per community in this country seems unlikely to increase. Nothing suggests that costs will fall. Television and suburbanization are driving ahead as fast as they can go. As monopoly continues to spread, the ancient check of competition can of course no longer be relied on.

This should lead to the burial of that consoling reference to Jefferson's Second Inaugural, an ever-present refuge in time of criticism, which made its last formal appearance in the statement of your committee commenting on the Report of the Commission on the Freedom of the Press. Jefferson said, in effect, that the people would make their views of a newspaper felt by refusing to read, believe, or buy it. The theory that the daily test of the market place is an expression of public criticism, and all that is needed, is reduced to absurdity when the public has no option, when it has to buy the newspaper that is offered or go without.

If we cannot look to competition to keep publishers from getting out of hand, what can we do to save their freedom from the consequences of their irresponsibility? My youthful suggestion of some endowed newspapers was designed to execute some publishers *pour encourager les autres.*[1] The object was to set some standards that publishers of unendowed newspapers might be held to. I take this proposal less seriously than I did twenty-five years ago. The *Christian Science Monitor* undoubtedly has a good influence on the press of this country, but the conditions under which it operates, with its foundations in heaven rather than on earth, are so different from the ordinary that any publisher has an adequate excuse for not following the *Monitor's* example. So I fear it would be with an endowed newspaper.

A trust such as that which controls the future of the Washington *Post* regulates the selection of stockholders, but gives the editor no explicit protection. The British trusts usually have the same object, that of preventing the ownership from falling into unsuitable hands. Although the British trusts reflect an attitude that an editor would find reassuring, no trust covering a daily newspaper leaves him formally any better off than he would be if there were no trust. The most that the Royal Commission was willing to say was, "A trust does not necessarily convert a newspaper from a commercial to a non-commercial concern or give it quality which it did not possess . . . A trust can be, however, a valuable means of preserving quality where quality already exists. We accordingly welcome the action of public-spirited proprietors who have taken such steps as lie in their power to safeguard the character and independence of their papers; and we hope that the number of papers so protected will grow."

A publisher's willingness to establish a trust shows that he could be trusted without it; still it is a way of extending the benevolence of the benevolent despot beyond the limits of his own life. When you have a newspaper worth protecting, a trust will help you protect it; but a trust does not guarantee you a newspaper worth protecting.

[1] To encourage the others.

The purpose of a newspaper, and the justification for the privileges of the press, is the enlightenment of the people about their current affairs. No other medium of communication can compete with the newspaper in the performance of this task. A newspaper that is doing this job well is a good newspaper, no matter how deficient it may be in astrology, menus, comics, cheesecake, crime, and Republican propaganda. A newspaper that is doing this job deserves protection against government, and it will certainly need it.

A newspaper that is doing this job will have to bring before its readers points of view with which it disagrees and facts that it deplores. Otherwise in monopoly towns the people cannot expect to be enlightened; for television and radio are unlikely to be in the same class with a well-run newspaper in telling what is happening and what it means. Television and radio are, moreover, controlled by a governmental agency, and one that does not inspire much confidence today.

A good many newspapers take seriously their responsibility to enlighten the people about current affairs. It is generally agreed that the best American papers are as good as any in the world and that the average is high. Our question is how to maintain the good newspapers in the faith and how to convert the others.

I think the opposition to the principal recommendation of the Commission on the Freedom of the Press ought to be reconsidered. This recommendation was that a new agency be established to appraise and report annually upon the performance of the press. The Commission said, "It seems to us clear that some agency which reflects the ambitions of the American people for its press should exist for the purpose of comparing the accomplishments of the press with the aspirations which the people have for it. Such an agency would also educate the people as to the aspirations which they ought to have for the press." The Commission suggested that this agency be independent of government and of the press; that it be created by gifts; and that it be given a ten-year trial, at the end of which an audit of its achievement could determine anew the institutional form best adapted to its purposes. The fact that the British commission independently reached an identical recommendation seems to me highly significant.

Such an agency should contain representatives of the press; it should also contain laymen. My guess is that the weakness of the Press Council in Sweden results from the fact that it is composed entirely of representatives of the newspapers. I believe that the British Council will go the same way because the press rejected the recommendation of the Royal Commission that the Council should have lay members and a lay chairman. If its first report is suggestive of its future, this group is likely to manifest its fearless and high-principled character by speaking sternly to newspapers on trivial subjects.

The Nieman Reports, the Press Institute statements, A. J. Liebling's "Wayward Press," Robert Lasch in the *Progressive*, occasional studies by schools of journalism, these are all we have in this country. They are too casual and limited, and, since most of them are directed at the press, they do not perform one function that the Commission on the Freedom of the Press regarded as essential: they do not "educate the people as to the aspirations which they ought to have for the press."

Your own efforts to act as a critical agency have come to nothing. You appointed a committee in 1949 "to examine the desirability of sponsoring an appraisal of the self-improvement possibilities of American newspapers." The Committee reported in 1950 as follows: "Our Committee recognizes and reiterates that the American Society of Newspaper Editors is, itself, and must be, a continuing committee of the whole on self-examination and self-improvement. But, in addition, we urge the Society to call upon its Board of Directors to take whatever action may be necessary from time to time to clarify understanding of American newspapers by the public, and to keep editors alert to their responsibilities in fulfilling the public's right to an adequate, independent newspaper press."

That sounds as though it was written by a public relations man. In these sonorous sentences we hear the cadence of the Psalms.

The great issues of our time are peace and freedom. A new critical agency might appraise the performance of the newspapers in correcting, or contributing to, our vast confusion on these subjects. We know that the peoples of the earth are now equipped to turn one another into radioactive cinders. Can you say that the press has given Americans the material they need to reach a conclusion on the course they should follow, on the choice between co-existence and no existence, the choice between seeking peace through purchase and intimidation and seeking it through total, enforceable disarmament, the choice between competing nationalisms and world law?

And what of freedom in the garrison state? Since most of you take the official line, that the only important fact of life is our imminent danger from international conspiracy, most of you have watched the erosion of freedom without a twinge. When the official line permitted, you have sallied forth, as when you gallantly led the troops from the rear in a belated attack on Senator McCarthy. You have filled the air with warnings of the sinister figures on the Left, but have printed almost nothing about the fat cats on the Right. You have allowed things to get to such a pass that some government departments now have guidance clinics in which the employee is taught how not to look like a security risk. Look at the Passport Division, interfering with the travel of Americans on their lawful occasions; at the Attorney-General's list, ruining the lives of thousands on the basis of hearsay; at the Post Office Department, saving us from *Pravda* and Aristophanes; at the State Department, adding the name of Corsi to those of Davies and Service and countless others. See the blacklist spreading in industry, merging with proposals that American Communists should be starved to death. Listen to the wire-tapping, to the cry of Fifth Amendment Communist, to the kept witnesses roaming the land. The most distressing part of it is not that these things happen, but the free press of this country appears to regard them as matters of routine.

You are educators, whether you like it or not. You make the views that people have of public affairs. No competition can shake you from that position. You will lose it only if you neglect or abandon it. As the number of papers per community declines, the responsibility of each one that remains increases. This is a responsibility that is discharged by being a newspaper, by giving the news. The editorial function is to make sure that it is given in such a way that it can be understood. The people must see the alternatives before them; otherwise they cannot be enlightened.

Enlightenment means telling the people where they are in time and space. It means engaging in systematic criticism. The criticism of current affairs has to be made in the light of some standard. This must be something more than a set of partisan slogans. The standard by which the American press must judge current events is derived from an understanding of and sympathy with the deepest aspirations of the American people, those for peace and freedom. A press that serves its country in this way need have no concern about the future.

April 21, 1955

THE EASY CHAIR
NUMBER 241

Bernard DeVoto

The Nieman Fellows are newspapermen who spend a year studying at Harvard in order, so the grant that finances them reads, "to promote and elevate standards of journalism" in the United States. At intervals writers and editors are invited to talk to them about problems of journalism, and some time ago this election fell on the editor of *Harper's*. He chose to discuss the kind of journalism that *Harper's* publishes. Before he got very far there was a question from the floor: what fees did he pay for contributions? They are not of Hollywood size and another question followed at once, "How do you get anyone to write for *Harper's?*" There was no problem, the editor said; the articles that *Harper's* publishes are written by people who want to write for *Harper's*. The magazine pays as much as it can afford to but for the *Harper's* writer the fee is not the first consideration, it is not even an important one. He wants to bring something to the attention of the public.

For many *Harper's* pieces there is only one other possible outlet, the *Atlantic*. I cite the articles about the struggle over the public lands that I have been running periodically in the Easy Chair and the body of the magazine ever since January 1947. Some have been straight news stories, some have been editorial comment, some have been primarily polemic; but whatever their nature, they have given the subject the only adequate coverage it has had anywhere. No newspaper has covered it well, and that goes for the *New York Times*. Apart from *Harper's* no magazine has more than glanced at it. Presumably I could have published most of my pieces in the *Atlantic*—but where else? Several magazines for sportsmen ran occasional articles about isolated parts of the struggle. In the first year after the story of the land grab broke—after I broke the story—*Collier's* ran two pieces about it. No other mass-circulation magazine would touch it. The weeklies never got past the fringe. But *Harper's* ran my articles; to run such articles is one of its functions.

Harper's and the *Atlantic* are the only survivors of what was called the Quality Group when I was in college. The phrase carries no implication that there is not journalism as expert in other magazines; it does imply that much quality group journalism is different in kind, context, or treatment from other journalism, and that it has some forms of its own. All the other original members of the group have died and only two magazines that can be considered to belong to it have been established, *Fortune* and the *New Yorker*. Some *Harper's* articles might well appear in one or the other of them; some others might appear in such magazines as the *New Republic* or the *Reporter*.

None of these magazines, however, shares more than a part of the *Harper's* field. In the Easy Chair of the Centennial Issue I described that field, and I explained that *Harper's* has survived because it assumed some functions that American journalism at large has either relinquished voluntarily or proved unable to perform. The "people who want to write for *Harper's*" perform those functions.

I appear to be the person who wants most to write for *Harper's*. I have kept a file of my publications but I know that it is not complete and so I cannot say exactly how many pieces I have published in this magazine. There must have been at least thirty text articles and I began writing the Easy Chair twenty years ago this month, with the issue of November 1935. The total must be at least eight hundred thousand words, and more likely it is nine hundred thousand—the equivalent of half a dozen long books. As my twentieth anniversary approached, it occurred to me with some force that I have written more for *Harper's* than anyone else now living.

When my turn to address the Niemans came, I reminded them that the Easy Chair is the oldest editorial feature in American journalism. It is subject to the conditions of monthly journalism but only one limitation is set on it, that of length. I used to work three weeks ahead of publication, but the breath-taking advance in technology that is called American know-how spread to printing establishments and for some years I have had to work seven weeks ahead. The limitation of length and the long time-lapse are a monthly test of a writer's professional judgment, not to speak of his luck. (My luck has been good; in twenty years I have had to make only one stop-press change because a situation had developed otherwise than I had judged it would.) Also, I have a deadline. The editors will tell you that I have never missed it, and I can tell you that I am scrupulous not to anticipate it. One of the satisfactions of being a *Harper's* writer is that you remain your own writer; your work is not taken down, reassembled, and rewritten by a committee; you are expected to provide your own structure, verification, and who-he. But even the writers who edit *Harper's* are editors; their fingers may be counted on to twitch if given time.

When the Niemans pressed me for a label that would describe the Easy Chair I could do no better than "cultural criticism," which is unsatisfactory. I have never formulated any principles for writing it but I have probably observed some. Such a column as this could not easily be pretentious and I have tried to keep it from being pompous. I have tried to avoid repeating myself, at short intervals anyway, and to keep the subject matter so varied that a reader would not know what to expect when he turned to the column. I have ranged so widely that I found I could not represent the full scope of the Easy Chair in a volume of selections from it which will be published about the time you read this, and which no virtuous person will fail to buy. I have assumed that there was no public demand for me to write about anything at all but that if I was interested in something, some readers would be interested in it too. But also I have written about a good many subjects not primarily because I wanted to write about them but because it seemed likely that no one else would. *Harper's* does some chores because it believes that journalism must not leave them undone; so does the Easy Chair.

Some implications of my job were obvious from the beginning; others became apparent to me only gradually. Fact pieces in the *New Yorker* have a formula which is intended to preserve the convention that Mr. Tilley's interest in anything is strictly dilettante. "When I met Mr. Chase the next morning, he suggested that I have coffee with Mr. Sanborn while the reports from the whatisits were coming in." For a time after I began writing the Easy Chair I went to equal length to give it an appearance of editorial anonymity. But the personal pronoun is a space-saver and I found myself more and more forced to make use of it. I was surprised to find that readers welcomed it. Not many places where personal journalism can be praticed legitimately remain; there seems to be a use for what is left of it.

Equally surprising is the value attributed to such editorial space as mine by press agents. In the name of our common culture and the American way they call on me to publicize goods, liquors, restaurants, business firms, crusading organizations, crackpot organizations, causes, people who pay to get their names in print, and one columnist whose social engineer keeps demanding that I explain to my readers how the American language has been enriched by the words he invents. These efforts are occasionally subtle but usually high-pressure, frequently elaborate, and sometimes so persistent that it would have been cheaper for the client to buy four pages of display space in *Harper's*. If any has succeeded, then it succeeded brilliantly for I did not know I was being taken. Sometimes a press agent's solicitation has resulted in my abandoning an Easy Chair I had intended to write.

Such eagerness does not inflate my ego, for there are counter-irritants. Some of my most enthusiastic readers are people who have been reading someone else, frequently Elmer Davis. Others understand that the Easy Chair is a department of the *Atlantic*. And things happen—as when an apparently sober publisher once thanked me for rescuing a book he had published. The sale was small and had dried up, he said, but following my Easy Chair about it, it revived and ran sixteen thousand copies. This was a flattering story but it had a hole in it, for I hadn't written anything about the book. And I get a lot of letters praising or denouncing pieces which neither I nor anyone else has written.

Readers write to me; newspapers run quotes from the Easy Chair and write editorials about it; other writers use it or refer to it in articles and books. These are the only means I have of judging the response to it. It has had enough supporters to count or I would have been fired. It has had opponents and even enemies, some of them habitual or occupational. I have annoyed quite a lot of people but though I have cost *Harper's* some subscribers there have been no lawsuits. A cheese-maker tried hard to suppress me and a publisher of books to censor me. Neither succeeded.

The Easy Chair is sometimes called controversial, even by Personal & Otherwise,[1] but the adjective is inaccurate. I have deliberately precipitated only one controversy, the one over the public lands I have mentioned, and I precipitated that one as a reporter. It took me some time to understand what the reality behind the inaccurate adjective is and why the Easy Chair has produced so much more heat than it has carried. My job is to write about anything in American life that may interest me, but it is also to arrive at judgments under my own steam, independently of others. With some judgments that is the end of the line; express them and you have nothing more to do. But there are also judgments that require you to commit yourself, to stick your neck out. Expressing them in print obliges you to go on to advocacy. They get home to people's beliefs and feelings about important things, and that makes them inflammable.

I seem most consistently to offend two groups that have in common a love of simplification and absolutes: writers of advertising copy and contributors to quarterlies that deal with epistemology and, trailing by some lengths, literature. Copywriters always run a mild fever, quite trivial stimuli can send it shooting up, and I am always wounding these poet-patriots without intending to. Commonly they assail me with one or the

[1]Another regular column or department in *Harper's*.

other of two libels: that only a Communist would disparage manufactured goods and that I could have made a fortune, as clearly I have not done, if I had gone into advertising. Often they are rhetorically belligerent and the announced ambition of one is to punch my nose. Still, I was once asked to address a meeting of advertising men, whereas so far as I know no quarterly has ever approved of anything I have written. The accusation here is on different grounds and there is no lament that I once had it in me to become a literary person. Instead there is a twofold anxiety, to establish that I am middlebrow, Philistine, superficial, the enemy—in a word, a journalist—and that I have betrayed or subverted literary thinking.

The condescension seems superfluous, a waste of energy. It is fully visible that I respect reality-judgments as requiring more intelligence than fantasy and think them a better instrument for critical analysis. Just as visibly I distrust the literary approach to experience, preferring direct approaches. The universals of *a priori* thinking are not for me, large abstractions will not fit my hand, and I work with complexities and tentatives. Certainly, I am a journalist. But who is using all those epithets? Long ago I got used to seeing ideas which were first expressed in this column, or in my books, turn up as the invention and fee-simple property of literary thinkers who scorned and denounced them when I published them.

More than that. When I was preparing the book that is to be published this month, I found clipped to one Easy Chair an article I had forgotten. The critic who wrote it proved me a Fascist, without disclosing that he knew what Fascism is but simmering with the same resentment that nowadays represents me as a red, and went on to say, "If Mr. DeVoto is a democrat, then I am not."

That may be a true statement but we have no way of knowing, for there is nothing to tell us what he is. I have been reading him for many years and I have yet to see him stick his neck out about anything except the symbol of the peach in "The Love Song of J. Alfred Prufrock." Getting out on that limb may have required courage but not of a kind that would make trouble for him, and I believe that some years later the peach proved to have been eaten by Edward Fitzgerald. Some battles cannot be fought after the fact and in journalism a writer runs into some he does not care to be above.

The first Easy Chair I wrote described some asininities committed by a New Deal agency. (Prophetically, it was a news story, one I had dug out for myself.) Various newspapers promptly admitted Mr. E. S. Martin's successor to the Republican party. The welcome was premature. I doubt if anyone was ever a 100 per cent New Dealer—obviously Mr. Roosevelt wasn't—but though many New Deal intellectuals had a much higher proof than mine, on the whole I had to go along. I got to that position by studying history, and the study of history has held me to the working principles of American liberalism.

Here, I believe, is where the accusation that I have betrayed literary thinking comes in, for fashions and events have required me, every so often, to show that literary liberalism is something else. I was at odds with the dominant fashions of literary thinking during the 1920s. Most of those who followed them seemed to me naïve and ignorant, ignorant especially of our history and of politics. During the 1930s I felt no impulse to seek comfort in Marx and Lenin, and it was again my job to point out that the literary thinkers who did were naïve and ignorant, ignorant especially of American history and of the politics which they told us they had mastered.

And today I feel no impulse to regress to Burke, Hobbes, Mandeville, or personal revelation. It is now high literary fashion to represent the fashionables of the earlier decades as naïve and ignorant, and this fact has a rich flavor, but the empirical grounds from which the representation is made seem worse than dubious. The thinkers are still practicing book reviewing. They have mastered politics just as their predecessors did, by making it up while gazing earnestly at their navels.

Nothing could astonish a journalist more than the fantasies regularly published in the literary quarterlies about the government of the United States, what its mechanism and energies are, how they are controlled. The practice of journalism has led me not only to work constantly with the reports of committees, commissions, and bureaus, but constantly to study Congress and the federal bureaus in action. I have had to know intimately many Senators, Congressmen, and bureau officials, and I have shared or assisted the work of a good many.

I have seen nothing to justify the literary critic's belief that he is more intelligent than the politician. And when I read what the quarterlies say about actions I know empirically—and say with a condescension that would be unbecoming in an archangel—I seldom find any realization at all of what the real energies at work are, or the real issues. I conclude that there is one infrangible virginity: literary criticism is not an approach to politics.

The Chicago *Tribune* put me on its list long ago and invented the word "DeVotoism" to classify one entire order of its phobias. The heaviest mail I have ever received was evoked not by the FBI piece that McCarthy lied about but by an Easy Chair a year before we entered the war which said that we ought to enter it and predicted that we would. Orders had gone out from the GHQ of America First to work me over. The organization charged its heirs to keep after me and they have been faithful to the trust. A lot of them are too pure in heart to sign their names.

If I have written as readily about disc jockeys as about *The Federalist*, that willingness too can be ascribed to the study of history. Library stacks as well as the town square taught me that no manifestation of American life is trivial to the critic of culture. Such a column as this could not easily avoid politics but no doubt I have felt an additional incentive to write about it because I was practicing history. Also, unlike much writing, political comment is a form of action. Sometimes it runs to prophecy too, and here I am entitled to brag. All but one of my prophecies have been borne out by the event, and if that one was a national-championship flop it originated in a mistake we are all prone to make. I underestimated the stupidity of Republican grand strategy.

My commonest political theme has been the erosion of the Bill of Rights. Before the war, and this is revealing, the Easy Chair was disturbed by such peripheral matters as literary censorship and our home-grown Catos. During the war it was usually suppression of the news, and I was uncomfortable for I had to take potshots at my friend Elmer Davis in order to get at the authorities who were muzzling him. Since the war the attack on our freedom has come closer to the jugular, and so I have been suspect in the indicated quarters. If I can judge by the quotations adduced by other committees, the file which the Un-American Activities Committee has on me contains little more than the *Daily Worker's* praise of the Easy Chair on the FBI. But most of the beagles have bayed at me (as their newly arrived imitators in Congress have begun to do) and I have been named on various private and commercial lists of subversives. Nomination to them is the diagnostic test of decency for everyone who has a public forum. We have fought at Arques[2]: where were you?

In twenty years I have published eight books and two collections of occasional pieces, I have edited a basic document of American history, and I have supported my family by writing for magazines more affluent than *Harper's*. And I have written the Easy Chair. Always I have written it under pressure of haste and with the morose knowledge that I was not writing it well enough. But in my private assignments it has always come first.

I hope that what I have said has been said gracefully and that sometimes it has been amusing, or informative, or useful. No one has got me to say anything I did not want to say and no one has prevented me from saying anything I wanted to. The Easy Chair has given me a place in the journalism of my time. No one knows better than a journalist that his work is ephemeral. As I have said elsewhere, it is not important, it is only indispensable. The life or the half-life of an issue of *Harper's* has never been calculated; the magazine has durable covers but even the copies kept in doctors' waiting rooms wear out and are dumped in the bay or ground up for pulp. But a historian knows that a lot of writing which has no castemark on its forehead gets dumped in the bay too, and that he can count on finding bound files of *Harper's* in library stacks. He has to use them; he cannot write history without them.

QUESTIONS

1. How does *confronting* in Hutchins's first sentence at once establish his attitude, the tactics of his speech? How does he soften the effect?

2. Why does Hutchins end his third sentence with the reference to

[2]One of the battles (1579) which assured the throne of France to Henry of Navarre.

television instead of the one to the atom, which is surely the more important problem? What does he mean by "before the suburbs"?

3. Study Hutchins's second paragraph. Whose side is he on: newspapers or educational institutions?

4. Explain the allusions in "Though I am neither prophet nor preacher."

5. In Paragraphs 4 and 5, Hutchins is rather trickily unfair to the editors; presumably he wanted to pay them back for some of their editorials about him. Can you describe his trick?

6. Pick out Hutchins's major points from his wise-cracks.

7. Liebling's *Minks and Red Herring*, which analyzes some famous news stories for evidence of journalistic ethics and responsibility, might be a good subject for a book review.

8. Why does De Voto (Paragraph 2) single out *The New York Times* in the sentence beginning, "No newspaper has covered it well"?

9. What are the characteristics of journalism in "the Quality Group"?

10. Discuss De Voto's journalistic creed. You can summarize, analyze, or criticize.

11. List the institutions, ideas, or bureaus that De Voto says he has criticized or attacked. What is your conclusion?

12. Both Hutchins and De Voto really diagnose the ills of American newspapers. Summarize the case in a sentence.

LEVELS OF STYLE:

SAD STORIES

Today Cobbett would be an editorial columnist, and it is interesting to speculate what papers might carry his column, or what columnists he is most like. In spite of Arnold's somewhat priggish view, which I quote in the introduction, Cobbett's style is a good one: quick, energetic, somewhat careless perhaps, but at the same time full of a kind of ordinary force that is quite ingratiating. The other selections are more literary, with more artfully designed periods and rhythmic units; and with also more selected vocabularies (though compare the question on Strachey's diction). The dying fall of Strachey's "last long lovely drifting sentence," as Forster calls it, is echoed again and again in the other two selections. The sentence bears study; though my own preference is for, say, Swift or Shaw, I have to admit that Strachey's sentence (indeed the design of the whole chapter) is the most simply but romantically beautiful object in this whole collection.

THE ROYAL FAMILY

William Cobbett

After the account of the Borough-mongers, which I have given in the last number, the reader will naturally have anticipated, that this is a very inferior set of persons in point of real importance. This is called a *"limited monarchy,"* and it really is very *limited* indeed, the person who fills the office of king having no more power of his own than has the bauble put upon his head, or the seat that he sits on. We usually call this branch of authority the *Crown*, or the *Throne*, and with great propriety, for the poor creature who wears the one, and sits on the other, is neither more nor less than a passive tool in the hands of those who own the seats in Parliament, and who, in fact, appoint all the Ministers, Ambassadors, Judges, and Commanders, and who, if they were to meet with a refractory king, or one who, from excessive folly, was troublesome to them, would very soon dispose of him, by shutting him up for life, or by some other contrivance, so as never to be pestered by him again.

Of all the objects which the Borough-mongers would most dread, next after free elections, would certainly be a king of sound understanding, good talents, aptness for business, and really desirous to promote the honour and happiness of the country. And, it must be confessed, that, in this view of the matter, they could hardly have been more fortunate than they are in the Guelphs,[1] not one of whom, since their being pitched upon to fill the throne of England, has ever discovered symptoms of a mind much more than sufficient to qualify the possessor for the post of exciseman.

It appears, at first sight, very strange that England should have for its sovereigns a race of *foreigners*, and that the marriages should be so made up as that no king should, supposing nothing illicit go on, ever have a single drop of English blood in his veins. But, if we consider these apparent sovereigns, as we ought, nothing more than mere puppets in the hands of the Borough-mongers, we shall find a very substantial reason for this seemingly strange taste. It is the interest of this body of men, to have upon the throne a person for whom the people have no regard. The English nation have a rooted hatred, or, at best, contempt, for all foreigners: yet, be they who or what they may, these foreign princes and princesses always surround themselves with Hanoverians, Brunswickers, and other Germans, and care is taken that the race shall never mix with any

[1] An allusion to emphasize the extreme un-Englishness of the House of Brunswick; the eighteenth century Kings of England were also Electors of Brunswick-Lüneburg (Hanover), in Germany, which in the Middle Ages had been a duchy held by members of the Guelf family. The Hanoverian connection lapsed on the death of William IV, since according to Hanoverian custom a woman could not rule.

English race; so that this contempt, on the part of the people, is constantly kept alive.

The language that is made use of in conversation, with regard to this family, would astonish any stranger. All sorts of names, expressions of contempt, are constantly used by all ranks of people towards them.

The "d——d Germans" they are called in a lump by the common people; and when the nobility and gentry reject vulgar epithets and terms, it is only to choose others more severe. This abuse is made use of by *all* parties; by all men in, as well as out of, office. When the war was declared against France, at the rupture of the peace of Amiens, the princes went to the House of Lords to support the address to the Throne. The Duke of Clarence made a speech upon this occasion, and I was standing with a crowd of others below the Bar (as it is called) at the time. The House, which was exceedingly full, were very merry at his expense; and two Peers, who sat close to the bar, at the side of the House on which I stood, indulged themselves in this sort: "What a Jack-ass!" said one: "What a great fool!" said the other: "did you ever hear such a beast?" And, towards the close of the speech, the Royal Duke having declared, that he spoke the sentiments *of his whole family,* a third Peer exclaimed: "*his* family! who the d——l cares about his family!" All this was said loud enough for twenty or thirty persons to hear, who stood or sat nearest to them. Other Peers were smothering a laugh; some affected to be blowing their noses; and the Lord Chancellor, ELDON,[2] sat and looked at the Duke with one of those smiles which contain the double expression of pity and contempt. To be sure the speech was a foolish rant; but, if it came from a Duke of Newcastle or an Earl of Lonsdale, or any other great Borough-monger, it would have been listened to with the greatest attention and apparent respect.

Strangers to the workings of this system wonder how it comes to pass, that we *obey* a family, whom we so abuse. The fact is, we do not obey them; and, the very lowest man in the country knows that we do not. The Borough-mongers, 23 of whom have from 140 to 200 votes, are our real rulers; and, it suits them to have the forms of monarchy, while they possess all the substance of its powers. If the family on the throne were really *English*, the people would have a regard for them, exclusive of the powerful connexions which an English Royal Family would have in the country, in consequence of marriage alliances. Such a family would be a formidable rival of the Borough-mongers; and might, like the Plantagenets, side with the people against those who have usurped their rights. In such a struggle the people might, perhaps, get some share of the power into their hands. Therefore, the Borough-mongers prefer this race of foreigners; and the lower and more paltry its origin, and the more despicable the character and conduct of the individuals belonging to it, the better it suits their purpose.

[2]Cobbett's point is that even Eldon, who was the son of a tradesman, was openly contemptuous of royalty. Eldon was among the most reactionary of the Tory politicians.

I have, since I have been acquainted with the real situation of the Royal family, often laughed at the old story about "an *influence behind the throne* greater than the throne itself." This is one of the numerous cheats that have been practised upon the world. *What influence* could there be of any practical consequence? *Charles Jenkinson*, who was afterwards Lord Hawkesbury and Earl of Liverpool, and whose son is Earl of Liverpool now, was looked upon as one of the *influencing* persons. As if this man, who was once a *Page* to the king's father, could have any weight in dictating measures, to which the Borough-mongers had been opposed! as if he and Lord Bute, and three or four other contemptible people, could have supported the king against old Lord Chatham, if the men who had three votes out of every four had not been on the same side?

The rejection of "Catholic Emancipation" was attributed to the "*conscientious scruples*" of the king; and by others to his "*obstinacy*." The poor old man had no more to do with it than had any one of the little land turtles in the American woods. It has always been foreseen, that, if the Catholics are "indulged," as it is impudently called, any further, they will next demand an "abolition of tithes," and the Church demesnes would follow of course. This is property, altogether, worth more annually than a fourth part of the *rent* of all the Land and Houses in Ireland. And to whom does this property belong? Why, to the nobility and a few commoners who own the seats in parliament. Three fourths of the Church Livings are their own *private* property. The rest, and the Bishopricks and other Dignities, they, in fact cause to be filled with their own relations, or by those who serve them, or whom they choose to have appointed. If, then, we find them in real possession of a quarter part of the rental of the kingdom of Ireland, by the means of the existence of a protestant Church, is it wonderful that they do such abominable acts as they notoriously do, in order to support the Church? Did it need any "conscientious scruples" on the part of an unfortunate old man, who had no interest in the rejection, to prevent the "*emancipation*" taking place? Besides, the Emancipation would have opened the place of Judge, Chancellor, Attorney, and Solicitor Generals, Master of the Rolls, Privy Councillor, Field and General Officer, Captain and Admiral, and of Parliament men, and Sixty Peers, to *Catholics*. Was it likely, that those who had, as we have seen in the last number, all these in their own hands, should call in more persons to share in the rich spoils? Is it usual for men to act thus? Did Cochrane and Cockburn, when they had packed up the plunder of Alexandria, call in the crews at Halifax or Jamaica to partake with them? Ireland is one of the *estates* of the Borough-mongers; and do men ever call in other men to participate in their rents?

Mr. Fox and his party, who brought forward this measure in 1807, stood *pledged*, however, to the Catholics. They had given the pledge when they were out of place, and, most likely, when they never expected to get in. But, still, it is surprising that they should have attempted the fulfilment; knowing, as they did, the all-ruling power that was naturally opposed to it. The truth is, they were deceived. Some seat-owners *appeared to acquiesce*; and the ministers, who were, in the *arts* of the trade, not half so deep as their opponents, thought that, if they carried their measure, they should have the Catholic Peers and Commoners with them; and should, thus, acquire permanent strength. The Borough-mongers took the alarm. Lords Eldon, and Hawkesbury, (now Liverpool,) and Perceval, were despatched to the king, who was told that he was about to act "in violation of his *Coronation Oath*," and that he *must turn out the ministers*.

The Foxites finding themselves undermined, endeavoured to keep their places by *withdrawing the Emancipation Bill* from the Table of the House of Commons, on which it was laid, and in which House it had been read a first time. But, it was now too late. The Borough-mongers could not trust them; and out they were driven. That *the king* was a mere instrument on this occasion is certain; else how came he *to approve of the Bill* before it was introduced? How came he first to do this, and then, all of a sudden, to turn out his ministers for having proposed the measure? Nay, how came he to put them out, even after they had withdrawn the Bill? If I am asked why the Borough-mongers did not *vote* out the Bill and the Ministers. I answer, that that would have been to expose themselves to great odium, especially in Ireland, every impartial man being for the measure. It was, therefore, much better to throw the failure of it upon the "*tender conscience* of the king." And to set up all through England, a tremendous cry of, "God bless the king, and *No Popery*," which the new minister did, and with such success, that when Mr. ROSCOE offered himself to be re-elected, the people of his own town, where his talents and his virtues were so well known, almost buried him with dirt and stones, amidst shouts of "Down with the *Pope*;" and that, too, as the event has proved, while they were paying loads of taxes to restore the Pope and the Inquisition.

But, if those who really *knew* any thing of the matter could have had any doubt upon this subject in 1807, the events of 1811 and 1812 would have completely removed such doubt; for the king was then shut up; he was put aside; his son was, in fact, put in his place. The king's *conscience*, therefore, was no longer an obstacle. The Prince Regent stood pledged to the Catholics both verbally and in *writing*. Yet he did not attempt to redeem the pledge. Suppose him, if you like, a *faithless* man; but faithless men do not, any more than others, *voluntarily* and gratuitously expose themselves to the hatred and contempt of mankind. At first, he had only *limited powers*. The Borough-mongers actually openly kept a part of the very exterior of royalty in their own hands, lest a man, on whom they could not depend, should be guilty of some thing that would rouse the people against them. But, at the end of a certain time, they enlarged his powers. To this time his old friends and companions looked with eagerness. The Catholics thought, to be sure, that they should *now* get their long-sought emancipation.

All London heard the execrations that were, upon this occasion, poured out upon the Prince. He was called every thing descriptive of baseness and perfidy; when he really had no more power with respect to Catholic Emancipation than I had. He might be perfectly sincere, when he pledged himself to the Catholics; nor is there any good reason to suppose that he was not sincere. As Duke of Cornwall he owns *two seats* in that County. His two Members voted *for* the Emancipation. Even Castlereagh, to make good *his* pledge, was suffered to vote for it, in 1812. But when there appeared so large a majority against it, was it not then become clear, that the *conscience* of the king had been a mere pretext? Could any man, however stupid, still be deluded by so stale a trick? What miserable nonsense is it, then, to talk of "an influence *behind the throne* greater than the throne itself!" Will any body believe, that any *favourites* of the Prince could have persuaded him thus to falsify his word? Why should they? His favourites had been Lord Holland, Mr. Tierney, Mr. Sheridan, and generally, the friends of Catholic Emancipation. He had supposed that some *real power* would come into his hands, when he should be king; but, he soon found his mistake; he found himself to be a mere tool in the hands of the owners of the seats in parliament; namely, about 120 Borough-mongers, who have, at all times, a dead majority; and who, though they very willingly would permit the Prince to do such odious things as the creating of Bate Dudley[3] a Baronet, and are glad to see him disgrace himself and disgust the people by his amours, his excesses, and his squanderings, take special care that he shall do nothing that shall trench upon their real and solid dominion.

Of the real nothingness of the king and the people called *his* ministers there were ample proofs in the history of PITT. It is very well known, that Pitt, who had formed to himself a hope of immortal fame from his financial schemes, went with extreme reluctance into the war with France in 1793. The account of the conversation between him and Mr. MARET, which was published in the Annual Register, from a translation of Mr. MARET's notes, proves, that the minister, who was thought to *rule* in England, was in *great fear*, lest the French Convention should, by their violence, give a handle to the Aristocracy here to force him into the war. His chief *reliance* was upon the *Opposition*, which was then formidable. He hoped that the great seat-owners, who belonged to that Body, and who had so long affected to *follow* Mr. Fox, would *continue firmly united against his ministry;* in which case, he could have resisted the warlike commands of his own masters, that is to say, the Borough-mongers on his side. But, his hopes were disappointed. It has been a thousand times stated, that the *Court Influence* drove him into the war. That the *king* told him "war, or *turn out.*" This was, indeed, the alternative; but, the *source* of the command was different; and, upon this occasion, it was *openly seen to be so.*

[3]In the eighteenth century Dudley had been something of a man about town with a reputation for quarrelsomeness, but probably Cobbett (writing in 1816) was alluding to his alleged trafficking in Church benefices; he was a clergyman.

A great body of Borough-mongers, who had, until now, been in the opposition, finding that the example of France might produce reform in England, the necessity of which reform, by the by, was most ably urged by men of great talent and weight, resolved to have for minister some man that should go to war with France. They found that Mr. Fox would not; and, after due preparations, over they came to Pitt, who would rather have had the company of Satan himself. Amongst the leaders of the seceders from Mr. Fox were the Duke of Portland, Lord Fitzwilliam, and Lord Spencer, each of whom having ten times the influence of Pitt himself. BURKE, who had been the trumpeter of the war, and who had been for two years labouring to work people's minds up to it, was a mere tool in the hands of Earl FITZWILLIAM, in one of whose seats he sat. He belied his conscience through the whole of his work; but, he received, not only his seat, but his very *bread,* at the hands of this opulent nobleman, who was bent upon preserving his borough powers and his titles, or, at least, to take the chances of war for that preservation. Earl SPENCER was, at the time of his leaving Mr. Fox, asked by a gentleman, who had long voted with that party, and who was opposed to the war, what were the *motives* that could have induced a man so worthy as his Lordship to join in such an enterprise. "I will be very frank with you," said Lord Spencer, "and save you the trouble of *discovering* my motives. My lot is cast amongst the nobility. It is not my fault that I was thus born, and that I thus inherit. I wish to remain what I am, and to hand my father's titles and estates down to my heirs. I do not know that I thus seek my own gratification at the expense of my country, which has been very great, free, and happy, under this order of things. I am satisfied, that if we do not go to war with the French this order of things will be destroyed. We *may* fall by the war; but we *must* fall without it. The thing is worth fighting for, and to fight for it we are resolved." The *substance* of this has been stated in print by Mr. MILES, in his letter to the Prince of Wales; but, I have here put down the words as I heard them from the gentleman who had the conversation with Lord Spencer, having made, in 1812, a memorandum of them in a few minutes after I had heard them.

When one gets thus behind the curtain, how amusing it is to hear the world disputing and wrangling about the motives, and principles, and opinions of *Burke!* He had no notions, no principles, no opinions of his own when he wrote his famous work, which tended so much to kindle the flames of that bloody war, which, in its ramifications, have reached even to the Canadian Lakes and the Mexican Gulf. He was a poor, needy dependant of a Borough-monger, to serve whom, and please whom, he wrote; and for no other purpose whatever. His defence of "our own Glorious Revolution," under the "deliverer *William,*" and his high eulogium of that king for introducing and ennobling a *Dutch* family or two, seem to be quite unaccountable to most readers, as they are disgusting to all; but, no longer wonder then, when we reflect, that Earl *Fitzwilliam* is the descendant of a natural son of *William the Third;* and that the ancestors of *Bentinck*, Duke of Portland, were Dutchmen, who came to England, and were here ennobled, in the same king's reign. And yet, how many people read this man's writings as if they had flowed from his *own mind;* and who seem to regard even the pension, which Lord Fitzwilliam soon after the change procured for him and for his widow after him, as no more than the proper and natural reward for his great and *disinterested* literary exertions in the cause of *"social order!"*

From this account of the real *cause* of the war of 1793, it is clear how the world, in general, have been deceived as to the *king's* commands upon that occasion. He, I dare say, *wished* for war. It was the cause of *kings* and *electors* as well as of Borough-mongers. But, his mere wishes were unsupported by any power of his own. And, as to PITT, if he had taken his place with Fox on the Opposition benches, he would have found, as he afterwards did, when he opposed his own understrapper, Addington, that out of his majority of four hundred and thirty votes, not more than thirty-seven would have gone over with him.

In 1801 Pitt resigned, because Catholic Emancipation was not permitted to be brought forward. But, when the Borough-mongers, in 1804, found, upon the renewal of the war, that Addington was insufficient for the purpose, they called Pitt, who, however, in spite of all his *pledges,* never dared to talk of Catholic Emancipation again, to the day of his death. Upon the occasion of this last change, it is notorious, that the king discovered his reluctance in all possible ways; and when it actually took place, it drove him into one of his fits of insanity. He personally liked Addington, who is a smooth supple creature, though very artful, and can be, when he chooses, very malignant. His father was a mad-doctor, had treated the king with great tenderness, while others used harsh, not to say cruel, remedies. Addington, who had always been an underling, behaved in that humble manner which the king and queen and royal family liked very much; and, besides, he did all their little *jobs* in the way of pensions and places for their personal friends. So that the life they led with him was perfect elysium, compared with what they were obliged to endure from the neglect and insolence of Pitt, who was domineering towards every living creature, the Borough-mongers excepted. But, the war was again begun. Addington was thought by the seat-owners unfit for their purpose; both sides of the House joined to put him out; and, a very little after he had left Pitt in a minority of thirty-seven, Pitt saw him (the Members being all the same persons) in a minority of about the same number! Where was *now* that *"influence behind* the throne greater than the throne itself?" What was become of it upon this memorable occasion? The truth was, that Pitt was thought, by those who had the real power in their hands, the fittest man to carry on the complicated machine; and, no sooner had they made up their minds, than they put out the poor thing who had filled his place for a couple of years, *keeping in almost all the rest of the ministry.*

Is it possible for any thing to show, more clearly than these facts do, the *nothingness* of the Royal Family and the Ministers, if considered in any other light than that of puppets and tools? When the present cabinet was formed, the Earl of Lonsdale, who owns *nine* seats, had made it a point that Lord *Mulgrave* should be Master General of the Ordnance. It being found difficult to comply with this request without clashing in another quarter, the Earl of Lonsdale was informed, that His Royal Highness the Prince Regent had *been graciously pleased to make an arrangement* by which Lord Mulgrave would have a very lucrative post *out* of the cabinet, sensible men, most likely, not wishing to have such an empty coxcomical[4] gabbler *in* the cabinet. Upon seeing this information by letter, at one of his country seats, it is said that Lord Lonsdale exclaimed: *"His Royal Highness* has been *pleased,* has he! Bring me my *boots!"* Whether this be true or not, it is very certain that he undid the arrangement, and that he put Lord Mulgrave into the Ordnance and the Cabinet. In fact, it is notorious, that the Prince has no power at all of any public consequence; that he cannot procure the appointment to any office of considerable trust or emolument; that it is not *he* that chooses Ministers, Ambassadors, Judges, Commanders, or Governors; that it is not *he* who grants pensions, or bestows sinecures; that it is not *he* who gives to the Dean and Chapters *leave* to elect Bishops any more than it is the "Holy Ghost" that inspires the said Deans and Chapters upon the occasions when these at once impious and farcical scenes are exhibited. Of all the *elections,* that ever the world hear of, *these* are the most curious.

When a Bishop dies, another must be put in his place. The Bishop is elected by the Dean and Prebends of the Cathedral Church of the Diocess.[5] The king, who is called the *head* of the Church, sends these gentlemen, who are called the Dean and Chapter, a *congé d'élire,* or a *leave to elect;* but he sends them, at the same time, the *name of the man,* whom, and whom only, they are to elect. With this name in their possession, away they go into the Cathedral, chant psalms and anthems, and then, in a set form of words, *invoke the Holy Ghost to assist them in their choice.* After these invocations, they, by a series of good luck wholly without parallel, always find that the dictates of the Holy Ghost agree with the *recommendation* of the king. And, now, if any man can, in the annals of the whole world, find me a match for this mockery, let him produce it. But even this shockingly impious farce loses part of its qualities, unless we bear in mind, that it is not the *king,* but some Borough-monger, in virtue of some bargain for votes, who has really nominated the Bishop; and, that the King, the Minister, the Dean and Chapter, and the Holy Ghost proceeding, are neither more nor less than so many tools in the hands of the said Borough-monger. Good and pious people wondered amazingly that the Holy Ghost, or even the king, should have pitched upon the present gentleman to fill the Archbishop's Chair of Canterbury; but, these good and pious Church people did not know, that the Duke of

[4]Neither a misspelling nor a pun; only a variant spelling.
[5]An old-fashioned spelling of *diocese;* the London *Times* used it as late as the 1870's.

Rutland[6] had, as he still has, *seven* or *eight* votes of his own in the two Houses, besides, perhaps, twenty more that he could, upon a hard pinch, make shift to borrow.

It makes me, and hundreds besides me, laugh to read in American and French publications, remarks on the men engaged in carrying on this curious government of ours. We laugh at the idea of the *influence of the Crown;* of the *party of Pitt;* of the *party of Fox;* of the intrigues of this Minister, of the *powerful eloquence* of that Minister; of those great men, the Wellesleys, and Liverpools, and Castlereaghs, and Cannings, on the one side; and the Tierneys, and Horners, and Broughams, and God knows who, on the other side; and the Thorntons, and Wilberforces, and Banks's, and Romillys, and the rest of that canting crew in the middle. We know them all; yea, *one and all,* to be the mere tools of the Borough-mongers; and, that, as to the *deciding of any question,* affecting the honour, liberty, or happiness of the country, the Duke of Newcastle, who was, only a few years ago, a baby in his cradle, had, even while he was living upon pap, more power than this whole rabble of great senators all put together; and, I dare say, now that he is grown up to be a young man, he pays much more attention to the voice of his fox-hounds than to the harangues of these bawlers, and that he has more respect for the persons and motives of the former than for those of the latter. One thing I can state as a certainty; and that is, that, if I were in his place, I should flee to the dog-kennel as a relief from that filthy den, the House of Commons.

"The king's friends" is an expression frequently used. Poor man! He has no friends, unless it be in his own family, and amongst his and their menial servants, the greater part of whom are Hanoverians and Brunswickers. The common people do not *hate* the Royal Family; they despise them too much to hate them. They listen greedily to all the dirty stories about the Queen and her Daughters, of which I have, for my part, never heard any thing bordering upon the nature of *proof.* Every body speaks ill of all the sons; they *blackguard* them in all manner of ways. In *print,* indeed, the Attorney General takes care that a little decorum should be observed; but, even he suffers the assailants to go pretty good lengths. The story at this moment (10th Feb.) is, that the Prince Regent is *mad.* In vain is there no *proof* of this; in vain do the physicians report, that his ailment is merely the *gout.* People will not believe this. They laugh at you if you affect to believe it. The life that the Prince has led may be easily guessed at from the following fact, for the truth of which I refer to publications in London notorious to every body. One Walter, now dead, the proprietor of a newspaper called the *Times,* which is now carried on by his son, published, during the first agitation of the Regency question, previous to the French war, some outrageously gross libels, very *false* as well as foul, against the Duke of York and the Prince of Wales. Walter, who was a very base and

[6]The Archbishop was Charles Manners-Sutton, a grandson of the third Duke of Rutland; it was the fifth Duke who, Cobbett suggests, used his influence to procure the election.

infamous fellow, was prosecuted by the Attorney General, sentenced to be imprisoned two years for each libel, and to pay a fine for each. The *Treasury*[7] itself (Pitt at the head of it) were the *authors* of the libels. Walters threatened *to give up the authors*. The Treasury gave him a sum of money to keep silence; and, after he had suffered the two years imprisonment for the libel on the *Duke*, the Prince obtained the scoundrel's pardon for the libel on himself, which WALTER repaid by every species of malevolence towards the Prince to the day of his death, the Prince's enemies being better able to *pay* the ruffian than he was!

Now, let any one suppose what the situation of this family must be, when the Treasury itself could unite, and cause to be published, infamous libels against two of the King's sons! And the truth is, that the whole family, the Prince Regent not excepted, are compelled to subsidize the newspapers, in order to blunt or repel, the shafts aimed, or launched forth, against them. If any one could paint this part of our press in its true colours, it would shock every man of common justice. The fears of the whole family are constantly kept alive. They know very well what is said about them. However false the story, they dare not attempt to contradict it; for the bare attempt alone would be produced as *proof* of their guilt. The sons and daughters cannot marry without *leave of the Borough-mongers*, as was recently shown in the case of the Duke of Cumberland. He *did*, indeed, marry, and by his brother's consent, which was precisely what the *law* required; but, because the Prince had not asked *their* leave, they would not give him a farthing of *money*, though such grants have always been customary in like cases. And, what is more, they prevented the Queen from receiving his wife at court. It is true, that very bad whispers had been long afloat about the Duke, and I do not say, because I do not know, that they were without foundation; but, I believe, his great sin, a sin for which most certainly there is no forgiveness for him in this world, was his very foolish attempt to uphold Addington against the Borough-mongers, and which attempt, nevertheless did not succeed for one single day. With what truth the story is told of the poor old king's expressing his resolution, upon one occasion, to *go off to Hanover*, I do not know; but really one can easily believe, that a man would go almost any where, and live almost any how, or with almost any body, to get out of such a state of mock-majesty and of real slavery.

The "Royal Dukes," as they are called, in order to gain a little popular favour, run about to Bible Societies, Lancaster schools, sometimes to societies for assisting *lying-in women*, and to the most popular Methodist Meeting Houses, when any Thundering Preacher holds forth on a popular occasion. Their names are in all great subscription Lists; and they make speeches on many of these occasions; and always give away some of their money. All this exposes them to ridicule. The Borough-mongers never expose themselves in this way. They are at their great country seats with their packs of hounds and troops of hunters, and with their good cheer

[7]That is, the Government, with Pitt as Prime Minister.

for their numerous guests. Not a single country seat has the Royal Family; not an acre of land; not a pack of hounds, except the Stag-hounds kept up *for the use of the old king!* The kings of England had, formerly, *immense landed estates.* They lived upon these estates. They wanted no *public money,* except for the purposes of war, and sometimes they carried on war out of their own purses.

The Borough-mongers took all these estates away from the Guelphs, in the early part of this king's reign; they have divided the greater part of them amongst themselves, and settled a pension, or, what they call a *Civil List,* on the king in lieu of them, thus exposing him and his family to all the odium that the annual exhibition of a great *charge upon the public* naturally excites and keeps alive.

After this view of the situation of this family how we must laugh at De Lolmes' pretty account of the *English Constitution.* After seeing that about three or four hundred Borough-mongers actually possess all the legislative power, divide the ecclesiastical, judicial, military, and naval departments amongst their own dependants, what a fine picture we find of that wise system of *checks* and *balances,* of which so much has been said by so many great writers! What name to give such a government it is difficult to say. It is like nothing that ever was heard of before. It is neither a monarchy, an aristocracy, nor a democracy; it is a band of great nobles, who, by sham elections, and by the means of all sorts of bribery and corruption, have obtained an absolute sway in the country, having under them, for the purposes of *show* and of execution, a thing they call a *king,* sharp and unprincipled fellows whom they call *Ministers,* a mummery which they call a *Church,* experienced and well-tried and steel-hearted men whom they call *Judges,* a company of false money makers, whom they call a *Bank,* numerous bands of brave and needy persons whom they call *soldiers and sailors;* and a talking, corrupt, and impudent set, whom they call a *House of Commons.* Such is the government of England; such is the thing, which has been able to bribe one half of Europe to oppress the other half; such is the famous "Bulwark of *religion* and *social order,*" which is now about, as will be soon seen, to surround itself with a *permanent standing army* of, at least, a hundred thousand men, and very wisely, for, without such an army, the Bulwark would not exist a month.

FAREWELL ON P STREET— AND MR TRUMAN SLIPS AWAY

Alistair Cooke

WASHINGTON, JANUARY 21.

Between the hours of breakfast and one o'clock yesterday there was quite a bustle going on in a a modest Georgian house on a side street in the Washington suburb of Georgetown. The bedroom windows were flung high to air the place out. A jovial coloured maid put her head out now and then to see if Gabriel was ready with his trumpet, to watch for the incoming flight of angels who would guard the place for the imminent great event. A coloured butler peeked out of the the cream-coloured door to see if Georgetown still stood.

It did. It was exactly as it has been since a little swarm of genteel persons descended on this old suburb a generation ago, cleaned up the classical porticoes, painted in black and red and green the old shutters, stripped many a little Georgian house of its Victorian crust and restored the place to its rambling eighteenth-century appearance. P Street is very typical. It has everything. Noble Federal houses lean up against little cottages. A Justice of the Supreme Court looks out from his bedroom on to a butcher's backyard.

What the butler saw at 2805 P Street was what he had seen since he had worked there. Across the street to the left is the bus stop, on a corner by a grocery store, next to a Chinese laundry, next to a cobbler's. The butler vanished at one o'clock when the host came home to get ready for the guest. The host was the owner of the house, Dean Gooderham Acheson, a whiskered Washington lawyer, formerly Secretary of State.

Then a motor-cycle cop came ripping up, straddled his cycle against the curb, and marched around in his leggings. He went to the corner by the grocery store and waved all cars and cabs off to the adjoining streets. A few stragglers stopped. A man in a leather windbreak, with a bubbling baby on his shoulder walked over to 2805 and balanced the baby on the railings. Two teen-age girls appeared with box cameras. Pretty soon there were twenty or thirty idlers. Then another cop. Then a black car with two plain-clothes men. Then a hundred, two hundred, maybe three hundred onlookers.

A long, shining, black car preceded by another motor-cycle cop shot up the street and stopped outside. And Mr Truman got out, handing down Mrs Truman and their daughter Margaret. He jerked his face up and

FROM the *Manchester Guardian Weekly* (Airmail Edition). Reprinted by permission.

around, scarcely believing his eyes. Who did they think he was, the President?

A ragged rebel cry went up: "We want Truman," "Good old Harry." They clapped in rhythm. He went in. So did a lot of other people, faintly familiar faces. Thirty-eight all told were to sit down to lunch. They were the old Truman Cabinet and their wives. When the door closed on the last guest, the little crowd set up a howl. The door opened and the small, square jaunty figure appeared. He did not seem to be able to get out what he wanted to say. He swallowed a couple of times and put his hands out to quieten the crowd.

"May I say," he began at last, "that I appreciate this more than any other enthusiastic meeting I attended as President, Vice-President, or senator. I'm just plain Mr Truman, a private citizen." He ducked and smiled and everybody cheered. He looked around nervously till old Alben Barkley appeared. Mr Barkley said he had been in Washington forty years. "I came here in knee pants. It's wonderful of you to come out here." They bowed and were going inside but the compact little crowd shouted for the host. A very grand tall man, in cutaway jacket and grey cravat, appeared. He has been called urbane so often that the word is useless for any further employment. His white whiskers bristled, but he could not say a thing. His eyes bulged more than ever. All he could stammer was, "I thank you from the bottom of my heart—for being—great to a bunch of has-beens."

The sun which had blazed for Ike was hiding now behind ramparts of grey clouds. The afternoon chill came on. A lot of people went away, but a lot stayed. The bubbling baby burped and smiled like a mechanical doll. The man in the leather jacket hoisted her anew for the long wait. The motorcycle cop twirled a long cigar between his lips. A smaller knot of people waited. They waited for more than two hours and broke into chatter whenever the butler came out to say, "Not yet."

At a quarter after three Mr Acheson's tall figure came out again. He was urbane again and chuckling and cheerfully flushed: a warming contrast with the dead sky and the darkening afternoon. "This," he said, "is my last press conference." But he had wanted to come out and tell us what went on inside. "We had a very gay time. We laughed a lot, told stories— on each other. We reviewed our experiences and we ended as we began —full of love and devotion to our chief, his wife, and daughter that has never, I dare say, been equalled in the history of the Presidency. Now we're going to sit here for a little while, and talk and laugh some more."

He went in again and about twenty minutes later the cream-coloured door opened wide. Mr Lovett came out. All sorts of dispensable famous faces, torn off the covers of national magazines, came bobbing out on legs and bodies. Then Mr Truman came out with his hat off and with his wife and daughter. The hundred or so people clapped hard again. He went down the few steps and towards the big black car. Mr Acheson was behind him. He leaned over and put his hand into the car. "Thank you, sir, again. It was a great joy." The Secret Service men bustled in. The motor-cycle cop tossed a cigar away and cranked up. The car whisked off. And Mr Acheson stood and watched the tail-light.

He had his arms folded but his eyes glittered and he did not move for many seconds. Then he said "Good-bye" to everybody else. He waved at the scattering crowd. The butler shut the door for the last time. The uncomplaining baby was hoisted again and the man said, "Well, that's it, baby." They stalked off and left P Street to the cobbler and the Chinese laundry and the grocery store (semi-self service). The New Deal had evaporated quietly into the twilight.

THE DEATH OF QUEEN VICTORIA

Lytton Strachey

The evening had been golden; but, after all, the day was to close in cloud and tempest. Imperial needs, imperial ambitions, involved the country in the South African War. There were checks, reverses, bloody disasters; for a moment the nation was shaken, and the public distresses were felt with intimate solicitude by the Queen. But her spirit was high, and neither her courage nor her confidence wavered for a moment. Throwing herself heart and soul into the struggle, she laboured with redoubled vigour, interested herself in every detail of the hostilities, and sought by every means in her power to render service to the national cause. In April 1900, when she was in her eighty-first year, she made the extraordinary decision to abandon her annual visit to the South of France, and to go instead to Ireland, which had provided a particularly large number of recruits to the armies in the field. She stayed for three weeks in Dublin, driving through the streets, in spite of the warnings of her advisers, without an armed escort; and the visit was a complete success. But, in the course of it, she began, for the first time, to show signs of the fatigue of age.[1]

For the long strain and the unceasing anxiety, brought by the war, made themselves felt at last. Endowed by nature with a robust constitution, Victoria, though in periods of depression she had sometimes supposed herself an invalid, had in reality through her life enjoyed remark-

[1] *Quarterly Review*, vol. 193, pp. 818, 836-7. [Author's note]

ably good health. In her old age, she had suffered from a rheumatic stiffness of the joints, which had necessitated the use of a stick, and, eventually, a wheeled chair; but no other ailments attacked her, until, in 1898, her eyesight began to be affected by incipient cataract. After that, she found reading more and more difficult, though she could still sign her name, and even, with some difficulty, write letters. In the summer of 1900, however, more serious symptoms appeared. Her memory, in whose strength and precision she had so long prided herself, now sometimes deserted her; there was a tendency towards aphasia; and, while no specific disease declared itself, by the autumn there were unmistakable signs of a general physical decay. Yet, even in these last months, the strain of iron held firm. The daily work continued; nay, it actually increased; for the Queen, with an astonishing pertinacity, insisted upon communicating personally with an ever-growing multitude of men and women who had suffered through the war.[2]

By the end of the year the last remains of her ebbing strength had almost deserted her; and through the early days of the opening century it was clear that her dwindling forces were only kept together by an effort of will. On January 14, she had at Osborne an hour's interview with Lord Roberts, who had returned victorious from South Africa a few days before. She inquired with acute anxiety into all the details of the war; she appeared to sustain the exertion successfully; but, when the audience was over, there was a collapse. On the following day her medical attendants recognised that her state was hopeless; and yet, for two days more, the indomitable spirit fought on; for two days more she discharged the duties of a Queen of England. But after that there was an end of working; and then, and not till then, did the last optimism of those about her break down. The brain was failing, and life was gently slipping away. Her family gathered round her; for a little more she lingered, speechless and apparently insensible; and, on January 22, 1901, she died.[3]

When, two days previously, the news of the approaching end had been made public, astonished grief had swept over the country. It appeared as if some monstrous reversal of the course of nature was about to take place. The vast majority of her subjects had never known a time when Queen Victoria had not been reigning over them. She had become an indissoluble part of their whole scheme of things, and that they were about to lose her appeared a scarcely possible thought. She herself, as she lay blind and silent, seemed to those who watched her to be divested of all thinking—to have glided already, unawares, into oblivion. Yet, perhaps, in the secret chambers of consciousness, she had her thoughts, too. Perhaps her fading mind called up once more the shadows of the past to float before it, and retraced, for the last time, the vanished visions of that long history—passing back and back, through the cloud of years, to older and ever older memories—to the spring woods at Osborne, so full of

[2] Lee, 536-7; private information. [Author's note]
[3] Lee, 537-9; *Quarterly Review*, cxciii, 309. [Author's note]

primroses for Lord Beaconsfield—to Lord Palmerston's queer clothes and
high demeanour, and Albert's face under the green lamp, and Albert's
first stag at Balmoral, and Albert in his blue and silver uniform, and the
Baron coming in through a doorway, and Lord M. dreaming at Windsor
with the rooks cawing in the elm-trees, and the Archbishop of Canterbury
on his knees in the dawn, and the old King's turkey-cock ejaculations, and
Uncle Leopold's soft voice at Claremont, and Lehzen with the globes,
and her mother's feathers sweeping down towards her, and a great old
repeater-watch of her father's in its tortoise-shell case, and a yellow rug,
and some friendly flounces of sprigged muslin, and the trees and the grass
at Kensington.

THE QUEEN GOES HOME

Amy Kelly

This is the worm that dieth not, the memory of things past.
Bernard of Clairvaux, *De Consideratione*

In those days when the foreshadow of some new order in the world was
dimly taking shape in the minds of men, and the appeal to "ancient custom" was giving place to new sanctions, the Britons took account of the
worsening of their lot since the steady, if heavy, hand of Henry Fitz-
Empress had been withdrawn. What demon had entered into the race of
the Angevins? The prestige of Queen Eleanor suffered in the general distrust of transmarine ties. She had doubled the Angevin empire for Henry
and enriched his house with a brilliant posterity; and when he had gone,
she had defended his empire with a political sagacity that had brought
the highest magnates to her counsels and earned for her the trust and
confidence of popes and emperors and kings. But now she became an object of calumny. Clerks, like Giraldus Cambrensis, with rancors of their
own to appease, asked to know what could be expected of the brood of
the "eagle of the broken pledge," of the Poitevin who had renounced the
pious King of the Franks for the Angevin king and abandoned one crown
for another. Hugh of Lincoln, that disciple of Saint Bernard, held that her
marriage with Henry was "adulterous" and the Angevin eaglets "spurious."
Although throughout her long history as Queen of England, no breath of
scandal had touched her good fame, the old legends the Franks had used
in the mid-century to discredit her—legends discreetly suppressed in

FROM *Eleanor of Aquitaine and the Four Kings*, by Amy Kelly. Cambridge, Mass.:
Harvard University Press, Copyright, 1950, by The President and Fellows of Harvard
College.

Henry's day—were brought out of limbo and refurbished and bequeathed to balladeers, who used them to season broadsides and chapbooks down to the seventeenth century. The impossible story of Eleanor's murder of Rosamond Clifford got its vogue and passed into folklore, and has never ceased to serve to her disparagement as theme for opera, romance, and poetry.

After Mirebeau Eleanor had withdrawn from the habitations of kings to her own ancestral provinces, to places familiar before she had dwelt with Louis Capet or Henry Plantagenet. She left the roar of hopeless war behind. She could no longer lead armies in the field, collect ransoms, scale mountain barriers, or deal with magnates or envoys in the interest of empire. In Poitiers she was safe among the loyal citizens of her own capital. Like Henry at the last, she was obliged to put off vainglory and echo his words, "Let all things go as they will. I care no more for aught of this world."

The eternal aspect of her earth, unchanged by all the ravages of conflict, must have renewed its patient poetry and solace. Beyond the rivers that moated the ancient high place of the Poitevin counts the land ebbed away, nursing on its bosom here a hamlet, there a mill, yonder a priory. The immemorial toil of ox and colon went forward in the field, and the tireless magpie skimmed the furrow. The chestnuts bloomed again. In the busy commune all about the palace were heard the creak of wheels, the slithering of horses' hoofs upon the cobblestones, the drumming of hammers, the rasp of the stonecutter's adz, the voices of housewives, and the cries of children; and over all the other sounds the dissolving resonance of bells—the bells of Saint Pierre, Saint Radigonde, Saint Porchaire, and Notre-Dame la Grande, proclaiming the office and the calendar of the everlasting church.

The great assembly hall where the duchess once held her courts of love is now used as an antechamber to justice and is known as the "hall of lost footsteps" (*la salle des pas perdus*). Already in the queen's day it thronged with ghosts, some of whose footfalls had died away in the long past: the ribald, philandering, musical troubadour, her grandfather, with his huge laughter and his inimitable travesties; the gay Countess of Châtellerault; her father, fire-eating Guillaume le Toulousain, of the gorgeous appetite and the reckless imbroglios; Louis Capet, young, wilted with the summer heat, and plainly dazed by his confusing role as king, bridegroom, count of the Poitevins; the lovely Countesses of Champagne and Flanders ushering in the areopagus of the courts of love, the marriage prizes of the south; André the Chaplain with his choir of poets and his corps of clerks polishing the peerless *Tractatus de Amore*; the troubadours of the Limousin and the valleys of Provence—Ventadour, Rudel, Vidal, and many more; Guillaume le Maréchal, brave and loyal, leading in her sons triumphant from the jousting fields, the beautiful young king, gallant Coeur-de-Lion, the clever Count of Brittany, with their households of *preux chevaliers*, their hair smoothed down with sweet-smelling unguents and their nostrils shaven; Marguerite and Alais of France, Constance of Brittany, Joanna of Sicily, and Eleanor of Castile; Thomas Becket, with the tall figure and the burning eyes . . . Thomas the Chancellor . . . Thomas Becket, Archbishop of Canterbury . . . Saint Thomas . . . Thomas Martyr! The grim figure of Henry Fitz-Empress on the threshold of her palace hall; the awful ghost of Falaise and Rouen, his spectral eyes still stricken with a horror that was mortal; the ghastly Channel crossings to and from the foggy island on the edges of the world. Salisbury Tower. This is the worm that dieth not, the memory of things past.

Tableaux from remoter times must have taken semblance and fled away, dismembered and recombined, strange interminglings of feudal palaces at the crossroads of Christendom, and of personages that made the century glow. Paris, the Île de la Cité moored like a barge in the Seine, teeming with students and clamorous with bells, stirred now by the love songs, now by the fulminations of Abélard, now by the subtle discourse of Abbé Bernard . . . Saint Bernard, "that well of flowing doctrine"; wise and temperate Abbé Suger; the Counts of Champagne; Petronilla and the one-eyed Count of Vermandois; nights on the Danube below Durrenstein; Byzantium crowned by the domes of Sancta Sophia set between the sweet and bitter waters of the West and East; sleek and crafty Manuel and his dowdy German empress, who had not learned, even in Byzantium, how to lay on her fards . . . The horrible geography of Paphlagonia, the unspeakable Turks; Antioch the glorious, the lilies of the field, the latter rains; Jerusalem, the Holy Sepulcher, the tottering dynasty of the Latin Kingdom, the stony pilgrim roads of Palestine . . . the pirates of Barbary, Pope Eugenius in Tusculum.

"This life," says the chronicler, "is but a journey and a warfare." In the day of every man's pilgrimage to holy shrines, the metaphor had special meaning. The duchess' long road, beset with every kind of accident and every sort of weather, had brought her home at last, but in a night of storm. Had she chosen the saints of her devotion, her route and destination, or had she been driven by the press of throngs and the waywardness of storm to unforeseen harborages, to havens not even on the map? Had Fate been capricious, or had she?

Above the Loire the masonry of Henry's empire, which she had helped to build and fortify, slid down under the blows of Philip Capet, Dieu-Donné, whom, according to Giraldus, heaven had sent in answer to the prayers of Louis and the Cistercian brotherhood to be "a hammer to the King of the English"; and not an Angevin stirred among the smoking rubble of its towns to retrieve the inheritance of his forebears. Only the echo of crashing ramparts reached her as one fortress after another from Rouen to Saint Michael-in-Peril-of-the-Sea fell to the son of Louis Capet. She did not live to hear of Bouvines or Runnymede; perhaps even the news of the surrender of Gaillard fell on deaf ears. But it was as if the messenger reporting the loss of that master fortress of the Angevins brought her summons too. On the sixth of March the castle hung out its white flag. Barely three weeks later the queen "passed from the world," "as a candle in the sconce goeth out when the wind striketh it." She was in her eighty-third year. Chroniclers are not even agreed about the place in which she died. The chronicle of Saint Aubin of Angers declares she ended her days in her own capital; but others say she was taken at the last to Fontevrault, where she put on the garb of a nun before closing her eyes.

In the terror and dismay that swept over the heritage of Henry, her death was hardly noticed. The nuns of Fontevrault, who knew her through many stages of her journey, gave her a paragraph in their necrology:

> She enhanced the grandeur of her birth by the honesty of her life, the purity of her morals, the flower of her virtues; and in the conduct of her blameless life, she surpassed almost all the queens of the world.

Matthew Paris ventures to say, "In this year the noble Queen Eleanor, a woman of admirable beauty and intelligence, died in Fontevrault."

But among the discreet chroniclers, whose records were subject to review by the clerks of various kings, the inscription is noncommittal and meagerly informative about Eleanor of Aquitaine and the four kings. Scanning a dozen entries yields no more than this: Anno 1204. In this year died Eleanor, Duchess of Aquitaine, who was divorced from the French king by reason of consanguinity, and then married Henry Fitz-Empress, and was the mother of Richard, called the Lion-Heart, and of John, who in turn succeeded him.

The queen's cortege brought her at any rate to Fontevrault, and her tomb was erected in the crypt. The nunnery had become, as Merlin was believed to have prophesied, the necropolis of the Angevins. The tombs, all crowned with effigies, were disturbed during the French Revolution, but were subsequently replaced in the crypt in new array, all of them damaged in detail by the ravages of time and war. The queen now reposes between Henry Fitz-Empress and Richard Coeur-de-Lion, whose scepters and crowned heads are epitaph enough. Nearby rest Joanna and Isabella of Angoulême. Here Eleanor lies serene, the play of a smile in her whole expression, in her hand a small volume, which one of her apologists has said need not be regarded as a missal. Tranquil, collected, engaged with her book, the queen seems to have found at last, beyond the wrath of kings and the ruin of the Angevin empire, that domain of peace and order to which her vast journeyings amongst the high places of feudal Christendom had never brought her. The highhearted Plantagenets are marble still. The dusty sunlight falls softly where they sleep.

1204: In hoc anno obiit Alianor.

THE DEATH OF LOUIS XIV

W. H. Lewis

At the beginning of August 1715 watchful courtiers noticed that the king's appetite was failing, and on the 10th he had a violent attack of indigestion at Marly: but recovered sufficiently to go round the gardens in a bath chair to give directions about the siting of a collection of statuary which had just arrived from Italy. At six that evening he set out for Versailles, having seen his beloved Marly for the last time.

On 11th August, after a bad night, he succeeded in getting through the routine of his day until the hour of the afternoon drive, which he cancelled, feeling too tired to face the jolting, and at his supper it was noticed that he looked worn out. On the following day he heard Mass, and dined in bed, but got up in the afternoon.

So far no one, and least of all the royal doctors, had taken the king's illness seriously, but by the 14th he was suffering intense pain in his left leg, and on the 19th he shut himself up in his private suite, which he was never to leave again.

Wednesday 21st had been fixed for the review of the Life Guard, but Louis was too weak to take the salute, even from his balcony, and the Duc du Maine acted as his deputy. By this time, there was no doubt at Court what was happening; the king was dying, the old oak was about to fall at last, and men looked at each other in bewilderment. Louis had often reminded them that he was mortal, but no one had realized the fact. The king was part of the fixed order of things, *was* in fact the fixed order of things in that thronged Versailles where there were not half a dozen people who could remember his predecessor. The incredible, often discussed but never wholly believed in, was happening at last; the longest reign in European history was drawing swiftly and terribly to its close.

But not even the onset of death could deter Louis from playing out his part to the end; to modify his plans to accommodate that grisly intruder would be an act unworthy of a man of quality and on the morning of the 22nd, the dying king began his day by choosing a coat to wear when he came out of mourning for Prince François de Lorraine; and after that held his usual meeting of the Council of State. Dying he was, but the world should see that he was still King of France. Nor did he so act in ignorance of his state, for on this day he refused rather abruptly to fill some vacant benefices, saying that in his condition he could not take it upon his conscience to meddle with a business which could be settled at leisure by his successor.

From *The Sunset of the Splendid Century*, by W. H. Lewis. Reprinted by permission of the Author.

On the 24th, black patches appeared on his leg, and he spent the day in great pain, but by sheer will-power kept the engine of State running. He dined and supped in bed in the presence of the Court, presided at a meeting of the Council of Finance, and saw his Chancellor on business.

Sunday 25th was his Feast-day, the Feast of St. Louis, and by the king's express command the usual ceremonial was observed. The drums and hautboys played beneath his window as soon as he was awake, and at his dinner he insisted on having his four and twenty violins, so as not to disappoint the musicians. Later in the day he did a little business, amongst other things adding a codicil to his Will, whereby the command of the civil and military Household was entrusted to the Duc du Maine. His wife and her ladies were with him in the evening until seven o'clock, when he fell asleep. He woke with his mind wandering, recovered himself almost immediately, and, with apologies to the ladies, sent for Cardinal de Rohan to administer the Sacrament to him; after which, the Duc d'Orléans was summoned, the room cleared, and a long private conversation took place. His concluding words to the Regent must dispel any lingering idea that he suspected his nephew of the horrible crime imputed to him, or that he deliberately deceived him as to the tenor of the Will:

"My dear nephew, remember me. I have made such arrangements as I thought fairest and most prudent for the good of the State, but one cannot foresee everything, and if there is anything that needs altering or amending, you will do whatever you think best."

Compare this with St. Simon's version:

"Awful to relate, at this moment when the Body of Our Lord had only just passed his lips, he assured him (the Regent) that he would find nothing in his will to displease him."

The first account, and a great many other interesting details of the last hours of Louis XIV, we owe to one Anthoine, the king's gun carrier, a servant so humble that he was apparently overlooked, or considered too unimportant to be excluded from the dying man's room, and whose journal deserves to be better known than it appears to be.

On the morning of the 26th, Louis rallied himself for the last effort; he had done with life, it only remained for him to say his farewells and be gone. For the last time, the whole Court assembled to hear its king:

"Gentlemen, I have to ask your pardon for setting you so bad an example. I thank you for the manner in which you have served me, and for the loyal attachment which you have always shown. I am sorry it has not been in my power to do as much for you as I could have wished; the bad times must be my excuse. I ask you to continue to serve my great-grandson with as much zeal and fidelity as you have shown me. He is a child, and may have many unpleasantnesses in store for him. I hope you will set an example which will be followed by all my subjects. Obey the commands which my nephew will give you. He is about to govern the kingdom; I trust he will govern it well. I trust you will all do your best to preserve unity, and, if you see anyone attempting to disturb it, you will bring him back into the right way. I feel that my emotions are becoming too strong for me: and I perceive that you also are moved. I am sorry if what I have said has been too much for your feelings. Farewell gentlemen, I hope you will sometimes think of me when I am gone."

It was then the turn of the servants, to all of whom, even the humblest as Anthoine tells us, he said goodbye, asking their prayers for his soul, and their pardon for any annoyance or pain he had ever caused them: a request which touched them the more, because, says Anthoine, there never was any gentleman more considerate towards servants. He then told them that he had given them the best of characters to the Duc d'Orléans, who would take care of them, warned the upper servants to treat those under them kindly, "as I have always done myself, to the best of my ability," and wound up by saying, "Goodbye, my good folk, this is all I have to say before I leave you."

Then came the turn of old Villeroi, followed by the princesses, for each of whom there was a kindly word: even for Mme. du Maine, who had been persuaded—with difficulty—to come up to Versailles to receive her father-in-law's last blessing.

Finally came Louis XIV's farewell to his natural sons, Maine and Toulouse, and of this interview we know nothing, except that it lasted a long time, behind closed doors. Never have we succeeded in penetrating the king's relations with his beloved sons or with his second wife; we say that Louis lived all his life in public. But not quite all. Even for the Grand Monarque there was a final locked door, guarding an inner privacy, that ultimate circle of intimacy without which life ceases to be human. We can but speculate on the tender outpouring of love with which that wise old brain endeavoured to forearm his sons, so alone in their perilous elevation and whose dangers he saw so clearly. According to Mlle. de Launay, the king told Maine the contents of his Will; "but," she adds, "it was too late for M. du Maine to profit by the knowledge, and he could only represent to the king the inconveniences which were in store for him." But we must remember that Mlle. de Launay's only source of information would be Mme. du Maine, and that Mme. du Maine knew no more of the interview than her husband chose to tell her.

As Mme. de Maintenon sat by Louis' bed that night, the dying man said suddenly, "One always hears it said that it is difficult to make up one's mind to die; I don't find anything difficult about it." And a little later, hearing her crying, he said "Come, Madame, are you allowing yourself to be upset at seeing me about to die? Haven't I lived long enough? I have thought of this for a long time, and prepared myself for it, knowing well that there is a King of Kings, whose orders must be obeyed."

On the morning of the 28th, when all hope had been abandoned, there arrived at Versailles a peasant from Marseilles; after the manner of the ancien régime, he found no difficulty in making his way to the king's bedside, where he explained that, hearing of His Majesty's illness, he had come to persuade him to try some of his elixir. The king was now in such a state that his futile and flustered physicians were prepared to let anyone try any remedy upon him. Fagon, First Physician of France, did indeed demur, but "was answered so roughly and rudely by the peasant, that he was left speechless with astonishment." "Life or death, God's will be done," said the king as he drained the draft; and, whether it was the elixir, or merely the last flare of the sinking candle, there was on the morning of the 29th some little improvement in his condition. But during the day, the transient hope was extinguished, and Louis himself dismissed the subject from his mind; to the Curé of Versailles, who came to tell him that prayers were going up all over France for his recovery, he said that the time had come to pray for his soul, not for his life. And the few people he saw during the day noticed that he no longer spoke of "The Dauphin," but of "The young king."

On the 30th the royal suite was shut to everyone except Mme. de Maintenon, the Duc du Maine, and the doctors; the innermost shrine of France, the central cell of the Versailles beehive, had ceased to function, and in the vast outer rooms the dazed courtiers buzzed to and fro, a swarm without a leader. Throughout the night the king was conscious, able to speak, but usually silent, and with his eyes shut. Who can say what thoughts passed through that weary old brain before the night paled into the dawn of his last day on earth? Further, ever further back would memory lead him, to the day when he had stood by the deathbed of a King of France, a solemn little boy in tight jerkin and embroidered breeches, and how the dying man, whose darkened eyes could no longer recognize his son, had asked, "Who is it?" and his own triumphant answer, "Louis XIV." And the long troubled years of the Regency; now there was another Regency, beginning tomorrow as like as not, and when he was gone, who was left who would remember his own minority? Dead, all dead, the silky, insinuating Mazarin, his beautiful mother with her slow smile, and her soft Spanish accent, behind whose ample skirts he used to hide from his tutors, and whose comfit box he and *Monsieur* used to rifle. *Monsieur* too was gone, how long ago, with his scents and his sulks; gone too *Monsieur's* bewitching wife, and her royal scamp of a brother, who, like himself, had been an unconscionable time in dying; how he envied Charles II that apology. And Marie Mancini, with the dark bright eyes and the imperious charm, and Beaufort and his Frondeurs, where were they all tonight? And that dreadful evening when he had lain in his State bed, pretending to sleep, as he did now, while the Paris mob had tiptoed to his bedside to assure itself that he was really there, and had not been smuggled out of Paris. But he would dismiss this nightmare with an uneasy sigh, and let his thoughts rest on the glorious years which had followed, sinking again into a restless doze before the kaleidoscope of that France whose splendour had dazzled the world, his great Captains, his Guards, the blood beating against his ears in the hour of victory, the triumphant return to savour the incense of that bright flowerbed, the youthful Court of France; flowers, flowers, great red roses, the heavy scented summer night at Fontainebleau, and La Vallière waiting for him in some secret arbour. But such thoughts would be dismissed as he started into wakefulness once more: *Mea culpa, mea culpa* the sad-faced watchers heard him murmur more than once, and also the single word, *Confiteor.*

On 31st August, the last day of his life, he was mostly unconscious. Mortification was running swiftly upwards from his gangrened leg, and all pretence at remedial treatment was at an end, though the king complaisantly swallowed whatever was presented to him, including a sovereign remedy sent by Mme. du Maine. At eleven in the evening the prayers for the dying were offered, Louis himself repeating them in a loud voice. To Cardinal de Rohan he said, "This is the Church's last favour." He never again spoke to a mortal, but at intervals during the night, he was heard to say *"Nunc et in hora mortis,"* and "Help me, O my God, haste Thee to Help me."

At a quarter past eight on the morning of Sunday, the 1st of September 1715, he died, aged seventy-seven years less three days, and having reigned for seventy-two years, three months, and eighteen days.

"Thus passed the glory of the world, *sic transit gloria mundi.*" So writes Anthoine, and yet we say that no man is a hero to his valet. "The glory of the world" sounds excessive to modern ears; but we cannot quarrel with the epitaph written for Louis XIV by a French man of letters of the Third Republic—"He walked into eternity with the same tranquil majesty with which he used to cross the Hall of Mirrors."

QUESTIONS

1. It has been said (by Herbert Read) that the chapter from *Queen Victoria* has been reprinted too often. Can you think why? In Strachey's favor, compare the description of the death of Louis XIV by W. H. Lewis, especially the passage beginning "Who can say what thoughts passed through that weary old brain. . . ."

2. Amy Kelly's book on Eleanor of Aquitaine is an example of academic writing at its best. Indeed, to the extent that her style is quite personal, it probably should not be called academic at all. Since she is a historian, perhaps she should be compared to Barraclough, especially in approach to material. How would you describe the way she views her subject or the business of writing history? Note the paragraph beginning "The great assembly hall where the duchess once held her courts of love is now used as an antechamber to justice. . . ." How would you rate it alongside the comparable paragraphs in Strachey and Lewis?

3. One of Strachey's curious characteristics as a writer is his use of clichés. Presumably he must have been aware of them, but what he intended I have never been able to see. Here, for example, the figure in the

first sentence is certainly a worn one. And what other first-rate writer would couple *evening* and *golden,* especially when *golden* doesn't mean a color? Then the country is *involved* in war, disasters are *bloody,* the nation is *shaken,* the Queen's spirit is *high,* and so forth. How many other examples can you find?

4. Strachey is described briefly by Keynes, and his work is mentioned by Forster. Can you get a single impression of him?

5. What is the effect of Cooke's first sentence? Note "quite a battle going on," and also that the house is modest and on a side street. What is the connection, in tone, between this sentence and the last one?

6. There were, Cooke says, two or three hundred people in the crowd. Can you think why he asks us to look only at the man in a leather windbreaker and the two teen-age girls?

7. Study Cobbett's analysis of the defeat of Fox over Catholic Emancipation. What characteristics of Cobbett's style here might justify Arnold's criticism that is quoted in the introduction? Read some of Arnold, then compare his and Cobbett's styles.

INTERLUDE

For the following breather no proper headnote is necessary. Enjoy it.

HERE, DEAR LIBRARY, ARE THE PAPERS

Stanley Walker

(*Author's Note to the Librarian of Congress: The following collection of documents was made in response to your letter suggesting that unless some other disposition has already been agreed upon, I bequeath my "papers" to the Library of Congress.*)

Gladly, sir, in memory of the great patron, Thomas Jefferson,
Do I give, devise, and bequeath these historic documents.

Use them as you please, for no strings are tied to this bequest.
Collate them, annotate them, and let the scholars paw them.

They shed a curious light upon the dark crannies of our time,
And thinkers now unborn will gasp, "Could such things be?"

They are the fruits of a long lifetime, and they repose
In an old shoe box, bound with a frayed hangman's noose.

When I die (maybe soon, maybe not), they all go to you,
To have and to hold in perpetuity. And this is what they are:

A note from Henry L. Mencken written in the spring of 1946: "What's this I hear? So you have gone home to Texas, leaving New York desolate. One report is that you are scheming to restore the old Republic of Texas and make yourself President, or Dictator. Another is that you are engaged in breeding freak animals for zoos and circuses. All this is very disturbing. Please enlighten me."

An appeal, in pencil, written on ruled paper, from an old cowhand serving a life term in Arizona State Prison: "I do not like it around here. They treat me fine, but it is all very boring. Don't you think it's about time you got me out?"

Memorandum on an envelope dated August, 1935, at Great Neck, Long Island: "Don Skene and John McNulty, who are resting in my house, spent most of the afternoon quarrelling. They do not like each other. They almost fought when Skene advanced the idea that 'We can sleep all day tomorrow' is the finest sentence in the English language. McNulty held out for 'No date has been set for the wedding.'"

Part of a letter from an old Denver editor, apparently referring to the failure of some miscreants to obtain clemency: "After all, you can't really blame the Governor. Remember these boys killed eight Mormons before breakfast."

A haunting sentence picked up in the lobby of the Paso Del Norte Hotel, in El Paso, in 1937, and recorded on a piece of hotel stationery: "There were these two brothers and they were bachelors and they had onions on both sides of the river."

Sentiment, by an author unknown to me, found written on a menu at Arnaud's Restaurant, in New Orleans: "This funny old Cajun named Quimper came down with a case of distemper."

Memorandum of a snatch of literary criticism overheard during a discussion of a new popular novelist in the Lafayette Restaurant, in New York, in 1933: "There are only two things wrong with his writing. He makes an unfortunate choice of words and then the bum places them in infelicitous juxtaposition."

Message on a Western Union blank from an unidentified informer: "This fellow fancies himself a cosmopolite and a social success because he knows that the M.-P. in the name of Grayson M.-P. Murphy stands for Mallet-Prevost. That's all he knows."

Verbatim quote, taken down on the spot, from a broad-hatted nabob who was getting off the Santa Fe's Texas Chief at Houston: "It's been a hard day all around. First, my wife's pet kangaroo has to go and get poisoned, and then somebody stole my midget butler's stepladder."

Excerpt from a letter from Chicago dealing with an acquaintance who had just died: "Well, he's gone. Somehow I'll miss him. He sang a beautiful tenor, but he was crazy as a peach-orchard boar."

Anonymous missive from someone, apparently not an admirer, in Atlanta, Georgia: "You cad! May your hair turn green and your eyeteeth dissolve in sheep dip. You are so lowdown you would rob a widow's bee tree."

Taunting postcard from a detective friend, addressed to me at the *Herald Tribune* (when I was its city editor) and postmarked Fairbanks, Alaska: "So you can't find Judge Crater, eh? I didn't think you could. But don't feel bad about it. I can't find him either."

Transcribed remarks of an aged barber at the Astor, who cut my hair while I was on a visit to New York, in March, 1956: "You remember Fritz Gutman? Used to have the first chair. Been here since the place opened, in 1904. Dead now. Guess you want to know what his last words were. Yes? Well, he was dying in the bedroom of his home, out in Queens. Cancer. Been in a coma for a day or two. You remember a big motion-picture man named Bernstein? Used to stay at the Astor when he was in town. He'd always have Fritz Gutman come up to his room to work on him. Tipped him big—maybe ten dollars a visit. Fritz thought a lot of him. Well, all of sudden, Fritz came out of his coma, and woke up and called to his wife, Emma—for that's her name. 'Emma,' he said, 'bring me my razor and my strop and the mug with my name on it and some witch hazel. I must go upstairs now to see Mr. Bernstein.' Then he died."

Letter from a Philadelphia dowager, written the morning after a lively party in the Warwick Hotel, in that city: "There is something about Philadelphia social life which I think you should understand. It seems that every time a Biddle gets drunk, he thinks he's a Cadwalader."

Note from William Muldoon, the aged Solid Man, written from his training camp in Westchester County shortly before his death: "The trouble with life, my young friend, is that when you get old enough to know what to do you are too old to do it."

Notation of a comment made by W. O. McGeehan, the sportswriter, concerning an editor for whom he had a low regard: "I think he has often really tried to fight the s.o.b. that's in him. It's no use. He's hopelessly overmatched."

And that, beloved Library of Congress, seems to be the crop;
Use it, pray, for the enrichment of the American Way of Life.

⸙ GEORGE BERNARD SHAW

A writer in the Times Literary Supplement *speaks of Shaw's "superb prose." The adjective is not unjust, nor is the encomium that follows: it is "a prose unmatched in our time for eloquence and that yet speaks itself, a prose that never breaks under the burden of thought and that can flash into intellectual indignation as beautifully as it can soar into moral passion." The selection here is intended to give you some taste of Shaw's style as it appears in works done under different circumstances and for different occasions. A full sample would, of course, have included something from one of the Prefaces, and you should at least read the Prefaces in the two volumes of* Plays Pleasant and Unpleasant, *in the second of which* Candida *was published.*

PREFACE TO LONDON
MUSIC IN 1888–89

When my maiden novel, called Immaturity, was printed fifty years after it was written, I prefaced it with some account of the unhappy-go-lucky way in which I was brought up, ending with the nine years of shabby genteel destitution during which my attempts to gain a footing in literature were a complete and apparently hopeless failure.

I was rescued from this condition by William Archer, who transferred some of his book reviewing work to me, and pushed me into a post as picture critic which had been pushed on him, and for which he considered himself unqualified, as in fact he was. So, as reviewer for the old Pall Mall Gazette and picture critic for Edmund Yates's then fashionable

REPRINTED by permission of The Public Trustee and The Society of Authors, London.

weekly, The World, I carried on until I found an opening which I can explain only by describing the musical side of my childhood, to which I made only a passing allusion in my Immaturity preface, but which was of cardinal importance in my education.

In 1888, I being then 32 and already a noted critic and political agitator, the Star newspaper was founded under the editorship of the late T. P. O'Connor (nicknamed Tay Pay by Yates), who had for his very much more competent assistant the late H. W. Massingham. Tay Pay survived until 1936; but his mind never advanced beyond the year 1865, though his Fenian sympathies and his hearty detestation of the English nation disguised that defect from him. Massingham induced him to invite me to join the political staff of his paper; but as I had already, fourteen years before Lenin, read Karl Marx, and was preaching Socialism at every street corner or other available forum in London and the provinces, the effect of my articles on Tay Pay may be imagined. He refused to print them, and told me that, man alive, it would be five hundred years before such stuff would become practical political journalism. He was too good-natured to sack me; and I did not want to throw away my job; so I got him out of his difficulty by asking him to let me have two columns a week for a feuilleton on music. He was glad to get rid of my politics on these terms; but he stipulated that—musical criticism being known to him only as unreadable and unintelligible jargon—I should, for God's sake, not write about Bach in B Minor. I was quite alive to that danger: in fact I had made my proposal because I believed I could make musical criticism readable even by the deaf. Besides, my terms were moderate: two guineas a week.

I was strong on the need for signed criticism written in the first person instead of the journalistic "we"; but as I then had no name worth signing, and G. B. S. meant nothing to the public, I had to invent a fantastic personality with something like a foreign title. I thought of Count di Luna (a character in Verdi's Trovatore), but finally changed it for Corno di Bassetto, as it sounded like a foreign title, and nobody knew what a corno di bassetto was.

As a matter of fact the corno di bassetto is not a foreigner with a title but a musical instrument called in English the basset horn. It is a wretched instrument, now completely snuffed out for general use by the bass clarinet. It would be forgotten and unplayed if it were not that Mozart has scored for it in his Requiem, evidently because its peculiar watery melancholy, and the total absence of any richness or passion in its tone, is just the thing for a funeral. Mendelssohn wrote some chamber music for it, presumably to oblige somebody who played it; and it is kept alive by these works and by our Mr Whall. If I had ever heard a note of it in 1888 I should not have selected it for a character which I intended to be sparkling. The devil himself could not make a basset horn sparkle.

For two years I sparkled every week in The Star under this ridiculous name, and in a manner so absolutely unlike the conventional musical criticism of the time that all the journalists believed that the affair was a huge joke, the point of which was that I knew nothing whatever about music. How it had come about that I was one of the few critics of that time who really knew their business I can explain only by picking up the thread of autobiography which I dropped in my scrappy prefix to Immaturity. For the sake of those who have not read the Immaturity preface, or have forgotten it, I shall have to repeat here some of my father's history, but only so far as is necessary to explain the situation of my mother.

Technically speaking I should say she was the worst mother conceivable, always, however, within the limits of the fact that she was incapable of unkindness to any child, animal, or flower, or indeed to any person or thing whatsoever. But if such a thing as a maternity welfare centre had been established or even imagined in Ireland in her time, and she had been induced to visit it, every precept of it would have been laughably strange to her. Though she had been severely educated up to the highest standard for Irish "carriage ladies" of her time, she was much more like a Trobriand islander as described by Mr Malinowski than like a modern Cambridge lady graduate in respect of accepting all the habits, good or bad, of the Irish society in which she was brought up as part of an uncontrollable order of nature. She went her own way with so complete a disregard and even unconsciousness of convention and scandal and prejudice that it was impossible to doubt her good faith and innocence; but it never occurred to her that other people, especially children, needed guidance or training, or that it mattered in the least what they ate and drank or what they did as long as they were not actively mischievous. She accepted me as a natural and customary phenomenon, and took it for granted that I should go on occurring in that way. In short, living to her was not an art: it was something that happened. But there were unkind parts of it that could be avoided; and among these were the constraints and tyrannies, the scoldings and browbeatings and punishments she had suffered in her childhood as the method of her education. In her righteous reaction against it she reached a negative attitude in which, having no substitute to propose, she carried domestic anarchy as far as in the nature of things it can be carried.

She had been tyrannously taught French enough to recite one or two of Lafontaine's fables; to play the piano the wrong way; to harmonize by rule from Logier's Thoroughbass; to sit up straight and speak and dress and behave like a lady, and an Irish lady at that. She knew nothing of the value of money nor of housekeeping nor of hygiene nor of anything that could be left to servants or governesses or parents or solicitors or apothecaries or any other member of the retinue, indoor and outdoor, of a country house. She had great expectations from a humpbacked little aunt, a fairy-like creature with a will of iron, who had brought up her motherless niece with a firm determination to make her a paragon of good breeding, to achieve a distinguished marriage for her, and to leave her all her money as a dowry.

Manufacturing destinies for other people is a dangerous game. Its results are usually as unexpected as those of a first-rate European war. When my mother came to marriageable age her long widowed father married again. The brother of his late wife, to whom he was considerably in debt, disapproved so strongly that on learning the date of the approaching ceremony from my mother he had the bridegroom arrested on his way to church. My grandfather naturally resented this manoeuvre, and in his wrath could not be persuaded that his daughter was not my granduncle's accomplice in it. Visits to relatives in Dublin provided a temporary refuge for her; and the affair would have blown over but for the intervention of my father.

My father was a very ineligible suitor for a paragon with great expectations. His family pretensions were enormous; but they were founded on many generations of younger sons, and were purely psychological. He had managed to acquire a gentlemanly post in the law courts. This post had been abolished and its holder pensioned. By selling the pension he was enabled to start in business as a wholesaler in the corn trade (retail trade was beneath his family dignity) of which he knew nothing. He accentuated this deficiency by becoming the partner of a Mr Clibborn, who had served an apprenticeship to the cloth trade. Their combined ignorances kept the business going, mainly by its own inertia, until they and it died. Many years after this event I paid a visit of curiosity to Jervis St., Dublin; and there, on one of the pillars of a small portico, I found the ancient inscription "Clibborn & Shaw" still decipherable, as it were on the tombs of the Pharaohs. I cannot believe that this business yielded my father at any time more than three or four hundred a year; and it got less as time went on, as that particular kind of business was dying a slow death throughout the latter half of the nineteenth century.

My father was in principle an ardent teetotaller. Nobody ever felt the disgrace and misery and endless mischief of drunkenness as he did: he impressed it so deeply on me in my earliest years that I have been a teetotaller ever since. Unfortunately his conviction in this matter was founded on personal experience. He was the victim of a drink neurosis which cropped up in his family from time to time: a miserable affliction, quite unconvivial, and accompanied by torments of remorse and shame.

My father was past forty, and no doubt had sanguine illusions as to the future of his newly acquired business when he fell in love with my mother and was emboldened by her expectations and his business hopes to propose to her just at the moment when marriage seemed her only way of escape from an angry father and a stepmother. Immediately all her relatives, who had tolerated this middle-aged gentleman as a perfectly safe acquaintance with an agreeable vein of humor, denounced him as a notorious drunkard. My mother, suspicious of this sudden change of front, put the question directly to my father. His eloquence and sincerity convinced her that he was, as he claimed to be, and as he was in principle, a bigoted teetotaller. She married him; and her disappointed and infuriated aunt disinherited her, not foreseeing that the consequences of the marriage would include so remarkable a phenomenon as myself.

When my mother was disillusioned, and found out what living on a few hundreds a year with three children meant, even in a country where a general servant could be obtained for eight pounds a year, her condition must have been about as unhappy and her prospects as apparently hopeless as her aunt could have desired even in her most vindictive moments.

But there was one trump in her hand. She was fond of music, and had a mezzo-soprano voice of remarkable purity of tone. In the next street to ours, Harrington Street, where the houses were bigger and more fashionable than in our little by-street, there was a teacher of singing, lamed by an accident in childhood which had left one of his legs shorter than the other, but a man of mesmeric vitality and force. He was a bachelor living with his brother, whom he supported and adored, and a terrible old woman who was his servant of all work. His name was George John Vandaleur Lee, known in Dublin as Mr G. J. Lee. Singing lessons were cheap in Dublin; and my mother went to Lee to learn how to sing properly. He trained her voice to such purpose that she became indispensable to him as an amateur prima donna. For he was a most magnetic conductor and an indefatigable organizer of concerts, and later on of operas, with such amateur talent, vocal and orchestral, as he could discover and train in Dublin, which, as far as public professional music was concerned, was, outside the churches, practically a vacuum.

Lee soon found his way into our house, first by giving my mother lessons there, and then by using our drawing-room for rehearsals. I can only guess that the inadequacies of old Ellen in the Harrington Street house, and perhaps the incompatibilities of the brother, outweighed the comparative smallness of our house in Synge Street. My mother soon became not only prima donna and chorus leader but general musical factotum in the whirlpool of Lee's activity. Her grounding in Logier's Thoroughbass enabled her to take boundless liberties with composers. When authentic band parts were missing she thought nothing of making up an orchestral accompaniment of her own from the pianoforte score. Lee, as far as I know, had never seen a full orchestral score in his life: he conducted from a first violin part or from the vocal score, and had not, I think, any decided notion of orchestration as an idiosyncratic and characteristic part of a composer's work. He had no scholarship according to modern ideas; but he could do what Wagner said is the whole duty of a conductor: he could give the right time to the band; and he could pull it out of its amateur difficulties in emergencies by sheer mesmerism. Though he could not, or at any rate within my hearing never did sing a note, his taste in singing was classically perfect. In his search for the secret of *bel canto* he had gone to all the teachers within his reach. They told him that there was a voice in the head, a voice in the throat, and a voice in the chest. He dissected birds, and, with the connivance of medical friends, human subjects, in his search for these three organs. He then told the teachers authoritatively that the three voices were fabulous, and that the voice was produced by a single instrument called the larynx. They replied that musical art had nothing to do with anatomy, and that for a musician to practise dissection was unheard-of and disgusting. But as, tested by results, their efforts to teach their pupils to screech like locomotive whistles not only outraged his ear but wrecked the voices and often the health of their victims, their practice was as unacceptable to him as their theory.

Thus Lee became the enemy of every teacher of singing in Dublin; and they reciprocated heartily. In this negative attitude he was left until, at the opera, he heard an Italian baritone named Badeali, who at the age of 80, when he first discovered these islands, had a perfectly preserved voice, and, to Lee's taste, a perfectly produced one. Lee, thanks to his dissections, listened with a clear knowledge of what a larynx is really like. The other vocal organs and their action were obvious and conscious. Guided by this knowledge, and by his fine ear, his fastidious taste, and his instinct, he found out what Badeali was doing when he was singing. The other teachers were interested in Badeali only because one of his accomplishments was to drink a glass of wine and sing a sustained note at the same time. Finally Lee equipped himself with a teaching method which became a religion for him: the only religion, I may add, he ever professed. And my mother, as his pupil, learnt and embraced this musical faith, and rejected all other creeds as uninteresting superstitions. And it did not fail her; for she lived to be Badeali's age and kept her voice without a scrape on it until the end.

I have to dwell on The Method, as we called it in the family, because my mother's association with Lee, and the *ménage à trois* in which it resulted, would be unpleasantly misunderstood without this clue to it. For after the death of Lee's brother, which affected him to the verge of suicide, we left our respective houses and went to live in the same house, number one Hatch Street, which was half in Lower Leeson Street. The arrangement was economical; for we could not afford to live in a fashionable house, and Lee could not afford to give lessons in an unfashionable one, though, being a bachelor, he needed only a music room and a bedroom. We also shared a cottage in Dalkey, high up on Torca Hill, with all Dublin Bay from Dalkey Island to Howth visible from the garden, and all Killiney Bay with the Wicklow mountains in the background from the hall door. Lee bought this cottage and presented it to my mother, though she never had any legal claim to it and did not benefit by its sale later on. It was not conveniently situated for rehearsals or lessons; but there were musical neighbors who allowed me to some extent to run in and out of their houses when there was music going on.

The *ménage à trois*, alternating between Hatch St. and Dalkey, worked in its ramshackle way quite smoothly until I was fifteen or thereabouts, when Lee went to London and our family broke up into fragments that never got pieced together again.

In telling the story so far, I have had to reconstruct the part of it which occurred before I came into it and began, as my nurse put it, to take notice. I can remember the ante-Lee period in Synge St. when my father, as sole chief of the household, read family prayers and formally admitted that we had done those things which we ought not to have done and left undone those things which we ought to have done, which was certainly true as far as I was personally concerned. He added that there was no health in us; and this also was true enough about myself; for Dr. Newland, our apothecary, was in almost continual attendance to administer cathartics; and when I had a sore throat I used to hold out for sixpence before submitting to a mustard plaster round my neck. We children (I had two sisters older than myself and no brother) were abandoned entirely to the servants, who, with the exception of Nurse Williams, who was a good and honest woman, were utterly unfit to be trusted with the charge of three cats, much less three children. I had my meals in the kitchen, mostly of stewed beef, which I loathed, badly cooked potatoes, sound or diseased as the case might be, and much too much tea out of brown delft teapots left to "draw" on the hob until it was pure tannin. Sugar I stole. I was never hungry, because my father, often insufficiently fed in his childhood, had such a horror of child hunger that he insisted on unlimited bread and butter being always within our reach. When I was troublesome a servant thumped me on the head until one day, greatly daring, I rebelled, and, on finding her collapse abjectly, became thenceforth uncontrollable. I hated the servants and liked my mother because, on the one or two rare and delightful occasions when she buttered my bread for me, she buttered it thickly instead of merely wiping a knife on it. Her almost complete neglect of me had the advantage that I could idolize her to the utmost pitch of my imagination and had no sordid or disillusioning contacts with her. It was a privilege to be taken for a walk or a visit with her, or on an excursion.

My ordinary exercise whilst I was still too young to be allowed out by myself was to be taken out by a servant, who was supposed to air me on the banks of the canal or round the fashionable squares where the atmosphere was esteemed salubrious and the surroundings gentlemanly. Actually she took me into the slums to visit her private friends, who dwelt in squalid tenements. When she met a generous male acquaintance who insisted on treating her she took me into the public house bars, where I was regaled with lemonade and gingerbeer; but I did not enjoy these treats, because my father's eloquence on the evil of drink had given me an impression that a public house was a wicked place into which I should not have been taken. Thus were laid the foundations of my lifelong hatred of poverty, and the devotion of all my public life to the task of exterminating the poor and rendering their resurrection for ever impossible.

Note, by the way, that I should have been much more decently brought up if my parents had been too poor to afford servants.

As to early education I can remember our daily governess, Miss Hill, a needy lady who seemed to me much older than she can really have been.

She puzzled me with her attempts to teach me to read; for I can remember no time at which a page of print was not intelligible to me, and can only suppose that I was born literate. She tried to give me and my two sisters a taste for poetry by reciting "Stop; for thy tread is on an empire's dust" at us, and only succeeded, poor lady, in awakening our sense of derisive humor. She punished me by little strokes with her fingers that would not have discomposed a fly, and even persuaded me that I ought to cry and feel disgraced on such occasions. She gave us judgment books and taught us to feel jubilant when after her departure we could rush to the kitchen crying "No marks today" and to hang back ashamed when this claim could not be substantiated. She taught me to add, subtract, and multiply, but could not teach me division, because she kept saying two into four, three into six, and so forth without ever explaining what the word "into" meant in this connection. This was explained to me on my first day at school; and I solemnly declare that it was the only thing I ever learnt at school. However, I must not complain; for my immurement in that damnable boy prison effected its real purpose of preventing my being a nuisance to my mother at home for at least half a day.

The only other teaching I had was from my clerical Uncle William George (surnamed Carroll) who, being married to one of my many maternal aunts (my father had no end of brothers and sisters), had two boys of his own to educate, and took me on with them for awhile in the early mornings to such purpose that when his lessons were ended by my being sent to school, I knew more Latin grammar than any other boy in the First Latin Junior, to which I was relegated. After a few years in that establishment I had forgotten most of it, and, as aforesaid, learnt nothing; for there was only the thinnest pretence of teaching anything but Latin and Greek, if asking a boy once a day in an over-crowded class the Latin for a man or a horse or what not, can be called teaching him Latin. I was far too busy educating myself out of school by reading every book I could lay hands on, and clambering all over Killiney hill looking at the endless pictures nature painted for me, meanwhile keeping my mind busy by telling myself all sorts of stories, to puzzle about my vocabulary lesson, as the punishments were as futile as the teaching. At the end of my schooling I knew nothing of what the school professed to teach; but I was a highly educated boy all the same. I could sing and whistle from end to end leading works by Handel, Haydn, Mozart, Beethoven, Rossini, Bellini, Donizetti and Verdi. I was saturated with English literature, from Shakespear and Bunyan to Byron and Dickens. And I was so susceptible to natural beauty that, having had some glimpse of the Dalkey scenery on an excursion, I still remember the moment when my mother told me that we were going to live there as the happiest of my life.

And all this I owed to the meteoric impact of Lee, with his music, his method, his impetuous enterprise and his magnetism, upon the little Shaw household where a thoroughly disgusted and disillusioned woman was

suffering from a hopelessly disappointing husband and three uninteresting children grown too old to be petted like the animals and birds she
was so fond of, to say nothing of the humiliating inadequacy of my
father's income. We never felt any affection for Lee; for he was too excessively unlike us, too completely a phenomenon, to rouse any primitive
human feeling in us. When my mother introduced him to me, he played
with me for the first and last time; but as his notion of play was to decorate
my face with moustaches and whiskers in burnt cork in spite of the most
furious resistance I could put up, our encounter was not a success; and
the defensive attitude in which it left me lasted, though without the
least bitterness, until the decay of his energies and the growth of mine
put us on more than equal terms. He never read anything except Tyndall
on Sound, which he kept in his bedroom for years. He complained that
an edition of Shakespear which I lent him was incomplete because it did
not contain The School for Scandal, which for some reason he wanted to
read; and when I talked of Carlyle he understood me to mean the Vice-
roy of that name who had graciously attended his concerts in the Antient
Concert Rooms. Although he supplanted my father as the dominant factor
in the household, and appropriated all the activity and interest of my
mother, he was so completely absorbed in his musical affairs that there
was no friction and hardly any intimate personal contacts between the
two men: certainly no unpleasantness. At first his ideas astonished us. He
said that people should sleep with their windows open. The daring of this
appealed to me; and I have done so ever since. He ate brown bread instead of white: a startling eccentricity. He had no faith in doctors, and
when my mother had a serious illness took her case in hand unhesitatingly
and at the end of a week or so gave my trembling father leave to call in
a leading Dublin doctor, who simply said, "My work is done" and took
his hat. As to the apothecary and his squills, he could not exist in Lee's
atmosphere; and I was never attended by a doctor again until I caught
the smallpox in the epidemic of 1881. He took no interest in pictures or
in any art but his own; and even in music his interest was limited to
vocal music: I did not know that such things as string quartets or symphonies existed until I began, at sixteen, to investigate music for myself.
Beethoven's sonatas and the classical operatic overtures were all I knew
of what Wagner called absolute music. I should be tempted to say that
none of us knew of the existence of Bach were it not that my mother
sang My Heart Ever Faithful, the banjo like obbligato of which amused
me very irreverently.

Lee was like all artists whose knowledge is solely a working knowledge:
there were holes in his culture which I had to fill up for myself. Fortunately his richer pupils sometimes presented him with expensive
illustrated books. He never opened them; but I did. He was so destitute
of any literary bent that when he published a book entitled The Voice,
it was written for him by a scamp of a derelict doctor whom he entertained for that purpose, just as in later years his prospectuses and press

articles were written by me. He never visited the Dublin National Gallery, one of the finest collections of its size in Europe, with the usual full set of casts from what was called the antique, meaning ancient Greek sculpture. It was by prowling in this gallery that I learnt to recognize the work of the old masters at sight. I learnt French history from the novels of Dumas *père*, and English history from Shakespear and Walter Scott. Good boys were meanwhile learning lessons out of schoolbooks and receiving marks at examinations: a process which left them pious barbarians whilst I was acquiring an equipment which enabled me not only to pose as Corno di Bassetto when the chance arrived, but to add the criticism of pictures to the various strings I had to my bow as a feuilletonist.

Meanwhile nobody ever dreamt of teaching me anything. At fifteen, when the family broke up, I could neither play nor read a note of music. Whether you choose to put it that I was condemned to be a critic or saved from being an executant, the fact remains that when the house became musicless, I was forced to teach myself how to play written music on the piano from a book with a diagram of the keyboard in it or else be starved of music.

Not that I wanted to be a professional musician. My ambition was to be a great painter like Michael Angelo (one of my heroes); but my attempts to obtain instruction in his art at the School of Design presided over by the South Kensington Department of Science and Art only prevented me from learning anything except how to earn five shilling grants for the masters (payment by results) by filling up ridiculous examination papers in practical geometry and what they called freehand drawing.

With competent instruction I daresay I could have become a painter and draughtsman of sorts; but the School of Design convinced me that I was a hopeless failure in that direction on no better ground than that I found I could not draw like Michael Angelo or paint like Titian at the first attempt without knowing how. But teaching, of art and everything else, was and still is so little understood by our professional instructors (mostly themselves failures) that only the readymade geniuses make good; and even they are as often as not the worse for their academic contacts.

As an alternative to being a Michael Angelo I had dreams of being a Badeali. (Note, by the way, that of literature I had no dreams at all, any more than a duck has of swimming.) What that led to was not fully explained until Matthias Alexander, in search, like Lee, of a sound vocal method, invented his technique of self-control.

I had sung like a bird all through my childhood; but when my voice broke I at once fell into the error unmasked by Alexander of trying to gain my end before I had studied the means. In my attempts to reproduce the frenzies of the Count di Luna, the sardonic accents of Gounod's Mephistopheles, the noble charm of Don Giovanni, and the supernatural menace of the Commendatore, not to mention all the women's parts and the tenor parts as well (for all parts, high and low, male or female, had to be sung or shrieked or whistled or growled somehow) I thought of nothing but the dramatic characters; and in attacking them I set my jaws and my glottis as if I had to crack walnuts with them. I might have ruined my voice if I had not imitated good singers instead of bad ones; but even so the results were wretched. When I rejoined my mother in London and she found that I had taught myself to play accompaniments and to amuse myself with operas and oratorios as other youths read novels and smoke cigarets, she warned me that my voice would be spoiled if I went on like that. Thereupon I insisted on being shewn the proper way to sing. The instructive result was that when, following my mother's directions, I left my jaw completely loose, and my tongue flat instead of convulsively rolling it up; when I operated my diaphragm so as to breathe instead of "blowing"; when I tried to round up my pharynx and soft palate and found it like trying to wag my ears, I found that for the first time in my life I could not produce an audible note. It seemed that I had no voice. But I believed in Lee's plan and knew that my own was wrong. I insisted on being taught how to use my voice as if I had one; and in the end the unused and involuntary pharyngeal muscles became active and voluntary, and I developed an uninteresting baritone voice of no exceptional range which I have ever since used for my private satisfaction and exercise without damaging either it or myself in the process.

Here I must digress for a moment to point a moral. Years after I learnt how to sing without spoiling my voice and wrecking my general health, a musician-reciter (Matthias Alexander aforesaid) found himself disabled by the complaint known as clergyman's sore throat. Having the true scientific spirit and industry, he set himself to discover what it was that he was really doing to disable himself in this fashion by his efforts to produce the opposite result. In the end he found this out, and a great deal more as well. He established not only the beginnings of a far reaching science of the apparently involuntary movements we call reflexes, but a technique of correction and self-control which forms a substantial addition to our very slender resources in personal education.

Meanwhile a Russian doctor named Pavlov devoted himself to the investigation of the same subject by practising the horrible voodoo into which professional medical research had lapsed in the nineteenth century. For a quarter of a century he tormented and mutilated dogs most abominably, and finally wrote a ponderous treatise on reflexes in which he claimed to have established on a scientific basis the fact that a dog's mouth will water at the sound of a dinner bell when it is trained to associate that sound with a meal, and that dogs, if tormented, thwarted, baffled, and incommoded continuously, will suffer nervous breakdown and be miserably ruined for the rest of their lives. He was also able to describe what happens to a dog when half its brains are cut out.

What his book and its shamefully respectful reception by professional biologists does demonstrate is that the opening of the scientific professions to persons qualified for them neither by general capacity nor philosophic moral training plunges professional Science, as it has so often plunged professional Religion and Jurisprudence, into an abyss of stupidity and cruelty from which nothing but the outraged humanity of the laity can rescue it.

In the department of biology especially, the professors, mostly brought up as Fundamentalists, are informed that the book of Genesis is not a scientific document, and that the tribal idol whom Noah conciliated by the smell of roast meat is not God and never had any objective existence. They absurdly infer that the pursuit of scientific knowledge: that is, of all knowledge, is exempt from moral obligations, and consequently that they are privileged as scientists to commit the most revolting cruelties when they are engaged in research.

Their next step in this crazy logic is that no research is scientific unless it involves such cruelties. With all the infinite possibilities of legitimate and kindly research open to anyone with enough industry and ingenuity to discover innocent methods of exploration, they set up a boycott of brains and a ritual of sacrifice of dogs and guinea pigs which impresses the superstitious public as all such rituals do. Thereby they learn many things that no decent person ought to know; for it must not be forgotten that human advancement consists not only of adding to the store of human knowledge and experience but eliminating much that is burdensome and brutish. Our forefathers had the knowledge and experience gained by seeing heretics burnt at the stake and harlots whipped through the streets at the cart's tail. Mankind is better without such knowledge and experience.

If Pavlov had been a poacher he would have been imprisoned for his cruelty and despised for his moral imbecility. But as Director of the Physiological Department of the Institute of Experimental Medicine at St. Petersburg, and Professor of the Medical Academy, he was virtually forced to mutilate and torment dogs instead of discovering the methods by which humane unofficial investigators were meanwhile finding out all that he was looking for.

The reaction against this voodoo is gathering momentum; but still our rich philanthropic industrialists lavish millions on the endowment of research without taking the most obvious precautions against malversation of their gifts for the benefit of dog stealers, guinea pig breeders, laboratory builders and plumbers, and a routine of cruel folly and scoundrelism that perverts and wastes all the scientific enthusiasm that might otherwise have by this time reduced our death and disease rates to their natural minimum. I am sorry to have to describe so many highly respected gentlemen quite deliberately as fools and scoundrels; but the only definition of scoundrelism known to me is anarchism in morals; and I cannot admit that the hackneyed pleas of the dynamiter and the assassin in politics become valid in the laboratory and the hospital, or that the man who thinks they do is made any less a fool by calling him a professor of physiology.

And all this because in 1860 the men who thought they wanted to substitute scientific knowledge for superstition really wanted only to abolish God and marry their deceased wives' sisters!

I should add that there is no reason to suppose that Pavlov was by nature a bad man. He bore a strong external resemblance to myself, and was well-meaning, intelligent, and devoted to science. It was his academic environment that corrupted, stultified, and sterilized him. If only he had been taught to sing by my mother no dog need ever have collapsed in terror at his approach; and he might have shared the laurels of Alexander.

And now I must return to my story. Lee's end was more tragic than Pavlov's. I do not know at what moment he began to deteriorate. He was a sober and moderate liver in all respects; and he was never ill until he treated himself to a tour in Italy and caught malaria there. He fought through it without a doctor on cold water, and returned apparently well; but whenever he worked too hard it came back and prostrated him for a day or two. Finally his ambition undid him. Dublin in those days seemed a hopeless place for an artist; for no success counted except a London success. The summit of a provincial conductor's destiny was to preside at a local musical festival modelled on the Three Choirs or Handel Festivals. Lee declared that he would organize and conduct a Dublin Festival with his own chorus and with all the famous leading singers from the Italian opera in London. This he did in connection with an Exhibition in Dublin. My mother, of course, led the chorus. At a rehearsal the contralto, Madame de Meric Lablache, took exception to something and refused to sing. Lee shrugged his shoulders and asked my mother to carry on, which she did to such purpose that Madame Lablache took care not to give her another such chance.

At the Festivals Lee reached the Dublin limit of eminence. Nothing remained but London. He was assured that London meant a very modest beginning all over again, and perhaps something of an established position after fifteen years or so. Lee said that he would take a house in Park Lane, then the most exclusive and expensive thoroughfare in the West-end, sacred to peers and millionaires, and—stupendous on the scale of Irish finance—make his pupils pay him a guinea a lesson. And this he actually did with a success that held out quite brilliantly for several seasons and then destroyed him. For whereas he had succeeded in Dublin by the sheer superiority of his method and talent and character, training his pupils honestly for a couple of years to sing beautifully and classically, he found that the London ladies who took him up so gushingly would have none of his beauty and classicism, and would listen to nothing less than a promise to make them sing "like Patti" in twelve lessons. It was that or starve.

He submitted perforce; but he was no longer the same man, the man to whom all circumstances seemed to give way, and who made his own musical world and reigned in it. He had even to change his name and his aspect. G. J. Lee, with the black whiskers and the clean shaven resolute lip and chin, became Vandaleur Lee, whiskerless, but with a waxed and pointed moustache and an obsequious attitude. It suddenly became evident that he was an elderly man, and, to those who had known him in

Dublin, a humbug. Performances of Marchetti's Ruy Blas with my sister as the Queen of Spain, and later on of Sullivan's Patience and scraps of Faust and Il Trovatore were achieved; but musical society in London at last got tired of the damaged Svengali who could manufacture Pattis for twelve guineas; and the guineas ceased to come in. Still, as there were no night clubs in those days, it was possible to let a house in Park Lane for the night to groups of merrymakers; and Lee was holding out there without pupils when he asked me to draft a circular for him announcing that he could cure clergyman's sore throat. He was still at Park Lane when he dropped dead in the act of undressing himself, dying as he had lived, without a doctor. The postmortem and inquest revealed the fact that his brain was diseased and had been so for a long time. I was glad to learn that his decay was pathological as well as ecological, and that the old efficient and honest Lee had been real after all. But I took to heart the lesson in the value of London fashionable successes. To this day I look to the provincial and the amateur for honesty and genuine fecundity in art.

Meanwhile, what had happened to the *ménage à trois;* and how did I turn up in Park Lane playing accompaniments and getting glimpses of that art-struck side of fashionable society which takes refuge in music from the routine of politics and sport which occupies the main Philistine body?

Well, when Lee got his foot in at a country house in Shropshire where he had been invited to conduct some private performances, he sold the Dalkey cottage and concluded his tenancy of Hatch Street. This left us in a house which we could afford less than ever; for my father's moribund business was by now considerably deader than it had been at the date of my birth. My younger sister was dying of consumption caught from reckless contacts at a time when neither consumption nor pneumonia were regarded as catching. All that could be done was to recommend a change of climate. My elder sister had a beautiful voice. In the last of Lee's Dublin adventures in amateur opera she had appeared as Amina in Bellini's La Somnambula, on which occasion the tenor lost his place and his head, and Lucy obligingly sang most of his part as well as her own. Unfortunately her musical endowment was so complete that it cost her no effort to sing or play anything she had once heard, or to read any music at sight. She simply could not associate the idea of real work with music; and as in any case she had never received any sort of training, her very facility prevented her from becoming a serious artist, though, as she could sing difficult music without breaking her voice, she got through a considerable share of public singing in her time.

Now neither my mother nor any of us knew how much more is needed for an opera singer than a voice and natural musicianship. It seemed to us that as, after a rehearsal or two, she could walk on to the stage, wave her arms about in the absurd manner then in vogue in opera, and sing not only her own part but everybody else's as well, she was quite qualified to take the place of Christine Nilsson or Adelina Patti if only she could get a proper introduction. And clearly Lee, now in the first flush of his success in Park Lane, would easily be able to secure this for her.

There was another resource. My now elderly mother believed that she could renounce her amateur status and make a living in London by teaching singing. Had she not the infallible Method to impart? So she realized a little of the scrap of settled property of which her long deceased aunt had not been able to deprive her; sold the Hatch Street furniture; settled my father and myself in comfortable lodgings at 61 Harcourt St.; and took my sisters to the Isle of Wight, where the younger one died. She then took a semi-detached little villa in a *cul-de-sac* in the Fulham Road, and waited there for Lucy's plans and her own to materialize.

The result was almost a worse disillusion than her marriage. That had been cured by Lee's music: besides, my father had at last realized his dream of being a practising teetotaller, and was now as inoffensive an old gentleman as any elderly wife could desire. It was characteristic of the Shavian drink neurosis to vanish suddenly in this way. But that Lee should be unfaithful! unfaithful to The Method! that he, the one genuine teacher among so many quacks, should now stoop to outquack them all and become a moustachioed charlatan with all the virtue gone out of him: this was the end of all things; and she never forgave it. She was not unkind: she tolerated Lee the charlatan as she had tolerated Shaw the dipsomaniac because, as I guess, her early motherless privation of affection and her many disappointments in other people had thrown her back on her own considerable internal resources and developed her self-sufficiency and power of solitude to an extent which kept her up under circumstances that would have crushed or embittered any woman who was the least bit of a clinger. She dropped Lee very gently: at first he came and went at Victoria Grove, Fulham Road; and she went and came at 13 Park Lane, helping with the music there at his At Homes, and even singing the part of Donna Anna for him (elderly prima donnas were then tolerated as matters of course) at an amateur performance of Don Giovanni. But my sister, who had quarrelled with him as a child when he tried to give her piano lessons, and had never liked him, could not bear him at all in his new phase, and, when she found that he could not really advance her prospects of becoming a prima donna, broke with him completely and made it difficult for him to continue his visits. When he died we had not seen him for some years; and my mother did not display the slightest emotion at the news. He had been dead for her ever since he had ceased to be an honest teacher of singing and a mesmeric conductor.

Her plans for herself came almost to nothing for several years. She found that Englishwomen do not wish to be made to sing beautifully and classically: they want to sing erotically; and this my mother thought not only horrible but unladylike. Her love songs were those of Virginia Gabriel and Arthur Sullivan, all about bereaved lovers and ending with a hope for reunion in the next world. She could sing with perfect purity of tone and touching expression

> Oh, Ruby, my darling, the small white hand
> Which gathered the harebell was never my own.

But if you had been able to anticipate the grand march of human progress
and poetic feeling by fifty years, and asked her to sing

> You made me love you.
> I didnt want to do it.
> I didnt want to do it.

she would have asked a policeman to remove you to a third-class carriage.

Besides, though my mother was not consciously a snob, the divinity
which hedged an Irish lady of her period was not acceptable to the British
suburban parents, all snobs, who were within her reach. They liked to be
treated with deference; and it never occurred to my mother that such
people could entertain a pretension so monstrous in her case. Her practice with private pupils was negligible until she was asked to become
musical instructress at the North London College. Her success was immediate; for not only did her classes leave the other schools nowhere
musically, but the divinity aforesaid exactly suited her new rôle as school-
mistress. Other schools soon sought her services; and she remained in
request until she insisted on retiring on the ground that her age made her
public appearances ridiculous. By that time all the old money troubles
were over and forgotten, as my financial position enabled me to make her
perfectly comfortable in that respect.

And now, what about myself, the incipient Corno di Bassetto?

Well, when my mother sold the Hatch Street furniture, it never occurred to her to sell our piano, though I could not play it, nor could my
father. We did not realize, nor did she, that she was never coming back,
and that, except for a few days when my father, taking a little holiday for
the first time in his life within my experience, came to see us in London,
she would never meet him again. Family revolutions would seldom be
faced if they did not present themselves at first as temporary makeshifts.
Accordingly, having lived since my childhood in a house full of music, I
suddenly found myself in a house where there was no music, and could
be none unless I made it myself. I have recorded elsewhere how, having
purchased one of Weale's Handbooks which contained a diagram of the
keyboard and an explanation of musical notation, I began my self-tuition,
not with Czerny's five finger exercises, but with the overture to Don
Giovanni, thinking rightly that I had better start with something I knew
well enough to hear whether my fingers were on the right notes or not.
There were plenty of vocal scores of operas and oratorios in our lodging;
and although I never acquired any technical skill as a pianist, and cannot
to this day play a scale with any certainty of not foozling it, I acquired
what I wanted: the power to take a vocal score and learn its contents as
if I had heard it rehearsed by my mother and her colleagues. I could manage arrangements of orchestral music much better than piano music

proper. At last I could play the old rum-tum accompaniments of those days well enough (knowing how they *should* be played) to be more agreeable to singers than many really competent pianists. I bought more scores, among them one of Lohengrin, through which I made the revolutionary discovery of Wagner. I bought arrangements of Beethoven's symphonies, and discovered the musical regions that lie outside opera and oratorio. Later on, I was forced to learn to play the classical symphonies and overtures in strict time by hammering the bass in piano duets with my sister in London. I played Bach's Inventions and his Art of Fugue. I studied academic textbooks, and actually worked out exercises in harmony and counterpoint under supervision by an organist friend named Crament, avoiding consecutive fifths and octaves, and having not the faintest notion of what the result would sound like. I read pseudo-scientific treatises about the roots of chords which candidates for the degree of Mus. Doc. at the universities had to swallow, and learnt that Stainer's commonsense views would get you plucked at Oxford, and Ouseley's pedantries at Cambridge. I read Mozart's Succinct Thoroughbass (a scrap of paper with some helpful tips on it which he scrawled for his pupil Sussmaier); and this, many years later, Edward Elgar told me was the only document in existence of the smallest use to a student composer. It was, I grieve to say, of no use to me; but then I was not a young composer. It ended in my knowing much more about music than any of the great composers, an easy achievement for any critic, however barren. For awhile I must have become a little pedantic; for I remember being shocked, on looking up Lee's old vocal score of Don Giovanni, to find that he had cut out all the repetitions which Mozart had perpetrated as a matter of sonata form. I now see that Lee was a century before his time in this reform, and hope some day to hear a performance of Mozart's Idomeneo in which nothing is sung twice over.

When I look back on all the banging, whistling, roaring, and growling inflicted on nervous neighbors during this process of education, I am consumed with useless remorse. But what else could I have done? Today there is the wireless, which enables me to hear from all over Europe more good music in a week than I could then hear in ten years, if at all. When, after my five years' office slavery, I joined my mother in London and lived with her for twenty years until my marriage, I used to drive her nearly crazy by my favorite selections from Wagner's Ring, which to her was "all recitative," and horribly discordant at that. She never complained at the time, but confessed it after we separated, and said that she had sometimes gone away to cry. If I had committed a murder I do not think it would trouble my conscience very much; but this I cannot bear to think of. If I had to live my life over again I should devote it to the establishment of some arrangement of headphones and microphones or the like whereby the noises made by musical maniacs should be audible to themselves only. In Germany it is against the law to play the piano with the window open. But of what use is that to the people in the house? It should be made felony to play a musical instrument in any other than a completely soundproof room. The same should apply to loud speakers on pain of confiscation.

Readers with a taste for autobiography must now take my Immaturity preface and dovetail it into this sketch to complete the picture. My business here is to account for my proposal to Tay Pay and my creation of Bassetto. From my earliest recorded sign of an interest in music when as a small child I encored my mother's singing of the page's song from the first act of Les Huguenots (note that I shared Herbert Spencer's liking for Meyerbeer) music has been an indispensable part of my life. Harley Granville-Barker was not far out when, at a rehearsal of one of my plays, he cried out, "Ladies and gentlemen: will you please remember that this is Italian opera."

I reprint Bassetto's stuff shamefacedly after long hesitation with a reluctance which has been overcome only by my wife, who has found some amusement in reading it through, a drudgery which I could not bring myself to undertake. I know it was great fun when it was fresh, and that many people have a curious antiquarian taste (I have it myself) for old chronicles of dead musicians and actors. I must warn them, however, not to expect to find here the work of the finished critic who wrote my volumes entitled Music in London, 1890-94, and Our Theatres in the Nineties. I knew all that was necessary about music; but in criticism I was only a beginner. It is easy enough from the first to distinguish between what is pleasant or unpleasant, accurate or inaccurate in a performance; but when great artists have to be dealt with, only keenly analytical observation and comparison of them with artists who, however agreeable, are not great, can enable a critic to distinguish between what everybody can do and what only a very few can do, and to get his valuations right accordingly. All artsmen know what it is to be enthusiastically praised for something so easy that they are half ashamed of it, and to receive not a word of encouragement for their finest strokes.

I cannot deny that Bassetto was occasionally vulgar; but that does not matter if he makes you laugh. Vulgarity is a necessary part of a complete author's equipment; and the clown is sometimes the best part of the circus. The Star, then a hapenny newspaper, was not catering for a fastidious audience: it was addressed to the bicycle clubs and the polytechnics, not to the Royal Society of Literature or the Musical Association. I purposely vulgarized musical criticism, which was then refined and academic to the point of being unreadable and often nonsensical. Editors, being mostly ignorant of music, would submit to anything from their musical critics, not pretending to understand it. If I occasionally carried to the verge of ribaldry my reaction against the pretentious twaddle and sometimes spiteful cliquishness they tolerated in their ignorance, think of me as heading one of the pioneer columns of what was then called The New Journalism; and you will wonder at my politeness.

You may be puzzled, too, to find that the very music I was brought up on: the pre-Wagner school of formal melody in separate numbers which seemed laid out to catch the encores that were then fashionable, was treated by me with contemptuous levity as something to be swept into the dustbin as soon as possible. The explanation is that these works were standing in the way of Wagner, who was then the furiously abused coming man in London. Only his early works were known or tolerated. Half a dozen bars of Tristan or The Mastersingers made professional musicians put their fingers in their ears. The Ride of the Valkyries was played at the Promenade Concerts, and always encored, but only as an insanely rampagious curiosity. The Daily Telegraph steadily preached Wagner down as a discordant notoriety-hunting charlatan in six silk dressing-gowns, who could not write a bar of melody, and made an abominable noise with the orchestra. In pantomime harlequinades the clown produced a trombone, played a bit of the pilgrims' march from Tannhäuser fortissimo as well as he could, and said, "The music of the future!" The wars of religion were not more bloodthirsty than the discussions of the Wagnerites and the Anti-Wagnerites. I was, of course, a violent Wagnerite; and I had the advantage of knowing the music to which Wagner grew up, whereas many of the most fanatical Wagnerites (Ashton Ellis, who translated the Master's prose works, was a conspicuous example) knew no other music than Wagner's, and believed that the music of Donizetti and Meyerbeer had no dramatic quality whatever. "A few arpeggios" was the description Ellis gave me of his notion of Les Huguenots.

Nowadays the reaction is all the other way. Our young lions have no use for Wagner the Liberator. His harmonies, which once seemed monstrous cacophonies, are the commonplaces of the variety theatres. Audacious young critics disparage his grandeurs as tawdry. When the wireless strikes up the Tannhäuser overture I hasten to switch it off, though I can always listen with pleasure to Rossini's overture to William Tell, hackneyed to death in Bassetto's time. The funeral march from Die Götterdämmerung hardly keeps my attention, though Handel's march from Saul is greater than ever. Though I used to scarify the fools who said that Wagner's music was formless, I should not now think the worse of Wagner if, like Bach and Mozart, he had combined the most poignant dramatic expression with the most elaborate decorative design. It was necessary for him to smash the superstition that this was obligatory; to free dramatic melody from the tyranny of arabesques; and to give the orchestra symphonic work instead of rosalias and rum-tum; but now that this and all the other musical superstitions are in the dustbin, and the post-Wagnerian harmonic and contrapuntal anarchy is so complete that it is easier technically to compose another Parsifal than another Bach's Mass in B Minor or Don Giovanni I am no longer a combatant anarchist in music, not to mention that I have learnt that a successful revolution's first task is to shoot all revolutionists. This means that I am no longer Corno di Bassetto. He was pre- and pro-Wagner; unfamiliar with Brahms; and unaware that a young musician named Elgar was chuckling over his irreverent boutades. As to Cyril Scott, Bax, Ireland, Goossens, Bliss, Walton, Schönberg, Hindemith, or even Richard Strauss and Sibelius, their idioms would have been quite outside Bassetto's conception of music, though today they seem natural enough. Therefore I very greatly doubt whether poor old Bassetto is worth reading now. Still, you are not compelled to read him. Having read the preface you can shut the book and give it to your worst enemy as a birthday present.

MID-ATLANTIC,
Sunday, 2nd June 1935.

ON REVIEWING

Letter to R. E. Golding Bright

Private.   29 Fitzroy Square W.
                                           2nd December 1894
Dear Sir
    The best service I can do you is to take your notice and jot down on it without ceremony the comments which occur to me. You will find first certain alterations in black ink. In them I have tried to say, as well as I can off hand, what you were trying to say: that is, since it was evident you were dodging round some point or other, I have considered the only point there was to make, and have made it. It came quite easy when I had altered your statement about Frenchmen at large to what you really meant—the conventional stage Frenchman. Always find out rigidly and exactly what you mean, and never strike an attitude, whether national or moral or critical or anything else. You struck a national attitude when you wrote that about the Frenchman and Englishman; and you struck a moral attitude when you wrote "She has sunk low enough in all conscience." Get your facts right first: that is the foundation of all style, because style is the expression of yourself; and you cannot express yourself genuinely except on a basis of precise reality.
    In red ink you will find some criticisms which you may confidently take as expressing what an experienced editor would think of your sample of work.
    You have not at all taken in my recommendation to write a book. You say you are scarcely competent to write books just yet. That is just why I

recommend you to learn. If I advised you to learn to skate, you would not reply that your balance was scarcely good enough yet. A man learns to skate by staggering about and making a fool of himself. Indeed he progresses in all things by resolutely making a fool of himself. You will never write a good book until you have written some bad ones. If they have sent you my Scottish article, you will see that I began by writing some abominably bad criticisms. I wrote five long books before I started again on press work. William Archer wrote a long magnum opus on the life and works of Richard Wagner, a huge novel, and a book on the drama, besides an essay on Irving and a good deal of leader work for a Scotch paper before he began his victorious career on The World. He also perpetrated about four plays in his early days. (By the way, you mustn't publish this information). You must go through that mill too; and you can't possibly start too soon. Write a thousand words a day for the next five years for at least nine months every year. Read all the great critics— Ruskin, Richard Wagner, Lessing, Lamb and Hazlitt. Get a ticket for the British Museum reading room, and live there as much as you can. Go to all the first rate orchestral concerts and to the opera, as well as to the theatres. Join debating societies and learn to speak in public. Haunt little Sunday evening political meetings and exercise that accomplishment. Study men and politics in this way. As long as you stay in the office, try and be the smartest hand in it: I spent four and a half years in an office before I was twenty. Be a teetotaller; don't gamble; don't lend; don't borrow; don't for your life get married; make the attainment of EFFICIENCY your sole object for the next fifteen years; and if the city can teach you nothing more, or demands more time than you can spare from your apprenticeship, tell your father that you prefer to cut loose and starve, and do it. But it will take you at least a year or two of tough work before you will be able to build up for yourself either the courage or the right to take heroic measures. Finally, since I have given you all this advice, I add this crowning precept, the most valuable of all. NEVER TAKE ANY-BODY'S ADVICE.

And now, to abandon the role of your guide, philosopher and friend, which I don't propose to revert to again until you report progress in ten years or so, let me thank you for the paragraph in the Sun, which was quite right and appropriate. I have no more news at present, except that I have nearly finished a new play, the leading part in which I hope to see played by Miss Janet Achurch, of whose genius I have always had a very high opinion. It is quite a sentimental play, which I hope to find understood by women, if not by men; and it is so straightforward that I expect to find it pronounced a miracle of perversity. This is my fifth dramatic composition. The first was "Widowers' Houses" of Independent Theatre Fame. The second was "The Philanderer," a topical comedy in which the New Woman figured before Mr. Grundy discovered her. The third was "Mrs. Warren's Profession," a play with a purpose, the purpose being much the same as that of my celebrated letter to the Pall Mall

Gazette on the Empire controversy. The fourth was "Arms and the Man," which was so completely misunderstood that it made my reputation as a playwright both here and in New York. The Independent Theatre has already announced "Mrs. Warren's Profession" for its forthcoming season. "The Philanderer" was written originally for that society; but on its completion I threw it aside and wrote another more suitable for the purposes of the society—Mrs. Warren. Wyndham asked me to do something for him on seeing "Arms and the Man"; and I tried to persuade him to play The Philanderer; but whilst the project was under consideration, Wyndham made such a decisive success with "Rebellious Susan" that he resolved to follow up the vein of comedy opened by Henry Arthur Jones to the end before venturing upon the Shawian quicksand. But this involved so long a delay that I withdrew the play, and am now looking round to see whether the world contains another actor who can philander as well as Wyndham. As I have always said that if I did not write six plays before I was forty I would never write one after, I must finish the work now in hand and another as well before the 26th July 1896; but I hope to do much more than that, since I have managed to get through the present play within three months, during which I have had to take part in the Schoolboard and Vestry elections, to keep up my work in the Fabian Society, to deliver nearly two dozen lectures in London and the provinces, and to fire off various articles and criticisms. The fact is, I took a good holiday in Germany, Italy, and in Surrey; and I accumulated a stock of health which I am dissipating at a frightful rate. The Christmas holidays will come just in time to save my life.

If any of this stuff is of use to you for paragraphing purposes—and remember that the world will not stand too much Bernard Shaw—you are welcome to work it up by all means when it suits you. Only, don't quote it as having been said by me. That is an easy way out which I bar.

I find that you have got an atrociously long letter out of me. I have been blazing away on the platform this evening for an hour and a half, and ought to be in bed instead of clattering at this machine.

yours, half asleep,
G. Bernard Shaw

R. Golding Bright, Esq.
Playgoers' Club.

(Golding Bright's Review with Shaw's Comments)

"ODETTE" AT THE PRINCESS'S

When a *man* (crossed out and "stage hero" substituted by Shaw) discovers firstly a Russian Prince creeping about his drawing-room at midnight, and secondly, his wife in undress standing at her bedroom door, whispering her lover's name, what course shall he pursue? A *passionate*

Frenchman would kill the wife and fight her seducer, whilst the more phlegmatic Englishman would seek redress in the Divorce Court. (Crossed out by Shaw, and the following substituted: "If a Frenchman, he must kill his wife and fight her seducer. If an Englishman, he is permitted to seek redress in the Divorce Court.") *Lord Henry Trevene, however, elected to do neither.* (Crossed out by Shaw, and the following witty paraphrase substituted: "Lord Henry Trevene, being in the impossible position of a French stage hero translated into English, finds both these plain paths of duty barred to him.") Accordingly, he denies the justice of a law which unties the nuptial knot only as a preliminary to uniting the guilty lovers. He can see full well what his own future will be—a hopeless blank. So be it! But Odette's life shall be no better. His wife she shall remain till the end, though he will no longer tolerate her presence under the same roof. Go she must and that very night, whilst he will retain their only child, an infant daughter.

Fifteen years elapse, the child Eva has developed into a charming girl of eighteen summers, who knows nothing of the past, but has been taught to believe her mother dead. Eva is engaged to Lord Shandon, and the only bar to their mutual happiness is his mother's sanction, which can be gained by a promise from Odette never to call herself by her married name again, and never to set foot either in Paris or London. At Nice, where all the parties are stopping, Lord Henry sends an ambassador in the person of Philip Eden to induce his wife to consent to these terms. She has sunk low enough in all conscience, living in an establishment that is neither more nor less than a gambling hell kept by an American quack doctor, who never loses at cards. (Here the underlining of the first clause is clear from the letter—Shaw objected to the moral attitude expressed; what his objection was to *loses* is not clear.) In debt, in difficulties, she none the less refuses the proposal of an increased allowance on such conditions. "Sweet is revenge, especially to women." It's her turn now, and she means to make the most of it; she demands to see her child for whom her maternal instinct, though dormant, is yet alive. To this proposition, Lord Henry very weakly consents, provided that she does not reveal her identity. The interview between mother and daughter takes place, when Odette strives to awaken her child's memory to herself, and failing, leaves husband and child alone once more.

Mr. Clement Scott has been pleased to designate this a problem play, thereby seeking to prove that long before "The Second Mrs. Tanqueray" was produced, London had dealt with the subject. *Frankly, I cannot see where the problem comes in, but then I am possibly dense. Dumas fils solved the enigma with the famous 'Tue-la' of La Femme de Claude. In England, a divorce suit would have obviated all the difficulties arising from Lord Henry's silly and inexplicable behaviour.* (The three sentences deleted by Shaw, and the following substituted: "But then every play that touches real life at all is a problem play. The only question that interests us is whether it is a 'solution-of-the-problem' play. And will anyone seriously contend that the course taken by Lord Henry is a solution of the problem of how to deal with an unfaithful wife. The famous 'Tue-la' of Dumas fils is reasonable in comparison, and our own divorce court appears a quite divinely wise institution beside the silliness of Lord Henry." After which, obviously pleased with his improvements, Shaw commented: "Here, having disposed of the problem business, you must start a new paragraph, criticising the play as a play solely.") It appears to me that Sardou blundered not once but many times in the construction of his play. (Shaw's comment: "And you mustn't tell a man like Sardou that it appears to you that he has blundered: you must point out what you object to & why you object to it.") It may be that, as it was written some fifteen years ago, and produced in England under the Bancroft régime in '82, it appears stilted and old-fashioned in thought and idea; but under no circumstances can it be called a great play. (Underlining here by Shaw. His comment: "It does not pretend to be a great play. The remark is equally true of Box & Cox, which is nevertheless a very good farce. The question is, is Odette a good play of its class, and what you mean is that it isn't.") One feels instinctively that Sardou got "no forrader," *whereas Mr. Pinero with "The Second Mrs. Tanqueray" really handles a dangerous theme most delicately & infused a strain of genius into his work.* (Foregoing italicized passage crossed out by Shaw. His comment: "You must make an oath never to mention Mrs. Tanqueray again, or even think of her. The one chief and damning disability of the young critic is that he always has some pet author and pet work for whose supremacy he is mortally jealous. He becomes a knight errant indicating the superiority of his Dulcinea over all other ladies, Mrs. Tanqueray is your Dulcinea; and you will never be worth a guinea a column until you grow out of her.")

When Mrs. Anna Ruppert made her début as Camille some four months since, she won the good opinion of Mr. Clement Scott, who informed his readers that the lady *had* (crossed out by Shaw and "possessed" substituted) every quality needed for a successful stage-career. *I do not for one moment wish to set myself up* (Foregoing italicized passage crossed out by Shaw. His comment: "Yes, you do wish to set yourself up, and you are going to do it in the next line. Why shouldn't you? Why deliberately say what you don't mean?") against so distinguished a critic, but I am quite unable to side with him on this point. "*I must be cruel only to be kind*" (This italicized passage, referred to in the letter as an example of taking a moral attitude, receiving this comment from Shaw in the manuscript— it *was* a *manu*script, not a typed notice, which Bright sent him: "Never say a thing like this. There is nothing more offensive to artists—and rightly so—than to make a show of sparing their feelings. It is right to be considerate, but horribly wrong to show it") *and when I state that so far as I could discover Mrs. Ruppert showed no sign even of latent talent, it must not be assumed that I am making the lady the subject of a critical attack.* (This longish passage was crossed out by Shaw; his comment: "This unnecessary & self-conscious exculpation is awful. The public is supposed to understand a critic's position without being told.") *Au contraire,* (Crossed out, with eloquent absence of comment, by Shaw) I admire her pluck in attempting to make a success out of a play which with the alluring personality of Modjeska failed to attract. But Mrs. Ruppert is unfortunately not an actress at all. Her performance was amateurish to a fault. *She has not learned the first principles of acting.* (Crossed out by Shaw. His comment: "You mustn't talk about first principles: they don't exist. Poor Mrs. R had been drilled to within an inch of her life in 'the principles' of elocution") nor can she even tread the stage with dignity. Her voice is hard, unsympathetic and monotonous, (Shaw's comment: "Now we are coming to something sensible. You are quite entitled to describe her voice: that is quite a different thing to talking about 'the principles of elocution & acting' ") and her *tragic* (Crossed out by Shaw) pathos is deliciously comic. She no more realized the light and shade of Odette's nature than would a schoolgirl appreciate the hidden beauty and poetry of Ophelia or the *sublime tragedy of Mrs. Tanqueray.* (Crossed out by Shaw. His comment: "No, Reginald, no. Not again.") In taking to the stage, Mrs. Ruppert has clearly mistaken her vocation, *and the sooner she realizes this fact the better it will be for her pocket.* (Foregoing crossed out by Shaw. His comment: "It is no part of a dramatic critic's business to make such a remark, which would have been equally true of a fine actress playing the best sort of dramatic poetry.") If the leading lady be weak, however, the rest of the company certainly are not. One piece of acting stands out most vividly, and may possibly drag the play into the quiet waters of success. The audience, annoyed by the incompetence of the manageress, readily appreciated Mr. Charles Warner's skilful impersonation of Lord Henry. We have been too apt to regard this actor as a breezy hero of melodrama only, but last night Mr. Warner proved how mistaken we all were, by playing this trying and difficult part, which is almost wholly in one key, to perfection. (Last word underlined by Shaw. His comment: "Rather strong, eh? It leaves no room for Salvini, or Irving.") *Undoubtedly* (Crossed out by Shaw. His comment: " 'Undoubtedly' is not the right way to put it. Many other critics doubted it and ridiculed it. You mean that it *seemed to you* one of the finest &c &c—") it is one of the very finest things he has ever done, worthy of a place next his hauntingly terrible Coupeau. Here and there, perchance, one could detect a false *emphasis* (Crossed out by Shaw, and "note" substituted), a misplaced emphasis; but the whole was so excellent, and played with so firm a grip and manly (never degenerating to maudlin) pathos, that such slight excrescences may readily be condoned. (Underlining by Shaw. His comment: "Now here you are saying something definite—you are writing criticism—you are describing what you saw. Don't you feel how much better it is than mere pompous and unmeaning phrase slinging like 'Undoubtedly it is one of the finest things he has done &c'?") Scarcely less deserving of praise was the cynic Johnny Stratford, sustained with rare skill (Shaw's comment: "This is all right— quite presentable.") and a keen eye for artistic effect by Mr. Bernard

Fourth, the only good line of pure rhetoric in Mrs Siddons's style:—

"Fear not: I'm empty of all things but grief."

Only, Shakespear, like an ass, spoils that line by adding, in words, all that the delivery of the line itself ought to convey. The words "Thy master is not there, who was, indeed, the riches of it" should not be spoken. If anyone says you left them out you can retort "I did not speak them; but I did not leave them out."

If you utter all that rubbish about false Æneas and Dido's weeping, I will rise, snatch the nearest family Shakespear, solemnly throw it at your head, and leave the theatre. The moment Pisanio says "Good Madam, hear me," cut him short with "Come, fellow, be thou honest"; and say it with something of the deep admonition which makes me remember your "Shylock: there's thrice thy money offered thee" since years and years ago. And when you have fairly started cutting the miserable attorney's rhetoric out of the scene, do it with a bold hand. Dont trouble about the Paragonese "Some jay of Italy" stuff, or the wretched impossible logic chopping. And oh, my God, dont read the letter. You *cant* read it: no woman could read it out to a servant. (Oh what a DAMNED fool Shakespear was!) You must manage it in this way. In the second scene of the third act, let Pisanio begin by reading the letter, from "Thy mistress, Pisanio, hath played the strumpet, etc." down to "lie bleeding in me." Then let him break off and exclaim "How! of adultery!" etc. down to "O my master, thy mind to her is now as low as were thy fortunes!" Then let him resume the reading of the letter to the end, when he will find himself with just the right cue for "How! That I should murder her . . . I! her! . . ." and so on. The audience will not forget what is in the letter after that; and when Pisanio hands it to you in the fourth scene, you can *play* the reading of it with the certainty that the audience will have the clue in their imaginations burning hot. The pantomime will be easy for you—it goes this way—the horrible shock of the first sentence—"*I* false!"—then the slow, significant look at Pisanio, the man who is to kill you (it is the majesty of death that raises you for a moment from your horror)—then the return to the subject of the accusation and the slipping away of consciousness. Then cut all the rubbish out of the scene which follows, thus:—

P. What shall I need to draw my sword? The paper
   Hath cut her throat already. What cheer, madam?
I. False to his bed, etc. (the whole speech uncut)
P. Alas, good lady (Imogen has nothing to do with this speech and
   should go straight on without hearing it)
I. *I* false! Thy conscience witness, Iachimo. (Everything can be conveyed in these 4 words)
P. Good madam, hear me—
I. (Turning on him with solemn sternness)

Come, fellow, be thou honest.
Do thou thy master's bidding, etc. etc. (the whole speech uncut)
P.   Hence, vile instrument
Thou shalt not damn my hand.
I.   (Sharply, not much impressed by his rhetoric at such a pass)
                                                    Why, I must die;
And if I do not by thy hand, thou art
No servant of thy master's. Prythee despatch.
The lamb entreats the butcher: where's thy knife, etc. etc.

All this will mean an intolerable load off your memory and off the real side of Imogen. Archer will complain in The World of the violation of the Bard's integrity; and I will declare in The Saturday Review that your dramatic instinct and delicacy of feeling have never guided you more unerringly than in rescuing the live bits of Imogen from the bombazine trappings of the Bishop's wife.

There is another point which puzzles me—in that other big scene— that nice Elizabethan morsel of the woman waking up in the arms of a headless corpse. I cannot for the life of me follow the business of that long speech without getting the words "A headless man" in the wrong place. For instance, you wake up, you sit up, half awake, and think you are asking the way to Milford Haven—*the blessed Milford,* since for the moment you have forgotten your unhappines. You lie down to sleep again, and in doing so touch the body of Cloten, whose head (or no head) is presumably muffled in a cloak. In your dim, half asleep funny state of consciousness, you still have the idea that you mustnt go to bed with anybody else but Posthumus, and you say "But soft, no bedfellow." Then in rousing yourself sufficiently to get away from this vaguely ap- prehended person, you awaken a little more at this very odd, dreamlike thing, that the bedfellow is covered with flowers. You take up a flower, still puzzly-dreamy, and look curiously at it. It is *bloody,* and then in an instant you are broad awake—"Oh gods and goddesses!" etc. But it is quite clear that you must not know that "this bloody man" is headless, as that would utterly spoil the point later on. He looks simply as if he had swathed his head in his cloak to sleep in. It is the blood under the flowers that makes him so horrible to be alone with. When you utter the prayer "If there be yet left in heaven as small a drop of pity as a wren's eye, feared gods, give me a part of it," I suppose you kneel and cover your eyes with your hands in the hope that when you remove them your prayer will be answered and the nightmare gone. You take down your hands and dare to look again. "The dream's here still. Even when I wake it is without me and within me, not imagined—felt." Now in the text, what follows is "A headless man!" That is what I cannot understand; and I believe it is an overlooked relic of some earlier arrangement of the business. For see how it plays if you omit it. Your attention is caught by the garment of Posthumus; you go on with the recognition step by step (confound those classical allusions; but they cant be helped); at last you lift the cloak to see the face, and then—"Murder in Heaven!" you go tearing, screaming, raging mad and rave your way to the swoon as best you can (a nice thing to play every night for 100 nights). But if you leave in the words "A headless man" the sequel is spoiled, and you are represented as being surprised at finding no face on a man, who, as you have already observed, has lost his whole head. Therefore, I submit that the "headless man" sentence must be left out.

These, dear madam, are the only ideas I have on the subject of Imogen. I daresay you know your own business better than I do; but no matter; your consciousness of your own view will only become more definite and determined if it contradicts everybody else's.

So you see I have no objection whatever to an intelligent cutting out of the dead and false bits of Shakespear. But when you propose to cut me, I am paralyzed at your sacrilegious audacity. I always cut myself to the bone, reading the thing over and over until I have discovered the bits that cant be made to play-act anyhow. *All* of Napoleon can be done if only the right touch is found. If a single comma is omitted, that will be because the actor has been beaten by the author. And I always like to beat the actor, and to beat the public, *a little*: it is the only way to keep screwing up the standard. I own I have certain misgivings about H. I. as Napoleon. Swift brute force, concentrated self-assertion, and the power of letting the electricity discharge itself in the meaning of the line, instead of in the look and tone of the stage figure, are all just what he has not got. His slowness, his growing habit of overdoing his part and slipping in an imaginative conception of his own *between* the lines (which made such a frightful wreck of Lear), all of which are part of his extraordinary insensibility to literature, are all reasons why he should avoid me, though his feeling for fine execution, and his dignity and depth of sentiment, are reasons why I should *not* avoid him. However, when Cymbeline is off his mind, I shall make him say Yes or No about The Man of Destiny. Meanwhile, I shall begin another play—a melodrama. After that I will write a real comic opera, to revive *that* industry a bit; and then I shall do whatever may come next.

You will observe how strictly I confine this letter to business. After the 22nd I decline further responsibility for my actions.

G.B.S.

8 September 1896

I have read carefully through that copy, but, worse luck, I must either write hurriedly or miss the post, as some people have arrived here and I have had to spend a lot of time mending punctures in female bicycle tyres. Therefore brief and blunt must I be, O Ellen. Fortunately there is not much to say. Our brains evidently work in the same way. At the same time I begin to doubt whether you can really be an actress. Most of 'em have no brains at all.

You have only once slipped out of the character in your plan, and that is in the scene between Imogen and Iachimo in the 2nd Act. Imogen is an impulsive person, with quick transitions, absolutely frank self-expression, and no half affections or half forgivenesses. The moment you abuse any-one she loves, she is in a rage: the moment you praise them she is delighted. It is quite easy for Iachimo to put her out of countenance by telling her that Posthumus has forgotten her; but the instant he makes the mistake of trying to gratify her by abusing him—"that runagate"—he brings down the avalanche. It is just the same with Cloten: she is for-bearing with him until he makes the same mistake. And Iachimo has nothing to do but praise Posthumus, and lay the butter on thick, and she is instantly as pleased as Punch, and void of all resentment. It is this that makes her pay him the extra special compliment of offering to take the chest into her own bedroom, *a thing she would never have done if she had not forgiven him* quite thoroughly—honest Injun. Therefore there is no subsiding storm, no "wary of him," no "polite—words, words, words." The words:—

> "—such a holy witch
> That he enchants societies to him:
> Half all men's hearts are his."

humbug her completely. The sun should come right out through the clouds when she says "You make amends."

You are unerring everywhere else.

On p. 4 the speech "O the gods! When shall we see again?" is really two separate speeches. When Posthumus puts the bracelet on your arm, look for a moment with delight at the present if you like, but that doesnt matter: the great thing is that you shiver with love at his touch on your arm, and say "O the gods!" as a sigh of rapture. It is when that subsides that you ask the question a woman always does ask—it being the nature of her sex never to be satisfied—"When will you come again?"

On the same page (4) comes the first quick transition. "I beseech you, sir, harm not yourself with your vexation" is thoroughly petulant and full of temper, Cymbeline having not only sent Posthumus away, but called him "thou basest thing." What she really means is "You may save your breath to cool your porridge, you old wretch."

On page 33—the last line—throw up your engagment and bid H. I. farewell for ever sooner than allow Pisanio to make "and too much too" a comic aside. It is a perfectly serious, tender, *nurselike* thing to say. Any Irish peasant would say "and too much too, darlint," quite naturally. I hasten on, lest I should use bad language.

I still think you should let Tyars read the letter. My reasons are that if you read it so as to convey your own feelings on seeing it you cannot also read it with the decision and point needed to enable the audience to take in the force of Posthumus's instructions to Pisanio. Further, I have a particular liking for the absolute truth of effect produced by the *acting* of the reading only, without the clumsiness of an aside, not to mention the force of effect derived from the audience's foreknowledge of what is happening to you; so that they can watch you without listening to the verbal instructions. However, I dont press that. Shakespear preferred to convey the foreknowledge by Pisanio's speech in the former scene, and the fact that his knowledge of his business was always a clever half-knowledge (the result of a hurry to get things done anyhow) is known to me only. So read the letter by all means; but just take another look at my way of cutting the following scene. At all events you must cut out "to pieces with me!" (p. 38) as it is not only unintelligible as it stands, but actually suggests a quite wrong idea. In the original it means "Now that there is another woman, to pieces with poor me!" As you have it, it represents Imogen as inviting Pisanio to carve her up like a chicken, which is ridiculous and spitefully out of character. And "Come: be honest—look" is nothing like so beautiful or expressive as "Come, fellow, be thou honest: do thou thy master's bidding etc." To cut out such fine bits and leave in such tawdry trash as "slander whose tongue outvenoms all the worms of Nile" is idiotic. The tearing of Posthumus's letters from her bosom seems to me very poor business—at least for you. Cut out the Roman courtesan on page 39: she belongs to the Bishopess side of the part, as you have noted.

But do *not* cut out the "clouted brogues" in p. 52; but rather "put thy shoes from off thy feet, for the place on which thou standest is holy ground." And I adjure you, do not cut out the prayer to heaven for "as small a drop of pity as a wren's eye" (54). You will find it a blessed relief (prayer is better than crying for that purpose) and to kneel and pray with your eyes covered will be beautiful. On p. 63 do not let them cut the speech of Lucius, "I do not bid thee beg my life, good lad, and yet I know thou wilt." It belongs to *your* part, your reply being important as a bit of play.

Generally speaking, the cutting of the play is stupid to the last extremity. Even from the broadest popular point of view, the omission of the grandiose scene about England and Cæsar for the queen, Cloten and the Roman, is a mistake. Cloten's part is spoiled. Every part is spoiled except "the governor's"; and he has actually damaged his own by wantonly cutting off your white and azure eyelids laced with blue of heaven's own tinct. Posthumus's exit on p. 32 is utterly spoiled by a fragment of another scene stuck in in the wrong place, lest Posthumus should complain that Iachimo was jealous of him and would not let him have that scene. The prudery of the cutting is silly: Pisanio says "disloyal" instead of adultery; Iachimo discreetly omits the lines "where, I profess, I slept not etc.," and Cloten's irresistibly turned remark that if Imogen doesnt like his serenade "it is a vice in her ears which horsehairs and calves' guts, nor the voice of unpaved eunuch to boot [a quite delightful bit of writing] can never amend"—is sacrificed to please the curates for whom the Lyceum seems chiefly to exist.

Forgive these splenetic remarks; but really H. I.'s acting versions of Shakespear are past all bearing. The man has no artistic sense outside his own person: he is an ogre who has carried you off to his cave; and now Childe Roland is coming to the dark tower to rescue you.

This letter I positively forbid you to answer: I should not have written it if it did not bear on your present business.

Did I tell you the name of my new play: You Never Can Tell. The Haymarket people—Harrison, Cyril Maude & Co.—appear to be making up their minds to ruin themselves with it.

Hark, hark, the lark—no, the post. This hurried kiss—adieu.

G. B. S.

16 September 1896.
Stratford St. Andrew.
(last day—leave tomorrow)

This will never do. Read *no* letters (except mine) until after the 22nd. The one thing that is quite certain about Mrs Siddons's "Yes" is that she did not get it out of the letter of an amateur, or even a professional eighty years out of date. What is more, if you did it exactly like Mrs Siddons, you would do it wrong, because you are not Mrs Siddons; and even if you are a worse actress—which cannot be proved—there is all the more reason why you should put her completely out of your head. Of course, if any trustworthy person remembers that Mrs Siddons made a great effect in such and such a line, it is quite worth considering where the tender spot she found in it lies, and then touching it in your own way; but very likely you would find that spot—if you detected it at all—one that has lost its tenderness with the wear and tear of the imagination and the growth and change of the human spirit since her time. Just imagine Duse (now *that's* acting if you like) playing Magda at Drury Lane in 1815. The thing is not more impossibly preposterous than Mrs Siddons playing Imogen at the Lyceum in 1896; and it is this absurd and monstrous effect that your good old people want you to produce. Did you ever see Cathcart playing Iago exactly as he used to rehearse it for Charles Kean? Nay, more horrible still, did you ever see Henry Irving, 20 years ago, trying to get Macready-Barry Sullivan effects in Richelieu? Or would you like me to rewrite The Man of Destiny in blank verse? Clear all superstitions out of your mind: there is nothing before you but Ellen Terry and Imogen; and the only letters that concern you are those which I shall write when I am 99 or so begging the newest leading lady of that time to do the wren's eye exactly as Ellen Terry did it (for you must die before me and get my rooms ready for me in heaven and tell the cook about my vegetarianism)—or, better still, the letters of the old men who are now boys, and whose first Imogen you will be. If you have the heart to fob them off with anything out of Wardour Street—anything that is not the very ownest own of your sacredest self—you are a wretch.

After all, how easy it all is! You will have a huge house, all convinced beforehand that whatever you do will be the right thing, all idiotically loyal and enthusiastic and devoted, except a few with a deeper and not idiotic feeling, and yet none of them expecting more than you can give them by merely existing as you are. There will be no traditions, no comparisons, no compulsion to retain a scrap of the dead, stupid, rhetorical, stagey past. As for me, I shall be there on the first night (for The Saturday Review must have its article on Cymbeline all in type on Thursday) with my nostrils writhing in scornful derision of the whole wretched show. I shant expect anything from you; my expectations, on my honor, will be so cynically tiny that you cannot help surpassing them—surprising, delighting me. All the other nasty critics will be like that too; and it will be easier for your pride to annihilate us than for your soft side to face the nice ones, who will believe anything you do beautiful, even if you introduce a skirt-dance out of jealousy of Mrs Pat's Juliet. Of course competition paralyses you; but what great artist *competes?* As the Boyg says to Peer Gynt, "the great Boyg does not fight: he conquers." After all, the real thing that you fear is your own criticism; but dont waste fear on it. Cæsar, Napoleon, all the big achievers have said the same thing; guard against everything you can foresee; and then—take your chance. Take your own Imogen as if it were *the* Imogen and play it for all you are worth; and dont relax your determination or look back disconcertedly on a missfire in this or that line until the last word is out of your mouth and the curtain down. Then go home to bed, and sleep comfortably with *your* part of the work done. However, you know all about this as well as I do; only it is aggravating to have you talking about so small a business as Imogen (however large it may loom in the amateur imagination) as if you could possibly be unequal to it. Dont you see that the real difficulty is that *there is not enough in it*—not enough to absorb your whole power of work and fill your embrace and occupy every corner of your energy and affection—that Imogen, an old mechanical thing with a few touches of simple nature, is too cheap for you instead of too big? Good Lord! did you ever see Duse play Shakespear? I did—Cleopatra! It was like seeing her scrubbing a scullery. Dont deceive yourself: what you have to do on Tuesday is to be a mother to Shakespear—to cover his foolishness and barrennesses, and to make the most of his little scattered glimpses of divinity. If you cannot believe in the greatness of your own age and time and inheritance, you will fall into the most horrible confusion of mind and contrariety of spirit, like a noble little child looking up to foolish, mean, selfish parents.

Oh, if people only would be modest enough to believe in themselves! Ha! there they rang the bell for grub. I am hungry. I leave this place tomorrow (Thursday) and shall spend Thursday night at the Bath Hotel, Felixstowe. Thereafter as God pleases until Monday (or perhaps Tuesday) and then Fitzroy Square.

Must I really give up calling you Ellen after twenty years? Impossible: Ellen Terry is the most beautiful name in the world: it rings like a chime through the last quarter of the 19th century. It has a lovely rhythm in it. Not like "Jorj," which is so horribly ugly and difficult that all attempts to call me by it are foredoomed to failure. I am, and always have been, and ever shall be, by pre-eminent brevity and common-sense, simply

SHAW

23 September 1896
29 Fitzroy Square, W.

Yes, that is all very well, but the real event is yet to come—the event that London is waiting for, to which the Lyceum business is the merest insignificant preliminary—that is G. B. S.'s article in the Saturday. I have to do that unaided and alone: nobody writes *me* sixteen or seventeen nice letters a day to encourage me, but no matter. If there is a thing I hate, it is ingratitude. Some people think of nobody but themselves. But I say no more.

My article is half written, and oh! isnt it nasty! All the natural malignity which I have been suppressing for weeks on your account is now simply boiling over. So it is to be "Madame Sans Gêne" after all. Oh VERY well, Sir Henry Irving. A homemade Napoleon isnt good enough for you, isnt it? Very good: we shall see. And you are going to play Richard III, are you? Then I think I know who is going to play Richmond: that's all.

I shall begin that article over again to-morrow: it's not half nasty enough.

I was greatly shocked by your entrance last night. You must have spent hours before the glass, getting up that success of personal beauty, merely to écraser Mrs Pat. Do you think, at your age, it is right?

I consider the way you went on with Posthumus postively indecent. Who is he, pray, that he should be made love to in that fashion? I consider myself to the full as good-looking a man.

Look here: I shall go again in a week or two. I am not satisfied: there is a crumple in the roseleaf here and there. You made one AWFUL mistake. You actually bawled out the words "a headless man!" before you had half seen him. Good heavens! you mustnt do that: it's ridiculous. You must simply start in horror, give the audience time to see in your face what is the matter, and then say "a headless man" in a frozen whisper. If you must make a noise, screech like mad when you start. Then it will be all right.

In playing Shakespear, play *to* the lines, *through* the lines, *on* the lines, but never between the lines. There simply isnt time for it. You would not stick five bars rest into a Beethoven symphony to pick up your drumsticks; and similarly you must not stop the Shakespear orchestra for business. Nothing short of a procession or a fight should make anything so extraordinary as a silence during a Shakespearean performance. All that cave business wants pulling together: from the line about " 'tis some savage hold" to "Such a foe! Good heavens!" you ought to get all the business of peeping and hesitating and so on packed into the duration of the speech, spoken without a single interval except a pause after the call. Otherwise it drags. Mind, I dont propose that you should omit or slur anything, but only that you should do it with the utmost economy of time.

The scene of the waking up should be moonlit: full bank holiday sunlight is too prosaic to make Imogen's dreamy condition and the uncanny effect of the mysterious body covered with flowers credible. On the other hand the low light in the scene where you read the fatal letter is not good. Somehow, at the Lyceum, the scenery is always imagined pictorially instead of dramatically.

How extra-OR-dinarily young and charming you have made yourself by that American trip! Or is it all tricks? Hurst put me five rows further back than usual. Heavens! am I the victim of a conspiracy!

Oh my article, my article, how am I to keep my style fresh if I sit up all night writing to you now that it is all over and I can be of no further use.

Can you recommend some horribly ugly person for the Strange Lady, now that Iachimo has deceived me? The villain! he has locked my play up for exactly a year. All your fault, yours, yours, yours, yours, and nobody else's. Ought to be ashamed of yourself.

G.B.S.

BLAMING THE BARD

Cymbeline. By Shakespeare. Lyceum Theatre, 22 September, 1896.

I confess to a difficulty in feeling civilized just at present. Flying from the country, where the gentlemen of England are in an ecstasy of chicken-butchering, I return to town to find the higher wits assembled at a play three hundred years old, in which the sensation scene exhibits a woman waking up to find her husband reposing gorily in her arms with his head cut off.

Pray understand, therefore, that I do not defend "Cymbeline." It is for the most part stagey trash of the lowest melodramatic order, in parts abominably written, throughout intellectually vulgar, and, judged in point of thought by modern intellectual standards, vulgar, foolish, offensive, indecent, and exasperating beyond all tolerance. There are moments when one asks despairingly why our stage should ever have been cursed with this "immortal" pilferer of other men's stories and ideas, with his monstrous rhetorical fustian, his unbearable platitudes, his pretentious reduction of the subtlest problems of life to commonplaces against which a

Polytechnic debating club would revolt, his incredible unsuggestiveness, his sententious combination of ready reflection with complete intellectual sterility, and his consequent incapacity for getting out of the depth of even the most ignorant audience, except when he solemnly says something so transcendently platitudinous that his more humble-minded hearers cannot bring themselves to believe that so great a man really meant to talk like their grandmothers. With the single exception of Homer, there is no eminent writer, not even Sir Walter Scott, whom I can despise so entirely as I despise Shakespeare when I measure my mind against his. The intensity of my impatience with him occasionally reaches such a pitch, that it would positively be a relief to me to dig him up and throw stones at him, knowing as I do how incapable he and his worshippers are of understanding any less obvious form of indignity. To read "Cymbeline" and to think of Goethe, of Wagner, of Ibsen, is, for me, to imperil the habit of studied moderation of statement which years of public responsibility as a journalist have made almost second nature in me.

But I am bound to add that I pity the man who cannot enjoy Shakespeare. He has outlasted thousands of abler thinkers, and will outlast a thousand more. His gift of telling a story (provided some one else told it to him first); his enormous power over language, as conspicuous in his senseless and silly abuse of it as in his miracles of expression; his humor; his sense of idiosyncratic character; and his prodigious fund of that vital energy which is, it seems, the true differentiating property behind the faculties, good, bad, or indifferent, of the man of genius, enable him to entertain us so effectively that the imaginary scenes and people he has created become more real to us than our actual life—at least, until our knowledge and grip of actual life begins to deepen and glow beyond the common. When I was twenty I knew everybody in Shakespeare, from Hamlet to Abhorson, much more intimately than I knew my living contemporaries; and to this day, if the name of Pistol or Polonius catches my eye in a newspaper, I turn to the passage with more curiosity than if the name were that of—but perhaps I had better not mention any one in particular.

How many new acquaintances, then, do you make in reading "Cymbeline," provided you have the patience to break your way into it through all the fustian, and are old enough to be free from the modern idea that Cymbeline must be the name of a cosmetic and Imogen of the latest scientific discovery in the nature of a hitherto unknown gas? Cymbeline is nothing; his queen nothing, though some attempt is made to justify her description as "a woman that bears all down with her brain"; Posthumus, nothing—most fortunately, as otherwise he would be an unendurably contemptible hound; Belarius, nothing—at least, not after Kent in "King Lear" (just as the Queen is nothing after Lady Macbeth); Iachimo, not much—only a *diabolus ex machinâ* made plausible; and Pisanio, less than Iachimo. On the other hand, we have Cloten, the prince of numbskulls, whose part, indecencies and all, is a literary masterpiece from the first line to the last; the two princes—fine presentments of that impressive and generous myth, the noble savage; Caius Lucius, the Roman general, urbane among the barbarians; and, above all, Imogen. But do, please, remember that there are two Imogens. One is a solemn and elaborate example of what, in Shakespeare's opinion, a real lady ought to be. With this unspeakable person virtuous indignation is chronic. Her object in life is to vindicate her own propriety and to suspect everybody else's, especially her husband's. Like Lothaw in the jeweller's shop in Bret Harte's burlesque novel, she cannot be left alone with unconsidered trifles of portable silver without officiously assuring the proprietors that she has stolen naught, nor would not, though she had found gold strewed i' the floor. Her fertility and spontaneity in nasty ideas is not to be described: there is hardly a speech in her part that you can read without wincing. But this Imogen has another one tied to her with ropes of blank verse (which can fortunately be cut)—the Imogen of Shakespeare's genius, an enchanting person of the most delicate sensitiveness, full of sudden transitions from ecstasies of tenderness to transports of childish rage, and reckless of consequences in both, instantly hurt and instantly appeased, and of the highest breeding and courage. But for this Imogen, "Cymbeline" would stand about as much chance of being revived now as "Titus Andronicus."

The instinctive Imogen, like the real live part of the rest of the play, has to be disentangled from a mass of stuff which, though it might be recited with effect and appropriateness by young amateurs at a performance by the Elizabethan Stage Society, is absolutely unactable and unutterable in the modern theatre, where a direct illusion of reality is aimed at, and where the repugnance of the best actors to play false passages is practically insuperable. For the purposes of the Lyceum, therefore, "Cymbeline" had to be cut, and cut liberally. Not that there was any reason to apprehend that the manager would flinch from the operation: quite the contrary. In a true republic of art Sir Henry Irving would ere this have expiated his acting versions on the scaffold. He does not merely cut plays: he disembowels them. In "Cymbeline" he has quite surpassed himself by extirpating the antiphonal third verse of the famous dirge. A man who would do that would do anything—cut the coda out of the first movement of Beethoven's Ninth Symphony, or shorten one of Velasquez's Philips into a kitcat to make it fit over his drawing-room mantelpiece. The grotesque character tracery of Cloten's lines, which is surely not beyond the appreciation of an age educated by Stevenson, is defaced with Cromwellian ruthlessness; and the patriotic scene, with the Queen's great speech about the natural bravery of our isle, magnificent in its Walkürenritt swing, is shorn away, though it might easily have been introduced in the Garden scene. And yet, long screeds of rubbish about "slander, whose edge is sharper than the sword," and so on, are preserved with superstitious veneration.

This curious want of connoisseurship in literature would disable Sir Henry Irving seriously if he were an interpretative actor. But it is, happily, the fault of a great quality—the creative quality. A prodigious deal of nonsense has been written about Sir Henry Irving's conception of this, that, and the other Shakespearean character. The truth is that he has never in his life conceived or interpreted the characters of any author except himself. He is really as incapable of acting another man's play as Wagner was of setting another man's libretto; and he should, like Wagner, have written his plays for himself. But as he did not find himself out until it was too late for him to learn that supplementary trade, he was compelled to use other men's plays as the framework for his own creations. His first great success in this sort of adaptation was with the "Merchant of Venice." There was no question then of a bad Shylock or a good Shylock: he was simply not Shylock at all; and when his own creation came into conflict with Shakespeare's, as it did quite openly in the Trial scene, he simply played in flat contradiction of the lines, and positively acted Shakespeare off the stage. This was an original policy, and an intensely interesting one from the critical point of view; but it was obvious that its difficulty must increase with the vividness and force of the dramatist's creation. Shakespeare at his highest pitch cannot be set aside by any mortal actor, however gifted; and when Sir Henry Irving tried to interpolate a most singular and fantastic notion of an old man between the lines of a fearfully mutilated acting version of "King Lear," he was smashed. On the other hand, in plays by persons of no importance, where the dramatist's part of the business is the nearest trash, his creative activity is unhampered and uncontradicted; and the author's futility is the opportunity for the actor's masterpiece. Now I have already described Shakespeare's Iachimo as little better than any of the lay figures in "Cymbeline"—a mere *diabolus ex machinâ*. But Irving's Iachimo is a very different affair. It is a new and independent creation. I knew Shakespeare's play inside and out before last Tuesday; but this Iachimo was quite fresh and novel to me. I witnessed it with unqualified delight: it was no vulgar bagful of "points," but a true impersonation, unbroken in its life-current from end to end, varied on the surface with the finest comedy, and without a single lapse in the sustained beauty of its execution. It is only after such work that an artist can with perfect naturalness and dignity address himself to his audience as "their faithful and loving servant"; and I wish I could add that the audience had an equal right to offer him their applause as a worthy acknowledgment of his merit. But when a house distributes its officious first-night plaudits impartially between the fine artist and the blunderer who roars a few lines violently and rushes off the stage after compressing the entire art of How Not to Act into five intolerable minutes, it had better be told to reserve its impertinent and obstreperous demonstrations until it has learnt to bestow them with some sort of discrimination. Our first-night people mean well, and will, no doubt, accept my assurance that they are donkeys with all possible good humor; but they should remember that to applaud for the sake of applauding, as schoolboys will cheer for the sake of cheering, is to destroy our own power of complimenting those who, as the greatest among us, are the servants of all the rest.

Over the performances of the other gentlemen in the cast let me skate as lightly as possible. Mr. Norman Forbes's Cloten, though a fatuous idiot rather than the brawny "beefwitted" fool whom Shakespeare took from his own Ajax in "Troilus and Cressida," is effective and amusing, so that one feels acutely the mangling of his part, especially the cutting of that immortal musical criticism of his upon the serenade. Mr. Gordon Craig and Mr. Webster are desperate failures as the two noble savages. They are as spirited and picturesque as possible; but every pose, every flirt of their elfin locks, proclaims the wild freedom of Bedford Park. They recite the poor maimed dirge admirably, Mr. Craig being the more musical of the twain; and Mr. Webster's sword-and-cudgel fight with Cloten is very lively; but their utter deficiency in the grave, rather sombre, uncivilized primeval strength and Mohican dignity so finely suggested by Shake-speare, takes all the ballast out of the fourth act, and combines with the inappropriate prettiness and sunniness of the landscape scenery to most cruelly handicap Miss Ellen Terry in the crucial scene of her awakening by the side of the flower-decked corpse—a scene which, without every accessory to heighten its mystery, terror, and pathos, is utterly and heart-breakingly impossible for any actress, even if she were Duse, Ristori, Mrs. Siddons, and Miss Terry rolled into one. When I saw this gross and palpable oversight, and heard people talking about the Lyceum stage management as superb, I with difficulty restrained myself from tearing out my hair in handfuls and scattering it with imprecations to the four winds. That cave of the three mountaineers wants nothing but a trellised porch, a bamboo bicycle, and a nice little bed of standard roses, to complete its absurdity.

With Mr. Frederic Robinson as Belarius, and Mr. Tyars as Pisanio, there is no reasonable fault to find, except that they might, perhaps, be a little brighter with advantage; and of the rest of their male colleagues I think I shall ask to be allowed to say nothing at all, even at the cost of omitting a tribute to Mr. Fuller Mellish's discreet impersonation of the harmless necessary Philario. There remains Miss Geneviève Ward, whose part, with the "Neptune's park" speech lopped off, was not worth her playing, and Miss Ellen Terry, who invariably fascinates me so much that I have not the smallest confidence in my own judgment respecting her. There was no Bedford Park about the effect she made as she stepped into the King's Garden; still less any of the atmosphere of ancient Britain. At the first glance, we were in the Italian fifteenth century; and the house, unversed in the cinquecento, but dazzled all the same, proceeded to roar until it stopped from exhaustion. There is one scene in "Cymbeline," the one in which Imogen receives the summons to "that same blessed Mil-ford," which might have been written for Miss Terry, so perfectly does its innocent rapture and frank gladness fit into her hand. Her repulse of Iachimo brought down the house as a matter of course, though I am convinced that the older Shakespeareans present had a vague impression that it could not be properly done except by a stout, turnip-headed matron, with her black hair folded smoothly over her ears and secured in a classic bun. Miss Terry had evidently cut her own part; at all events the odious Mrs. Grundyish Imogen had been dissected out of it so skilfully that it went without a single jar. The circumstances under which she was asked to play the fourth act were, as I have explained, impossible. To wake up in the gloom amid the wolf and robber-haunted mountain gorges which formed the Welsh mountains of Shakespeare's imagination in the days before the Great Western existed is one thing: to wake up at about three on a nice Bank-holiday afternoon in a charming spot near the valley of the Wye is quite another. With all her force, Miss Terry gave us faithfully the whole process which Shakespeare has presented with such dramatic cunning—Imogen's bewilderment, between dream and waking, as to where she is; the vague discerning of some strange bedfellow there; the wondering examination of the flowers with which he is so oddly covered; the frightful discovery of blood on the flowers, with the hideous climax that the man is headless and that his clothes are her husband's; and it was all ruined by that blazing, idiotic, prosaic sunlight in which everything leapt to the eye at once, rendering the mystery and the slowly growing clearness of perception incredible and unintelligible, and spoiling a scene which, properly stage-managed, would have been a triumph of histrionic intelligence. Cannot somebody be hanged for this?—men perish every week for lesser crimes. What consolation is it to me that Miss Terry, playing with infinite charm and delicacy of appeal, made up her lost ground in other directions, and had more than as much success as the roaring gallery could feel the want of?

TO GRANVILLE BARKER

Ayot St. Lawrence, Welwyn, Herts.
15th November 1908.

My dear Barker,

Taylor Platt came to Liverpool yesterday (Saturday) to tell me that he had left you at 104°. Irish temperature is fortunately 2° higher than English; but still even 102° is pretty warm. Let us know when you get down to normal; for Charlotte would certainly have gone over to nurse you yesterday but for the fact that she was herself in bed in much the same plight: I sent your telegram on to Wheeler; but I now learn that it will not reach him until this evening. Therefore you will hear from him a day later than I had counted on. Liverpool also threw me back a day: I delivered a noble address there and ended with a soul-stirring appeal for a municipal theatre.

The Bacchae was, on the whole, good business for Lillah: it brought out the sort of thing she can do that nobody else can do; and the mesmeric scene came off immensely. But of course the performance was an absurdity all the same. The four women yowled inhumanly. They remembered my precepts fairly well in the first chorus; but they soon got hysterical; and if some property on the lines of the Wooden Horse of Troy, but shaped like a tom cat had come forth, fascinated by their wailings, the effect would have been superb. As it was, nothing better was to be expected than Max's article in the Saturday. The gay chorus leader sang prettily and spoke clearly; but she was not classical; and some of her music would have revolted the Girls of Gothenburg. And then the curtains were a horrible mistake. Greek plays require the open air: and Duchess of Malfi effects are no use in them. Lillah's entrance was most trying. She had to step out from behind a dark curtain into a crude blaze of light which was all wrong for her open air costume, and produced a haggard, raw, eyeball-insulting effect. I have persuaded her to be discovered next time in a robe-cloak, with her back to the audience, and to turn on them for her opening lines instead of entering. On Friday morning I went through the part with her, and acted the first scene with Pentheus with such superb realism that she got uncomfortable and finally stopped and said "It's no use: I cant act with you; you make me feel that you dont believe in me a bit." I never even told her that the sceptic was Pentheus, not G.B.S. because I wanted to get on to the later scenes.

Some of the cuts are very stupid. Poel doesnt understand Lillah technically, and doesnt understand Dionyseus temperamentally. He pulls off the big bits, and gets the story across the footlights; but he throws away a good deal too, and does not quite realize how very bad is the best that his choreoguses can do.

The National Theatre is being organized apace. Esher and I have imposed a sound democratic constitution on it: the director must carry a Standing Committee of seven with him; and I have imposed the yoke of the treasurer heavily on him. The staff is to be Director, Treasurer, and Man of Letters: three *not* in one, nor one in three. Pinero had a fancy for allowing the Director one play of his own choice, whether his mother would let him or no (so to speak); but on closer consideration we all saw that it would not do. As Esher and I are the oldest hands at public committee work, we get our own own way pretty well. We have now finished our statutes (or think we have) and are about to start on the bye-laws. Meanwhile, we are agreed that we must get £100,000 in the hat before it goes round, or we shall get £5 notes from people who ought to give us a thousand. The £100,000 is called my uncle's banknote. Said uncle was a clergyman. When he preached a charity sermon, he always put a bank note in the plate before the churchwarden started with it. He replaced it in his pocket subsequently. I told this to the committee: hence the phrase above quoted.

Esher thinks we may get a Knighthood for Pinero next June. He approves warmly.

I saw Forbes-Robertson in the Jerome play on Thursday. It was quite as good as I thought it when I read it. The third act is the weak spot; but the first and second would carry a worse one through.

Hankin, bedridden in Brompton Square, writes endless letters to everybody, and talks of an operation. What is the matter with him? It is time for him to get to work at De Mullin if he means to assist in the production.

The Fabian Basis meetings are developing into a series of personal attacks on one another by the leaders of the Society. Headlam's paper was an attack on "the bureaucratic Collectivist" (Webb); and Pease's paper was an attack on me as an absurd imposter in economics. I up and said "Who will be Mr. Hobson's victim"? (Roars). The women asked urgency for a resolution calling on the Home Secretary to put Mrs. Pank and Christabel in the first division. The Nursery protested because they had not been allowed to move the Grayson resolution last time. Hobson said he would allow the resolution to be put provided it passed without discussion. "Is there any opposition"? said he. "Yes," shrieked the Nursery. "I appeal to you," said Hobson. "Is there any opposition?" The Nursery—molto crescendo—"Yes." Hobson looked pained. "For the third time, is there any opposition?" he repeated. The Nursery—con tutta la forza—"Y E S." "Then I declare the resolution carried," said Hobson. Struck dumb by this coup, and intimidated by the triumphant cheers of the Feminists, the Nursery subsided until after Pease's lecture, when Blanco White moved that Hobson leave the chair. Sidney Herbert seconded; and Hobson put it to the meeting. FOR 2. AGAINST, all the rest. Applause and curtain.

I am summoned away and must break off.

G.B.S.

TO MRS. PATRICK CAMPBELL

The Mitre, Oxford.
22nd February 1913

What a day! I must write to you about it, because there is no one else who didnt hate her mother, and even who doesnt hate her children. Whether you are an Italian peasant or a Superwoman I cannot yet find out; but anyhow your mother was not the Enemy.

Why does a funeral always sharpen one's sense of humor and rouse one's spirits? This one was a complete success. No burial horrors. No mourners in black, snivelling and wallowing in induced grief. Nobody

REPRINTED by permission of Curtis Brown, Ltd. for the Trustees of the Estate of the late Mrs. Patrick Campbell; from *Bernard Shaw and Mrs. Patrick Campbell: Their Correspondence*, New York, Alfred A. Knopf, Inc., London, Victor Gollancz, Ltd., 1952.

knew except myself, Barker and the undertaker. Since I could not have a splendid procession with lovely colors and flashing life and triumphant music, it was best with us three. I particularly mention the undertaker because the humor of the occasion began with him. I went down in the tube to Golders Green with Barker, and walked to the Crematorium; and there came also the undertaker presently with his hearse, which had walked (the horse did) conscientiously at a funeral pace through the cold; though my mother would have preferred an invigorating trot. The undertaker approached me in the character of a man shattered with grief; and I, hard as nails and in loyally high spirits (rejoicing irrepressibly in my mother's memory), tried to convey to him that this professional chicanery, as I took it to be, was quite unnecessary. And lo! it wasn't professional chicanery at all. He had done all sorts of work for her for years, and was actually and really in a state about losing her, not merely as a customer, but as a person he liked and was accustomed to. And the coffin was covered with violet cloth—not black.

I must rewrite that burial service; for there are things in it that are deader than anyone it has ever been read over; but I had it read not only because the parson must live by his fees, but because with all its drawbacks it is the most beautiful thing that can be read as yet. And the parson did not gabble and hurry in the horrible manner common on such occasions. With Barker and myself for his congregation (and Mamma) he did it with his utmost feeling and sincerity. We could have made him perfect technically in two rehearsals; but he was excellent as it was; and I shook his hand with unaffected gratitude in my best manner.

At the passage "earth to earth, ashes to ashes, dust to dust" there was a little alteration of the words to suit the process. A door opened in the wall; and the violet coffin mysteriously passed out through it and vanished as it closed. People think that door the door of the furnace; but it isnt. I went behind the scenes at the end of the service and saw the real thing. People are afraid to see it; but it is wonderful. I found there the violet coffin opposite another door, a real unmistakable furnace door. When it lifted there was a plain little chamber of cement and firebrick. No heat. No noise. No roaring draught. No flame. No fuel. It looked cool, clean, sunny, though no sun could get there. You would have walked in or put your hand in without misgiving. Then the violet coffin moved again and went in, feet first. And behold! The feet burst miraculously into streaming ribbons of garnet coloured lovely flame, smokeless and eager, like pentecostal tongues, and as the whole coffin passed in it sprang into flame all over; and my mother became that beautiful fire.

The door fell; and they said that if we wanted to see it all through, we should come back in an hour and a half. I remembered the wasted little figure with the wonderful face, and said "Too long" to myself; but we went off and looked at the Hampstead Garden Suburb (in which I have shares), and telephoned messages to the theatre, and bought books, and enjoyed ourselves generally.

By the way I forgot one incident. Hayden Coffin suddenly appeared in the chapel. *His* mother also. The end was wildly funny, she would have enjoyed it enormously. When we returned we looked down through an opening in the floor to a lower floor close below. There was saw a roomy kitchen, with a big cement table and two cooks busy at it. They had little tongs in their hands, and they were deftly and busily picking nails and scraps of coffin handles out of Mamma's dainty little heap of ashes and samples of bone. Mamma herself being at that moment leaning over beside me, shaking with laughter. Then they swept her up into a sieve, and shook her out; so that there was a heap of dust and a heap of calcined bone scraps. And Mamma said in my ear, "Which of the two heaps is me, I wonder!"

And that merry episode was the end, except for making dust of the bone scraps and scattering them on a flower bed.

O grave, where is thy victory?

In the afternoon I drove down to Oxford, where I write this. The car was in a merry mood, and in Notting Hill Gate accomplished a most amazing skid, swivelling right round across the road one way and then back the other, but fortunately not hitting anything.

The Philanderer, which I came down to see (Mona Limerick as Julia) went with a roar from beginning to end. Tomorrow I drive to Reading and thence across Surrey into Kent to the Barkers. The deferred lunch at the German Embassy will take place on Monday. Unless I find at Adelphi Terrace before 1.15 a telegram forbidding me ever to see you again, I *know* I shall go straight from the Embassy to your bedside. I must see you again after all these years.

Barrie is in bed ill (caught cold in Oxford a week ago) and ought to be petted by somebody.

I have many other things of extreme importance to say, but must leave them until Monday. By the way you first said you were leaving Hinde St on the 23rd; but you said last time to Lady Jekyll "Another ten days." If you are gone when I call I shall hurl myself into the area and perish.

And so goodnight, friend who understands about one's mother, and other things.

G.B.S.

TO DAME LAURENTIA
McLACHLAN

St. Patrick's Day in Damascus, 1931

DEAR SISTER LAURENTIA

This Holy Land is in a queer situation from the Crusader's point of view, which is officially your point of view. The British representative in Jerusalem is also the representative, precisely, of Pontius Pilate; and when Communist Messiahs turn up, as they actually do from time to time under Russian influences, he is bound to handle the case on Pilatical lines. What would any medieval Christian saint—or say Richard Coeur de Lion —say if miraculously resuscitated in Jerusalem today? Saladin and the followers of the accurst Mahound vanquished at last by the Christian British Empire. The circumcised crucifiers of Christ scattered through the ghettos of Europe. The Cross triumphant over all the Promised Land, over Christ's birthplace, over his sepulchre, over the Mount of the Beatitudes and over the bloodstained plain (which Christ overlooked from that Mount) on which Saladin smashed the last effort of the Crusaders to resist him, over Galilee and Samaria, Bethlehem, Nazareth, Capernaum, over the waters on which he walked and the hillsides from which he preached, over Nain and Cana and Bethany, over Jordan in which he was baptized, and the unknown Golgotha on which he was duly executed according to the official routine by the predecessor of Mr. Keith Roach.

So far, praised be God, Richard would say, probably adding a stentorian Hep, hep, hep!

But when Richard was further informed that the use England had made of its victory was to hand over all that sacred territory to the descendants and co-religionists of Saladin and to those of Annas and Caiphas, having promised it to both for their help in the war, and that Pontius now had his hands full with the job of keeping the peace between them, he would surely either start a new crusade or return to his tomb in disgust with a world gone entirely mad.

I ask myself whether I shall persuade Sister Laurentia to get a hundred days indulgence, a tailor-made short skirt, gaiter boots, a Fair Isle pullover, a smart waterproof, a field glass and camera, a brown sun umbrella lined with red, and a Revelation suit case, and hasten hither to see for herself what she has imagined at Stanbrook. I leave the question unanswered; but I will tell you what might happen to you because it has happened to me.

You would enter the Holy Land at night under a strong impression made on you in Egypt, not by the Tutankhamen trash which the tourists

FROM *In A Great Tradition*, New York, Harper & Brothers, London, John Murray, Ltd., 1957. Reprinted by permission of The Public Trustee and The Society of Authors, London.

are now mobbing, but by something seen under the pyramids. A pyramid is just as big as its royal builder is old; and it is always finished. If he dies a baby, there is his monument ready for him, like this: △. If he grows

up, his tomb grows with him 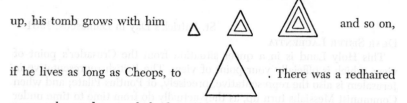 and so on,

if he lives as long as Cheops, to [triangle] . There was a redhaired queen who made a tomb for herself and her daughters, deep under tons of pyramid and rock, and set two great artists, Rahay a painter and Yentaf a sculptor, to work in it. Whether the redhaired one and her brood were very fine ladies, or whether the two fine artists made fine ladies of them I do not know; but when you see that row of sculptured women come alive in a hundred candle power electric sunlight without a shadow of death or fear on their shining faces and pleasantly courteous eyes or a line or contour in their whole bodies that is not exquisite, and when you turn to their magnificently designed portraits on the wall, the impression you receive is beyond description in our lower language, as of an order of beings completely redeemed from sin and vulgarity and all the plagues of our degradation, and yet not in the least geniuses, as Michael Angelo would have made them, but girls whom you might enlist for Stanbrook without expecting them to excel in doing as well as in being. You might question their vocation on the ground that they seem to have no religion nor to need any, having achieved excellence and being content to leave it at that; but the impression would be all the more astonishing. And that to those who served them fifty tons of solid stone seemed as easy to move and handle as a little water in a spoon, gets far beyond our miracles which are wondered at as miracles and taken as divine testimonies, and lifts us into a region in which the miraculous is no longer miraculous but gigantically normal, and immortality a thing to be achieved in a turn of the hand.

Under such impressions you find yourself in the Holy Land by night, with strange new constellations all over the sky and the old ones all topsy turvy, but with the stars soft and large and down quite close overhead in a sky which you feel to be of a deep and lovely blue. When the light comes you have left the land of Egypt with its endlessly flat Delta utterly behind, and are in a hilly country, with patches of cultivation wrested from the omnipresent stones, which you instantly recognize with a strange emotion which intensifies when you see a small boy coming down one of the patches, and presently, when he has passed away, a bigger boy of about thirteen, beginning to think, and at last, when he too has vanished, a young man, very grave and somewhat troubled, all three being dressed just as Christ dressed. (Here I break off, to resume on the night of the 20th, between Cyprus and Rhodes, at sea.) The appearance of a woman with an infant in her arms takes on the quality of a vision. On this first hour you do not improve. It gives you the feeling that here Christ lived and grew up, and that here Mary bore him and reared him, and that there is no land on earth quite like it.

Later on the guides try to be more exact. This, they tell you, is the stable in the inn. This is the carpenter's shop. This is the upper chamber where the Last Supper was served. You know that they are romancing—that there is not a scrap of evidence for the possible identifications and that no inn or stable ever existed in a natural cavern in the limestone rock without light or fresh air. In Nazareth you know that Mary used the well in the street because there was (and is) no other well in the town to use; but the water she drew is gone, and the new water, with taps affixed by the British mandatory Government, is anybody's and everybody's water. Everything else in Nazareth except its natural beauty as a hill town is a fraud, meanly commemorated by an unattractive and unimpressive church. But for these frauds every stone in Nazareth would be sacred with possibilities. Because one muddy bend of the Jordan is labelled as the spot on which the dove descended, the whole river is desecrated to make trade for the stall that sells the mud in bottles. I swam in the lake of Tiberias with a pleasant sense that this, at least, was Christ's lake on which nobody could stake out the track on which he walked or the site from which the miraculous draught of fishes was hauled. It is better to have Christ everywhere than somewhere, especially where he probably wasnt.

The hills rise almost into mountains over the train to Jerusalem, which winds between them so sinuously that you can see its tail from the window. When you arrive you are surprised: the place has a flourishing modern suburban air, and the new fashionable villa-land is mentioned as The New Jerusalem. When your very modern hotel has completed your disenchantment you make for the old Jerusalem and the church of the Holy Sepulchre. And the only possible comment on it is that of Dean Inge (he is with us on this trip) "Why seek ye the living among the dead? He is not here." (When Dean Inge says the right thing it is so very right that he is privileged to say a hundred wrong things that dont matter). A sort of case can be made for the sepulchre: it is at least possible that what remains of the chamber in the rock after its smashing up by the Moslem persecutions may be the family vault of Joseph of Arimathea; but when on the same floor a few yards off they show you Calvary (not a hill) with the sockets of the three crosses, it is irresistibly revealed to you that Saint Helena was a humbug who, when the court was ordered to turn Christian, was quite determined to outshine the Queen of Heaven by a galaxy of visions and miracles that would show the world that Roman queens would enter the new temples as goddesses and not as Syrian peasants cradling their infants in mangers. I know that sort of woman almost as well as you must. I have seen her court in the mosaics of Ravenna, where the attempt of the imperial court ladies to look pious is ludicrously unsuccessful.

The church of the Holy Sepulchre, to eyes accustomed to western architecture of the same period, is a second rate affair; and the squabbles of the sects over their "rights" in it are not edifying. I duly squeezed myself into the sepulchre, and tipped the queerly robed priest who touched my hands with oil to the extent of five piastres, looking as credulous as I could so as not to hurt his feelings; but my thought was that you would be disappointed. For the rest of the day I damned Jerusalem up hill and down dale; and when they took me to the Mount of Olives (practically oliveless) and showed me the famous view of the city my only comment was "Just like Buxton." But one's appreciation is more complex than that. When you stand on the stone from which the Ascension took place you feel at the same moment everything that the legend means you to feel and a purely comic amusement at the notion of Jesus going up to the highest attainable point as a taking-off place for his celestial flight. Your faith and your tourist's observation jostle one another in the queerest fashion.

Next day I discovered Jerusalem. I went to the great plain of stone on which the Temple stood, and on which the Mosque of Omar (who didn't build it) stands. And there I found the charm and sanctity of Jerusalem. Christ has been worshipped in both the mosques; Omar was a man after God's own heart; and Mahomet's horse sprang to heaven with him from the great rock which the mosque of Omar enshrines, and which is a nobly beautiful building in spite of the utterly anachronistic Corinthian capitals of the red pillars of granite which bother one all over the Holy Land, and which are so Roman and common. The Kaiser gilt the Corinthian heavily so that they might hit you harder in the eye. Mahomet respected Christ and taught his followers to do the same; and it is perhaps the failure of the Christians to respect Mahomet equally that makes Islam and Israel more impressive in the east than Christendom. Still, the history of the place is such a record of iconoclasms, massacres, persecutions, spoliations, demolitions, and delendings (in Cato's sense) by Turks, Romans, and any conqueror who happened to come along, that the only general verdict possible is that of the King of Brobdingnag. God must feel sick when he looks at Jerusalem. I fancy he consoles himself by turning to Stanbrook.

You asked me for a relic from Calvary. But St. Helena's Calvary is only a spot on a church pavement, jealously guarded, and with nothing removable about it. Where the real Calvary is nobody knows; for the hills outside the city are innumerable. The alleged Via Dolorosa I traversed in a motor car hooting furiously at the children to get out of the way. The praetorium can be reasonably identified as in the palace of Herod, which Titus kept as a fortress for his garrison when he as nearly as possible left not one stone on another of the rest of the city; but as you cannot tell where Calvary was you cannot tell the way from the praetorium to it.

So off I went to Bethlehem, a beautifully situated hill town; and from the threshold of the Church of the Nativity I picked up a little stone, a scrap of the limestone rock which certainly existed when the feet of Jesus pattered about on it and the feet of Mary pursued him to keep him in order; for he was a most inconsiderate boy when his family was concerned, as you would realize if you travelled over the distance (at least a day's journey without a Rolls Royce) his mother had to go back to look for him when he gave her the slip to stay and argue with the doctors of divinity. In fact I picked up two little stones; one to be thrown blindfold among the others in Stanbrook garden so that there may always be a stone from Bethlehem there, though nobody will know which it is and be tempted to steal it, and the other for your own self. You shall have them when I return, unless I perish on the way, in which case I shall present myself at the heavenly gate with a stone in each hand, and St. Peter will stand at attention and salute the stones (incidentally saluting ME) when he has unlocked the gate and flung it open before me. At least he would if it were ever locked, which I dont believe.

I have been writing all this in scraps; but there must be an end to everything, even to a letter to you; besides, I finished with the Holy Land at Patmos three days ago, the intervening two days having been spent among heathen idols in and around Athens. For climbing up that frightfully stony road to the top of the mountain where the Greek monastery stands I shall claim indulgence for every sin I ever committed and a few hundred which I still hope to commit. The man who wrote the Book of Revelations, who was *not* the John of the fourth gospel (the Dean assures me that his Greek was disgracefully ungrammatical) ought to have married St. Helena. I *know* he was a drug addict, as all the wickednesses of which he accuses God, all the imaginary horrors, all the passings of a thousand years in a second and the visions of universes breaking into three pieces, are the regular symptoms of drug action and delirium tremens. The book is a disgrace to the Bible and should never have been admitted to the canon.

I began this on the 17th March and it is now the 26th! You can spend a week of your scanty leisure in reading it, and then sell the manuscript to Cockerell for the Fitzwilliam and endow a chapel to St. Bernard at Stanbrook with the proceeds. The writing of it has been very restful to the soul of your brother.

affectionately
G. Bernard Shaw

"Brother Bernard's is a splendid document," was Dame Laurentia's brief comment, "the least merit being its brilliancy. I believe his criticisms are such as I should have made myself if I had been there, and his appreciations seem to me to be most just. The tenderness of some passages is beautiful and reveals, I imagine, the soul of the real G.B.S."

On June 12 he forwarded one of the two stones to which his letter refers with the cryptic remark: "This is for the garden. Your particular one will come later: the delay is not *my* fault; and the explanation will be satisfactory."

Meanwhile Dame Laurentia was quite seriously ill; overwork had affected both heart and blood pressure, and the doctor ordered complete rest. In September, therefore, a letter arrived to ask her if she were able to receive a visit as the Shaws were in Malvern for the Festival:—

Unless your unenclosed lady who opens the door for me telephones to the contrary before twelve tomorrow, we will call on our way back from Cheltenham. If at that moment you are tired and cannot bear us, it will not upset any of our arrangements: it will only shatter my hopes. I have just been in Russia—the oddest place you can imagine. They have thrown God out by the door; and he has come in again by all the windows in the shape of the most tremendous Catholicism. I hope they strapped you down in bed and kept the door locked until your overwork had been cured by a spell of thorough laziness. Your affectionate Brother Bernard.

On the Saturday appointed, Mr. and Mrs. Shaw arrived, bearing with them the stone from Bethlehem intended to serve as Dame Laurentia's personal memento. To her delighted amazement she was presented with an exquisite example of the silversmith's art, almost a foot in height, constructed on the model of a medieval reliquary and cunningly devised to focus attention upon the small object enshrined, for which its own beauty is but a setting.

Dame Laurentia was enchanted with the beauty of the gift, and a fortnight later showed it to Sydney Cockerell. Noticing that it lacked any mark of its donor's identity, he suggested that it should bear an inscription to indicate its origin. Dame Laurentia accordingly wrote and asked Bernard Shaw to supply a text, assuring him at the same time that he had the gratitude and prayers of the whole community. Her request met with the following reply:—

London, Oct. 25, 1931

DEAR SISTER LAURENTIA

. . . Why can it not be a secret between us and Our Lady and her little boy?

What the devil—saving your cloth—could we put on it?

Cockerell writes a good hand. Get him a nice bit of parchment and let him inscribe it with a record of the circumstances for the Abbey archives, if he must provide gossip for antiquarian posterity.

We couldn't put our names on it—could we? It seems to me something perfectly awful.

"An inscription explaining its purpose"! If we could explain its purpose we could explain the universe. I couldn't. Could you? If Cockerell thinks he can . . . let him try, and submit the result to the Pope.

Dear Sister: our finger prints are on it, and Heaven knows whose footprints may be on the stone. Isn't that enough?

Or am I all wrong about it?

faithfully and fraternally

BROTHER BERNARD

P.S. I don't mind being prayed for. When I play with my wireless set I realize that all the sounds in the world are in my room; for I catch them as I alter the wave length receiver—German, French, Italian and unknown tongues. The ether is full of prayers too; and I suppose if I were God I could tune in to them all. Nobody can tell what influence these prayers have. If the ether is full of impulses of good will to me so much the better for me: it would be shockingly unscientific to doubt it. So let the sisters give me all the prayers they can spare; and don't forget me in yours.